# The Roots of Blitzkrieg

# The Roots of Blitzkrieg

## HANS VON SEECKT AND
## GERMAN MILITARY REFORM

James S. Corum

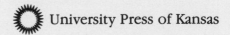 University Press of Kansas

Published by the University Press of Kansas (Lawrence, Kansas 66049), which was
organized by the Kansas Board of Regents and is operated and funded by Emporia State
University, Fort Hays State University, Kansas State University, Pittsburg State University,
the University of Kansas, and Wichita State University

Library of Congress Cataloging-in-Publication Data

Corum, James S.
    The roots of Blitzkrieg : Hans von Seeckt and German military
reform / James S. Corum.
        p.   cm. — (Modern war studies)
    Includes bibliographical references and index.
    ISBN 0-7006-0541-X (cloth)     ISBN 0-7006-0628-9 (pbk.)
    1.  Germany—Armed Forces—History—20th century.   2.  Military
doctrine—Germany—History—20th century.   3.  Lightning war—
History.   4.  Seeckt, Hans von, 1866–1936.   I.  Title.   II.  Series.
UA710.C67   1992
355.02′0943—dc20                                                                    92-5178

British Library Cataloguing in Publication Data is available.

Printed in the United States of America
10 9 8 7 6 5 4 3 2

The paper used in this publication meets the minimum requirements of the American
National Standard for Permanence of Paper for Printed Library Materials Z39.48-1984.

# CONTENTS

# ILLUSTRATIONS

# PREFACE

In January 1933, when Adolf Hitler became chancellor of Germany, he inherited the best-led, best-trained, and arguably the most-modern army in the world. The process of creating the tactical doctrine of this army and the incorporation of this doctrine into the army's weapons, organization, and war plans are the primary concerns of this work. In the immediate aftermath of World War I, German Army leaders, on their own initiative, began to analyze the lessons of that war carefully, and they set out to create a military system that would be a great improvement on the admittedly impressive one of the old Imperial Army.

This book should provide some insights into the question of military reform in the interwar era. Every major military power had to face the issues of the new weaponry and tactics created during World War I. Many British, American, and French officers offered a variety of operational analyses and worked to develop the new technologies. The German Army was not unique in attempting to deal with the new conditions of warfare. It was the methodology that differed.

The General Staff's process of creating a tactical doctrine and then building an army around it was a comprehensive one—very unlike the more haphazard approach of the victorious Allied armies in their postwar assessment and reorganization. In Germany, as soon as the General Staff created a new tactical doctrine, the whole army—from generals to privates—was trained in it. The new army would become more technically minded than its counterparts or its predecessor and an effective system of weapons development would be inaugurated. Furthermore, by the mid- and late 1920s, the German army's training and command system established an efficient process in which the new tactical ideas, unit organization, and equipment would be continuously tested, adapted, and improved. This process of rebuilding the German Army is one of the most impressive and significant military accomplishments of the twentieth century.

For the historian, the German Army of the Weimar Republic is intrinsically interesting. The Wehrmacht and its military victories from 1939 to 1941 were firmly rooted in the Reichswehr of 1919–1933. The German military leaders of World War II were selected and trained by the Reichswehr, that organization created from the wreckage of the Imperial Army.

Many of the best-known World War II weapons were either designed in the Reichswehr period or stemmed from Reichswehr weapons programs. Most important, the tactics of blitzkrieg warfare in the era between 1939 and 1941 originated in the military doctrine and training of the 1920s Reichswehr.

Owing to the Reichswehr's pivotal role in the Weimar Republic, many of its aspects have already been carefully examined. Much of the post–World War II scholarship on the interwar German Army has tended to focus on its role in domestic and foreign policy, assessing its share of responsibility for the collapse of the republic and the rise of the Nazi regime. Some of the excellent studies that examine the political side of the army's history in the Weimar era include F. L. Carsten's *The Reichswehr and Politics, 1918–1933* (1966) and Gordon Craig's *The Politics of the Prussian Army, 1640–1945* (1955). Many other aspects of the Reichswehr have inspired good scholarly work. The sociology of the Reichswehr and its officer corps was thoroughly examined in Karl Demeter's *Das Deutsche Offizierkorps in Gesellschaft und Staat, 1650–1945* (1962) and Hans Hofmann's *Das deutsche Offizierkorps, 1866–1960* (1980). One of the most intriguing episodes of the Weimar Republic's history is the story of the army's private foreign policy initiatives, which resulted in its own foreign policy, the main feature being the close cooperation with the Red Army and Soviet government. Until the Soviet archives of this era are completely opened to historians, a truly satisfactory history of this episode cannot be written. With the limited number of documents available, John Erickson's *The Soviet High Command: A Military-Political History, 1918–1941* (1984) is the best and most thorough analysis of the Reichswehr–Red Army relationship. Gaines Post's *The Civil-Military Fabric of Weimar Foreign Policy* (1973) stands out as one of the best of several books on the Reichswehr's role in foreign policy.

In the last quarter-century, a variety of good specialized studies of the Reichswehr have appeared. A thorough and well-documented study of the German Army's early rearmament plans and its relationship with German industry is provided by Ernst Hansen in *Reichswehr und Industrie* (1978). Another useful book on German military-industrial policy is Georg Thomas's *Geschichte der deutschen Wehr und Rüstungswirtschaft, 1918-1943/45* (1966). Even some relatively esoteric aspects of Reichswehr history have inspired major, detailed studies. Walter Spielberger has written a good study of the Reichswehr's motorization program in *Die Motorisierung der deutschen Reichswehr, 1920–1935* (1979). The Reichswehr has not lacked good general histories either. Harold Gordon's *The Reichswehr and the German Republic, 1919–1926*, though written in 1957, is by no means out-of-date. This detailed book remains an excellent starting point for research on the Reichswehr. More recently, Adolf

Reinicke's *Das Reichsheer, 1921–1934* (1986) has proven to be a good general history. One of the most important books for any student of the German Army is Hans Meier-Welcker's *Seeckt* (1967), a long and meticulously researched biography of the Reichswehr's commander. Of several books written on von Seeckt, Meier-Welcker's is the definitive biography.

The raison d'être of an army, however, is to plan, train for, and fight wars, and this obviously important aspect of the Reichswehr has not been adequately explored. Although the origin and development of the Reichswehr's tactical doctrine has been touched on in many books, only a few have provided any real depth. S. J. Lewis has contributed some good scholarship toward certain aspects of Reichswehr military thinking in *Forgotten Legions: German Army Infantry Policy, 1918–1941* (1985). Jehuda Wallach has also made a useful contribution in *The Dogma of the Battle of Annihilation* (1986), wherein he examined some of the tactical and strategic debates that took place within the German Army in the 1920s. David Spires has provided a detailed study of Reichswehr officer and General Staff training in *Image and Reality: The Making of the German Officer, 1921–1933* (1984). Still, not one of these books provides a comprehensive picture of Reichswehr tactical doctrine.

In my research I have come across numerous explanations of Reichswehr tactics. For many years after World War II, military historians virtually ignored Reichswehr-era tactics, except for the ideas of General Heinz Guderian. Many historians, discussed later in this study, proffered the theory that the tactics of the interwar German Army were essentially imports, adopted by the Germans and used to great effect in 1939-40. One political scientist, Barry Posen, argued in *The Sources of Military Doctrine* (1984) that the German General Staff's conservative tendencies led it to revert to a traditional mode of offensive warfare after World War I. Robert Citino's *The Evolution of Blitzkrieg Tactics* (1989) provides a useful study of the German-Polish military confrontation and the German war plans against Poland but draws the very broad conclusion, from a narrow field, that the German Army developed blitzkrieg tactics in the 1920s in response to the Polish threat.

None of these studies or theories seems to me to provide either an adequate description of the Reichswehr's military doctrine or an adequate explanation of how the Reichswehr arrived at its tactical methods. After all, the German General Staff was a complex instrument with a strong tradition of studying warfare carefully. The notion that the General Staff, which showed great ability and innovation in conducting offensive warfare in World War I, could be bound by traditionalist inertia after the war seemed implausible. Another doubtful explanation was that the organization that did so well in developing new tactics would, after the war, discard its own experience and adopt foreign theories. The lack of plausible explanations was the starting point for my own studies of the Reichswehr. The following questions needed to be pondered: What exactly was the tactical doctrine of the Reichswehr? What role did it play in the later development of blitzkrieg tactics? How did the Reichswehr develop its tactical doctrine? Recognizing that the German General Staff was not a monolithic bureaucracy but a collection of individuals—many of them officers of imagination and brilliance—what debates and disputes over military doctrine took place within the General Staff and army as a whole?

This book is intended as a military-intellectual history of the Reichswehr and its conception of strategy and tactics. As such, it will focus on the military thought of the Reichswehr and particularly that of the General Staff. I shall refrain from any in-depth commentary on the Reichswehr's role in politics, its sociology, its relationship to industry, or its foreign policy role, for these issues have already been carefully examined in the works of F. L. Carsten, Gordon Craig, Ernst Hansen, Hans Hofmann, and Gaines Post, Jr. I would recommend all of these books to the reader who is interested in obtaining a comprehensive picture of the Reichswehr or of the political relationship between Hans von Seeckt and the Weimar Republic. I see my own work on the Reichswehr's military doctrine as a supplement to these historical works on the Reichswehr.

This book will concentrate on the Reichswehr in the era of Hans von Seeckt, General Staff chief from 1919 to 1920 and army commander from 1920 to 1926. It was during this period that the most important decisions on tactical doctrine, military organization, and training were made. By the time von Seeckt left in 1926, the Reichswehr had a clear standardized battle doctrine and theory of future warfare that was amended and adapted only slightly during the remaining years of the Weimar Republic. Indeed, the tactics of the 1939 and 1940 campaigns were, for the most part, developed in the early 1920s. This study is organized into three major sections. Chapters One through Three examine the creation of the Reichswehr's tactical doctrine, based on the very thorough analysis made by the General Staff under von Seeckt's direction between 1919 and 1921. At that time, the German Army attempted to create a military doctrine that would correct the mistakes made in World War I. Although the majority of the General Staff favored an offensive doctrine of mobile war, there was also considerable dissent and debate within the army, and alternative theories were proffered. This debate is covered in Chapter Three.

The second major section of the work is the development of the Reichswehr's tactics as set down by von Seeckt and the General Staff in Army Regulation 487, *Leadership and Battle with Combined Arms*, the primary expression of the German Army's doctrine of future warfare. Chapters Four through Seven examine how the army's training organization and weapons development were geared to the tactical doctrine cre-

ated after World War I. A study of early German armor and air force doctrine is also included, for both of these aspects of military tactics were
viewed as important elements of future warfare. In both of those fields,
the German Army made great progress that would directly affect the development of those arms in the 1930s and 1940s. The third major section
is Chapter Eight, which examines the Reichswehr in its maturity, during
the mid- to late 1920s, when the tactical doctrines had been created and
the army trained in them. In this period, the Reichswehr would practice
its tactical system in large-scale maneuvers and exercises, gaining proficiency in the art of carrying out a mobile war using combined arms.

This work is not meant to be a biography of Hans von Seeckt, though
von Seeckt is the dominant figure of the interwar German Army, and his
ideas on warfare definitively shaped German military thought, from army
mobilization programs to air force doctrine. The German Army that
marched into Poland in 1939 and into France in 1940 was more a creation
of Hans von Seeckt than anyone else. Military historians have generally regarded von Seeckt's ideas as important and interesting, but not particularly innovative. I disagree. I intend to demonstrate in this study that Hans
von Seeckt was in many ways an original military thinker, whose clarity of
vision, comprehensive view of future warfare and ability to impose these
views on the German Army made him one of the most important military
thinkers of the twentieth century.

Even though a great commander might provide the vision and set the
army's grand strategy, all of his effort would be for nought unless the
framework of his grand vision were fleshed out by the detailed work of
capable staff officers and military specialists. Great commanders and military theorists are useful only to a point. A brilliant theory is useless if the
officers who have to make it a reality are mediocre. The Reichswehr had a
very competent, high-quality officer corps. There were many staff and
line officers who were very sound military thinkers in their own right, capable of turning von Seeckt's outline of tactics and strategy into a practical reality. Some officers would even amend and improve von Seeckt's
outline.

There seems to be a prejudice among many historians to study the great
military theorists almost to the exclusion of the lower ranking officers
who made the theories effective. In this work, I hope to correct this tendency by focusing attention upon certain lesser-known, but still important, lower ranking tactical thinkers of the Reichswehr. Officers like Ernst
Volckheim, Germany's first major armor tactician, and Helmut Wilberg,
the Reichswehr's premier air tactician, did not publish any grand strategic
principles, but they did quietly create a body of practical and effective
tactics for armored and aerial warfare that played a central role in the development of the Reichswehr and later the Wehrmacht. There is, unfortu-

nately, relatively little mention of either Volckheim or Wilberg by either German or English-language military historians. A more thorough examination of both of these officers is long overdue. Helmut Wilberg, in particular, deserves his own biography.


ON VOCABULARY

Throughout this work, the terms "Reichswehr" and "German Army" are used interchangeably. The official title of the German Army from 1919 to 1935 was actually the Reichsheer (Reichs Army); the navy was the Reichsmarine, and together, their official title was the Reichswehr. I realize this linguistic discrepancy and justify it by common usage. Even in Germany in the 1920s, the army was commonly referred to as the Reichswehr— witness the contemporary term "Black Reichswehr" to describe secret *army* reserves. In 1933 Hans von Seeckt wrote a book about the army entitled *Die Reichswehr*. Harold Gordon, author of an excellent general history of the German Army from 1919 to 1926, normally uses the term Reichswehr. Even though it is technically incorrect, most German military historians today feel comfortable using the word Reichswehr to describe the army of the Weimar Republic. Another term—the Provisional Reichswehr—can also be confusing. The Provisional Reichswehr was the official title of the army from March 1919—when it was an ad hoc collection of Freikorps and former Imperial Army units—until January 1, 1921, when it was drawn down to its treaty organization and permanent strength of 100,000. Henceforth, it was just the Reichswehr.

I have also used the terms "General Staff" and "Truppenamt" (Troops Office) interchangeably. Legally, of course, the German Army possessed no General Staff in the 1920's. General Staff officers were officially regarded as "Führergehilfen" (leadership assistants). I also justify the term "General Staff officer" by contemporary usage. The Truppenamt *was* the General Staff. Even in official correspondence, German Army officers often slipped and used the term "General Staff officers." I doubt that any German General Staff corps officer of the 1920s would have called himself a "leadership assistant" unless he was standing in front of Allied inspectors of the Interallied Military Control Commission. As regards other standard military terms such as "strategy" and "doctrine," I generally follow the accepted American military definitions. To an American, strategy means army and army group operations—war on a grand scale. The political side of large-scale warfare is normally called grand strategy. The Germans normally refer to what we call strategy as operations, and grand strategy as strategy. The term "doctrine" is a common military term in English, but not common in German. In fact, in that word one sees much of the difference between the American approach to war and the German one. The American term implies a rigidity of tactics, the "proper" way to employ the principles of war. The Germans, before World War I, did not define the tactics and strategy in any manner that would imply dogma. The closest language equivalent the Germans would have had is "concept." Military tactics were general guidelines—they were not meant to be literal formulas or principles of warfare. Doctrine is a simple and convenient word to use to describe the standardized military tactics of the German Army. In the absence of a clear German term for standardized tactics, I will use the term "doctrine" without implying the additional meaning of "dogma" that the American military has added to it.

## ON SOURCES

The primary emphasis of this work is on the German military thought of the Weimar Republic era using contemporary sources. I was most fortuitously assisted in researching this study by the events of German reunification. Western historians are once again allowed into the formerly closed archives of the People's Army of the German Democratic Republic. I was able to visit these archives and use material that has been unavailable to Western scholars since World War II. Otherwise, the material I used in my research is generally available in major collections on the German Army, especially the U.S. National Archives German Records Collection and the German Federal Military Archives in Freiburg im Breisgau in West Germany. Of particular importance has been the Crerar Collection of the Royal Military College of Canada in Kingston, Ontario. This collection is, after the U.S. National Archives, the best German Army collection in North America. The Crerar Collection contains many books, periodicals, and military manuals from the 1920s and 1930s, enough material to build a clear picture of German tactical doctrine in the 1920s. I have also added an extensive bibliography that goes well beyond the specific focus of this volume and includes works on the British, French, and American tactical doctrine of the period, so that readers might have a good basis for comparison between the tactics and organization of the Reichswehr and those of the World War I Allies.

Although most of the documents I used have been readily available to historians for many years, I used them in an original manner. The main priority for scholars using these documents for a quarter-century after World War II has been from the perspective of political history: to examine the role of the Reichswehr in the Weimar Republic. Until recently, tactical regulations such as Army Regulation 487 have gone relatively unnoticed, while the Reichswehr-government correspondence has been minutely examined. This applies to German as well as non-German historians. My approach was to analyze these regulations and to analyze the role of the post–World War I studies in making German tactics. These important documents, and the works of men like Ernst Volckheim and Helmut Wilberg, have been overlooked, and as a consequence, the quality and content of German military thought of the early 1920s has been relatively ignored. In this study, I hope to rediscover the main trends of Reichswehr military thought and offer a case for their central importance in the later development of German military theory and practice.

## LESSONS TO BE LEARNED

A study of the Reichswehr can offer several lessons to modern military leaders. The first is the effective methodology of reform worked out by von Seeckt and the General Staff in the immediate postwar period. The questions that von Seeckt proposed in 1919, the basis for examining the army's wartime lessons, are as pertinent today for the study of operational doctrine as they were then. The comprehensive nature of the postwar survey, a program that employed several hundred officers, is a model of an effective and objective study of the lessons of war. The survey critically analyzed the wartime performance of the German Army, including its mistakes, and developed some clear and (as it turned out) sound operational and tactical solutions.

The second lesson is the intellectual atmosphere engendered by von Seeckt and the Reichswehr command. While insisting that the army adopt a common operational and tactical doctrine, the Reichswehr avoided intellectual stagnation—one of the great enemies of any army—by allowing flexibility and tolerating debate on military matters. Officers who dissented from the new operational concepts, such as Kurt Hesse, were allowed to argue openly for radical alternatives without penalty. As a result of the high command's attitude, the mobile-war doctrines of the 1920s were gradually transformed into the blitzkrieg concepts of the 1930s.

A third lesson is the primacy of training. The Reichswehr emphasized the training of soldiers, especially leaders, from lance corporals to senior General Staff officers. The Reichswehr training system, which introduced numerous innovations, excelled in training both large units and individual soldiers. Sound tactical theory aside, it was in training that the Reichswehr surpassed all its contemporary rivals, ensuring the battlefield efficiency and tactical success of the German Army in 1939-40. Ironically, the German system was built directly upon the foundations of the military defeat of World War I.

In the end, a study of the Reichswehr provides a lesson on the importance of the individual in history. Hans von Seeckt was the core of the effort to rebuild and reform the German Army, and a major share of the result should be credited to him. Other German military leaders of the period possessed little of the ability, prestige, and intellectual vision necessary to inspire a defeated army and thereby dramatically remold its system and doctrine. Considering the circumstances and opposition, von Seeckt's achievement is remarkable.

I would not have been able to write this book without the advice, assistance, time, and encouragement of several people. Professor Gunther Rothenberg of Purdue University has critiqued my drafts and offered encouragement over the last two years. Professors Robert Hopwood and Lucien Karchmar of Queen's University, Canada, have made numerous suggestions to improve the text. Harry Riley and Robin Cookson of the U.S. National Archives and Völker Ernst of the East German Army Archives all provided excellent research support. Last, but never least, I wish to thank my wife, Lynn, who is an excellent scholar in her own right. She is the best proofreader a scholar could wish for, and as a computer whiz she carried me through all aspects of layout and word processing.

Any errors of commission or omission in this work are the sole responsibility of the author.

*Hans Von Seeckt*

CHAPTER ONE

# The Lessons of World War I

In the midst of crisis and defeat at the end of 1918, the civilian leaders of Germany were demoralized and confused. Germany's military defeat had brought about the collapse of the Imperial government, the proclamation of a republic virtually by accident, and the establishment of a government whose authority was not recognized even on the streets of Berlin. On the surface, the army appeared to be in the same state. The rear units had taken part in the overthrow of the monarchy, and the field armies were being brought home and demobilized. Behind the scenes, however, the high command and the General Staff were not as confused and uncertain as civilian leaders. Even before the civil war ended in Berlin and Munich, the General Staff had absorbed the lessons of World War I and begun rebuilding the army. From its frank assessment of its strengths and weaknesses in the war, the army was able to remold its organization and tactical doctrine.

By any normal application of the principles of economics, international politics, and military history, the German Empire never stood a chance of winning World War I. It was a case of Germany against the world: Germany, bolstered by three weak allies—Austria-Hungary, Turkey, and Bulgaria—was pitted against France, Russia, the British Empire, the United States, Italy, and several other nations. Despite the odds, Germany nearly won the war on the battlefield. As late as June 1918 the German Army was on the offensive, pushing back the Allied armies in France. The Germans had fought so well and been victorious so often that when the collapse came only five months later, some generals—most notably Erich von Ludendorff—refused to acknowledge that the Imperial Army had been defeated on the battlefield, blaming the collapse instead on a "stab in the back" by traitorous politicians and civilians on the home front.

Most generals and experienced officers did not share Ludendorff's view. They knew that the Imperial Army had been defeated militarily, but even this awareness did not replace the conviction that Germany could—should—have won the war. Since a defeated army has more incentive to study the lessons of the war, many German officers began to write histories, memoirs, studies, and articles filled with criticism and support of wartime leadership, tactics, and strategy. General Staff training had traditionally emphasized the study of military history, and the smoke had

1

barely cleared before officers were interpreting the war's lessons. Thus by
the end of World War I, a consensus on the strategic, tactical, and technological lessons of the army's experience could be found within the General Staff Corps. These conclusions would be reinforced by further study,
debate and reflection.


## THE STRATEGIC LESSONS OF WORLD WAR I

The "stab in the back" theory, which explained Germany's defeat as the
result of betrayal by Social Democrats and leftists at home, was a useful
myth for postwar Germany's extreme right and for Germany's de facto
wartime dictator, General Ludendorff. However, few General Staff officers
or higher commanders actually believed it. The senior officers were painfully aware that Germany had been defeated on the battlefield and that
the defeat had been caused primarily by grand strategic mistakes on the
part of the army high command. In their correspondence during and after
the war as well as in their postwar books, German generals were often
ruthlessly critical of the military decisions made by Germany's wartime
army chiefs: General Helmuth von Moltke, chief of staff until September
1914, General Erich von Falkenhayn, chief of staff until August 1916, and
Ludendorff, military dictator of Germany until November 1918.

Many of the General Staff's most capable officers believed that the war's
greatest strategic mistake had been committed by von Moltke in the first
months of the war. Von Moltke's poor execution of the Schlieffen Plan had
lost Germany its last chance to end the war quickly by one decisive
stroke. Count von Schlieffen, chief of the General Staff until 1906, had
created a war plan against the French calling for an enormous envelopment of the French army: Thirty-six German corps were to drive around
the French flank through Belgium. The Schlieffen Plan is one of the most
intriguing "might-have-beens" of military history, for it came within a
hairbreadth of actually deciding the war for Germany within two
months.[1]

The soundness of the Schlieffen Plan has been a major subject of debate within military history circles for the last seventy-five years. However, the debate about von Schlieffen's strategy was pretty one-sided in
Germany.[2] Most of the General Staff believed in it. Indeed, its most articu-
late postwar advocate was Lieutenant General Wilhelm Groener, a highly
regarded General Staff officer and ardent disciple of Count von Schlieffen
who took over Ludendorff's post as quartermaster general of the German
Army in October 1918 and who later served as Reichswehr minister for
the Weimar Republic. After the war era Groener wrote two detailed studies of the 1914 campaign that firmly placed the blame for the Schlieffen

Plan's failure on the shoulders of von Moltke. According to Groener, von Moltke had shown weak leadership. He had violated von Schlieffen's dictum of focusing the German effort on one flank by engaging a large part of his forces in a strategically senseless battle in Lorraine on the left flank and losing effective control of the German right flank.[3]

The strategic handling of the war's next phase by von Falkenhayn, new chief of the General Staff, also came in for intensive criticism both during and after the war. In 1915, with the western front settling into fruitless trench warfare, German senior officers on the eastern front saw opportunities to inflict a decisive defeat on the Russians. In the winter of 1914/15, Paul von Hindenburg and Ludendorff, in command on the northeastern front, planned a gigantic pincer movement that would not only capture Poland but also surround the main Russian armies.[4] Given enough troops, the German commanders in the east probably could have knocked Russia out of the war in 1915. After Hans von Seeckt was transferred to the eastern front early in 1915 he also became an advocate of the Eastern Strategy, arguing that the military opportunities lay there and not in the west.[5] Yet von Falkenhayn sent only limited reinforcements to the eastern front in 1915 and engaged large German forces in the west in a futile attempt to break the Allied Front in Flanders. In contrast, the limited offensives authorized in the east in 1915 succeeded in overrunning Poland and inflicting over one million Russian casualties.

Von Falkenhayn's greatest strategic blunder was the Battle of Verdun. In a notable departure from German military tradition, von Falkenhayn planned not for a decisive battle, a breakthrough, or even the seizure of strategic territory, but rather for a campaign that would simply produce so many French casualties that the French Army would be bled white. Von Falkenhayn was right on the last point: the French Army suffered an estimated 377,200 casualties in the ten-month battle. But the German Army was also badly weakened, with an estimated 337,000 casualties.[6] The Verdun strategy was seen as so disastrous that in the summer of 1916, a delegation of senior staff officers from von Falkenhayn's own staff at the army high command visited the emperor to request that von Falkenhayn be relieved.[7]

In August 1916 General von Hindenburg was brought from the east to replace von Falkenhayn as chief of the army high command. Hindenburg's chief of staff, Ludendorff, became quartermaster general of the army and dictator of the war effort. Ludendorff was a brilliant tactician, perhaps the best of the war. Under his direction, the western front was stabilized, Romania overrun in 1916, and the Russians knocked out of the war in 1917. Yet, for all of Ludendorff's acknowledged brilliance as a soldier, he was seen by many German generals as a man whose emotional fanaticism and poor grasp of grand strategy brought about the collapse of the German Army in 1918.

Up until the summer of 1918, Ludendorff believed that Germany could decisively win the war. Accordingly, he opposed government efforts to negotiate a favorable peace. In fact, the general came close to winning the war for Germany in the brilliantly conceived and executed German offensive of March 1918. By using surprise and superior infantry and artillery tactics, the German Army shattered the British Fifth Army near St. Quentin, breaking through the British lines into open country in one day, March 21, 1918. The remarkable success of the German offensive of 1918 nearly panicked British Headquarters. By March 23 the Germans had achieved a 40-mile breach in Allied lines. Exhaustion of the attacking troops, however, combined with the difficulty of bringing reinforcements, supplies, artillery, and ammunition up to the new battle line, slowed the German offensive. In March 1918 the Germans had a slight numerical superiority of 191 divisions to 169 Allied divisions and had established a favorable troop and artillery ratio at the point of the offensive.[8] But the marginal German troop superiority meant that the Allies could maintain a considerable force in reserve while still holding the rest of the line. In response to the German offensive, General Ferdinand Foch, Allied Supreme Commander, committed these reserves and established a new, unbroken front.

From March to July 1918 Ludendorff carried out a series of major offensives in northern France, each one forcing back the Allied lines and gaining territory. The allies stopped each offensive, and soon the troop and material superiority on the western front switched decisively to them. By midsummer 1918, strong Allied forces went on the offensive supported by thousands of tanks, aircraft, and fresh American troops against German divisions that had been "fought out"—and that Germany, with little manpower left to provide, had no hope of reinforcing. After the initial failure of the German offensive in March 1918, the subsequent offensives had little hope of success.

Many of the German generals were highly critical of Ludendorff's strategy. General von Lossberg, chief of staff of the Fourth Army in Flanders, expressed doubt as to the outcome of the Ludendorff offensives in April 1918.[9] Colonel Wilhelm Ritter von Leeb pointed out that "we had absolutely no operational goal! That was the trouble."[10] Wilhelm Groener echoes this view in his memoirs.[11] One of the most interesting critiques of Ludendorff's war strategy appears in a letter of July 1919, written by General Georg Wetzell, former chief of the General Staff Operations Section to General von Seeckt. In it, Wetzell regrets that Ludendorff might have been talked out of his strategy if von Seeckt had been at the army high command and not kept away due to Ludendorff's professional jealousy. Wetzell recounts Ludendorff's rejection of his proposal to ship a considerable German force to the Italian front, where German and Austrian forces had just delivered a crushing blow to the Italians at Caporetto. A sustained German offensive in Italy, he argued, would threaten to knock Italy out of the war, forcing the Allies to divert all their troop reserves to Italy simply to hold the line and thereby making an Allied offensive on the western front impractical[12]—certainly a superior strategic concept to Ludendorff's 1918 offensive gamble.

The most comprehensive critique of Ludendorff's strategy was done by a special Reichstag committee that took testimony on the causes of the German collapse in 1918. Eight volumes of documents, commentaries, and statements were published in 1928.[13] The "stab in the back" explanation was refuted simply by printing the status reports of German corps and divisions in October and November 1918. It was clear that most units were scarcely combat effective in the last months of the war.[14] In 1918, even Hans Delbrück, Germany's premier military historian, became a leading critic of Ludendorff's strategy.[15]

## THE TACTICAL LESSONS OF WORLD WAR I

If the German officer corps had ample reason to be dissatisfied with the way the army high command had handled military strategy, they could take some consolation in the fact that German battlefield tactics had generally been superior to those of the Allies throughout the war.

The Imperial Army entered World War I with a more realistic and balanced tactical doctrine than its major opponents. In addition to this, the Germans had a command tradition that allowed subordinate leaders greater flexibility and more independence, which proved to be of great value on the battlefield. Karl von Clausewitz had stressed that friction and "the fog of war" were intrinsic to hostilities. The elder von Moltke, victor of the 1866 war with Austria and the 1870 war with France, built on the Clausewitz tradition by training his General Staff officers to expect friction in war and to command by general directives that allowed subordinate commanders considerable tactical independence in fulfilling their missions. Rigid adherence to plans was not emphasized but a uniform battle doctrine was assured by an elite corps of a few hundred highly trained General Staff officers spread throughout the army.

The Imperial Army went to war in 1914 with a sound respect for modern firepower. In the Field Service Regulations of 1908, fire superiority was considered an essential element of a successful offense.[16] The Germans, like the French and Russians, relied on the relatively flat-trajectory, short-range light field gun as a weapon to gain fire superiority. The French Army provided one hundred twenty of the excellent 75-mm light guns to each corps, as compared with the German allowance of one hundred eight 77-mm light fieldpieces per corps. But the French divisions and corps possessed no medium or heavy artillery, whereas each German division had eighteen 105-mm light howitzers and each corps had sixteen 150-mm heavy howitzers. In all, the French Army had only three hundred heavy guns in comparison with two thousand German heavy guns and howitzers and fifteen hundred light howitzers.[17] This balanced artillery support enabled the Germans to effectively execute a wide variety of fire operations, including long-range missions and the reduction of fortifications, while French artillery was limited to short-range offensive fire support.

From Field Marshal von Moltke the Elder's time, the German tactical preference was to avoid frontal assaults and to use envelopment whenever possible.[18] The Germans were also better trained in using cover and terrain than other European armies.[19] While the French Army had developed a doctrine of carrying out a constant offense under all circumstances—the *offensive à l'outrance* (offensive to the extreme)—and disdained field fortifications as a detriment to troop morale, the Germans had practiced building field fortifications and entrenching before the war.[20] The German Army tactics of 1914 suffered from certain drawbacks such as close attack columns and infantry platoons of eighty men, which were much too large to command effectively. Still, the Germans had much less to unlearn in 1914 than any other major power.

Once the war began, the cohesive and well-trained German General Staff Corps enabled the army to adapt quickly to the new tactical conditions. The General Staff officers at the front acted as the eyes and ears of the high command and army commanders. Membership in the General Staff Corps meant that even a junior captain would be given important tasks and the younger and lower ranking General Staff officers had direct access to the commanders and senior staff members. Lower ranking General Staff officers were assigned special studies on tactics, weaponry, and battlefield conditions. The constant dialogue between the General Staff officers assigned to front units and those at the army headquarters and the high command ensured that the latter had a clear picture of front-line conditions and tactical problems. Accurate information through the General Staff system combined with tactical flexibility enabled the Imperial Army to remain a skip or two ahead of the Allies.

A good example of the German "way of war" is the order written by the army's chief of staff, von Seeckt, for the German Eleventh Army at the Gorlice offensive in May 1915. The order emphasized the subordinate commanders' flexibility in the offense:

> The attack . . . must be pushed forward at a rapid pace. . . . Thus the Army cannot assign the attacking corps and divisions definite ob-

jectives for each day, lest by fixing them the possibility of further progress may be obstructed. . . . Any portion of the attacking troops which is successful in pushing on will expose itself to the danger of envelopment. Thus the troops which least deserve it may meet with disaster as a result of their own rapid advance. Consideration of this possibility makes it necessary for the Army to fix certain lines, which should be reached by the force as a whole, and if possible simultaneously. Any progress beyond these lines will be thankfully welcomed by the Army and made use of.[21]

This is in strong contrast to the extremely detailed orders issued to British units at the Somme in 1916, which set maximum, not minimum, lines of advance and insisted upon an exact alignment of advancing troops as well as strict timetables.

Almost all of the tactical experience of the British, French, and American armies in World War I came from the western front, where the war was dominated by the problem of attacking or defending a continuous front of strong trenches. The Germans' experience was dramatically different from the Allies' because a large part of the Imperial Army served on the eastern front, where an extremely long front, open terrain, and fewer soldiers per mile meant that the war of maneuver was a normal feature of eastern tactics. In August 1914 the outnumbered German Eighth Army, using the superior mobility of the German rail system and possessing more artillery firepower, surrounded and destroyed the Russian Second Army at Tannenberg. In May 1915 the German Eleventh Army, commanded by General von Mackensen with Colonel Hans von Seeckt as his chief of staff, opened the Gorlice offensive with a short but heavy artillery barrage and rolled over the Russians with the whole army. For six weeks the Germans advanced at a rate of 6.5 miles per day, capturing 240,000 prisoners and 224 guns for a loss of 40,000 casualties.[22]

An excellent example of German tactical inventiveness occurred in November 1916 as the Germans swept into Romania. After the Germans broke through the Transylvanian mountains in the north at Vulcan Pass, the strong Romanian forces continued to hold out at the Iron Gate region of the Danube, which straddled the major rail line needed by the Germans for their advance. General von Falkenhayn, commanding the Ninth Army attacking Romania in the north, assembled a motorized task force consisting of a battalion of the 148th Infantry (four rifle companies), three machine-gun platoons (twelve guns), two truck-mounted antiaircraft guns for fire support, a radio detachment, and a cavalry patrol from the Tenth Dragoons. Heavy trucks (2.5-ton vehicles) were detached from the divisional motor battalion to support the attack. The whole constituted a five-hundred-man force under Captain Picht, who was given the simple order,

"Open the Iron Gate." Picht took his motorized force 50 miles to the Iron Gate without being spotted. In a surprise night attack he overran some Romanian garrisons in the rear of the Iron Gate and, in effect, blocked off the division-sized Romanian force defending it. Picht's force established a defensive position and beat off Romanian counterattacks until relief came and the Romanians were forced to evacuate their vital position across the transportation lines.[23] This small rapid-moving campaign by an independent motorized force was almost as neatly done as some large motorized operations of World War II. Surprise, mobility, good communications, a well-balanced force as well as a clear understanding of the transport net and terrain were all elements of this successful operation.

On the eastern front, in Romania, and in Italy, the Germans carried out numerous successful offensives. In the open terrain of Poland, Russia, and Romania, cavalry divisions were still tactically useful. As cavalry disappeared from the western front, the Germans developed tactics for mixed cavalry-infantry formations.[24] In the Romanian campaign of fall 1916, the Germans managed to overrun the country in two months. Remember that the Allied leaders of World War II (for example, Bernard Montgomery, Charles De Gaulle, and George Patton) had fought World War I in places like the Somme, Verdun, and the Meuse-Argonne. Most of the German generals of the 1940s (for example, Erwin Rommel, Albrecht Kesselring, Ewald von Kleist, Erich von Manstein, Karl von Rundstedt), in contrast, had seen extensive service on the eastern front in World War I.

As that world war progressed, the Germans rapidly developed new methods of artillery support and infantry offensive tactics that restored maneuver to the western front. The chief originator of the new artillery tactics was Lieutenant Colonel Georg Bruchmüller. Bruchmüller increased the accuracy of artillery pieces by developing for each gun individual firing tables that combined survey information, meteorological data, and live-fire data for each gun tube. By maximizing the accuracy of their artillery, the Germans were able to provide accurate artillery support without the ranging fire that gave warning of impending offensives. By using this system, the Germans managed to achieve surprise at Riga in September 1917 in a 13-division attack. The liaison between the infantry and supporting artillery was stressed, and infantry unit commanders down to the platoon level were carefully briefed on the artillery support plan. The attack at Riga, which combined new infantry storm tactics following a surprise heavy-artillery barrage, cost the Russians Riga, 25,000 men, and 262 guns in a three-day campaign.[25]

The greatest German tactical achievement of the war was the development of stormtroop tactics. Storm tactics were not created by any one man but rather evolved during the course of the war with contributions by many officers.[26] Ludendorff officially endorsed the new tactics and, by late 1917, battalions, regiments, and even divisions had been trained as elite attack formations. During the course of the war, the Imperial Army dropped the old rigid, linear attack formations and developed squad tactics emphasizing infiltration, rapid advance, disregard for flanks, and bypassing of enemy strongpoints by the first wave of assault troops. The infantry squad was efficiently restructured into a seven-man rifle section as the maneuver element and a four-man light machine gun team as the fire element commanded by a noncommissioned "officer" (NCO).[27] The object of combining Stormtroop tactics with new artillery tactics was to restore surprise and mobility to the offensive so as to break through the Allied front line into the open country beyond and the Allied rear organization.

Stormtroop tactics were used on the Italian front by the Austrian-German armies during the Caporetto offensive of October-November 1917. This offensive not only knocked the Italian Army across the Piave River but also cost the Italians 10,000 killed, 30,000 wounded, 293,000 taken prisoner and 400,000 deserted, at only a fraction of the casualties for the attackers.[28] In a counterattack against the British at Cambrai on November 30, 1917, the Germans used storm tactics on a grand scale for the first time on the western front; the 20-division German attack was almost as successful as the British mass tank attack only 10 days before. Catching the British by surprise, the German forces, without tanks, quickly overran and captured 158 British artillery pieces, took 6,000 prisoners, and pushed the British back—in some places, beyond their original front.[29] Using entire divisions of storm troops on the first day of the March 1918 offensive, the German Eighteenth Army under General von Hutier broke open the entire front line of the British Fifth Army. The British lost over 21,000 prisoners on March 21.[30] The German offensive was slowed and eventually halted, more by the Germans' inability to bring supplies and artillery support rapidly to the new front lines than by Allied tactical proficiency.

As in the case of offensive tactics, German development of defensive tactics stayed well ahead of the Allies. When Hindenburg and Ludendorff took over the high command in 1916, they decided to revise the defensive tactics of the army, particularly on the western front. The army would no longer keep most of its troops in the front line. Instead, they would be withdrawn well behind the forward trenches, where they would be less vulnerable to Allied artillery fire. The forward positions would be held lightly, and heavy-duty defensive strongpoints, many of reinforced concrete, were to be built behind the lines, preferably on the reverse slope of a hill or ridge to inhibit Allied observation. The defense was to be kept mobile and the German reserves in strongpoints and directly behind the front would, in case of an Allied attack, counterattack immediately, before the attackers could consolidate their positions. Local commanders had the leeway to create their own variations of the defensive system, to authorize counterattacks, and to commit local reserves.[31]

The new German defensive tactics were employed against the French spring offensive of 1917. Between April 16 and April 25 the French Army lost over 96,000 men in exchange for a minimal gain in ground and considerably lower German losses.[32] This bloody repulse of the French led directly to the mutiny of much of the French Army in the spring and summer of 1917. The British Army did not learn the lessons of German defensive tactics. In March 1918, at the point of the German attack, the British had two-thirds of their troops in the forward zone, vulnerable to German artillery and offensive tactics, with one-third of their forces in the rear available for counterattacks. The German defense reversed these proportions, with only one-third of the forces in the forward zone and two-thirds well to the rear.[33]

## TROOP TRAINING

The world has long admired the effectiveness of German troop training. From the army of the Great Elector of Prussia to the modern Bundeswehr, the German Army has shown a particular talent for training soldiers. The German military tradition gave top priority to the thorough training of soldiers, and this became central to the German way of making war. Even before the French Revolution, Prussian drill regulations and military organization were so highly regarded that the French seriously considered their adoption.[34] When Germany and France went to war in 1870, a German army composed largely of well-trained conscripts and reservists defeated France's highly regarded professional army.

Beginning with Scharnhorst and the Prussian Army at the start of the nineteenth century, the German Army has gone through several reformations in organization and training. By the outbreak of World War I, an effective system of training General Staff officers, line officers, noncommissioned officers (NCOs), and soldiers was established. Many prewar officers were educated in old-fashioned cadet schools that combined rigid military discipline and drills with civilian subjects. A growing number of officer aspirants, however, were receiving an education that would allow them to enter a university. Even in the nineteenth century, the Bavarian Army required an *Abitur* (university matriculation certificate) of all aspiring officers, and the percentage of Abitur holders among officer aspirants in the Prussian, Saxon, and Württemberg armies grew from 35 percent in 1890 to 65.1 percent in 1912.[35] The prewar cadet attended an officer school for his particular army branch, such as cavalry or infantry, for one year before being commissioned. After three or four years of troop service, the officer, usually a senior lieutenant, could take the General Staff examination and compete for a place at the Kriegsakademie in Berlin.

During the last years before World War I, about eight hundred officers each year took the Kriegsakademie entrance examinations. Of these, about 20 percent passed and were accepted as students for the General Staff course.[36] The course lasted three years. The curriculum stressed military history, tactics, logistics, and operational problems rather than politics or world economics. It was an education geared toward creating an elite group capable of effectively commanding divisions, corps, and armies on the battlefield, rather than toward a corps well versed in the broad political/strategic aspects of war.[37] Once an officer was admitted to the General Staff Corps, his career would be carefully managed and would include alternating periods of regimental duty and unit command with service on the higher army staffs. Membership in the General Staff Corps assured an officer of faster promotion and greater opportunity to rise to high command than service as a line officer.

The average German soldier was a conscript. Since the army required only about 60 percent of the men eligible for military service before the war, the standards could be kept high. The average prewar German conscript was healthy, literate, and generally first-rate soldier material. He was also trained by probably the best NCO corps in the world. These NCOs were career professionals, carefully selected to high standards, and they enjoyed considerably greater prestige in society than NCOs in Britain, France, or the United States. The German NCO, upon completing his military career, was guaranteed a pension of 1,500 marks as well as preferential hiring in the civil service, railroads, and postal system. Local governments preferred former NCOs as employees because they were competent, reliable, and diligent.[38] Becoming a career NCO was a great social step up for many men from farms and factory towns, guaranteeing a good future and entry into the lower middle class.

High-quality officer and NCO corps combined with an abundance of suitable conscripts ensured that German soldiers and small units would be adequately trained. For the training of commanders, higher staffs, and large units, the Prussian Army had pioneered the use of large-scale, peacetime maneuvers for divisions and corps. Even before the 1870 war, the Prussian Army had established a maneuver system that included independent umpires and the free play of unit against unit.[39] The yearly corps and divisional maneuvers provided the General Staff officers with experience in directing large troop movements and the commanders and junior officers with the opportunity to test the effectiveness of their battlefield tactics.

The Germans entered World War I with the best-trained army in Europe and managed to keep its training advantage throughout the war. The Kriegsakademie was shut down for the duration, but the General Staff examination system was maintained and special short courses were set up for General Staff aspirants. Once an officer was granted General Staff probationer status, he was sent to gain additional experience serving under seasoned staff officers in front units. Officer courses were established for wartime commissionees. Lieutenant Ernst Jünger, a 1914 volunteer who served for four years on the western front, was sent back to Germany by his regiment in 1915 to attend a basic officer course. In April 1916 he attended another officer course under the direction of his divisional commander. In January 1917 he was sent to a four-week company-commander course.[40] The intensive army training program, which emphasized the training of NCOs and officers, provided the German Army with good leadership at the lowest levels. The senior commanders trusted the abilities of their most junior leaders to carry out missions and, in the more mobile war of 1918, German squad, platoon, and company commanders would accordingly be given far more tactical independence than their British or American counterparts.

As the tactics of war changed, the high command initiated a program to retrain virtually the whole army. Nine artillery schools were set up on the western front for training artillery officers in the new gunnery tactics.[41] The entire artillery force was rotated to ranges behind the front in 1917-18 in order to re-register every gun and retrain the officers and gun crews in the new tactics.[42] By September 1916, courses for company and battery commanders in the new style of defense were established behind the lines. There is no exact record of the total number of officers who attended these courses, but one army group, that of Crown Prince Wilhelm, "sent 100 officers and 100 NCO's through the five to six week courses late in 1916."[43] In preparation for the 1918 offensive, whole divisions were brought out of the line for training. Jünger's unit was brought behind the front in early 1918 for several weeks' training in storm tactics, including live-fire exercises that resulted in accidents and casualties.[44] Ludendorff described his training program for the 1918 offensive: "In the West we revived courses of instruction for higher commanders and staff officers, as well as for juniors down to group commanders [squad leaders], whose functions were so important a factor in success. Marked activity became apparent throughout the army. I commenced with unit training, and ended in exercises by formations of all branches, or on the ranges. The barrage was practiced with live ammunition, and the infantry trained to follow close behind it."[45]

As units rotated to the rear for rest or relegation to reserves, they were expected to conduct intensive small-unit training. The high command developed a flexible two-week training program for company and battalion commanders to use while their units were in reserve. By 1918 marksmanship was again stressed, as were tactics of attack, counterattack, and ma-neuver.[46] Small units were expected to carry out their own live-fire exer-cises and to set up realistic hand-grenade ranges behind the front lines.[47]

The thoroughness of German wartime training was especially evident in the air war. German fighter pilots were first trained in Germany and then passed on to a special fighter school at Valenciennes, France, where they learned the ropes from experienced fighter pilots before going into action. From 1916 on, the instruction program for the German two-seater observa-tion and battle pilots consisted of initial flight instruction and a solo flight for a standard pilot's license. Then the pilot had to undertake a program of twenty-five landings, five at night. A second array of tests included flights of various heights and distances. Twenty more landings under more diffi-cult conditions were then required, as well as practice dogfights and four long-range overland flights. A third test was then given, which consisted of a written examination, a 250-kilometer flight, and high-altitude flying with at least thirty minutes over 3,500 meters. Only then would the pilot be con-sidered qualified.[48] Training deaths accounted for one-quarter of the Ger-man wartime pilot casualties, in sharp contrast to the British, who lost more than 50 percent of their casualties in training, not battle.[49] Although the Germans were consistently outnumbered in the air by the Allies at a 2:1 ra-tio, they not only held their own, but for much of the war they also held air superiority. The quality of German pilot training had much to do with this. By 1917 the British were sending pilots to the front who had only fifteen hours of flying time, sometimes less.[50] Compare that with the standard training program for the German fighter and observation pilots and it is no surprise how the Germans shot down two to three Allied pilots for every pilot of their own lost.

No less an admirer of the German Army than General Charles de Gaulle credited the superior training of the Germans as the primary cause of Ger-man tactical successes: "Even in the gloomy hecatombs to which the ex-clusive system of nations-in-arms led during the Great War, the superiority of good troops was abundantly clear. How else is one to explain the pro-longed success of the German armies against so many opponents? For the 1,700,000 deaths which they counted in all, the Germans, better trained than anyone else, killed 3,200,000 enemies; for the 750,000 prisoners which they lost, they took 1,900,000."[51]

## THE LESSONS OF THE AIR WAR

The German Army's Air Service (Luftstreitkräfte), like its ground forces, emerged from the war with more-sophisticated tactics than the Allied air forces, as well as a more accurate evaluation of tactical air support for ground troops and the worth of strategic bombing. In 1914 the airplane appeared to the major powers not as a weapon in its own right but rather as an element of reconnaissance and artillery observation. The idea of bombing the enemy rear forces or using aircraft in a ground attack had not been discussed seriously.[52] With the rapid evolution of aerial technology, however, bomber and fighter aircraft became a major element of every air service by 1916. That same year, gaining air superiority over the battlefield became a tactical imperative for mounting a successful offensive. The artillery had become dependent on observation and reconnaissance aircraft for locating enemy targets, and the inability to freely operate observation aircraft made effective artillery support extremely difficult.

From the Somme offensive in the summer of 1916 to the German offensive in March 1918, the German Army maintained a defensive posture on the western front. Following the ground strategy, the German Air Service also decided upon a defensive air battle doctrine of denying the air space behind German lines to the Allies. This defensive strategy gave the Germans several advantages. First, their aircraft, if damaged, could easily land behind their own lines. Second, the Germans built a comprehensive observer and communications network that warned them of Allied strikes, enabling the Air Service to concentrate fighters to meet the threat. The offensive force would not only have to fight enemy airplanes but would also have to face considerable antiaircraft fire. And third, the German defenders could choose to give battle under favorable conditions, while the Allies were forced to keep attacking in order to keep the initiative.

In the fall of 1916, Hindenburg and Ludendorff created a central headquarters and staff for the German air units, with General Erich von Höppner as the Air Service commander and Colonel Hermann von der Lieth-Thomsen as his chief of staff. Although the Air Service was not yet an independent air force, it did have its own chain of command and was answerable only to the army high command. General von Höppner and his senior staff officers, Colonels Wilhelm Siegert and von der Lieth-Thomsen, had an excellent grasp of air organization, tactics, and logistics. They provided top-notch leadership for the Air Service until the end of the war.

Since the Allies normally had a 2:1 superiority of aircraft over the western front, the Air Service met the situation by concentrating its aircraft into larger units. In 1916 the German air detachments were reorganized into squadrons of ten to twelve aircraft. In April 1917 the Air Service combined flights from four fighter squadrons in order to create a tactical battle formation of over twenty aircraft. The object was to concentrate planes in a particular sector to gain local air superiority. The large formation experiment was a success, and in June 1917 the Air Service created the first fighter group, Jagdgeschwader 1, which comprised the Fourth, Sixth, Tenth, and Eleventh fighter squadrons under the command of Baron Manfred von Richthofen.[53]

The large fighter groups were highly mobile. Their entire support apparatus and ground staff could be moved quickly by truck and rail from one threatened area of the front to another, then rapidly set up in tents and temporary airfields. The mobility of the German air groups meant that the Air Service could redeploy and concentrate against each new threat. Thus it was able to hold its own against the British in support of the Arras offensive in April 1917: That month the Germans shot down 151 British airplanes for a loss of 66 of their own.[54] In March 1918, in support of the Ludendorff offensive, the German Air Service was able to establish numerical air superiority over the attacking armies' front by secretly concentrating 730 aircraft to oppose 579 British planes.[55] Even though the Allied powers produced 138,685 aircraft to the Central powers' 53,222 and generally maintained numerical superiority, the Germans were able to keep an effective force in the air until the war's end.[56]

In 1917 and 1918, the Air Service headquarters even specified that aircraft be built with rapid deployment in mind. The American Air Service general, William ("Billy") Mitchell, commented on the German Fokker DVII fighter planes, which he examined at the war's end: "The Fokkers impressed us all greatly. They could be shipped on the train with their wings off, which were laid back against the sides of the fuselage. The gas tank remained, full of fuel, and the engine was ready to start. They could be wheeled off the flatcars, the wings put on in about fifteen minutes, the engine cranked up and they were ready for combat. Their ammunition belts were even full of ammunition. There was no airplane on the Allied side which could be handled in this way."[57]

During the war, the Germans moved ahead of the Allies in developing specialized aircraft and tactics for ground-attack planes. In 1917 the German Air Service deployed the world's first all-metal—steel and aluminum—aircraft, the Junkers J-1. The crew and engine were protected by 5 millimeters of chrome-nickel steel plate, and since it was built expressly for ground attack, it carried three machine guns and a bomb load.[58] Other partially armored aircraft were produced in 1917-18; these gave excellent service in ground attacks, particularly the Halberstadt C1II and the Hannover C1II, both of which were used in the offensives at Cambrai in 1917 and in the major German offensives of 1918.[59] By the end of 1917, 10.5 percent of the German aircraft were ground-attack planes.[60] Although the Allies also employed aircraft in ground attacks, they never designed specialized aircraft for that role, using standard fighters instead.

By 1918 the high command was emphasizing the role of the "battle planes" as offensive breakthrough weapons that would substitute for the

German lack of tanks in providing mobile firepower and shock effect for the first waves of assault troops. In February 1918 the Air Service commander outlined a system of tactical air support by which aircraft would not merely fly preplanned ground-attack missions—some battle-plane detachments would remain in reserve and ready to fly immediate support missions at the request of the forward infantry commanders.[61] A training manual of January 1918 outlined the support that ground-attack aircraft could provide for the infantry and established training exercises for infantry and air units to practice together.[62] The German offensives in the spring of 1918 demonstrated how vital tactical air support had become for the Imperial Army. For the three German armies that attacked on March 21, 1918, twenty seven ground-attack squadrons provided support. Four squadrons of heavy bombers carried out night attacks on enemy headquarters and airfields, and thirty five fighter squadrons flew cover missions to protect the bombing, attack, and observation aircraft.[63]

During World War I the Germans also gained considerable experience in strategic bombing. In 1915 they initiated the first strategic bombing campaign by using Zeppelin airships to bomb London and other British cities. In the course of two years, 220 Zeppelin sorties were made against Britain, 175 tons of bombs dropped, and 500 Englishmen killed. The German losses were 9 Zeppelins to British planes and gunfire and a larger number to operational accidents.[64] The early raids, though a severe blow to British morale, were not very damaging materially. Hindenburg and Ludendorff therefore revised the German strategy and ended the raids by the vulnerable airships, deciding instead to build the heavy bomber force of Gotha G4s into 100-plane contingents for attacking British cities.[65] The German hope was that the submarine blockade combined with an assault on British cities would put Britain out of the war. This is the first time in history wherein strategic bombing of the enemy's homeland was expected to have a decisive, war-winning effect.

The strategic bombing campaign began in earnest in May 1917 with attacks upon England by the two-engine Gothas. On June 13, 1917, a contingent of 17 Gothas flew over London in broad daylight at high altitude, dropped 4.4 tons of bombs, and killed 162 Londoners while injuring 432; there were no German losses.[66] These raids prompted the British government to create a large fighter and antiaircraft force for home defense. Soon the defense started to take its toll, as did the high accident rate, always a major problem with the early aircraft. The greatest technical problem of the strategic-bombing forces was the relatively small bomb capacity of the planes. The early-model Gothas carried only a 200-kilogram bomb load for long-range flights,[67] and the later German heavy bombers, the Riesen ("giant") aircraft, carried a bomb load of 1,800 kilograms.[68] By May 1918 the German strategic bombers had carried out a total of 27 raids on England, inflicting 2,807 casualties and causing 1.5 million pounds' worth of damage. This gain was at the cost of 62 bombers shot down or destroyed in crashes.[69]

In May 1918 the German high command called off the bombing campaign against Britain. The cost in aircrew and aircraft was simply too high to justify the marginal effect the bombing had had upon the enemy. One German officer's analysis of the giant bomber program concluded, "Although the R-bombers dropped a total of 27,190 kilograms of bombs on England, this amount was not in proportion to the immense effort which went into their construction and the vast apparatus required for the maintenance and servicing their machines."[70] For the rest of the war, the heavy bombers would be relegated to night bombing of enemy railyards, depots, and other military targets in support of the ground forces.

As the Germans were concluding that strategic bombing was a failure, the Royal Air Force (RAF) in June 1918 created its first strategic force, the Independent Air Force, under the command of General Hugh Trenchard. Bombing missions had been flown against Germany since 1915, but Trenchard, who planned for a force of 60 squadrons, was a true believer in strategic bombing and expected to break the German will and disrupt war production by bombing German cities and industries.[71] The German Army was not impressed with this Allied campaign. A report to the commanding general of the Air Service written on August 7, 1918, analyzed the 31 bombing raids against German cities in July 1918. There were several big Allied attacks in which there had been no German casualties at all. Most casualties occurred in the first attack on a city and the vast majority were easily avoidable: People would stand outside to watch the attack rather than taking cover. The 31 Allied bombing attacks had killed a grand total of 33 people that month. The German Air Service was not alarmed.[72]

Since western German cities had been subject to intermittent bombing since 1915, the Air Service had developed an efficient homeland fighter defense force by 1918. Western Germany was divided into 5 air-defense regions, and several anti-aircraft (*Flak*) artillery commands developed around the industrial areas.[73] By the time Trenchard began his strategic bombing campaign, his pilots faced a force of 896 heavy flak guns, 454 searchlights, 204 flak machine guns, and 9 fighter squadrons covering the German homeland.[74] British and Allied casualties were heavy. From June to November 1918, the Independent Air Force dropped 543 tons of bombs on Germany for a loss of 352 aircraft badly damaged or destroyed, 29 aircrew killed, 64 wounded, and 235 missing.[75] Total German losses to bomb raids in 1918 were 797 dead, 380 wounded, and 15 million marks' worth of damage.[76] Considering that the British air offensive was only part of the total air offensive against German cities in 1918, the Independent Air Force lost as many casualties as they inflicted—in this case, a trained airman and aircraft was traded for a civilian bystander. The wastage rate of aircraft was 1 aircraft for every 1.54 tons of bombs dropped.[77] The one Allied advantage in the air had been production capacity. Otherwise, the German Air Service generally fought the better war. Even in 1918, when the Allies had a great numerical superiority, the German Air Service managed to destroy 3,732 enemy aircraft for a loss of 1,099 of its own from January to September.[78] By 1918 the Germans had developed probably the best fighter plane of the war: the Fokker DVII.[79] The Germans had developed superior ground support aircraft and had introduced some commonsense technology. In 1918 German pilots had parachutes, but no Allied air service had made parachutes standard equipment.[80] The Germans, like the British, had learned to create an effective air defense system. However, while the German Air Service drew the correct conclusions and called a halt to their strategic bombing program, the Allies were increasing theirs. By 1918 the German Air Service had become, in modern terms, a tactical air force geared to supporting the ground armies—a mission it pursued to the end of the war with considerable effectiveness.

## THE TECHNOLOGICAL LESSONS OF WORLD WAR I

World War I constituted the most rapid period of technological change in world history, which is why recent military historians such as Rod Paschall view the Great War's military leaders with considerably more sympathy than have earlier historians.[81] Aside from the development of the atomic bomb, the pace of technological change in World War II can scarcely be compared to that of World War I. The weaponry, tactics, and organization of American, British, German, and Soviet infantry companies did not change dramatically between 1939 and 1945. Many 1939 aircraft—for example, the B-17, the ME 109, and the Spitfire—were still in service in 1945. Even the most advanced weapons—for instance, radar—were developed and modified from already deployed prewar weapons. In contrast, the German, French, and British infantry companies of 1918 scarcely resembled the 1914 units in organization, tactics, or weaponry. In 1918, soldiers wore steel helmets, carried gas masks and fought with an array of weapons undreamt of in 1914: submachine guns, flamethrowers, poison gas, light mortars, antitank rifles, and rifle grenades. No army of 1914 considered the light machine gun to be the primary infantry weapon. In 1914 aircraft were slow, frail machines used for artillery spotting. In 1918 armies received support from fast, heavily armed aircraft. The British and French soldiers in 1918 would make their most dramatic advances behind a wave of tanks. By 1918, aside from the rifle, the maxim gun, and some artillery pieces, the armies possessed all new weapons as well as radically new concepts of fighting.

From the point of view of wartime commanders, the primary problem after the fall of 1914 was to restore maneuver to the battlefield. This could be accomplished in two ways: by increasing firepower—all prewar armies taught the necessity of gaining fire superiority—and by increasing the mobility of the army. In order to gain fire superiority, the major combatants dramatically increased the number of machine guns while decreasing their weight to make the infantry more mobile. The addition of light machine guns, mortars, and rifle grenades increased the firepower of infantry units at least fivefold between 1914 and 1918. All the armies also greatly increased their artillery firepower in terms of the number of guns, their range, and their size.

The Germans made one of the great technological breakthroughs of the war by developing the battlefield use of poison gas, a weapon that would dramatically increase the firepower of the attacker. It was logical that the Germans would effectively exploit chemical technology, for the German chemical industry was Europe's largest and most advanced. Research into gas shells was begun in the autumn of 1914. By January 1915, tear-gas shells were being shipped to the eastern front to be used against the Russian Army at Bolimow; however, the tear gas froze in the extreme cold and the war's first gas attack was a flop.[82] As the war progressed, the Germans became extremely proficient in gas warfare. After the German gas attack at Ypres in 1915, the Allied powers would also develop gas warfare. They never caught up with the Germans in the toxicity of gas, nor did they develop as sophisticated tactics for using it.

The total gas production of Germany during the war was 68,100 tons, roughly equal to the combined British, French, and American production of 68,905 tons.[83] By 1917 the Germans had developed successful chemical tactics. Artillerymen would first fire salvos of shells containing sternutators or extremely potent sensory irritants such as diphenylchlorarsine or diphenylcyanarsine (called blue cross for markings on the shells). The tiniest whiff of these would cause sneezing and coughing, making it difficult for the defender to put on his mask. Then the defender would be hit by a concentration of phosgene shells (known as green cross for their markings). Phosgene is an acute lung irritant that can incapacitate or kill in doses as small as 200 parts to 10 million. A third type of shell, dichlorethylsulfide (mustard gas, or yellow cross), was rarely lethal but produced burning and blisters on the body and could blind its victims. The advantage of mustard gas was its extreme persistence: Concentrations of mustard gas would remain dangerous for weeks, rendering an area shelled with it difficult to cross.[84]

At Cambrai in November 1917 and in the spring offensives in 1918, the

Germans used a sophisticated mix of blue and green cross shells to incapacitate units about to be attacked. Yellow cross concentrations were
fired on the flanks of the assault troops to create a chemical barrier between them and Allied counterattackers. By the end of the war, German
poison gas had killed at least 78,198 Allied troops and wounded 908,645.
The Allied powers, using as much gas as the Germans but with less finesse, killed 12,000 Germans and Austrians and wounded another
288,000.[85] Gas warfare has been largely ignored by military writers because it is a particularly ugly form of warfare with no tradition behind it
like the infantry has and no romanticism attached to it like the cavalry and
fighter pilots have. Yet gas dramatically increased the German Army's firepower, and the high command came to rely upon it in all offensive operations—sometimes in defensive ones as well. In 1917 and 1918, gas came
close to being the war-winning weapon.

The Allies' greatest technological creation, the tank, did more than any
other weapon to tip the balance of power decisively toward the Allies: It
combined firepower and mobility. The German Army's failure to consider
the tank as a major weapon until too late was the high command's greatest
technological mistake. The tank was a simple idea that merely combined
items of existing technology into one weapon. The caterpillar-tracked
tractor had been in wide commercial use throughout the world for over a
decade by 1914. At the start of the war, all the major powers put the Holt
Company's caterpillar tractor to work hauling artillery through rough
ground. As the war became locked in the trenches in the winter of 1914-
15, both the British and the French began developing the caterpillar tractor as a weapon to break the stalemate.[86] The prototype French tanks created by the Schneider Company in 1915-16 were nothing more than a
Holt tractor chassis topped by a steel box that was armed with a cannon
and two machine guns. The British created a different design, with a
rhomboidal shape to give it greater trench-crossing ability.[87]

The early tank models were extremely unreliable. In the first tank attack in history, on September 15, 1916, at the Somme, few of the 49 British Mark I tanks reached their objectives; most of them broke down before reaching the front lines. The few tanks that did not break down,
ditch, or succumb to shellfire provided useful support.[88] This first, disappointing experience did not deter the British or the French. In the spring
of 1917 the British employed 60 Mark I tanks, and on the Aisne in April
the French employed over 180 tanks.[89] Again, the tanks did not prove to
be effective weapons due to mechanical breakdowns and the inexperi-
ence of both tankers and infantrymen in using them. However, by this
time, both the British and the French had developed improved models
and initiated mass production of tanks.

The German high command only moved to consider developing tanks after the British used the weapon in September 1916; even then the Germans moved slowly. Ludendorff found the first tank attack to be "inconvenient" but was not alarmed.[90] A committee to develop tanks was formed by the high command, but there was little progress until March 1917, when Captain Wegener of the motor troops was appointed as liaison officer between the high command and the tank committee. Before that, there had been little coordination between the tank designers and the army.[91] Ludendorff showed a remarkable lack of interest in a German tank program. In 1917 he claimed that he could not release workmen or materials for tank construction.[92] After the war, Ludendorff recalled that "we formed detachments of captured tanks. I had a look at the first one in February 1918 at an exercise by one of the assault battalions. It did not impress me. Our own tank detachments suffered heavy losses in the fighting without effecting anything."[93]

Any nation with an advanced automobile and heavy engineering industry can produce a tank. The Germans proceeded to design and build tank prototypes that were, for the standard of the time, quite satisfactory. German engineer Joseph Vollmer acquired a tractor chassis from the Holt Company's Austrian subsidiary, modified and improved it by putting three sprung bogie units on it instead of one as Holt had done, and designed an armored body to carry a 57-mm gun and six machine guns. The result was the A7V tank, 30 tons with a crew of eighteen and up to 30 millimeters of armor. Like any tank of the war, it was subject to frequent mechanical difficulties. The A7V's design gave it poorer cross-country capability than the British heavy tanks, but its 200 horsepower and sprung suspension gave it twice the speed—8 miles per hour—of the suspensionless British Mark I through Mark V tanks.[94]

German designers, notably Vollmer, would design and build prototypes of other tanks during the war. One prototype, the A7V/U, combined the British lozenge shape for improved cross-country performance with components of the A7V, and was armed with two 57-mm guns and four machine guns; it was tested in June 1918 and was accepted by the army. Vollmer also designed and built two light tank models in 1918. The first, the LKI, was designed around a truck chassis and engine; it was shaped much like a British Whippet tank surmounted by a revolving turret and gave a similar performance to a Whippet. The 7-ton vehicle was designed to be cheap and simple to build. The second tank, also built on a truck chassis, was an improved light tank of 10.2 tons with a 57-mm gun.[95]

The high command gave tanks a low production priority, and only 20 A7Vs were ever delivered. These reached the army in December 1917, and three A7V companies were formed. One hundred A7Vs were ordered in 1917, 20 A7V/Us in September 1918, and 580 LKIs in June 1918.[96] Only the A7Vs saw combat. Eighty other tanks used by the Imperial Army were captured British tanks, for a total tank corps of eight companies.[97]

If Ludendorff was not impressed by tanks, the front-line soldiers certainly were. On November 20, 1917, a force of 476 British tanks led a surprise six-division attack at Cambrai that shattered the German lines on a 12-kilometer front within just a few hours. As they seized their objectives, the British inflicted heavy casualties, taking 4,200 prisoners and 100 guns.[98] At Amiens, on August 8, 1918, a surprise attack led by 456 tanks ruptured the German defense, carried the British to a 6-mile advance on the first day, and enabled the British to capture 16,000 prisoners in exchange for low British losses.[99] Although British tanks of 1918 had a battle endurance of only one to three days before they broke down, they always managed to cut through fortified zones and into open country. The French also used masses of tanks in 1918. Their most successful assault was made by 346 tanks at Soissons on July 18, resulting in a 4-mile advance and 25,000 German prisoners.[100] By the end of the war, the British had built 2,636 tanks,[101] and the French 3,900.[102] Thousands more were on order for the 1919 campaign.

Many German officers after the war gave credit to the tank as one of the main factors in the Allied victory. Lieutenant General D.W. von Balck, wartime commander of the Fifty-First Division, called the tanks "at first a grossly underestimated weapon" that developed into "an extremely potent attack weapon."[103] Von Balck also asserted that German defenses could not withstand mass tank attacks.[104] Lieutenant General Max Schwarte wrote about tanks in 1923, "All of our opponents recognized the significance of the motor vehicle early on and brought that technology to its logical conclusion."[105] General Hermann von Kuhl attempted to defend Ludendorff's policies before the Reichstag Committee after the war but had to admit that by 1918 the tank had become a decisive weapon.[106]

Von Kuhl argued before the Reichstag that the high command had asked for tanks and it was industry's fault that they had not been produced.[107] Von Kuhl's statement was not plausible. The Allies had seized upon the tank idea two years before the Germans. German engineers had shown that they could quickly develop tanks equal to the Allied models, but tank production was given the lowest industrial priority. At the same time that workers and steel could not be found for tanks, the high command authorized the production of two enormous railroad-mounted "Paris Guns," that could shell Paris from 70 miles away. These guns, built with great effort and at great expense, fired a total of 367 shells—weighing 229–307 pounds each—at Paris in 1918, the approximate explosive weight of an aircraft bombing raid.[108] Putting Krupp to work on enormous guns while minimizing tank production is one of the clearest examples of military-industrial mismanagement in World War I. General J. F. C. Fuller

asserted that for the 1918 offensive the Germans should have cut cannon
production and built tracked tractors instead: "By the end of March 1918
the German attack 'petered out' for want of supplies. . . . Had the Germans possessed on March 21 and May 27, 5,000 to 6,000 efficient cross-
country tractors, each of which carried five tons of supplies, all the hosts
of brave men which the United States of America could have poured into
France, could not have prevented a separation of the British and French
Armies from being effected."[109]

Ludendorff might have been a better tactician than Foch and Haig, but
the latter two commanders possessed the imagination to grasp the funda-
mentals of mechanized war that Ludendorff did not. The first Allied tank
theorists, Britons Fuller and Colonel Swinton and Frenchman Colonel Es-
tienne, received full support from their respective high commands and
were given the resources to develop their ideas by the British and French
cabinets.

The sharpest criticism of the German Army's approach to technology
came from within the army itself. Colonel Kurt Thorbeck, president of
the Rifle Testing Commission, wrote a blistering thirty-three-page study
for the General Staff in 1920 on the technical and tactical lessons of the
war. His underlined conclusion was that "the German General Staff did
not properly recognize the material demands of a world war and therefore did not correctly prepare for the war in peace. This was the basic
mistake of the war."[110] Thorbeck pointed out that the prewar General Staff
had not properly studied the effects of the machine gun and magazine rifle. The General Staff had been filled with tacticians—no weapons technicians were given a place on the General Staff.[111] Thus once the war began,
there were no technically trained infantry officers at the high command to
represent the infantry. If there had been, the army might have developed a
better light machine gun.[112] Thorbeck asserted that much of the equipment ordered during the war was a waste of money and effort, owing to
the technical ignorance of the General Staff. For example, Thorbeck said,
the 82.5 million marks used to produce heavy body armor for the infantry should have been used for building tanks.[113] For Thorbeck, there was
certainly "no stab in the back"; the army's disregard for technology had
brought about national defeat.

CONCLUSION

During the First World War from 1914 to 1918, Germany mobilized
eleven million men and suffered 6 million casualties. The Allies mobilized
twenty-eight million men against Germany alone and suffered twelve million casualties, not counting those lost fighting other Central Powers.

Colonel Trevor N. Dupuy took these statistics and other battle statistics
and created a scoring system for military effectiveness. Against the British,
the German average effectiveness superiority was 1.49 to 1; against the
French 1.53 to 1. Against the Russians, the Germans scored at a ratio of
5.4 to 1.[114]

The lessons of World War I reinforced the German Army's belief in the
superiority of its flexible and mobile tactics in offense and defense.
Through tactics alone, the Germans had found a means to break the
trench stalemate. They were also confident of the superiority of their
training system and of their aerial strategy and tactics. The negative lessons of the war—the strategic failures of the high command and the superiority of Allied technology over German technology—would pro-
foundly affect the German Army's training, organization, and tactical
thought in the 1920s. The first problem, poor wartime strategy, did not
lend itself to any ready solutions except to a retrospective study of the
war. The second problem, appreciating the effect of technology on warfare, was solvable. Solving this problem was the primary reason for re-
forming the postwar General Staff and officer training.

CHAPTER TWO

# Von Seeckt and Rethinking Warfare

In December 1918, as soon as the Imperial Army marched back into Germany, it virtually dissolved overnight. Germany was wracked by civil war, with Communists attempting to seize power in Berlin, Bavaria, and other areas. Many officers remained at their posts and a few Imperial Army units maintained a small cadre, but it is fair to say that in the first two months following the armistice, Germany effectively had no military force. It had to rely on short-term volunteers for well over a year after the war's end. Germany would have to create a new army and command system in an atmosphere of uncertainty, violence, military defeat, and partial occupation.

This job would be done well. The army that was intended by the Allies to become no more than a border guard or police force would soon be considered a first-rate small army capable of forming the basis for rapid German rearmament. The architect of this force, its theorist and its primary trainer was Hans von Seeckt, first commander of the General Staff, or Troops Office (Truppenamt), and second army chief of the Reichswehr. Von Seeckt would have the opportunity to do what few military men have ever done: create an army from scratch, fashioning its organization and doctrine after his own theories. Von Seeckt would serve as General Staff chief and army chief from 1919 to 1926, but he was by far the dominant figure of the German Army for the interwar period.

GENERAL HANS VON SEECKT

Hans von Seeckt was born to a noble Pomeranian family in 1866. His father was a Prussian officer who would eventually attain the rank of general. Unlike most sons destined for the army, Hans did not go to a cadet school but rather to a civilian Gymnasium (preparatory school) in Strasburg, where he achieved his Abitur in 1885. That year he was enrolled in the Kaiser Alexander Guard Regiment of the Prussian Army as an officer cadet. He was commissioned in 1887 and in 1893 was accepted for the three-year General Staff course at the Kriegsakademie. In 1897 he was one of the small number of officers selected for the General Staff Corps. From 1896 to 1914 he rose steadily through the ranks, serving as a battalion

25

*Von Seeckt greets Hindenburg at an army review in 1925. (From Friedrich von Rabenau,* Seeckt: Aus seinem Leben, 1918–1936 *[Leipzig: Hase-Koehler Verlag, 1941])*

commander and on several staff assignments. Probably because of his civilian education, von Seeckt showed a much greater breadth of mind than the average Prussian officer. He was fluent in several languages and well traveled: In the prewar period, he visited Egypt and India as well as virtually all the European countries. He particularly enjoyed reading English authors, including the works of John Galsworthy and George Bernard Shaw.[1]

Von Seeckt was highly regarded in the General Staff Corps. The outbreak of World War I found him in an important position as chief of staff to the Third Army Corps on the right flank of the great advance through Belgium and France. The early part of the war made von Seeckt's reputation as a leader and tactician. One staff officer who served with him in August and September 1914 described him as "always radiating calmness" and "maintaining control" in battle.[2] At the end of October 1914, von Seeckt organized a limited corps attack to seize a French position on the Aisne. Rounding up all the artillery support he could muster, he planned for a strong surprise attack preceded by a heavy artillery barrage. The plan worked and the position was quickly taken along with 2,000 French prisoners.[3] In January 1915, in response to a French advance near Soissons, von Seeckt orchestrated the German counterattack that threw the French back to their original positions and netted the Germans 5,200 prisoners and 35 guns. The January 1915 battle made von Seeckt's reputation within the army.[4]

In March 1915 von Seeckt was appointed chief of staff to the Eleventh Army, which was being organized on the eastern front with General von Mackensen commanding. Von Seeckt planned the 11th Army's offensive against the Russians at Gorlice in Galicia, one of the greatest German victories of the war. Along a broad front of 40 kilometers held by 6 Russian divisions, the Germans secretly concentrated 14 divisions and 1,500 guns. After a short but intensive bombardment on May 2, 1915, the Eleventh Army broke through the Russian line. Instead of turning and enveloping the Russian flanks, the army kept advancing, effecting a deep penetration of the Russian rear. In 12 days, the Germans advanced 80 miles and broke the new Russian defense line on the San River. By June 22, 1915, Russia had lost all of Galicia and 400,000 men, mostly as prisoners.[5] The Eleventh Army continued the advance during the summer campaign, while Hindenburg's troops in East Prussia attacked southward. By the middle of August, Poland was overrun and another 350,000 Russian prisoners taken.[6] After the Gorlice campaign, von Seeckt was promoted to major general.

In the autumn of 1915 Bulgaria entered the war on the side of the Central powers. The scene of action on the eastern front switched to Serbia, where the German Eleventh Army was sent to reinforce the Austrian Third Army and two Bulgarian armies. Von Mackensen was put in command of this army group, with von Seeckt as his chief of staff. On October 6, 1915, the Austro-German-Bulgarian armies, following von Seeckt's plan, attacked and, in an efficient campaign, Serbia was overrun by the end of November. The Allied expedition to support the Serbs landed in Salonika too late. With their retreat cut off, the Serbs were forced to abandon most of their equipment and withdraw into Albania.[7]

In 1916 von Seeckt was again employed against the Russians. The Russian Brusilov offensive in the summer of 1916 shattered the Austrian Army's front and Romania entered the war on the side of the Allies. Von Mackensen was given command of an Austro-German army group on the Romanian front, again with von Seeckt as army group chief of staff. During June, with the whole Austrian front in retreat, von Seeckt effectively took command of the Austrian Seventh Army and fought to delay the Russians. In July von Seeckt became chief of staff to the newly created army group under the nominal command of Austrian Archduke Josef. For three months von Seeckt fought a defensive battle, retreating slowly and plugging holes in the line. By October the delaying tactics had served their purpose and worn the Russians and Romanians down. The Germans and Austrians were ready to attack the Russian-Romanian front line with both Mackensen's and Archduke Josef's army groups. The offensive went well for the Austro-German forces, and by December 6, in a campaign of two months, Bucharest fell and the Romanians were effectively knocked out of the war.[8]

Von Seeckt saw further service on the southern portion of the eastern front with Archduke Josef's army group in 1917. From 1915 to 1917 von Seeckt demonstrated great strategic and political abilities in warfare. He worked well with the Austrians and Bulgarians. He showed acute political perception when, in 1915, he advised the German high command that once the Bulgarians had beaten their traditional enemies, the Serbs, and seized Serbian territories, their war aims would be satisfied. The only practical reason for having Bulgarian Army stay at that point would be to use it on the Salonika front to hold the large Allied army in check.[9]

In a letter to his friend Joachim von Winterfeldt in August 1916, von Seeckt predicted that Russia would have a political upheaval after the war. He pointed out that one of Russia's greatest problems was the weakness of mid-level leaders.[10] Austrian duke Windischgrätz would write of von Seeckt, "He was one of the very few who truly understood our complicated relationships and understood not only Austria's weaknesses but their causes."[11] Archduke Josef remarked in 1917, "Ludendorff sees in Seeckt a rival. . . . My view is that Seeckt possesses even more military talent than Ludendorff."[12] Von Seeckt also maintained his reputation as a tactician. As the high command issued new tactical directives, which were primarily influenced by the western front experience, von Seeckt would analyze them, adjusting Ludendorff's tactical directives to the different conditions that prevailed on von Seeckt's front.[13]

In December 1917 the high command ordered von Seeckt to Turkey to serve as chief of staff to the Ottoman Field Army, a post he held to the end of the war. Von Seeckt went into a situation that was "unsalvageable," according to his ordnance officer, (later General) Ernst Köstring.[14] Von Seeckt attributed his assignment to a backwater front to Ludendorff's jealousy toward him.[15] However, von Seeckt made the best of things and, with his political and strategic talents, developed a close working relationship with the Turkish generals, especially with Minister Enver Pasha.[16] Many generals believed that a man of von Seeckt's capabilities should have been employed on a more decisive front, yet the move to Turkey probably helped von Seeckt's reputation. He had been continuously victorious from 1914 through 1917, and at the war's end, he was associated neither with Ludendorff nor with his failed strategy.

After the armistice, von Seeckt was an obvious candidate for chief of the General Staff. In the immediate postwar upheaval, however, he was ordered to Königsberg in January 1919 to take command of Grenzschutz Nord. In this special command, created to deal with the postwar emergency, von Seeckt was responsible for withdrawing the German armies from Russia, carrying out the anti-Bolshevik military campaign in the Baltic countries, and defending the eastern borders from Poles and Russians. From January to April 1919, von Seeckt successfully withdrew the armies from Russia and brought order to the eastern provinces.[17]

From April to June 1919 von Seeckt served as General Staff representative to the Peace Conference of Versailles, where he unsuccessfully attempted to get the Allies to soften their demands for virtually disarming Germany.[18] After the German acceptance of the Versailles Treaty in June 1919, von Seeckt was appointed chairman of the Commission for the Peacetime Army Organization, which would reorganize the German Army in accordance with the Versailles provisions.

Von Seeckt also served as acting chief of the General Staff. In November 1919 he officially dissolved the General Staff by order of the Allied powers, becoming chief of its successor organization, the Truppenamt.[19] As chief, von Seeckt initiated a program to rethink and rewrite the entire body of German military doctrine in accordance with the experience of World War I and von Seeckt's own ideas. In March 1920, in the aftermath of the failed Kapp Putsch, General Walter Reinhardt—von Seeckt's greatest opponent in politics, tactics, and army organization—was relieved and von Seeckt appointed chief of the army command. In this position, von Seeckt was subordinate only to the defense minister and the president. Thus, until his own relief in October 1926, von Seeckt was able to remold and retrain the army as he envisioned.

Although von Seeckt would elucidate many of his military theories in speeches, army reports, and postwar writings (especially *Thoughts of a Soldier* and *Die Reichswehr*), his basic ideas were already clearly formed in 1919. In a report to the army high command on February 18, von Seeckt broke dramatically with German military tradition by advocating the creation of a small, elite professional army based on voluntary recruitment rather than conscription.[20] (It is important to note that von Seeckt's advocacy of an elite professional army and his conviction that a war of maneuver was the superior military method was already firmly developed three months before the Allies imposed a professional army upon the Germans at Versailles.) Von Seeckt's concepts of warfare and military organization became the Reichswehr's primary body of interwar military doctrine.

Von Seeckt proposed an army of twenty-four divisions with a minimum of 200,000 men: "With full awareness, I would like to see the present conscript army replaced by a professional army, if you will, a type of mercenary army."[21] Volunteers would initially enlist for two years; material conditions—pay, housing, and so on—would be favorable enough to ensure a high proportion of recruits each year. Conscription would be considered only if not enough volunteers could be found.[22] The volunteer army would be equipped with the best weapons, equipment, and training devices.[23] For von Seeckt, one advantage of a highly disciplined and professional force would be its reliability in upholding the domestic authority of the government—a major consideration in February 1919, when Germany was experiencing a wave of Communist revolutions, including the seizure of Bavaria by a soviet government and civil war on the streets of Berlin.

The professional army would be backed by a national militia based on a mandatory three-month military training program for all able-bodied eighteen-year-old males, with additional militia training of shorter duration for another two years. Special courses would be instituted for militia officers. Although the militia was conceived primarily as a means of developing a trained reserve of manpower for wartime mobilization, militia units would not be used as wartime forces except in an emergency.[24]

Von Seeckt had been brought up in the military tradition of von Moltke and von Schlieffen, which affirmed that wars are won by destroying the enemy army and that the offensive and the use of maneuver were the primary means of achieving that goal. Von Seeckt accepted the basic Moltke-Schlieffen tenet: "The soldier knows only one aim of war: the destruction of the enemy forces."[25] However, von Seeckt broke with von Moltke and von Schlieffen over the importance of a mass army. Von Moltke's great campaigns aimed at achieving numerical superiority over the enemy on the battlefield. This was done by rapid mobilization and the use of reserve units with the regular field army. It worked surprisingly well for him at Königgrätz in 1866 and at the French border in 1870. Later, von Schlieffen and the General Staff also devised a plan that would guarantee the German Army superior numbers in the invasion of France, especially on the right flank where the Germans expected the major battles to be fought.

The experience of the eastern front, where well-trained, well-led, and well-equipped Germans had consistently defeated larger enemy forces, convinced von Seeckt that numbers were no longer the key to victory:

> To what military success did this universal levy in mass, this gigantic parade of armies lead? In spite of every effort the war did not end with decisive destruction of the enemy on the field of battle; for the most part it resolved itself into a series of exhausting struggles for position until, in the face of an immense superiority of force, the springs which fed the resistance of one of the combatants, the sources of its personnel, its materiel, and finally of its morale dried up. . . . Perhaps the principle of the levy in mass, of the nation in arms, has outlived its usefulness, perhaps the *fureur du nombre* has worked itself out. Mass becomes immobile, it cannot maneuver and therefore cannot win victories, it can only crush by sheer weight.[26]

For von Seeckt, the key to future victory was mobility. The small, professional force would be better led and equipped than the mass armies, and it would use mobility and maneuver far more effectively. According to von Seeckt, "The whole future of warfare appears to me to lie in the employment of mobile armies, relatively small but of high quality and rendered distinctly more effective by the addition of aircraft, and in simultaneous mobilization of the whole defense force, be it to feed the attack or for home defense."[27] In addition, "the smaller the army, the easier it will be to equip it with modern weapons, whereas the provision of a constant supply for armies of millions is an impossibility."[28]

Rather than rely on the cumbersome mobilization arrangements of pre-1914 armies, von Seeckt proposed that his mobile, professional army be stationed on the frontiers in a state of readiness, primed to move with a minimum of mobilization fuss. Unlike the armies of other nations, von Seeckt's army could launch an offensive with little delay. While the regular army attacked, the militia would be called up to defend the borders and to train and to serve as a replacement pool for the regulars to sustain their offensive.[29]

A strong air force was essential to von Seeckt's concept of mobile war. After the war, he hoped that the army could retain a strong air service and he fought hard at the Versailles peace conference to hold onto the air arm.[30] He thought of the air force as a tactical weapon for support of ground offensives, not as a strategic weapon. Von Seeckt affirmed that in the Great War, the air force had assumed a position of equality with ground and sea forces. In a future war,

> the war will begin with an air attack on both sides, because the air forces are the most immediately available for action against the enemy. It is not the chief towns and supply centers which will form the immediate object of the attack, but the opposing air forces, and only after the defeat of the latter will the attack be directed against other objects. . . . We must lay emphasis on the fact that all great concentrations of troops provide easy and important targets. The disturbance of the mobilization of men and supplies is one of the chief objects of attack by air. . . . The attack initiated by the air force will be pressed with all possible speed by all available troops, i.e. in essence, by the regular army.[31]

In the tactical sphere, von Seeckt's emphasis upon mobile war and his wartime experience on the eastern front led him to support the maintenance of a strong cavalry arm. Trench warfare on the western front had put an end to cavalry in that type of conflict, but in the east, "where the conditions of warfare and topography were often more favorable, cavalry did useful work."[32] Cavalry charges were a thing of the past, but von Seeckt saw cavalry in terms of all-arms light divisions for independent operations,

> for extensive operations of this nature cavalry requires the support of infantry; because without this its firing strength would fall too rapidly. . . . This infantry support must be maintained and made mobile by motor transport. . . . The variety of objectives assigned to a cavalry division necessitates a supply of mobile but effective artillery. . . . In such extensive operations, when the base is left far behind, it is obvious that the communications service—especially the wireless service—plays an important role. Cooperation with the airmen is of very particular importance, and suitable aircraft formations must be placed at the disposal of the cavalry division.[33]

For units on independent operations, von Seeckt recommended aerial transport of supplies as a solution.[34]

The eventual motorization of the whole army was a long-term possibility, but von Seeckt proposed giving the cavalry first priority for motor vehicles for their supporting arms.[35] Not only did motor vehicles provide transport for men, guns, and supplies; for von Seeckt, they constituted a new arm as well. Armored cars also constituted a new arm of the army—alongside the infantry, cavalry, and artillery.[36]

Von Seeckt rarely discussed defensive tactics; for him, the defense was a temporary condition from which one goes on to the offensive. The particular mode of the offense was whatever the commander found sensible. Von Seeckt strongly criticized the prewar army and the Schlieffen School's preference for envelopment. The prewar army, von Seeckt suggested, had made a dogma of envelopment: "It has been a distinct proof, to my mind, of the power of catchwords and of military precepts in general that in post-war maneuvers the desire for envelopment at any price and the extension of the front until it ceased to be a front at all had to be combated as though there had never been a war to teach us. The consequences which this craze for envelopment produced in the war were inevitable."[37] He argued, "Should no possibility of any kind of envelopment arise—and we have known cases of the kind—then the general cannot simply declare that he is at his wit's end; he will be acting quite in the spirit of Count Schlieffen, if, with a clear object in view, he launches his masses at the most effective point—even though it be in a frontal attack, for the success of which Schlieffen, we must admit, coined the sarcastic term 'ordinary victory.' "[38] Von Seeckt, who had been innovative in the war and had pioneered the "breakthrough" battle at Gorlice stood against the Schlieffen School in favor of tactical flexibility.

In von Seeckt's view, one of the greatest advantages of a small, professional army over the mass army was its superior leadership. The professional army needed to cultivate leadership at all levels, especially in the General Staff, and to promote technical education within the NCO and officer corps. In 1916 von Seeckt remarked that the mass of Russian soldiers had performed better than he expected but that the Russian Army's greatest problem was its weakness in leadership.[39] By 1916 the British had built an impressive mass army. Having analyzed the British Army, von Seeckt argued that not since Marlborough and perhaps Wellington have the British developed a military leadership that could command a large army. This made the British force considerably less dangerous despite its wealth in men and matériel.[40] Realizing that technical training was essential to the modern officer, von Seeckt in his report of February 1919 proposed sending officers to civilian technical courses while the army was being reorganized.[41] Only the technically trained officer could effectively operate modern weapons:

> The greater the advance of technical science, the more effectively can it devote its inventions and instruments to the service of the army and the higher will be the demands it makes on the soldier who manipulates these technical aids. Anyone who has the smallest idea what technical knowledge, what numerous instruments, operated only by carefully trained experts, what highly disciplined mental faculties are necessary for the effective control of modern artillery fire, must admit that these essential qualities cannot be taken for granted with men whose training had been brief and superficial, and that such men, pitted against a small number of practiced technicians on the other side, are "cannon fodder" in the worst sense of the term.[42]

Von Seeckt set extremely high education standards for officers and NCOs of the postwar army and particularly stressed technical education.

Most important, von Seeckt strove to preserve the General Staff's personnel and training for the army. This was von Seeckt's most important postwar battle with other German officers. Reinhardt, as army chief, ordered in 1919 that preference for officer selection for the Reichswehr go to the front officers, the wartime commissionees who had distinguished themselves. General Maercker, one of the senior Freikorps (Free Corps) commanders, echoed this view.[43] Young front officers, while brave, nevertheless did not have the education or military background of General Staff officers. Von Seeckt wanted to give officer retention preference to the General Staff Corps members because of their experience in army organization and higher command planning. Without General Staff officers, he pointed out, the Freikorps could never have been organized or the army rebuilt. Von Seeckt insisted that the General Staff officer was indeed a "front officer." Even though the General Staff was unpopular at the time, von Seeckt argued that it had preserved the Reich since the November Revolution.[44] General Groener, who—fortunately for von Seeckt— was Ludendorff's replacement, would passionately support von Seeckt's position to not only retain the General Staff and its prestige but to also ensure that as many General Staff officers as possible would be accepted by the Provisional Reichswehr (the official name of the army from March 1919 until January 1921, when it reached the 100,000-man strength mandated by the Versailles Treaty).[45] Von Seeckt and Groener, both first-rate military minds, cannot be described as close friends, but they saw eye-to-eye on most military matters.

Von Seeckt's decision to retain a disproportionately high percentage of General Staff officers was right for the army and the nation. It was less democratic than Reinhardt's vision, but von Seeckt was correct in recognizing the organizational and technical abilities of the General Staff as having first priority. Many of the wartime commissionees may have been brave storm platoon leaders, but the undisciplined postwar behavior of many members of the Freikorps, who were led by such officers, dismayed von Seeckt. Some of the Freikorps were no more than "mobs," and part of the border-troop Freikorps were characterized as "bandit gangs" by von Seeckt in 1919.[46]

RESHAPING THE GENERAL STAFF

The period 1919-1921 was one of confusion for the army. In accordance with the Versailles Treaty, the government forces, which numbered perhaps 350,000 in June 1919, would have to be reduced to 100,000 by January 1921.[47] Of the 100,000-man army, only 4,000 officers were permitted. Maximum limits for divisional and other organizations were specified; an infantry division, for example, could contain no more than 410 officers and 10,830 soldiers, a cavalry division no more than 275 officers and 5,250 soldiers.[48] Germany would be allowed to form seven infantry and three cavalry divisions along with schools, arsenals, high headquarters, and a defense ministry. Heavy artillery, tanks, and aircraft were disallowed and careful limits placed on the quantities of other weapons.[49] The General Staff was to be abolished. In June 1919 Germany accepted the Versailles provisions literally at the point of Allied guns: Nonacceptance would have meant an Allied invasion of Germany. Groener and von Seeckt, realizing that the army could not mount an effective resistance, argued for compliance with the treaty. Hindenburg, Reinhardt, and most of the generals preferred fighting a hopeless battle to preserve Germany's honor and argued this position to the government. Even though the more realistic view in favor of treaty compliance prevailed, there was great anger within the officer ranks toward the Versailles Treaty and toward the government for having accepted it.

Several laws were passed from 1919 to 1921 that created a framework for the army's reorganization. The first law, of March 6, 1919, dissolved the Imperial Army and called for an army "built on a democratic basis." It was this law—which provided that officers be chosen from those who had served at the front and that officer ranks be opened to NCOs—that caused the Groener–von Seeckt argument with Reinhardt.[50] In October 1919, further steps were taken to create a senior command organization for the army, and the office of defense minister was established. The defense minister would oversee the budget of both the army and the navy, and hold political responsibility for the armed forces before parliament. The army would be headed by the chief of the army high command, and all army major commands, administrative departments, and the newly modeled General Staff would be answerable to him.[51]

In November 1919 when von Seeckt officially dissolved the General Staff, its core, the Operations Section, was preserved in the Truppenamt, which consisted of about sixty officers. Other sections of the old General Staff were simply transferred to other government departments. The Military History Section of the General Staff was transferred to the Interior Ministry, where it became a section of the Reich Archives. The General Staff Survey and Map Section was also transferred to the Interior Ministry, where it became the Reich Survey Office. Part of the General Staff Transportation Section became a section of the Reich Transportation Ministry.[52] As the new command system evolved between 1919 and 1921, the old General Staff's economic and political sections would be revived as separate offices directly under the control of the chief of the army command. The core of the General Staff was retained as four sections of the Truppenamt: T-1, the Army Section (actually the Operations and Planning Section); T-2, the Organization Section; T-3, the Statistical Section (actually the Intelligence Section); and T-4, the Training Section.

As von Seeckt dissolved the General Staff, he proclaimed that "the form changes, the spirit remains the same."[53] In an address to Truppenamt officers, von Seeckt praised the historical record of the old General Staff and asked for the help, trust, and obedience of all the officers in order to transform the staff organization.[54] The Truppenamt was successful in carrying on much of the form, efficiency, and training of the General Staff. Even though the General Staff Corps as a separate branch of the army was officially abolished along with the Kriegsakademie, the Truppenamt would carry on with a revised training program and continue to treat staff officers as a separate branch of the army. Officially, the new General Staff

Corps members were called leadership assistants (Führergehilfen), but even in official correspondence, the Reichswehr officers would continue to refer to "General Staff officers" and to the Truppenamt as the "General Staff."[55] The Truppenamt would maintain the same prestige within the Reichswehr as the old General Staff.

In addition to the Army Personnel Office and the Army Administrative Office, which took care of pay, budget, procurement, and so on, the headquarters of the new army high command (Heeresleitung) would consist of two additional large staffs on par with the Truppenamt. First was the Weapons Office, which handled all ordnance and equipment testing and development. The Weapons Office consisted of sixty to sixty-five officers, about the same number as the Truppenamt.[56] Also on par with the Weapons Office and Truppenamt were nine different branch inspectorates, each of which had a staff of four to seven General Staff officers. The branch inspectorates were set up as follows: IN-1, the Inspectorate of Weapons Schools; IN-2, the Inspectorate of Infantry; IN-3, the Inspectorate of Cavalry; IN-4, the Inspectorate of Artillery; IN-5, the Inspectorate of Pioneers and Fortresses; IN-6, the Inspectorate of Transport Troops, which was divided into two staffs, one for horse transport and one for motor transport; IN-7, the Inspectorate of Signal Troops; SIN, the Army Medical Inspectorate; and VIN, the Veterinary Inspectorate. The different inspectorates had no command authority over their respective branches of service; rather they served primarily to direct the training and doctrine of each branch. Inspectorates would supervise the branch schools, write training manuals, and advise the Weapons Office on weapons and equipment development.

The relationship between the Truppenamt, Weapons Office, and inspectorates was fairly intricate. All had to cooperate in the creation of military doctrine. T-1, the Operations and Planning Section, was responsible for assessing strategic situations and drawing up war plans and operational orders for the army. In creating mobilization plans, T-1 worked closely with T-2, the Organization Section, which handled the drafting of organization and equipment tables. T-2 also coordinated the program for aerial rearmament by maintaining a special air staff. T-4, the Training Section, was responsible for supervising training throughout the army. Although branch inspectorates did most of the routine work in training and compiling manuals, all training programs, manuals, and materials had to be approved by T-4. The Training Section would ensure that the military training and doctrine developed by the branch inspectorates would conform to the unified operational doctrine and organization established by T-1 and T-2. The Training Section of the Truppenamt also had direct responsibility for training General Staff officers, as well as for creating and supervising the armywide testing program for officers and NCOs.[57]

In 1925 the old General Staff's Economic Section was revived within the high command's headquarters as the office for Economic Mobilization (Wehramt). In the early 1920s the Truppenamt contained a Transportation Section, T-7 (the Truppenamt never had a T-5 or a T-6 section). The essential form of the high command had thus been formulated by von Seeckt by 1921, with only superficial changes in the ensuing thirteen years until Hitler came to power. The militarily most important departments of the army high command—the Truppenamt, the Weapons Office, the branch inspectorates, the special staffs, and the army commander's personal staff—contained about two hundred officers in the 1920s. Almost all were members of the General Staff Corps. Despite its small size, the high command was an efficient and practical organization for war planning and for developing military doctrine and training. It was an effective tool in the hands of von Seeckt and his successors.

RETHINKING TACTICS

One week after officially dissolving the General Staff and taking over the Truppenamt, von Seeckt initiated a comprehensive program to collect and analyze the experiences of World War I to create a new body of military doctrine for the Reichswehr. In a directive issued to the Truppenamt, the Weapons Office, the branch inspectorates, and all the major Reichswehr departments as well as to particular officers, von Seeckt outlined a program to form fifty-seven committees and subcommittees of officers who would put together studies of tactics, regulations, equipment, and doctrine.[58] Von Seeckt wrote, "It is absolutely necessary to put the experience of the war in a broad light and collect this experience while the impressions won on the battlefield are still fresh and a major proportion of the experienced officers are still in leading positions."[59] The officers named to committees were to write "short, concise studies on the newly-gained experiences of the war and consider the following points: a). What new situations arose in the war that had not been considered before the war? b). How effective were our pre-war views in dealing with the above situations? c). What new guidelines have been developed from the use of new weaponry in the war? d). Which new problems put forward by the war have not yet found a solution?"[60]

Von Seeckt's directive follows with a list of the fifty-seven different aspects of the war to be examined, ranging from military justice and questions of troop morale to flame throwers, river crossings, and the military weather service. Military leadership, from leadership of an army group to large artillery formations, took up the largest single part of the plan (seven committees). Each inspectorate was also expected to assemble and analyze the recent tactical experiences of its branch. Committees were even appointed for such highly specialized aspects of warfare as tank and mountain warfare. In addition, 109 officers and former officers were appointed by name to serve on the committees. Von Seeckt sought out those with the highest reputations in specialized fields to contribute their expertise: Major General Bruchmüller was appointed to the Artillery Committee; Major General von Below, who had commanded the German Army at Caporetto, was placed on the Mountain Warfare Committee; and Major General von Lettow-Vorbeck, who had fought brilliantly in German East Africa for four years, headed the Committee on Colonial Warfare. Captain Wegener, who had commanded the First Heavy Tank Company in the war, was named to the Tank Committee.[61] Most of the officers named to the committees were of the General Staff corps, but some specialists, such as Captain Wegener, were not on the General Staff. Since virtually every inspectorate and department of the Defense Ministry, about 300 officers in all, were expected to work on these studies in addition to the officers specifically requested by von Seeckt, the total effort for compiling Germany's war experiences was done by over 400 officers.[62]

The Training Section of the Truppenamt was given responsibility for collecting and reviewing the work of the committees. T-4 was ordered to recommend committee changes regarding the opening up of new subjects of study and the appointment of additional committee officers. T-4 was also to edit the reports for possible use in army manuals and regulations.[63] During 1920 the Training Section would initiate a further twenty-nine studies on subjects not covered by von Seeckt's directive of December 1, 1919. The Training Section appointed mostly its own officers to carry out these studies but solicited contributions from retired officers and some officers outside of T-4 as well. Some of the studies were specific and tactical and thus more suitable for direct application as sections of the new tactical manuals, such as "How Should Tactical Units Be Organized for Mountain Warfare?" and "Should Supply Trains Be Placed under Divisional Control or under Higher Headquarters?" Others were on more general subjects, such as "The Economy and the Two-Front War."[64]

At the same time, the Air Service officers within the Truppenamt organized a similar program for assessing the aerial warfare experience, citing von Seeckt's directive as their guideline for asking questions and developing solutions.[65] Special committees were formed, and over one hundred airmen, including the senior Air Service commanders and a high proportion of the former squadron commanders, would contribute studies.[66]

Counting the original committees, the additional officers who conducted studies for the Training Section, and the efforts of the Air Service, by mid-1920 over five hundred of the most experienced German officers were involved in a program to mold their war experiences into system of modern tactics and military organization. The victorious nations also rewrote their tactics, but neither the British, nor the French, nor the Americans approached the study of the war in so comprehensive a manner or employed the efforts of so many of their best officers as the Germans did. The professionalism of the German General Staff and the seriousness with which the German officers studied tactics after the war can be gauged by comparing them with the British Army's postwar tactical analysis. Whereas the Germans assigned experienced officers to analyze tactics—the lowest ranking army officers assigned to tactical doctrine studies in 1919–1920 were experienced captains who had been admitted to full membership in the General Staff corps[67]—the British War Office in 1920 assigned the task of rewriting the infantry tactical manual to Basil H. Liddell Hart, a twenty-four-year-old lieutenant of limited experience.[68] At one point, when the War Office did not like a particular chapter of Liddell Hart's manual, it simply deleted it and reinserted a chapter from the 1911 infantry manual, even though the British infantry organization had changed completely since then.[69] In 1920 the British Army considered creating an Inspectorate of Training for the Empire—an idea that might have greatly improved the British Army's indifferent attitude toward tactical doctrine. The idea was soon dropped, however, and with it went a good opportunity for the British to study tactics in a systematic manner.[70]

Most of the Reichswehr studies of 1919-20 have been lost; the greatest proportion of extant studies are from the Air Service. The ground forces tactical studies that are still available show a clear link with the committee work and the new regulations and manuals that started to be issued in 1921. One study on the delaying battle, conducted by the Training Section in 1920, clearly forms the basis for that portion of the new Army Regulation 487: *Leadership and Battle with Combined Arms*, Part 1. The concepts of the study and even some of the exact wording are in the formal tactical doctrine.[71] So many officers were involved in writing studies to develop new regulations that it is impossible to determine exactly who wrote what in 1920–1923. In any case, several new regulations were issued that demonstrate a high standard of tactical thought. They refute the notion that nothing good comes out of a committee.

The primary tactical regulation for the Reichswehr was Army Regulation 487 (*Leadership and Battle with Combined Arms*). Part 1, Chapters 1–11, was issued by the Truppenamt Training Section and signed by von Seeckt on September 1, 1921. Part 2, Chapters 12–18, was issued in June 1923.[72] In the introduction to Part 1, von Seeckt pointed out that "this regulation takes the strength, weaponry and equipment of a modern military major power as the norm, not that of the Peace Treaty's specified German 100,000-man army."[73] Even though Germany had been stripped of aircraft, heavy artillery, and tanks, the army should still train for modern war with a modern enemy. "Great mobility, better training, superior use of terrain and constant night operations offer partial substitutes" for modern weapons.[74]

*Leadership and Battle* is a clear exposition of von Seeckt's military concepts, which in turn are a combination of the Moltke-Schlieffen tradition and von Seeckt's wartime experiences. The regulation states, "The attack alone brings the decision. . . . Especially effective is the envelopment of one or both flanks and to attack the enemy's rear. In this way, the enemy can be destroyed. All attack orders must carry the stamp of decisiveness. The leader's will to victory must be communicated to the lowest-ranking soldier. The majority of force must be employed at the decisive point."[75] The spirit of the regulation is oriented toward offensive warfare, even though a major portion of it outlines defensive tactics. In the first section, on high command, the dislike of defensive thinking is made clear: "The defense is only justifiable against a greatly superior enemy and only to make possible an attack at another point or at a later time."[76]

In proper Seecktian fashion, *Leadership and Battle* recommends that if a flank attack is not tactically possible, a breakthrough attack through the enemy's front should be considered. The regulation also recommends, in line with von Seeckt's wartime experience, that a breakthrough attack must include deep penetration of the enemy's position; only in that way can real victory be achieved.[77] All stages of an offensive war of maneuver were described in detail in the two-volume, 609-page regulation. Although *Leadership and Battle* was written primarily for senior commanders at the regimental level and above, the regulation advocated considerable independent tactical authority for junior leaders as well. In the pursuit phase of the war of movement, the regulation stated, "as soon as the enemy before them weakens, the junior leaders should immediately, and without waiting for orders, and without regard to the fatigue of troops, carry on the pursuit of the defeated enemy. They [the junior leaders] must act with daring and independence."[78]

*Leadership and Battle* takes Clausewitz's "fog of war" into account. It was expected that in a war of movement many battles would be meeting engagements of units on the march that collided with enemy forces: "Insecurity and a confused situation are the norm in the war of movement. Usually, when air reconnaissance fails, knowledge of the enemy forces comes upon contact. . . . The leader on the spot has a special responsibility. He ought not to make his decisions based upon time-consuming reconnaissance. He must often make orders in a confusing situation and he can assume that the enemy is no more prepared for battle than he."[79] In the war of movement, commanders—even division commanders—need to be close to the front so that the situation can be observed and orders

*Von Seeckt observes maneuvers in East Prussia, 1922. (From Friedrich von Rabenau,* Seeckt: Aus seinem Leben, 1918–1936 *[Leipzig: Hase-Koehler Verlag, 1941])*

quickly issued. The higher commanders need to observe the situation personally.[80]

The importance of combined arms was implicit in the title of Army Regulation 487. The primary arm of military decision was still the infantry, but the infantry officer was expected, as in the wartime experience, to work closely with the artillery. In the 1921 regulation, it was foreseen that each infantry regiment would possess its own battery of infantry support cannons, which might be assigned even down to company level for particular missions.[81] This meant that the modern German infantry officer not only had to know how to employ riflemen, machine guns, mortars, and flame throwers, he also had to become something of an artilleryman. Tanks and aircraft were given full emphasis in *Leadership and Battle*; Part 2 of the manual devoted a chapter each to tanks and aircraft.[82] The tactical use of tanks and aircraft was also stressed in Part 1. Nevertheless, the doctrine of the 1920s viewed these two weapons primarily as support for the infantry division and not as independent forces.

Since the army cavalry division was given the mission of independent strategic operations, it was to be reinforced to become a mobile, all-arms force: "Large scale operations by large cavalry formations against the enemy's line of communications often provide the cavalry a particularly worthwhile field of activity. In this case it is necessary to reinforce the cavalry establishment with mobile support troops—bicycle troops, motorized infantry and artillery."[83]

*Leadership and Battle* spends a great deal of time with the more mundane aspects of higher leadership. Most of Part 2 deals with supply and transportation matters. Chapter 1 provides the most important lessons, among them the directions for higher leadership: "It is the special art of leadership to unite all available force at the point of decision. Our own inferiority of numbers must often be equalized by superior mobility."[84]

The tactical regulations for the other branches of the Reichswehr quickly followed the publication of the first part of *Leadership and Battle*. The official infantry regulations of 1906 had long been superseded by wartime events, and in the immediate postwar period the Reichswehr used the wartime tactical manuals that had been issued by the high command in 1917–1918.[85] The new infantry regulation, *Training Regulation for the Infantry*, abbreviated in German as AVI, was issued in October 1922; it incorporated all of the tactical developments of 1917 and 1918. The ten-to-twelve-man infantry squad composed of a light machine gun section and a rifle section was accepted as standard. The fluid squad fire-and-maneuver tactics of the stormtroop attack were also endorsed. As with *Leadership and Battle*, the AVI departed from the 1917–1918 tactics in accepting a war of movement as the norm. Attacking enemy trenches was still a major part of the AVI, but more emphasis was given to warfare in open country. The infantry manual also refused to limit its tactical considerations to Versailles Treaty armament: Infantry cannons, forbidden by Versailles, were considered part of normal unit armament.

The new training manual issued in 1923 for the horse transport troops, Army Regulation 467, contains some useful examples of the combined-arms concepts of the interwar period. That every soldier should be trained as an infantryman, and should be able to fight as an infantryman, was not a new concept to the German Army or to other armies. Due to its shortage of troops, however, the Reichswehr carried the idea of cross training further than other armies. Like the artillery units, the transport troops worked extensively with horses and so were seen as suitable units to cross train as artillerymen. The transport troops regulation required that every transport company train twenty of its wagon drivers as cannon gunners. A six-week training course was envisioned.[86] The transport troops, who normally handled supply columns, were also ordered to undergo some engineer training, especially in the handling of bridge columns and the assembly of field bridges.[87] As with the infantry and cavalry, the junior officers and NCOs of the transport troops were expected to be "independent thinkers."[88]

After new tactical regulations were issued for all branches of the Reichswehr between 1921 and 1923, a variety of short handbooks were written that contained excerpts and summaries of the most important sections of *Leadership and Battle* and the 1923 infantry manual. These simplified versions of the regulations were for the NCOs to ensure that the principles of leadership and the tactics of a war of maneuver were understood at all levels of the army.[89] The same basic leadership characteristics that were expected for higher officers in *Leadership and Battle* were expected of corporals and sergeants: The leader was to set the example, be fit, possess a firm character, take joy in responsibility, be decisive, put the concern of his men first, and be militarily knowledgeable. The NCOs were enjoined not only to know the basics of other army branches, but also to truly be able to employ combined arms in battle.[90]

TACTICAL ORGANIZATION

The Versailles Treaty carefully specified limits on the personnel, unit size, and weaponry for Reichswehr infantry and cavalry divisions. An infantry division was allowed three regiments of infantry, each regiment to have no more than 70 officers and 2,300 men. Also included were three trench mortar companies, a cavalry squadron, a pioneer battalion, a signals battalion, a medical unit, and supply columns. The artillery available to a division was only one regiment of three battalions, twenty-four field guns,

and twelve medium howitzers—essentially, the artillery strength of a
1914 division. The total personnel of an infantry division was not to exceed 410 officers and 10,830 men.[91] The three cavalry divisions of the
Reichswehr were each to total no more than 275 officers and 5,250 men.
The division was composed of a small headquarters, six cavalry regiments
of four squadrons of 165 men each, a pioneer battalion, a signals section,
and an artillery battalion of twelve light guns.[92]

The Versailles Treaty envisioned the German Army as a lightly armed
border guard and internal security force. The Reichswehr, however, had
other notions. Drawing on their war experience, the committees that fash-
ioned *Leadership and Battle* also outlined in detail the infantry and cavalry divisions that the Reichswehr would ideally have. Tables of organization for modern infantry and cavalry divisions were compiled and
published in Part 2 of *Leadership and Battle*.[93] The divisional organization tells us a great deal about the Reichswehr's and von Seeckt's concepts
of war in 1923 (see Appendix).

The "triangular" division that the Versailles Treaty allowed the Germans to have was actually a German innovation dating from 1915. The
old "square" infantry division consisted of two infantry brigades, each
commanding two regiments. In 1914 it was the corps of two divisions
that formed the German Army's primary tactical element. By 1915 the division had become the most important unit on the battlefield, and the
high command found the square division's organization to be tactically
awkward. Starting in 1915 the Germans simplified the divisional structure
by dropping the extra layer of command on the brigade headquarters and
by reorganizing the division into a unit of three regiments, each of which
reported directly to division headquarters. The Germans were the first to
adopt this "triangular" division, found to be more flexible and responsive
than the old division.[94] Thus the Reichswehr was satisfied with the framework of the infantry division, which included much of the wartime organizational system. In the Reichswehr, the smallest unit was the squad, led
by a sergeant. Four squads constituted a platoon, led by a lieutenant or a
master sergeant. A company, commanded by a captain, contained four
platoons. The battalion was formed by three rifle companies and a machine-gun company. Three battalions formed a regiment.[95]

Even though the framework of the infantry division was sound, it was
far too weak in supporting weapons, mobile weapons, and reconnaissance forces to be of much use in a mobile war. The regiment's only heavy
supporting weapons were the two heavy mortars and six light mortars in
the regimental mortar company.[96] The only reconnaissance force of the
infantry division was one squadron of cavalry detached from one of the
cavalry divisions. The proposed infantry division of 1923 rectified these
faults. Each infantry regiment was allotted its own battery of six infantry

*Heavy mortar and crew on field exercises near Potsdam, 1924.*

guns for direct-fire support. The divisional artillery firepower was more than doubled. A second field artillery regiment was added to the divisional establishment. Whereas only one battery of the Reichswehr's nine divisional artillery batteries was motorized, the proposed organization contained six fully motorized batteries. Furthermore, in the proposed organization, an antiaircraft battalion of four batteries was allocated to the divisional artillery.[97]

In the proposed infantry division, the reconnaissance force grew from one cavalry squadron to a full reconnaissance battalion with two cavalry squadrons, a bicycle company, a detachment of four armored cars and a mobile signals detachment. The signals detachment of the 1923 division is greatly increased over that of the Versailles-approved organization. An extra signals company was added to the two-company Reichswehr signals battalion, and signals detachments were allotted to each regiment, as well as to the reconnaissance battalion. Since communication is so much more difficult and much more important in a war of movement, the doubled signals support of the 1923 division shows that the General Staff had thought through this problem. For reconnaissance and artillery observation, each of the proposed infantry divisions was to receive a full squadron of observation planes to come under the control of the divisional headquarters. The proposed infantry division probably would have about 15,000 to 16,000 soldiers. All of the service units were expanded accordingly, with strength increases proposed for the medical unit, supply columns, motor battalion, and engineers. The artillery commander would receive an observation and survey company, and the divisional headquarters a mounted military police platoon and a motorcycle platoon—units also useful for courier duties.[98]

The Reichswehr cavalry division is almost unrecognizable in the proposed organization of the 1923 regulation (see Appendix). The cavalry strength of twenty-four squadrons organized into six regiments was not increased at all, but so many supporting arms were added that the proposed division would have been double the size of the Versailles-imposed unit. *Leadership and Battle* proposed that the six regiments be organized in a triangular fashion, with three brigades of two regiments each. Although each regiment would still have four cavalry squadrons, it would also have a machine-gun company instead of a section, a section of two cannons, and its own mounted communications section. The equivalent of an infantry regiment was added to the cavalry division by including one infantry battalion, one bicycle battalion, and one machine-gun battalion. As with the infantry division, the artillery of the cavalry division was doubled from one battalion to two, with the second battalion of twelve guns to be fully motorized. A motorized flak battalion of four batteries was also added. Further supporting weapons not allowed by the Versailles Treaty were an engineer battalion, a signals battalion, an observation squadron of twelve planes, and an armored car battalion of twelve armored cars. The Versailles Treaty did not allow the cavalry divisions their own medical, supply, and motor transport units; all of these were provided by *Leadership and Battle*.[99]

The infantry division proposed in 1923 was a formidable organization for a war of movement. With ninety field guns, counting the infantry guns, the divisional commander possessed sufficient firepower to carry out a variety of missions, ranging from the short-range direct-fire support of infantry cannons to the long-range interdiction and counter-battery fire of heavy howitzers. The strong emphasis upon signals units and the motorization of much of the artillery were a response to the communications and fire-support difficulties that had plagued the German offensives of 1918. The infantry division organization outlined in *Leadership and Battle* was so sound that it would become the basic infantry division organization when Germany went to war in 1939, with only a few changes, notably the addition of an antitank company in each rifle regiment and the elimination of the divisional air squadron.

The cavalry division proposed in *Leadership and Battle* was similar to von Seeckt's view of the cavalry as an all-arms force for mobile war. Much of the 1923 organization comes from the German experience on the eastern front, where infantry units were commonly attached to cavalry units; the 1923 organization simply regularized the practice. Because the Germans had also successfully used armored cars and cavalry together on the Romanian front in 1916 and in the Baltic countries in 1919, this became standard as well. By more than doubling the cavalry's artillery and providing the division with a full complement of supply columns, engineers, and other special troops, the proposed cavalry division of 1923 had the firepower and support to carry out independent operations deep behind enemy lines.

The Reichswehr was able to turn several of the military provisions of the Versailles Treaty to its advantage. The Germans' realization that the Versailles-ordained triangular division was a superior organization has already been noted; the Allies, however, were not so quick to catch on. The Americans, for example, would keep the square infantry division until 1940. The Versailles Treaty strictly limited the number of Reichswehr officers to 4,000 and kept unit staffs small. To illustrate, the headquarters of an infantry division was only allowed a maximum of 33 officers, including the staffs of the infantry and artillery commanders.[100] The Reichswehr followed this Versailles provision: In the 1920s, the normal infantry division headquarters had 32 officers.[101] The Reichswehr was hardly crippled by this shortage of officers; rather, a lean and efficient headquarters developed, free of the many bureaucratic inessentials that preoccupied officers in other armies. This Reichswehr habit was carried into the Wehrmacht. During World War II, German divisional staffs tended to have about 30 officers and officials, and they functioned efficiently.[102] By contrast, the U.S. Army's infantry division headquarters contained 79 officers. However, no evidence has been proffered to indicate that American divisional headquarters were more efficient than German ones.[103] Historians such as Martin van Creveld and Trevor N. Dupuy have argued convincingly that the smaller German staffs were by far the more effective of the two.[104]

The greatest single loophole in the Versailles Treaty was the lack of any limit on the number of NCOs in the Reichswehr. The Germans used this Allied oversight to maximum effect. In 1922 the Reichswehr had 17,940 senior NCOs and 30,740 junior NCOs—corporals and lance corporals—for a total enlisted structure that was more than half NCOs. The numbers of senior NCOs would increase to 18,948 by 1926. The number of corporals would also increase after 1922, so that by 1926 there were 19,000 corporals and lance corporals budgeted, leaving the German army with only 36,500 privates.[105] The Reichswehr felt free to use NCOs in positions that other countries would designate for officers. For example, German NCOs were commonly platoon leaders. When rearmament began in

1933–1934, many Reichswehr sergeants would become officers.[106] NCO standards were set extremely high. It was more difficult to become an NCO in the Reichswehr than it had been in the Imperial Army. Strict examinations were required for promotion from the lowest ranks.[107] With this excellent NCO corps, von Seeckt could point proudly to the Reichswehr as the Führerheer (leaders army), which would in time serve as an efficient framework for a larger army. The NCO system was strong in the German Army before the Versailles Treaty; the Allied provisions merely inspired the Germans further along those lines. Martin van Creveld remarked, "Whereas the intelligent, thinking NCO had been an exception in 1914, he became the rule twenty-five years later."[108]

The German Army regulations developed in the 1920s emphasized all of the principles necessary to a war of movement: the offensive, combined arms, maneuver, independent action by officers, and intelligent, effective leadership at all levels. The small size of the Reichswehr also made it necessary to cross train specialist troops for other duties and to consider freely employing specialist units for a greater variety of tasks than could be done in other armies. This flexibility of organization and tactics must also be added to the Reichswehr's principles of the war of movement.

CONTRAST WITH FRENCH DOCTRINE

The vision of postwar German military doctrine is especially striking when compared with the revised French military doctrine published in 1921. The French counterpart for *Leadership and Battle—The Regulation for the Tactical Employment of Large Units*—was, like the German regulation, intended primarily for officers and higher commanders. There are only a few additional similarities. For example, the French concluded, like every other army of the era, that victory could only be gained by offensive action.[109] Otherwise, the French battle doctrine is almost 180 degrees from the German. Lip service, but little more, is paid to maneuver. In the meeting engagement, when two forces collide unexpectedly, the French regulation advises not to attack: "One should. . . . fight the battle only in a planned manner and only after bringing up all available fire support."[110] The trench warfare of 1914–1918 taught the French the power of defense, so the primary weapon of the French Army became the artillery: "The attack always begins under the protective fire of the entire artillery mass."[111] All movement in battle would be under artillery support.[112] "Fire is the most important factor in battle. . . . The attack is bringing fire forward. The defense is fire that stops."[113]

The French Army's military doctrine of 1921, which remained its tactical manual into the mid 1930s, was essentially a tactical system frozen in time somewhere between Verdun and the autumn offensive of 1918. In the introduction, the French Army Commission spoke of planned motorization of the army and the creation of partially mechanized light divisions and then discussed the new chain of proposed border fortifications that would become the Maginot Line.[114] There is little in the manual, however, that would lend itself to supporting the principles of mobile warfare. Battles must be fought by plan, there is little consideration for the "fog of war," and individual initiative is not encouraged. The French offensive doctrine was pure 1918: Use plenty of tanks for troop support and only attack when one has numerical and fire superiority. Once the attack succeeds, the artillery must be repositioned forward. It was a cumbersome, slow means of conducting offensive war. The most striking difference between the German and French regulations is the absence in the latter of any clear concept of military leadership. *Leadership and Battle* begins with a short treatise on the characteristics of military leadership applicable to corporals as well as to generals. The German doctrine emphasized the use of independent judgment down to the lowest command levels. All of this is lacking in the French manual. The job of the lower-ranking French leader was to follow the plan and little more. It was the doctrine of an army that had learned to rely more upon its artillery pieces than its officers and sergeants.

## VON SEECKT'S GREATEST ACCOMPLISHMENT

The task of a commanding general is to set broad strategic guidelines for operations and policy. In a well-functioning military system, the plans, details, and tactics of implementing these guidelines are properly left to subordinate officers. Von Seeckt had to create a system from the flotsam of defeat and postwar revolution. Once the Truppenamt was organized, the Reichswehr had an effective operations staff that preserved the best of the old General Staff—this was von Seeckt's greatest accomplishment.

Von Seeckt did not write the postwar operations manual, although much of *Leadership and Battle* seems to come straight from his writings. Von Seeckt's role was to give firm guidance and direction; the postwar regulations all bear the stamp of his concept of the war of maneuver. Von Seeckt set up the most comprehensive program for studying the lessons of war ever carried out by a General Staff. The von Seeckt–inspired military doctrine of *Leadership and Battle* served the Reichswehr well for a decade. When new weaponry and tactics mandated a revision of the doctrine in 1930, the result—Army Regulation 300—would draw much of its content from *Leadership and Battle*. The new regulation's chapter on leadership, which has been highly praised by Martin van Creveld as a model of military thinking,[115] uses *Leadership and Battle* as its primary source. Von Seeckt's doctrines continued to influence the Reichswehr and Wehrmacht into World War II.

The Reichswehr's commanding general was not a pure theorist; his concepts of an elite, professional army were based upon his own practical war experience, as well as upon the Clausewitz-Moltke-Schlieffen tradition of the General Staff. Von Seeckt took a direct interest in the daily workings of the Truppenamt's organization and training sections. Albrecht Kesselring, later a field marshal, served in both of these sections in the 1920s. He left the following account of von Seeckt: "Professionally the Berlin years were a schooling for me. What could have replaced the debates, often held in my room, in the presence of Lieutenant-General von Seeckt, who knew so well how to listen and then sum up in a way that always hit the nail on the head? What a model General Staff officer and leader of men!"[116]

Von Seeckt's war doctrine was enthusiastically accepted by most of the Reichswehr, but only after considerable opposition and debate.

# CHAPTER THREE

# Debate within the Reichswehr

Von Seeckt's theories of war were not accepted without question by the Reichswehr. There was intensive debate within the armed forces throughout the 1920s; as a result, several competing ideas arose within the officer corps as the wartime experience was carefully analyzed. Several historians have asserted that the popularity of von Seeckt's military theories within the Reichswehr sprang from the conservative nature of the General Staff's military training and thought and that von Seeckt's conception of a war of movement was not innovative, but rather a return to the German Army's traditional way of war. Martin van Creveld calls von Seeckt "a restorer rather than an innovator."[1] Waldemar Erfurth points out that the strategic thought of von Moltke the Elder and von Schlieffen—which emphasized the importance of encirclement, the decisive battle, and annihilation of the enemy force—remained the major theoretical foundation for the postwar Truppenamt, just as it had been for the prewar General Staff.[2] Thus, avoiding the impasse of trench warfare and returning to a doctrine of mobility was natural to officers trained before the war.[3] Jehuda Wallach believes that the Schlieffen School predominated in the Reichswehr. After all, a whole generation of General Staff officers had been trained and molded by von Schlieffen before World War I.[4] According to Wallach, Schlieffen School officers strongly influenced the interpretation of the war and, through a large number of books and articles, kept von Schlieffen's principles to the forefront of German operational doctrine until World War II. Dozens of books by former leading officers of the Imperial Army, among them General Wilhelm Groener's *Das Testament des Grafen Schlieffen*, analyzed and praised von Schlieffen's vision.[5] Martin Kitchen asserts that von Schlieffen's admirers were so numerous and influential among military historians and commentators that any deviation from his principles was ridiculed and almost instantly dismissed.[6]

It is true that admirers of von Schlieffen's military thought were persuasive in the Reichswehr officer corps and in the Truppenamt. Von Seeckt himself was an admirer of both von Moltke and von Schlieffen, and he regularly quoted both.[7] Von Seeckt's own concepts of war certainly used von Moltke's and von Schlieffen's ideas as a major part of their foundation. However, to assert that von Seeckt's theories were merely a variation of the Moltke-Schlieffen tradition is an oversimplification.

The General Staff of 1918-19 preferred von Seeckt over Reinhardt as army chief, largely because the officers believed that von Seeckt would uphold the tradition of the officer corps and General Staff, whereas Reinhardt was much less reliable on these central issues. Groener passionately attacked Reinhardt for "character weakness" and for "attempting to democratize the army" when he wanted to give preference to front officers over General Staff officers in personnel retention and to reduce the central role of the General Staff.[8] As far as Groener was concerned, von Seeckt was not only the superior soldier and strategist, he would also preserve the character and tradition of the Imperial Army General Staff.[9] Major Joachim von Stülpnagel of the high command wrote to von Seeckt in June 1919, asking him not to resign but rather to remain on active duty because "in my opinion it is absolutely essential that an officer corps with monarchical convictions and of the old stamp should be preserved for the miserable creature of the new army."[10]

Although von Seeckt's preservation of the General Staff was a central part of the program to hold on to as much of the Imperial Army tradition as possible, he also deviated strongly from much of the Schlieffen and Prussian traditions of army organization, strategy, and tactics. Von Moltke and von Schlieffen relied upon superior numbers of men and guns to win battles and therefore looked to reservists to provide the additional troops on the front lines. In 1914, under the Schlieffen Plan, the German regular divisions after mobilization contained an average of 46 percent reservists.[11] Von Seeckt placed little faith in reservists' battlefield performance in a war of maneuver; he planned to use his reserves in a purely defensive role or as a replacement pool for the regular forces. The weight of numbers was not as essential to von Seeckt as it was to von Moltke and von Schlieffen. Since the traditional German military thinkers were tactically oriented, they saw little value in the technical education of officers. Von Seeckt believed in technical training, realizing that the modern German officer needed to understand modern technology. Von Schlieffen relied upon a detailed mobilization plan to bring a large conscript/reservist army to the front faster than the enemy. Von Seeckt preferred to start the war without prior mobilization and to gain surprise by using the highly mobile regulars for a first strike. Even in basic battle tactics, the disagreement between von Seeckt and von Schlieffen is plain. Von Schlieffen preferred encirclement, while von Seeckt was flexible on that point—if encirclement was not possible, then a direct breakthrough was also a sound alternative.

One of the best interpretations of von Seeckt's military philosophy is found in Herbert Rosinski's *The German Army* (1966). Rosinski speaks of the "restorative character" of von Seeckt's position rather than simply labeling him a military traditionalist. In politics, von Seeckt was certainly a traditionalist, holding the Bismarckian Reich and the monarchy as his ideals. According to Rosinski, von Seeckt was "remarkably open-minded in all matters of detail and ready to accept and utilize the methods and instruments of the new age, yet fundamentally rooted in the old and disinclined to accept any radical alteration or even criticism of its foundations."[12] Rosinski explained that German military theory tended to stress either operations (army-level strategy) or tactics. Scharnhorst stressed the tactical factor; von Moltke balanced the two; and von Schlieffen put all his effort into developing the operational factor, virtually ignoring the tactical side. During World War I, Ludendorff came to the conclusion that tactics took precedence over strategy.[13] With von Seeckt, the one-sided emphasis of von Schlieffen was corrected and the tactical and operational factors were once again equally balanced. Rosinski stated that von Seeckt probably would have preferred to stress the operational aspect, but the tactical study of the war in the 1920s kept that factor in full consideration.[14]

Note that von Seeckt's original conception of an elite, professional, volunteer army was such a major break with German tradition that a true traditionalist like Wilhelm Groener disagreed with it. In the spring of 1919, Groener argued that the army needed to be at least 350,000 men strong and that accordingly he favored conscription.[15] The real conservatives among the officers are epitomized by Groener, who not only favored retaining the traditional General Staff, conscription, and a large army, but who also was an unabashed disciple of Count von Schlieffen. One German general said of Groener, "He described the World War as a battle of the railroads"—a statement much in line with the doctrines of von Moltke and von Schlieffen.[16] In contrast to Groener, a man who expressed the operational/tactical views of probably a majority of the General Staff officers of 1919, von Seeckt cannot be labeled simply as a "traditionalist" or "conservative." His departures from the Moltke-Schlieffen tradition are numerous and sufficiently noteworthy to underscore that von Seeckt was an original and innovative military theorist. The General Staff officers, however, even though they were conservative, came to support von Seeckt partly because of his war reputation, partly because of his conservative political and military nature, and partly because of his obvious breadth of vision.[17]

Some General Staff officers, notably his early supporters, Joachim von Stülpnagel and Werner von Blomberg (both later generals), characterized von Seeckt as insufficiently innovative in his military thought. In von Blomberg's memoirs, two instances are mentioned to demonstrate this:

Our suggestions for new developments in the Reichswehr were not readily accepted by General von Seeckt. . . . I suggested abandoning the use of lances of the cavalry soldiers so as to increase the firepower of our three cavalry divisions. . . . Seeckt replied, "For the same reason during the war I suggested relinquishing the lances. This was refused. Now the cavalry can retain the lances as far as I am concerned." . . . We wanted to make a very modest attempt to open the road to motorization and proposed to put the companies of bicyclists on motorcycles. . . . Seeckt replied literally, "Dear Blomberg, if we want to remain friends, then you must refrain from such suggestions."[18]

These two comments provide a weak basis upon which to build a case that von Seeckt stifled innovation; they are better illustrations of von Seeckt's irritation and anger.

Von Seeckt, who had to put up with an attempted coup by some of his own generals in the Kapp Putsch of 1920, and who was forced to relieve General von Lossow and several other officers for sympathizing with Hitler and the Nazis during the 1923 Putsch, had so many problems with overzealous and disloyal officers during the Reichswehr's early years that it is no wonder he occasionally lost his temper and belittled the ideas of his most enthusiastic officers. In fairness, however, he did enable the careers of von Blomberg and other innovative officers to prosper. On the whole, von Seeckt's record is one of supporting tactical and technical innovation. For example, he strongly supported the development of modern tanks and aircraft, as well as a wide range of thoroughly modern weapons (see Chapters five and eight).[19]

Some General Staff officers were highly critical of von Seeckt's ideas. Yet he still managed to imbue the whole Reichswehr with his military doctrines during 1919–1927. A few members of the officer corps were also critical of von Seeckt. General M. Faber du Faur, in his memoirs, referred to von Seeckt contemptuously as a schemer and "inflation man."[20] Such a view was, however, a minority opinion within the army. Although von Seeckt was cold and often difficult, the officer corps came to respect his leadership and ability and to accept his military ideas.[21] Harold Gordon pointed out that the officer corps as a whole stood solidly behind von Seeckt and his policies. Even some who later sympathized with the Nazis considered him a great soldier and followed him loyally while he commanded the Reichswehr.[22]

It was Guenther Blumentritt (later a general) who expressed an opinion of von Seeckt typical of the Reichswehr officer corps: "But Colonel General von Seeckt deserves even greater praise for having gradually strengthened this modest instrument of the new republic (the Army) inwardly and for having given it such training as might be termed model considering the times."[23] Franz von Papen, a former General Staff officer and later chancellor of Germany, compared von Seeckt to von Moltke and von

Schlieffen, calling him "the best representative [of the Reichswehr] and an outstanding personality in the early twenties."[24] The most definitive assessment of von Seeckt's impact upon the Reichswehr officer corps comes from a postwar study by Harold Gordon. Gordon surveyed over fifty German World War II generals who had served in the Reichswehr, including Generals Guderian, Heinrici, von Leeb, von Arnim, and Kesselring. They were asked, "Were the majority of your comrades satisfied with General von Seeckt and his policies? What do you think of General von Seeckt and his policies? What do you think of General von Seeckt as a man and a soldier?" The respondents were unanimous in their belief that the officers of their regiments accepted General von Seeckt and his policies with enthusiasm. They were also agreed in praising him as a man and soldier despite the coolness of his demeanor.[25] The description of unanimous support for von Seeckt's policies is overstated, but apparently his military doctrines came to be generally accepted by the officer corps. Aside from some opposition from the traditional advocates of the mass, conscript army, there were three other schools of military thought within the Reichswehr of the 1920s that advocated doctrines different from von Seeckt's.

## SCHOOLS OF MILITARY THOUGHT
## WITHIN THE REICHSWEHR

### The Defensive School

While von Seeckt and most of the General Staff concluded from their study of the war that a war of maneuver was the superior form of warfare—indeed, it was the "war of the future"—a minority within the army had learned the lessons of trench warfare all too well. They argued that the defense now had the military advantage. General of Infantry Walther Reinhardt was, until his death in 1930, the most prestigious opponent of von Seeckt's theory of strategy and tactics and the most eloquent advocate of the power of the defense.[26]

In June 1919 Reinhardt counseled the government to refuse to accept the Versailles Treaty and to continue fighting. This ran counter to the advice of von Seeckt and Groener, who saw resistance against the Allies as hopeless. Reinhardt, however, believed that armed resistance to Allied demands was a matter of honor and probably believed that a defensive position might actually hold the enemy. Reinhardt desired to call the nation to arms like Scharnhorst had in 1813, and he naively believed Germany would answer. Yet these two beliefs—the effectiveness of a national militia and the effectiveness of the defense—became the foundation of Reinhardt's thought.

Reinhardt had spent almost all of the war on the western front in hard battles like Verdun and the Somme. As a result of these experiences, he, like many other officers, naturally favored the defense. After Reinhardt's death his brother Ernst, also a general, edited the essays of the former Reichswehr commander, publishing them as *Wehrkraft und Wehrwille*.[27] This book would propose a military system completely at odds with von Seeckt's military philosophy. Herbert Rosinski fairly characterized Reinhardt as an officer who saw the lesson of World War I from the same perspective as the French Army: Mobile war was a thing of the past and the mass army and firepower gave an advantage to the defense. The semi-mobile war of 1918, with firepower rather than mobility as the primary factor of the offense, was Reinhardt's essential tactical conception.[28]

In direct contrast to von Seeckt's conception of a militia solely as a manpower and replacement pool for the professional field army, Reinhardt considered the military worth of such a reserve force to be greater than ever. Due to the mobility of many modern armies, he argued, the German army needed depth in the defense against a motorized opponent. The war experience, in which many thousands of older and less fit men were called to serve in the rear or as defense troops in quiet sectors, proved its worth to Reinhardt. He believed that the moral strength of a national militia would add to the army's defensive fighting power.[29] Simple mass of numbers was still important for Reinhardt. He offered the Swiss militia, in particular its national small-arms training program, as a model for Germany.[30]

According to Reinhardt, defensive works were particularly valuable in modern war, for the attacker exhausted his military power in trying to overcome them. The French fortifications system then under construction was praised by Reinhardt.[31] He proposed a program of national defense in which the border road and rail lines were to be cut and obstacles erected—all manned by a militia force that would halt, or at least delay, the invader and try to hold as much ground as possible.[32] In Reinhardt's view, the increased firepower provided by modern technology served the defender more than the attacker.[33]

Reinhardt also drew upon the German military tradition to justify his position, citing Clausewitz and von Moltke. He also recalled recent experience. Verdun and the 1918 offensives taught Reinhardt the value of mass: "Anyone who believes that you can have too many good soldiers is wrong. Superior force is and will remain the most important factor of war."[34] Von Seeckt and his military theories were repeatedly attacked by name.[35]

General Hermann von Kuhl was also an admirer of French postwar ideas.[36] In the 1920s von Kuhl wrote eleven books and dozens of articles on World War I.[37] Like Reinhardt, von Kuhl believed that the German Army could have held on and continued fighting in 1918. The Germans could have carried out a slow withdrawal to the Antwerp-Meuse Line—if necessary, successfully retreating behind the Rhine River—while causing heavy Allied casualties and forcing the enemy to reconsider any further attacks.[38] The battles of 1918 were as influential for von Kuhl as they had been for Reinhardt, and von Kuhl had an even greater appreciation for the French Army view.[39] Von Kuhl insisted that the war had proven that the time of the mass army had not passed: "It would seem . . . that holding on to universal military service is the correct course and that in war it is necessary from the first day on to employ the whole power of the nation. . . . The mass army has survived very well."[40]

Military historians have tended to view Reinhardt more sympathetically than they have von Seeckt, attaching greater importance to the former's views than they truly deserve. In the years shortly after World War II, Reinhardt was seen as the "democratic" general of the Weimar Republic, in contrast to the "undemocratic" von Seeckt. General Faber du Faur and Rosinski praised Reinhardt for his democratic views,[41] and both asserted that the Reichswehr would have been politically different had Reinhardt remained chief. This is certainly true, but Reinhardt was too unpopular with the General Staff and officer corps to have been an effective commander. Besides, there is little evidence that the views of Reinhardt or von Kuhl had any real following in the army. The *Militär Wochenblatt*, the primary journal of the German Army, sometimes published articles like "The War of Movement or Trench Warfare?"[42] or "The Commander and Mass."[43] These military commentaries, however, came down on the side of von Seeckt rather than Reinhardt or von Kuhl. The Germans carefully studied the French postwar tactics of mass and dependence upon fire support and rejected them. General von Taysen, inspector of infantry, wrote a critique of the French infantry in 1922, wherein he praised French weaponry but said French tactics were so dependent upon the artillery that it was hard for the French infantry to attack without massed fire. He maintained that in an encounter between infantry and infantry, the French would perform poorly. It was clear to him that the French system of attack would lead to trench warfare.[44]

### The Psychological School

The new variations on mobile warfare worked out by von Seeckt and the General Staff were not imposed without some resentment and debate from the lower ranks of the officer corps. In the early 1920s the majority of the four-thousand man officer corps were lieutenants and captains, many of them wartime volunteers and commissionees whose whole knowledge of warfare consisted of the trench war and storm attacks of the western front. An officer of that period, Franz von Gaertner, recounted the resentment of those sent through the infantry officer's course at Dresden, where they were taught the new mobile tactics. When some of these young officers disagreed with the content of the training, emphasizing their years of front-line service, the inspector of army schools, General von Metzsch, called them together and bluntly told them that as far as he was concerned, they had "war reminiscences but no war experience."[45]

Two young veterans of the western front, Lieutenants Ernst Jünger and Kurt Hesse, challenged the General Staff's model of war, proposing one based on their own experiences. Hesse acted consciously as a spokesman for a whole new approach to warfare, and Jünger served to represent the emotional side of the young officers who had served in the storm troops and who were reluctant to accept any concept of war that smacked of the prewar tradition. Hesse and Jünger both published books in the early 1920s attacking the traditional and the new models of warfare expressed by the General Staff. While the General Staff emphasized operational factors in military operations, Jünger and Hesse promoted a war model in which morale and psychology played primary roles.

Jünger, a storm troop company commander and winner of the pour le mérite, opened the debate in 1920 with *The Storm of Steel* (Das Stahlgewittern), a vivid and detailed account of his four years on the western front. This bestseller was followed by a book of essays on war, *The Battle as Inner Experience* (Der Kampf als inneres Erlebnis), in 1922 and in 1924 *Copse 125* (Das Wäldchen 125), ostensibly about the battle for a small forest in 1918 but also an extensive study of the philosophy and psychology of war.[46]

Jünger's books are a glorification of the indomitable spirit of the World War I German soldier combined with a detailed depiction of trench warfare and assault tactics. Both Jünger and Hesse viewed war from the worm's-eye vantage of the company officer, showing little understanding of higher strategy or operations. In Jünger's books, staff officers are always referred to disparagingly, especially when compared with company-grade front officers.[47] There is no reverence for drill, army traditions, or even the prewar distancing between officers and men, all aspects of the General Staff officer's mind set. It is the will of the soldier, his ideals, and his willingness to die that are, for Jünger, the essential attributes of the German Army. In *The Storm of Steel*, he related: "I learned this from the very four years' schooling in force and in all the fantastic extravagance of material warfare that life has no depth of meaning except when it is pledged for an ideal, and that there are ideals in comparison with which the life of an individual and even of a people has no weight."[48] Of postwar

Germany, Jünger remarked: "An official and officious patriotism, together with the forces that oppose it, must be swallowed up in a frenzy of faith in Folk and Fatherland, blazing out from every rank of society, and everyone who feels differently must be branded as a heretic and rooted out. We cannot possibly be national—yes, nationalistic—enough."[49]

Both quotations are typical of the emotional tone of Jünger's works and ideology. Jünger, who served in the Freikorps and then as a Reichswehr officer until 1923, voiced the more extreme views of the Freikorps era and of the young officers who disobeyed the General Staff's orders to fight on the Baltic in 1919 or who joined the Kapp Putsch of 1920 and the Hitler Putsch of 1923—or, at least, sympathized with those who did.[50] Like many young front officers, Jünger viewed his war experience through a thick, emotional haze. In contrast, the General Staff officers who were elucidating the new doctrines of the maneuver war analyzed the lessons of World War I from a traditional historical perspective.

Although Jünger was a strong nationalist, to the right of much of the General Staff (he was heavily involved in the politics of the Stahlhelm in the mid-1920s),[51] he never carried his nationalism to the extreme by becoming a Nazi. Despite being considered an advocate of the Psychological School, Jünger was much more acceptable to the General Staff than Hesse. Jünger agreed with the new infantry tactics adopted by the Reichswehr in 1922 and wrote about them in the *Militär Wochenblatt*.[52] Jünger's books were praised by Major General Georg Wetzell, a protégé of von Seeckt and one of the leading Truppenamt officers (he was chief of the Truppenamt from 1926 to 1927).[53] He saw them as "excellent representations of battle tactics. They will always be educationally useful."[54] Jünger left the army to pursue a writing career, not because of any disagreement with army policy.

The other notable young dissenter from the General Staff's model of war, First Lieutenant Kurt Hesse, held a doctorate in psychology and expressed the views of the officers of his generation in a more academic and specific manner than Jünger.[55] Hesse actually expounded a new approach to understanding war—the Psychological School. In numerous books and articles written in the early 1920s, he asserted that the old Imperial Army and the old General Staff had lost the war because they did not understand individual and mass psychology and that incorporation of a deeper psychological understanding in battlefield tactics would be the key to victory in the next war.[56] Hesse would, not unfairly, claim Ernst Jünger as an advocate of the Psychological School in 1924.[57]

In *The Psychology of the Commander* (Der Feldherr Psychologos), his first major work, Hesse spent the first six chapters in a detailed psychological analysis of the German defeat at Gumbinnen in August 1914, in particular the panic and rout of one regiment. The rest of the book strays among various topics including Clausewitz, psychology, and a psychological analysis of World War I. Sometimes Hesse sounds very similar to Jünger, with his glorification of the front soldier, and many of Hesse's conclusions are similar—for example, "The power of the race lies primarily in its spiritual health"[58] and "The German soul seeks suffering."[59] Hesse quoted Clausewitz to support these points. Hesse argued that a thorough program of psychological instruction should be given to all army officers and NCOs, and that psychology should be incorporated into all army branch instruction.[60] Hesse's style is even more difficult to follow than Jünger's turgid, passionate one, for he jumps from psychological analysis to Kantian philosophy to tactics. But some points are clear in both writers: The Great War had destroyed the traditional Prussian conceptions of warfare, and many traditions and modes of thought carried over from the old army needed to be discarded.

The General Staff's answer to the Psychological School came from Major Friedrich von Rabenau. In the course of his service in the Truppenamt's Training Section in the 1920s, von Rabenau shared responsibility for training the army in the war of maneuver. He was a military intellectual, a prolific writer, and later a general of artillery.[61] Von Rabenau, who wrote several books on tactics and military history in the interwar period, gave an extensive rebuttal of Hesse's military philosophy in *The Old Army and the New Generation* (Die alte Armee und die junge Generation).[62]

Insofar as anyone could apply a comprehensive analysis to Hesse's work, von Rabenau attempted a point-by-point refutation. First he defended the old General Staff tradition of the war of maneuver: "I am of the conviction that the older military generation possessed and taught a fairly correct image of war so far as it is humanly possible."[63] Von Rabenau used a common-sense approach to dismiss Hesse's long psychological analysis of the defeat at Gumbinnen by remarking that the German retreat was less than a rout and more a retreat caused by green troops receiving shellfire from friendly batteries. Such things "happen in every war."[64] Von Rabenau also took issue with Hesse's—and Jünger's—idealization of the common soldier. Von Rabenau argued that the army of the future might be a large one in time of war, but it would also rely more upon the technical abilities of the educated middle class and the mechanical background of skilled workers.

Von Rabenau was a strong advocate of the Seecktian General Staff concept of modern mobile warfare. In 1935 he wrote a military history/tactics book, *Operational Victories against Numerically Superior Forces* (Operative Entschlüsse gegen eine Anzahl überlegenen Gegner), that examined a series of major battles in which outnumbered German forces decisively defeated enemy armies by the use of maneuver.[65] The Battle of Tannenberg was the primary example—a battle in which superior German mobility, firepower, training, and leadership utterly destroyed the Russian Second Army in 1914. The Battle of Tannenberg was, in fact, a favorite example of General Staff officers to illustrate the power of smaller, more capable forces opposed to a clumsy mass army.

Other leading members of the Truppenamt also dismissed Hesse's theories of war. Major General Wetzell, in a review of Hesse's *The Old Army and the New Generation* in the *Militär Wochenblatt*, held that the proper way to study war experience was through traditional military-historical analysis. Hesse's dismissal of the old General Staff particularly irritated Wetzell: "One is astounded by the views of a young officer concerning the old army—which he never really knew. In our splendid old army, which for 100 years was the great educational institution for the whole German nation . . . the army which showed the highest military performance of all time in the horrible four-year war . . . does he think that it could have performed so well if it did not understand psychology?"[66]

General von Taysen, a first-rate tactician, a prolific writer, and one author of the new tactical regulations, commented on "First Lieutenant Hesse's latest thoroughly confused outpourings" in a paper on infantry tactics.[67]

Even General von Seeckt, who introduced modern psychological testing into the German Army and had progressive views on the use of psychology in soldier recruitment and leadership, was angered at Hesse's lack of respect for the tradition of the General Staff. In *Thoughts of a Soldier*, von Seeckt aimed some barbs at Hesse: "A youthful school of military writers recently discovered the term 'General Psychologos.' Platitudes have their periods of rejuvenation. As though the true arts of statesmanship and war had ever been imaginable without psychology!"[68]

There was never much chance of the Hesse-Jünger psychological model of war prevailing over the General Staff's model within the army. First of all, the younger officers came to accept the General Staff's concept of mobile warfare as the army was retrained in the 1920s. Second, the psychological model was largely incomprehensible to the average officer. In his critique, von Rabenau remarked, quite fairly, that he was unsure of what Hesse was trying to say. The General Staff officer and the average line officer of the Reichswehr were, above all, practical men, neither theorists nor philosophers. The Seecktian–General Staff model of war could at least be understood on the practical level.

The Hesse debate, however, does uncover a bit of generational conflict within the Reichswehr's officer corps. After von Rabenau and Wetzell attacked Hesse's doctrine, Major Benary defended Hesse in the *Militär Wochenblatt*—perhaps it was not so much a defense of Hesse's ideas as a plea for tolerance and sympathy within the officer corps for younger officers who bucked the mainstream thought. Benary argued that much of the experience of the young front officers was valid and ought to be reviewed more sympathetically by the officers who learned their trade in the old Imperial Army.[69]

In fact, Hesse was granted a great deal of tolerance within the officer corps. If leading General Staff officers publicly attacked his views, it certainly did not affect Hesse's promotions and assignments, nor was Hesse ever silenced or forced out. When he left the army for academic life in 1929, he was invited back to lecture at the cavalry and artillery schools; he also kept his status as a reserve officer. In the Reichswehr, if an officer had a good record and was competent in his duties, he was free to write and publish on military subjects and to disagree with the Reichswehr's tactical doctrines—as long as he trained his soldiers efficiently in the tactical doctrines laid out by the General Staff. Soldiers with radical military theories were probably tolerated more in the Reichswehr than in other armies of the period.

### The "People's War" School

In the first half of the 1920s, a few officers within the Reichswehr studied the "people's war" as an alternative to the war of maneuver. The concept of a people's war (*Volkskrieg*) is difficult to define, for there are many variations to the concept. The basic principle was that the Great War had broken down the traditional barriers between soldiers and civilians and between military and civilian targets. The strategic bombing campaign carried out, however primitively, by both sides signified that the worker in the factory was now as much a military target as the soldier in the trench. Henceforth, wars would not be seen as limited conflicts with limited goals—like the war with France in 1870 or the war with Austria in 1866. It was generally believed that future wars would be like the Boer War of 1899–1902—a contest of national survival—or like the Great War, in which both sides employed every manpower and economic resource to ensure victory and overthrow the enemy. The Volkskrieg concept not only turned the enemy's civilians into legitimate targets but also meant that the invader ought to be resisted by all means—particularly by sabotage and by armed irregulars practicing guerrilla war.

In one way, von Seeckt's concept of warfare was traditional. Like most of the General Staff, he advocated a conventional doctrine—wars were fought between soldiers. Von Seeckt and most of the officer corps were not interested in imposing victory by blockading ports, bombing cities, or other indirect means. The goal of the army was to be no different from what von Moltke had practiced or von Schlieffen had advocated: Trap and destroy the enemy armies in a battle of annihilation.

Germany's militarily helpless position after November 1918 caused the army to consider planning for a people's war, but it was not considered as a national policy. The idea of Volkskrieg was a measure of desperation in the immediate postwar period. In April 1919, when many Germans expected an invasion of Germany by Czechoslovakia, volunteer border guard regiments were formed, much like the Freikorps, and positioned along the Polish and Czech borders.[70] The 1919 defense plan of one of these units on the Czech border recommended that if superior Czech forces attacked, the guards could carry out a guerrilla war of sabotage, retreat, and ambush. In case of attack, the unit was authorized to mobilize and arm the local men. Since most Germans believed the Czechs would probably attack,[71] the absence of war plans or an organized army meant that desperate measures were seen as the only possible military response.

In 1923, when the French Army invaded the Ruhr and some of the territory beyond, the anger, fear, and frustration of the Germans prompted some consideration of a strategy of Volkskrieg, and in particular guerrilla war, within the General Staff. Lieutenant Colonel Joachim von Stülpnagel of the Operations Section hoped that the Reichswehr would sponsor a popular uprising in the French-occupied zone. Industrialist Fritz Thyssen and General von Wetter (retired) wanted to form a volunteer underground military organization to conduct full-scale guerrilla warfare against the French to drive them out.[72] Ludendorff, representing elements of the Freikorps and the extreme right, offered the services of these paramilitary groups to the government. At the same time, however, he refused to guarantee complete obedience to von Seeckt and the army. Von Seeckt refused the arrangement.[73] Von Stülpnagel continued to push for the adoption of some sort of guerrilla warfare doctrine by the Reichswehr as the most suitable method for a weakly-armed nation to oppose a stronger one.[74]

In a strategic study entitled "The War of the Future," written in March 1924, von Stülpnagel proposed that Germany adopt a Volkskrieg strategy and tactics, since Germany's weak position put it on the strategic defensive: "We ought to strive for a strategy of exhausting the enemy rather than destroying him. . . . In the battle of delay the object is to wear down the enemy forces."[75] Sabotage and organized resistance behind enemy lines would play a major role in defeating an invasion.[76] According to von Stülpnagel, guerrilla warfare needed to be organized and directed by the high command, but exactly how the high command could carefully control such a war was never explained.[77] Von Stülpnagel urged the Reichswehr to establish additional border units and new reserve formations and train them for the Volkskrieg.[78]

Von Seeckt saw guerrilla warfare as an impractical strategy and supported the government's view that passive resistance, including strikes and all manner of noncooperation, was the best course. Von Seeckt did allow a sabotage organization to be set up by von Stülpnagel and funded by the Reichswehr, but this was more a means of harassing and embarrassing the French in their effort to establish an independent Rhineland than a serious attempt to inflict military damage.[79] Von Seeckt's major objections to a guerrilla war or Volkskrieg were that these strategies were not only defensive (and therefore at the opposite end of his philosophical spectrum), they also could not be controlled by the professional soldiers.

For most of his career as chief of the army command, von Seeckt was bedeviled by the lack of discipline of the Freikorps. In the Kapp Putsch of 1920 and in the Hitler Putsch of 1923, some of the Freikorps tried to topple the government. In 1919 the Freikorps almost caused the Reichswehr to fire on itself; in 1920 and 1923, they caused mutiny within the army. Any attempt at creating a Volkskrieg or guerrilla war would, in effect, leave the initiative to the extreme right's paramilitary groups and not in the hands of the army. This was abhorrent to von Seeckt, who loved old-fashioned Prussian discipline.

During the crisis of 1923, the army enlisted and trained thousands of short-term volunteers. It also placed many paramilitary groups on call in case a mobilization against the French should prove necessary. In every instance, these secret reserves, called the Black Reichswehr, were clearly under the command and control of the army as its militia force and not as guerrilla units.[80]

Aside from von Stülpnagel, few in the army seem to have been interested in guerrilla warfare. One Truppenamt study of the early 1920s recommended modern fortresses and strategic defense zones as useful in a Volkskrieg or guerrilla war, but this is one of the few times either idea was mentioned in Reichswehr documents.[81] In 1925, after the Ruhr crisis, the Operations Section of the Truppenamt declared in its summary of goals for the next year's mobilization plans that the concept of guerrilla warfare would not be considered as a defense option.[82] The main supporter of Volkskrieg and guerrilla warfare, General Ludendorff, was now outside the army. In 1931 he wrote a bloodcurdling description of future war, *The Coming War*, in which mass armies of French, Czechs, Poles, and others would invade Germany in the most ruthless manner. Civilians would be treated brutally and towns would be burned as German irregulars fought behind the lines and carried out sabotage.[83] In 1935, in *Der Totale Krieg*, Ludendorff presented a similar view supporting the total war philosophy of the Volkskrieg, wherein civilians become the fighters.[84] Such views may have been popular among the Nazis and within the Freikorps, but they do not appear to have had the slightest effect upon the Reichswehr.[85]

The Military History Research Office of the Reich Archives, which was essentially a disguised General Staff Historical Section, conducted several studies of guerrilla warfare about 1930, concluding like von Seeckt and the Truppenamt that it was not a practical strategic option for the German Army. One classified study of the regions of Germany under Allied occupation pointed out that the behavior of German civilians living in the Rhineland was disappointing: In the General Staff's opinion, the civilians cooperated too much with the Allied occupation. The study estimated that, during the 1923 Ruhr invasion, approximately two thousand Germans had worked as paid French agents—certainly not a situation in which the civilians would join in a do-or-die war of national liberation.[86]

An extensive study of guerrilla warfare and Volkskrieg was conducted by several military historians at the Reich Archives at the Truppenamt's request. The editor, Archivrat Liesner, concluded that for a Volkskrieg to be successful most of seven elements had to be favorable: (1) popular support, (2) good leadership at the top, (3) preparation, (4) character of the terrain, (5) length of the war, (6) political position of the enemy, and (7) sympathetic foreign powers.[87] Few of these factors were in Germany's favor. The German Communist party was strong and divided the nation; preparation for a Volkskrieg was minimal, and the borders were not easily defended; a long war would mean a blockade that would devastate the national economy; and only Austria and Hungary could be numbered as allies, while Germany's major enemies—France, Belgium, Poland, and Czechoslovakia—could be counted on to hold together against Germany.[88]

Liesner was unable to estimate the worth of a militia or Freikorps against modern armies. He nevertheless believed that the old soldiers, recalled to the colors and militia, could be as effective as the Landeswehr and Landsturm reservists of the Great War—but only in a defensive battle. He concluded that such troops had little value in a war of maneuver.[89] Liesner did believe that with training in guerrilla warfare, the Freikorps might be relatively effective. Still, the power of the forty-nine available French divisions, the thirty Polish divisions, and the twenty Czech divisions was still too strong for Germany to consider conducting a war with any hope of success.[90] Liesner, however, was clearly partial to the military use of the Freikorps. Even after von Seeckt's retirement in October 1926, Reichswehr policy remained the same: Organizations not willing to place themselves under full military obedience to the Reichswehr would not be considered military reserves, nor would they receive arms, training, or equipment from the Reichswehr.

Since the army ultimately rejected the concept of Volkskrieg, the interest shown by von Stülpnagel and the Military History Research Office serves mainly to demonstrate the breadth of debate that existed within the Reichswehr concerning viable tactics and strategy for national defense.


CONCLUSION

Military historians have overstressed the continuity of the German Army's doctrine of maneuver warfare and understressed von Seeckt's divergence from tradition and the important role of debate within the Reichswehr. Certainly, the Schlieffen tradition was strong, but Jehuda Wallach[91] and Martin Kitchen[92] have overstated its importance to the Reichswehr. Officers with important posts, such as von Stülpnagel and Reinhardt, were willing to break dramatically with tradition and elucidate their own views.

The least acceptable interpretation of the postwar German doctrine of mobile warfare was proffered by Barry Posen in *The Sources of Military Doctrine*. Posen argued that the Reichswehr's adherence to a doctrine of maneuver is an example of organization theory, which states that military organizations like offensive doctrines and do not like to innovate.[93] Posen missed the point. Postwar German military doctrine represents considerable innovation, and armies prefer the offense because it wins wars. Von Seeckt and the General Staff were extremely conservative in political matters, but the enormous postwar effort in establishing committees to critically examine army doctrine and organization refutes the image of the General Staff as military traditionalists.

The Reichswehr adopted its doctrine of a quick war of maneuver leading to an early decision and rapid annihilation of the enemy force as simply the most sensible military doctrine for a future war. The idea of striking first and quickly offered some chance for straightforward victory—once the army was expanded and weapons were acquired. A defensive war, as Reinhardt and others advocated, could hurt and exhaust the enemy, but the Great War and the contemporary international situation demonstrated that Germany was far more vulnerable than its enemies to a war of attrition. If the Reichswehr accepted Reinhardt's view, it would mean returning to the trenches in wartime, with a military stalemate at best and certain economic collapse in the long term. After World War I, the prevailing sentiment was to avoid a war of attrition and trench warfare. Von Seeckt's concepts offered the army a chance for victory on the battlefield once the German forces were prepared. Given a choice between a doctrine of attrition and decisive victory on the battlefield, most Reichswehr officers clearly opted for the latter. It was a choice made not only with regard to recent military history and German tradition but also after consideration of the alternatives and careful appraisal of the French doctrine of war. The events of 1939 and 1940 would show that von Seeckt and the Reichswehr had chosen more wisely than their opponents.

# CHAPTER FOUR

# Training the Reichswehr

The period from November 11, 1918, through January 1921 was an especially turbulent time for the German Army as the old army was dissolved and a new army, organized in accordance with the provisions of the Versailles Treaty, was formed. Despite great difficulties, for the first few years after the 1918 armistice the training of soldiers, small units, and regiments proceeded much as it had during the war.

Under the old Imperial system, training for new conscripts consisted of several weeks of intensive basic training in recruit companies of the regular army regiments. In peacetime, entire companies would often be trained and kept together for the full cycle of their military service. As war broke out, however, the recruit companies became basic training units stationed at the regiment's home depot, with the primary mission of providing trained replacements for the parent regiment. The whole system worked to create considerable unit cohesion. Men who trained together were generally kept together. The regiment was responsible for its own unit and individual training program, and the men were often trained by the very sergeants and officers who would lead them into battle. Therefore, the regimental NCOs and officers had a strong interest in fashioning programs that were tough and comprehensive.

In the postwar Provisional Reichswehr, the primary difficulty was organizing an effective and cohesive force while also carrying out military campaigns against Communist insurgents and protecting the eastern border from the newly formed Polish nation. Carrying out these tasks while creating a new military force in a time of inflation, political confusion, and demobilization of field armies was next to impossible—but somehow accomplished. Holding an effective military force together after the armistice was one of the most impressive testimonies to the efficiency of the old General Staff.

Initially, the Provisional Reichswehr was created from the cadre of remaining Imperial Army units and the Freikorps (which had been formed to combat the Communists and protect the borders). Since the Freikorps soldiers were relatively well paid and there were plenty of unemployed veterans, there was little difficulty recruiting a military force large enough to combat internal rebellion and protect the eastern border. From 1919 to 1923, these would be Germany's predominant strategic problems. The

Provisional Reichswehr and the post-1921 Reichswehr were so busy coping with these tasks that until 1923-24 large unit training or division-sized maneuvers were scarcely possible. It is difficult to come by exact casualty figures, but existing statistics for Reichswehr casualties between 1919 and 1923 testify to the serious fighting that was necessary to suppress Communist uprisings in the industrial parts of Germany. In the campaign to put down the Bavarian Soviet Republic in April-May 1919, the Reichswehr and Freikorps lost thirty-eight soldiers dead and hundreds wounded.[1] In fighting the Communist insurgency in the Ruhr in March 1920, the Freikorps and Reichswehr lost five hundred men killed or wounded.[2] The Provisional Reichswehr was so involved in suppressing internal rebellions that in 1919 and 1920 a manual outlining the tactics for urban warfare was distributed throughout the army.[3]

In such a tumultuous situation, while the Truppenamt worked to create new manuals, tactics, and concepts, the 1918 tactical manuals and regulations remained in effect and soldier and unit training in the Provisional Reichswehr continued to be a modified version of the Imperial Army's until 1921–1924, when the new manuals and regulations were issued. Since the 1918 tactics and training methods were effective, this was no great disadvantage. Even amid internal strife tantamount to civil war, the Provisional Reichswehr maintained the old army's emphasis upon soldier and specialist training. Unit records of the Provisional Reichswehr regiments in Saxony in 1919–1920, largely preserved, show that units set up special machine-gunner, mortar-man, and artilleryman training courses for their soldiers.[4]

General von Seeckt's concept of an elite professional army was largely frustrated by the Versailles Treaty, which saddled Germany with an army much smaller than von Seeckt's ideal of a 200,000-300,000-man force backed by a militia. Throughout 1919 and 1920, the Germans negotiated with the Allies for a relaxation of the treaty requirements. The Germans requested permission to create an army of 200,000 soldiers armed with the full array of modern weaponry. The Allies' denial of such a force pushed von Seeckt to modify his elite army concept in 1921. The new army would henceforth serve two purposes: It would act as Germany's elite military strike force and it would be able to expand quickly to a twenty-one-division high-quality, professional army. This latter force was seen as the minimum force necessary for an adequate national defense. Of necessity, the entire army would become a leaders army, or a Führerheer, in which every officer, NCO, and soldier would immediately be able to function in at least the next higher rank.[5] Privates ought to be able to command fire teams, sergeants platoons, lieutenants companies, and so on. Soldiers and officers not capable of stepping into leadership positions were not to be retained.

A Führerheer would require much higher personnel standards than any force previously fielded by Germany. Therefore, in order to attract high-quality recruits, military life had to be improved. Pay was increased, the rigid discipline of a conscript army was tempered, and the living standards of professional soldiers were dramatically improved. Starting in 1920–1921, the army barracks were remodeled and renovated into more-comfortable troops quarters. Henceforth, each NCO would have his own room, and only four to eight privates would share pleasant, well-furnished rooms resembling college dormitories, a striking change from the bunks in large troop bays common in the Imperial Army.[6] Good food would be emphasized, and units would have a full range of recreation and sports facilities, unit libraries, and soldiers' clubs. A whole system of special trade and high-school courses was instituted within the army to teach each long-term soldier a profession to prepare him to succeed in civilian society upon completion of his twelve-year term of enlistment.[7]

All of this was a significant departure from the Prussian military tradition, which assured a Spartan existence for the conscript soldier. Still, it worked well in attracting the type of soldier that the Führerheer needed. A young German man had to be above average in physical condition and mental ability to join the Reichswehr. In the Ninth Infantry Regiment, a typical unit, 12 percent of the enlisted men had a middle school or high school education, 55 percent had worked for or been trained in a business trade, 18 percent had been educated in a manual trade, and 15 percent came from the farm.[8] Historian Hermann Teske described the enlisted men of the Ninth Regiment as high quality; the large recruiting pool and the small size of the army offered the Reichswehr the chance to select only the best applicants.[9] When the regiment was formed in 1920, the majority of NCOs were veterans of the front, which was typical of other regiments as well.[10] The history of the First Cavalry Regiment remarks that in the postwar period, there were far more volunteers than open positions, so that the new soldiers could be carefully selected.[11] In the Reichswehr as a whole, there were by 1928 fifteen applicants for every enlisted position.[12] The recruiting of privates was normally in the hands of the company and battery commanders. Harold Gordon asserted, "As a result of the decentralized recruiting system, local officers could influence the selection of enlisted men according to their own desires, but there are no complaints of widespread abuse of this privilege. The Reichswehr wanted good soldiers and it got them."[13]

Scholars who study the history of the Reichswehr agree that it was a first-rate force with regard to the quality of its officers and men. Gordon called it "a truly professional army. Not merely the officers, but the enlisted men as well, had entered the army for a significant proportion of their lives and were expected to study their profession as they would if they were doctors, lawyers, or academicians."[14] It is no exaggeration to assess the Reichswehr as, man for man, the best army of its time.[15]

The Reichswehr was distributed throughout the country in small garrisons of battalion or sometimes regimental size.[16] This practice of placing most of the garrisons in small cities and towns was inconvenient, but it helped insulate the soldiers from leftist propaganda and agitation that would have been directed against them in larger cities.[17] In the early 1920s, the Reichswehr soldier received his initial training in this small garrison environment; he would see the whole regiment assembled for training only occasionally. After the political situation stabilized in the mid-1920s, regiments and divisions came together for training more often.

The training of the Reichswehr recruit, a thorough course in basic infantry and soldier skills, normally lasted about six months. Hans Meier-Welcker, who joined the Reichswehr as an officer candidate in 1925 and who underwent the recruit training course, described it as strict and comprehensive. The training battalion of the Fourteenth Infantry Regiment, which Meier-Welcker joined, emphasized athletics as well as traditional drills.[18] Much of the training took the form of numerous night and day tactical exercises. Tactical handbooks were issued to the soldiers, who were expected to study their profession in their spare time.[19]

Soldiers in every branch of the Reichswehr received a basic infantry training in addition to specialized branch training. For example, soldiers assigned to the motor transport troops were given a course of infantry training during their first two years of service as well as the mechanics, technical training, and drivers' courses.[20] The branch of the army that changed its training program the least from the prewar norms was the cavalry. Even though fighting dismounted alongside the infantry had been part of the pre-1914 program, riding remained the core of postwar cavalry training, and the cavalryman was still outfitted with and trained to use the lance and the saber.[21] The essence of all cavalry training was, of course, learning to ride properly individually, and in formation. Formation riding, however—though the postwar cavalry training program still devoted considerable time to it—was of little practical use in warfare by the 1920s. The cavalry was by far the most conservative branch of the army. To describe much of the cavalry's higher officer corps as militarily reactionary would not be an overstatement. The primary manual for the cavalry was Army Regulation 12, originally published in 1912. A new edition with only a few minor changes was published by the Reichswehr in 1926.[22] After World War I, the junior officers of the cavalry were all in favor of eliminating the lance, but all of the Reichswehr's cavalry regiment commanders insisted upon retaining this picturesque but useless weapon. It was not until October 1927 that the army commander, General Wilhelm

*Reichswehr bicycle company on maneuvers, circa 1924–1927.*

Heye, overrode the cavalry colonels' opposition and ordered the lance abolished.[23]

As the army developed, late spring through early autumn became the season for regimental and divisional field maneuvers, culminating in multidivisional maneuvers in September. From November to March the company was the center of soldier training. Small units remained in garrison and used nearby training areas. A 1927 report by the American military attaché to Germany details German unit training during the winter. His report sheds light on Reichswehr training from the early 1920s to rearmament in 1934.[24] The American attaché was impressed by the classroom tactical training given by the company commander for the whole company. A large (2- × -4-meter) sand table was commonly used for war games and instruction—a much larger and more detailed sand table than that used by the U.S. Army. Scale models of buildings and equipment were used in this representation of a company battle zone, as well as a figure representing each soldier in the company. As the company commander talked the men through each stage of the tactical problem, constant questions were posed and answered, "the question being asked first and the class being given the name of the man to answer. The questions and answers are given snappily and there is not a second's pause between ques-

*Crew mans a 77-mm artillery piece during maneuvers of the Fifth and Seventh divisions in Bavaria and Baden-Württemberg, 1926.*

tion and answer or between the answer and the next question; every man must be intensely on the alert."[25]

The attaché considered German military physical training to be far superior to anything in the American military. The Reichswehr imposed more strenuous marches upon its soldiers than the U.S. Army normally did: "As regards agility and suppleness, the German is very much more highly trained physically than our own men";[26] the "impression of extraordinary alertness" was the American observer's comment.[27] In accord with von Seeckt's conception of creating a Führerheer, the platoon leader's position for the various tactical problems in company field exercises was rotated among the NCOs to give them practical experience. Even privates were given the chance to act as squad leaders in rotation for tactical problems. The company problems observed by the American included the company acting as advance guard for the regiment, an attack upon an entrenched position, and an attack upon machine-gun positions. A mock infantry gun as well as machine guns were used to add realism to the exercise. The whole maneuver was conducted "with great enthusiasm"; as for the leadership, "although the orders to the platoon and squads were given by junior noncommissioned officers and privates, they were well given and the leadership was first-class throughout."[28]

Other accounts of the Reichswehr's company-level training also relate how strenuous and serious it was. Reichswehr units normally would spend most of their time outdoors. Franz von Gaertner, a lieutenant in the early 1920s, recalled that his infantry company, commanded by future field marshal Erich von Manstein, regularly spent four days a week in field training. Three days would be spent on marches and tactical exercises and one day at the firing range. Only one day was set aside for barracks duties.[29]

## VON SEECKT'S TRAINING GOALS

General von Seeckt's policy was to organize and train the army by stages. First, the new professional army had to be organized. Second, a modern military doctrine had to be provided. Third, a comprehensive training program for the whole force needed to be established. With a new doctrine in place, the training would begin with platoon and company exercises, progressing to battalion and regimental exercises. When the individual and small-unit training levels were deemed to have attained a high standard, the army would be trained in divisional and multidivisional exercises. Von Seeckt made training the Reichswehr his top priority. He spent about one-third of his time during the year visiting garrisons throughout the country to observe training. Even the smallest detachments were not overlooked by the army chief.[30]

Von Seeckt expected his subordinate generals to do likewise, as indicated by his surviving records.[31] In a letter of instruction entitled "The Foundation of Training the Army," von Seeckt insisted that every officer of every branch of the Reichswehr had to be constantly aware of his role as teacher and exemplar to the troops.[32] A manuscript history of the Sixteenth Infantry Regiment refers to this step-by-step training of the Army. In 1921 the unit was formed. In 1922 the unit training program emphasized retraining the squads, platoons, and companies in accordance with the new infantry regulations.[33] The year 1924 saw a revision of soldier and NCO training in accordance with the experience gained in 1921–1923.[34] Also in 1924 a series of battalion and regimental exercises was conducted.[35] In 1926 divisional maneuvers were done.[36]

Von Seeckt's observations on troop and unit training were the subject of the annual *Observations of the Chief of the Army Command* (Bemerkungen des Chefs der Heeresleitung). In 1920 von Seeckt stipulated that the first three months of each new year were to belong to the company commander for his training program.[37] That same year, von Seeckt stated that "the most difficult mission of the leadership is the use of combined arms."[38] He made a negative example of a garrison he had visited that contained an infantry battalion and an artillery battery that rarely trained together. Another garrison he visited consisted of an infantry battalion without an artillery unit, yet the infantry were constantly trained in the use of mock infantry guns because there were some experienced artillerymen on the garrison staff who had created the program. Von Seeckt

*A motorized 77-mm gun during maneuvers of the Fifth and Seventh divisions, 1926.*

ordered that every infantry officer learn to operate artillery pieces and be able to command a gun section. The same order applied to the cavalry and other branches as well.[39]

Von Seeckt also criticized the tendency toward trench warfare tactics that he observed, insisting that the new tactics emphasizing mobility be employed. In 1922 he urged the infantry to concentrate on mobility and flank attacks.[40] Von Seeckt was especially critical of the artillery's tendency to train for positional warfare: "The artillery operations orders were often written for trench warfare and much too long. Battalion orders of 10-15 sections are impossible in battle."[41] He added, "Only one time in a war of maneuver is the rolling barrage ever used (it takes not less than 12 hours to prepare for a simple one). It is better not to use the rolling barrage in a war of maneuver and give the artillery missions in another form."[42] Von Seeckt continually stressed the innovation and flexibility of mobile warfare over the carefully planned methods of trench warfare. In an advance he recommended an attack from the march, arguing that the "elastic spirit" of the German Army and its quick reactions were some of its strong points.[43]

In 1923 von Seeckt again insisted that the main goal of the army was to train for a war of maneuver. The ability of troops to march for long distances was essential.[44] Von Seeckt emphasized the importance of short, clear orders in a war of maneuver, as opposed to the complex orders of trench warfare. He stated that the army's leaders still needed much more practice in giving orders suitable to a mobile war.[45] Finally, in 1925, von Seeckt expressed real satisfaction with the army's retraining in mobile warfare: "The field maneuvers show that finally the Army is succeeding in loosening the still binding chains of trench warfare. Mobility is a primary necessity of the Army. These principles which have been set out in our regulations must be incorporated into our training goals."[46]

## TRAINING THE NCO CORPS

Creation of an effective NCO corps was a central pillar of von Seeckt's concept of fashioning a Führerheer. "It is of fundamental significance that our junior leaders are taught to be independent-thinking and acting men. This will be achieved when they . . . understand when to act independently and when to wait for orders."[47] Von Seeckt directed that NCOs share in aspects of military leadership that had previously been the responsibility of officers. In addition, he ordered that senior NCOs be included with the officers in conferences summarizing field exercises and training maneuvers.[48] Von Seeckt's emphasis upon NCO training and development was accepted by the officer corps as its own ideal. Officer-NCO relations in the Reichswehr were excellent, not only because both groups respected each other as true professionals but also because the officers realized that when the time for army expansion came, many of the NCOs were likely to become officers.[49] In the 1920s, the First Cavalry Regiment included the regiment's senior NCOs with the officers on staff rides and leaders' terrain exercises.[50] This seems to have been a standard Reichswehr practice. The attitude of these officers was best represented by Walter Model, a junior officer and later field marshal, who saw it as his duty as company commander in the 1920s to turn every sergeant into a first-class platoon leader.[51]

If the German NCO corps was vital to the army's high performance before and during World War I, it was even more important to the Reichswehr after the war. The officer corps of the 100,000-man Reichswehr was restricted to only 4,000 men, but no restrictions were placed by the Allies upon the size of the NCO corps. The Reichswehr took advantage of this treaty loophole by relying as much as possible upon the NCOs to take over many of the leadership positions that in other countries were held by officers. By 1926 the middle and senior NCOs down to the rank of sergeant (unteroffizier) numbered 18,948. The lower leadership ranks of the Reichswehr—corporal (obergefreite) and lance corporal (gefreite)—had risen by 1926 to 19,000 of each rank, for a total of 38,000 junior NCOs or

NCO trainees. In 1926 the German Army contained only 36,500 privates.[52]

In the Reichswehr, NCO promotion was by examination and performance—not solely by seniority, as was the norm in the British and U.S. armies. After three years of service, a Reichswehr private was allowed to take the NCO probationer's examination, a test on general knowledge and military subjects. If he passed this examination, the private was promoted to lance corporal.[53] Henceforth, the soldier would have higher pay, a private or semiprivate room in the barracks, and mess with the NCOs. With the majority of enlisted soldiers serving as NCOs or lance corporals, virtually the whole army was converted to a large NCO academy, stressing constant practice as squad, section, and platoon leaders in tactical exercises. The period as lance corporal was one of intensive training. The soldier who passed the NCO examination could be promoted to sergeant in his fourth year of service. Further promotion from sergeant to staff sergeant (unterfeldwebel) came after two years' service as a sergeant. To become a senior NCO, or master sergeant (feldwebel), another examination was required.[54] The senior NCOs were often expected to serve as platoon leaders.

In the immediate postwar era, the army insisted upon education for the enlisted men and especially the NCO's. As early as June 1919, special high school courses for military personnel were organized and taught largely by the officers. Officers and Reichswehr civilian officials were assigned to education duties by the higher headquarters.[55] As in other armies, special military technical courses, such as on gas warfare, were set up for officers and NCOs.[56] In general, the opportunities for the military education of NCOs of the Reichswehr were about the same as in other modern armies, while the opportunities for obtaining a civilian education were the best of the era.

TRAINING THE OFFICERS

The turbulence and confusion of the immediate postwar era had a pronounced effect upon training within the officer corps. The prewar professional officers had come from the nobility and middle class. A large number had been educated in the strict and traditional cadet schools, which stressed military training and the Prussian virtues of discipline, frugality, and industry. The middle class provided reserve officers as well.[57] World War I changed much of this. Many men who would never have become officers in the old army received wartime reserve commissions. Many NCOs, men without the Abitur or a high school education, including some NCOs of the prewar professional army, received their lieutenancies during the war. The efficiency of these men as company-grade officers was unquestioned, but the prewar regular officers quite reasonably doubted the future performance of officers whose sole higher education consisted of wartime officer courses. The good storm trooper and former NCO platoon leader might not be suitable to serve on the regimental staff or have the sophistication to command effectively in units larger than a company.

Most of the General Staff officers and senior officers of the army would probably have been delighted to return to the prewar officer training and selection system. With a socialist government in power in Germany, and with the abolition of the old cadet schools under the provisions of the Versailles Treaty, such an option was impossible.[58] In any case, the war had broken down too many social barriers. Thus, in the period of the Provisional Reichswehr (1919–1921), hundreds of former NCOs-turned-officers were retained by the army as one means of adjusting to more democratic times. Other NCOs who had been commissioned in the war were taken into the newly-formed paramilitary security police.[59] The question of officer selection became crucial, for the Versailles Treaty allowed the German Army only a limited number of commissioned officers, including officials of officer rank.[60]

The thirty-four-thousand-man officer corps of 1918 had to be reduced to four thousand by January 1921.[61] In order to prevent the Reichswehr from building up a reserve of trained officers, the Allies ordered that German officers were to enlist for twenty-five-years' service. Moreover, only a small percentage of the officer corps would be granted permission each year to resign before their term of service was up. Whereas General Reinhardt favored allowing as many former NCOs as possible to serve as officers, von Seeckt, when he took over as chief of the army command in 1920, initiated policies emphasizing the educational level of the officer aspirant. In effect, he severely limited the intake of officers from the enlisted ranks by raising officer education standards to their highest level ever. An officer candidate now had to have an Abitur, as well as be of good character and in excellent physical condition.[62] Much of this policy can be explained by the social conservatism of von Seeckt and the majority of the General Staff. It was also a reflection of an understanding that war had become more technological: Only a well-educated elite could grasp the intricacies that chemistry, aeronautics, and mechanical engineering had presented to the battlefield.

Provisions were still made for the enlisted man who had joined the service without the Abitur to become an officer. Promising enlisted men who passed through a series of junior leader courses and passed academic examinations similar to the Abitur could become officers. It would take such soldiers six years from the date of enlistment to be commissioned.

For a young man with an Abitur who enlisted specifically as an officer candidate, the process to gain a commission would take about four years. The road to becoming an officer in the Reichswehr was a steep one indeed, and the way was particularly difficult for enlisted men. In 1928, only 117 officers of the Reichswehr were former NCOs. Between 1924 and 1927, only 11 enlisted men who had not completed a secondary education were commissioned.[63]

Since there were plenty of applicants to fill the few vacancies in the officer corps in 1924, von Seeckt directed that the academic standards for the officer candidates be raised, so that those who didn't pass the tests would be young enough to make a career change. No officer candidate was to be "on the borderline."[64] During the early 1920s, the Reichswehr planned on accepting only 250 officer candidates per year.[65] By the end of the Reichswehr era, there were only 120–180 positions per year to be filled by new officer candidates.[66] With numbers like these, the Reichswehr could afford to be selective.

The most important agency for officer training was Inspectorate 1 of the army command, the Inspectorate for Education (the name was changed in 1928 to the Inspectorate of Branch Schools). This inspectorate, commanded by a general, was charged with overseeing officer branch education. The Allies allowed the Reichswehr to have four branch schools for officer training: the Infantry School, first in Munich and later in Dresden; the Cavalry School, in Hannover;[67] the Artillery School, in Jüteborg (established in 1919); and the Pioneer School, in Munich.[68] As it evolved from 1919–1921, the branch-school system provided a sufficient framework for officer instruction. The Infantry School was the most important, because all officer candidates, except for the medical and veterinary candidates, had to spend one year there taking general officer courses. In the second year of academic branch instruction, the officer candidates of the artillery, cavalry, and pioneers went to their corps schools for a more branch-specific instruction.

The combat-support branch officers were trained within special sections of the four branch schools. The motor transport troops would eventually establish their own branch school, but for most of the 1920s, these officer candidates were trained in the Infantry School. The wagon transport officer candidates and the officer candidates for the signal corps were trained at the Artillery School.[69] To ensure that all officers were well trained in the basics of soldiering, even the medical corps officers had to serve for six months as officer candidates in a combat-arms branch of the Reichswehr before being accepted as army doctors. Medical students would enroll in the army, go on leave to do their studies during the school year, and then serve with the army during summer vacation.[70] Similar provisions were made for the veterinary officer trainees.[71] All of the army schools had a quota of qualified General Staff officers present and a selection of the best line officers as instructors. Service as an instructor in a branch school was prestigious duty that did not hurt an officer's career.

While the army was changing from the Provisional Reichswehr to the Reichswehr in 1919–1921, the priority of the officer schools was not to train new officers but rather to establish some kind of homogeneity of training and doctrine for the junior officers selected for retention in the Reichswehr. The officers of this period comprised several diverse groups: prewar regular officers of the General Staff who had undergone the full three-year Kriegsakademie course; prewar regular officers who had entered the General Staff via the abbreviated wartime course; prewar regular officers of the line; and former NCOs and wartime reserve officers with Abiturs whose training consisted of wartime officer courses. To bring some uniformity of outlook and training to the company-grade officers— the majority of the officer corps, 3,080 of 4,000 officers in 1922[72]—the first priority of the branch schools was to institute officer instruction courses of several months for the wartime commissionees.[73] From 1919 to 1922, the wartime commissionees were given a more thorough academic grounding in their profession than the wartime courses had allowed. These courses had turned out good platoon and company commanders, but staff work, battalion and regimental tactics, and army administration had been ignored, as had such basic academic subjects as chemistry and military history. The postwar officer courses were designed to rectify these shortcomings while also providing the General Staff with the opportunity to retrain the junior officers in the new tactical concepts and methods of maneuver warfare.[74]

One of the best descriptions of the Reichswehr's officer training program is provided by Hans Meier-Welcker, who entered the Reichswehr as an officer candidate in 1925, served in the Reichswehr, Wehrmacht, and Bundeswehr, and eventually became chief of the Federal German Military Archives. In a long article written in 1976, Meier-Welcker not only described the officer training system in detail using the official documents, but also augmented this information with his own letters, notes, and experiences of the period.[75] The Reichswehr's basic officer training program was laid out in Army Regulation 29A of November 1920 and would remain in force until 1931.[76] Not until 1921–22 did the officer schools start training non-veteran officer candidates. After an initial review of the system in 1924, von Seeckt issued directives to raise the individual standards for admission as an officer candidate as well as the standards for the academic training program in the branch schools.[77]

Meier-Welcker began his training as an infantry officer in April 1925, only a short time after he had completed his Abitur. Normally, each officer candidate spent six months undergoing the standard regimental recruit

*Reichswehr pioneers on a bridging exercise, mid-1920s.*

training that enlisted men received. At the end of this training, the officer candidate would be posted to a regular line company. In Meier-Welcker's case, every company in the garrison was assigned two officer candidates, who participated in normal company training. In large-scale maneuvers and in the company exercises, they were treated like any enlisted soldier. During fall and winter garrison training, the candidates would perform their company duties and training in the morning. In the afternoon, all officer candidates in the garrison would assemble for classes taught by the regiment's officers. Tactics, weaponry, military administration, a study of the other army branches, and horsemanship were all part of the instruction program in the candidate's first year of training. During this year with the regiment, the candidate would serve as a junior NCO section leader. Special lectures and tactical exercises were also arranged for the officer candidates. Eighteen months after enlisting—six months of recruit training and one year with the regiment—the candidate would be promoted to corporal; he was now called an ensign rather than a candidate.[78]

After three more months with his regiment and participation in the full divisional maneuvers as an NCO, the candidate would be promoted to sergeant and sent to the branch school. In Meier-Welcker's case, it was the Infantry School in Dresden. He described the school as consisting of brand-new or well-renovated buildings with comfortable quarters for the candidates.[79] After the ensign examinations had been taken, the academic year began, in which the officer candidates of all branches had courses in tactics, aerial warfare, signaling, motor technology, mapping, camouflage, riding, civics, and foreign languages—among other subjects.[80] Several hours a week were devoted to athletics. At this point in an officer candidate's education, tactics were taught within the framework of a reinforced battalion. Meier-Welcker found the academic instruction very interesting and found his instructors highly qualified.[81] After about six months, candidates were required to take an intermediate examination of military and civilian subjects. Those who failed were sent back to their regiments and usually discharged from the army. This examination was extremely difficult: In 1927, fifty-eight ensigns failed it.[82]

After the first academic year in the Infantry School, the officer candidates for the cavalry, artillery, signal corps, pioneers, and transport troops were transferred to their own officer schools. The second year at the Infantry School and the other branch schools was similar to the first, except that there were more military courses, with tactics as the main theme. In this year, students were also given driving instruction and received a motorcycle license. After the second year, more examinations were given over a six-week period, including orals. A few more candidates were removed from the officer program as a result of these examinations.[83]

The remaining candidates were called senior ensigns. They were returned to their regiments to undergo the last phase of officer instruction. The candidates served for a few months as troop leaders in the regiment and continued with an instruction course that included lectures, staff rides, and foreign language lessons. At the end of this last phase, the officer candidates were officially approved by the regimental officers and the colonel of the regiment. If the regimental officers expressed doubts about a candidate's suitability for admission to the officer corps, the decision was passed on to the Reichswehr minister. Successful candidates would become officers approximately four years after their enlistment.[84]

The officer instruction program of the Reichswehr was one of the most strenuous officer training systems ever devised. Before World War I, the German Army's officer instruction lasted for one year in the "War School." The postwar officer instruction was another major break with the Prussian Army tradition. The year and a half that the Reichswehr lieutenant spent with the troops as a recruit and junior NCO was a valuable one; he received more troop and leadership experience than lieutenants of other armies. Consequently, the Reichswehr lieutenant had more re-

*Using a light trench mortar in a direct-fire role in Potsdam, 1924.*

spect from, and authority over, soldiers and NCOs than had been the case before the war. The two years in the officer schools were geared toward practical academic instruction rather than toward theoretical instruction. For example, in the first year at Dresden, twenty-four hours a week were devoted to academic classes and thirteen hours to practical training. The academic instruction included six hours of tactics, two hours of geography, two hours of civics, three hours on weaponry, three hours on military engineering, one hour on aerial warfare, and one hour on motor vehicles, among other subjects. The fifteen hours of practical training included infantry and pioneer exercises, mortar and artillery instruction, and machine-gun instruction, as well as four hours of athletics and three hours of riding.[85]

The Reichswehr intended to modernize officer training as much as possible, discussing warfare and tactics in light of the latest technology. In both years of instruction, in all branches, there were classes on motor vehicles, including a study of motorization in the German and other armies, a review of the latest motor vehicle developments, a course on the armored cars and tanks of other armies, and classes in the latest tank tactics.[86] In both academic years at the Infantry School, the officer candidates were given a course on the use of air power in modern warfare, including air squadron organization, air reconnaissance, antiaircraft defense, and air support of ground forces.[87] In the second academic year, about half of the instruction was common to all the officer schools and half was branch-specific. The subjects common to all branches were military history, army administration, aerial warfare, geography, and weaponry. Tactical training and practical exercises were geared to the branch. Part of the academic training was also branch-specific. For example, the curriculum of the Cavalry School included three hours a week on riding theory and two hours of veterinary instruction.[88]

The initial proposals for setting up the officer branch-school curriculum rather idealistically proposed that military history stress the era of Frederick the Great and Napoleon as well as the last war. The history of warfare, it was proposed, would be comprehensively viewed through the works of Clausewitz and the principles of leadership would be studied in light of von Schlieffen's book *Cannae*.[89] By 1926–27, this ambitious program was scaled down. Meier-Welcker recalled that in his time at the officer course in Dresden, there was indeed plenty of military history instruction, but by the mid-1920s, books written about the most recent war were stressed—Clausewitz's works were "virtually unknown" and there was no mention of von Schlieffen.[90] In tactical instruction, the military classics were again ignored; the main texts were the army's new tactical manuals and regulations.[91] Such changes in the officer training curriculum show a considerable degree of common sense among the staff of Inspectorate 1. After all, the goal of the officer schools was to train young men to be effective troop leaders at the platoon, company, and battalion levels. There was no conceivable need for company-grade officers to know Clausewitz or grand strategy. Clausewitz was accordingly cut to make way for company and battalion tactics.

The officer training program of Inspectorate 1 also shows a good understanding of the type of young men who became Reichswehr junior officers. While the officer candidates were highly intelligent, capable young men of twenty to twenty-one, the vast majority were more inclined to the practical than theoretical side of tactics and soldiering. There was neither any need nor any expectation for every officer to be a military intellectual. Most of the young Reichswehr officers would spend their careers on the line, not on the General Staff. The few most intellectually adept would later be accepted for the General Staff, where they would study higher strategy. It is important to remember, however, that many of these Reichswehr junior line officers of the 1920s proved themselves to be superior tacticians and excellent large-unit commanders in World War II without reading Clausewitz or von Schlieffen. If the performance of the Wehrmacht in World War II is taken as a standard of military effectiveness, then Reichswehr officer training must be judged as first-rate.

FURTHER OFFICER EDUCATION

The military education of a Reichswehr officer was by no means completed upon achieving an officer's commission. The regimental commander was responsible for the further education of his officers. Therefore, lectures and evening seminars on political, military, and economic topics would be set up, especially during winters in garrison. The regimental commanders were also responsible for leading their officers on staff rides—that is, visits to nearby regions with discussions of how a location could be attacked or defended in a tactical situation. Staff exercises in garrison, in which the officers were presented with tactical problems and expected to come up with the necessary plans and orders, were also led by the regimental commander and were a normal part of officer training.[92]

The most important feature of junior officer training in the Reichswehr was the preparation for the Military District Examinations. These were essentially the old General Staff corps entrance examinations, but von Seeckt had added a new feature to the system. In the old army, once an officer was commissioned he was no longer required to take any tests. If he desired to remain in regimental duty, it was his choice. The General Staff entrance examination, which a candidate had to pass before entering the Kriegsakademie of the Imperial Army, was voluntary. In 1919 von Seeckt decided to introduce the Military District Examinations the next year, making them mandatory for army officers.[93] According to von Seeckt, the examinations would provide "a useful overview of the level of military knowledge and general education in the officer corps."[94]

The test was normally administered to senior first lieutenants. All officers were expected to achieve at least satisfactory marks. In case of failure, the test could be repeated the next year,[95] but more than one examination failure could result in the loss of one's commission. The top-scoring officers, 10 percent–15 percent of the total taking the examinations, would enter the General Staff training program. Von Seeckt's policy had three major results: (1) An additional hurdle was placed before the less-educated officers. This made the Reichswehr officer corps an even more elite organization. (2) All Reichswehr junior officers were forced into an intensive study program. (3) Whereas there had been an element of self-selection into the General Staff before World War I, in the postwar army the entire officer corps would become a recruitment pool for the General Staff corps.

The Military District Examinations, so called because they were administered annually in the headquarters of the seven military districts, were written every year by the T-4 Section of the Truppenamt. The examinations lasted several days and consisted of the following: three papers on applied tactics, one paper on theoretical tactics, one paper on military engineering, one paper on map reading and sketching, and one paper on weaponry and equipment. Different questions were posed, depending on the officer's branch. The general-knowledge examinations covered the following subjects, with one paper on each subject: history, civics, economic geography, mathematics, physics, chemistry, and athletics.[96]

These tests were strictly timed in order to put the officer under psychological stress. The general-knowledge questions were at the Abitur level, and a well-educated officer with a Gymnasium education probably only needed to review his old school texts in order to achieve a passing mark. The foreign language examination, for example, consisted of a couple of fairly simple pages from a foreign military journal, which the examinee had to translate into German. A choice of languages was offered. This part of the examination would not have been difficult for an officer with an Abitur. In the early 1920s, however, it would have presented a real barrier to former NCO officers and less-educated wartime commissionees.[97]

The military part of the examination was the most difficult. The only relatively easy sections of the test were the questions on map reading and military engineering, subjects that were thoroughly covered in officer branch-school instruction. The tactical problems, on the other hand, were designed to test the officer well past the limits of tactical instruction at officer schools. The problems were based on using the reinforced rifle regiment, whereas the lessons of the officer schools dealt with companies and battalions. Complicated problems were given, complete with maps, and officers were permitted a limited period to write a set of plans and orders. The tactical problems were contemporary and covered all modern weapons: Armored cars, tanks, aircraft, and gas were supposed to be taken into consideration. In order to ensure that no favoritism tarnished the system, the examination results were graded centrally by the T-4 Section in Berlin, and the test-taking officers remained anonymous. Each examination was corrected by three different officers to ensure objectivity.[98]

Preparation for the Military District Examinations was a major event in an officer's career. Junior officers would form study groups within the garrison, and a six-month correspondence course was available to assist in preparation.[99] Since the chiefs of staff of the seven military districts had the responsibility to ensure officers were ready for the examinations, the districts reviewed the correspondence course program and also organized winter conferences to prepare the officers.[100] In addition, numerous study guides and tactical textbooks were written by General Staff officers. For example, Captain Ludwig von der Leyen, an officer assigned to the T-4 Section of the Truppenamt in the early 1920s, was a prolific writer on tactics.[101] One of his books, *Tactical Problems and Solutions* (Taktische Aufgaben und Lösungen; 1923), presented ten tactical situations that concencentrated on the supply problems of large units in battle.[102] Another book by von der Leyen, *On Combined Arms* (An verbundenen Waffen; 1925), outlined the tactical methods of the Reichswehr's new manuals.[103] *Tactical Lessons in the Framework of the Reinforced Infantry Regiment* was edited by several officers and appeared in several editions in the 1920s.[104] The editors wrote that the book was "offered as a worthwhile aid to the junior officer preparing for the Military District Examinations."[105] It was also recommended to more senior officers for setting up war games and exercises.[106]

Tactical textbooks such as these were the primary literary expression of the 1920's Reichswehr officer. The tactical textbooks were usually based on the new tactics of Army Regulation 487 (*Leadership and Battle*). They served to flesh out and reinforce the tactical instruction of the officer schools. While von Seeckt and the Truppenamt officially proclaimed that only the offense wins the decisive victory, the tactical textbooks emphasized the full range of tactical situations common to modern warfare, including attack, defense, movement to contact, reconnaissance, and withdrawal. The Military District Examinations' tactical problems typically covered most of these situations.[107] Even though the offense was preferred, the Reichswehr's tactical education seems to have been well balanced. In practice, an officer was expected to be capable of reacting to all conceivable tactical demands.

Since Reichswehr officers were forbidden to participate in political activity of any sort, few wrote articles or books on grand strategy or on the politics and economics of warfare. The intellectual energies of these officers were turned away from the grander aspects of strategy and pushed toward the operational side of warfare. Serving officers rarely mentioned politics or economics in the *Militär Wochenblatt*, but virtually every issue of the 1920s includes their articles on tactics and weaponry; any articles on politics and grand strategy tended to be written by retired officers. The image of the Reichswehr officer corps is one of officers at all levels carefully studying the military tactics and operations in isolation from the politics and economics.

An example of the high quality of thought produced by this intensive study of tactics in the Reichswehr is the writing of Erwin Rommel. Rommel was an infantry line officer who won the pour le mérite in World War I but never served on the General Staff. As a captain stationed as an instructor at the Infantry School in Dresden from 1929 to 1932, he wrote several tactical pamphlets based on his extensive wartime experience. In 1936 these pamphlets were put together and edited as a book, *Infantry Attacks* [Infanterie Greift An!], a best-seller that went through eighteen printings and over 400,000 copies sold.[108] Rommel's style is clear, vivid, and straightforward. He discussed infantry tactics from the platoon to the

*Motorized infantry of the Fourth Division on maneuvers near Naumberg,
1927.*

regimental level in analyzing his wartime experience for practical lessons.
Rommel, though a brilliant practitioner of warfare, had no time for theories. He examined the tactical situations that he faced, including attacks,
raids, and defense, carefully detailing how each situation was handled. In
this respect, Rommel's book is very much like the standard Reichswehr
tactical textbook of the 1920s—only better written. Yet Rommel, like
most Reichswehr officers, cannot be proclaimed a military intellectual or
theorist. Although he obviously studied his profession closely, his diaries,
letters, and published writings give no evidence that he ever seriously
read Clausewitz or von Schlieffen. In any case, this deficiency seems not
to have impaired his generalship in the least.

A further opportunity for military education was granted to line and
General Staff officers in the form of foreign travel. Reichswehr officers
were encouraged to travel abroad for one to three months—ostensibly to
improve their language skills, but also to observe foreign military developments. A special allowance was provided to officers for overseas travel.
No exact figures exist on how many Reichswehr officers took this opportunity to go to France, Italy, Spain, Great Britain, and the United States,
but surviving records and accounts indicate that it was a common prac-

tice. The surviving Reichswehr documents of the 1920s contain dozens
of reports filed by Reichswehr officers upon their return from foreign
countries.[109] Memoirs by former Reichswehr officers also commonly refer
to their overseas travels in the 1920s.[110]

Another von Seeckt innovation in officer training, one that shows his
involvement in the continuing education of officers, was the training of
generals and senior officers. Since one of the problems in 1914 had been
the lack of coordination among senior German officers, von Seeckt conducted a series of staff rides for generals every year in which problems
such as defense against the French and Czechs were studied. The Truppenamt also conducted such exercises for the divisional staffs.[111] Von
Seeckt began his program of generals' training in 1921, and the annual
generals' staff ride became a tradition, continued by successive commanders of the Reichswehr. Von Seeckt would personally set the problems for his senior commanders and conduct the critique. He explained
his innovative methods in the following words: "Few commanding generals had the desire to become active in the training of their subordinate
generals and critique their tactical problems. The idea that a commanding
general still needed to learn was unusual. However, the result was that the
General Staff was trained in a set of common principles."[112]

TRAINING THE GENERAL STAFF

When the Versailles Treaty officially abolished the German General Staff
corps and closed the Kriegsakademie down, the Reichswehr simply re-
named the General Staff officers "leader's assistants" and created a comprehensive program of General Staff instruction that was conducted
through the Military Districts and in the Reichswehr Ministry. A new
three-year General Staff course was instituted that was just as thorough
and even more selective in its intake than the old Kriegsakademie program. Aside from the euphemisms used to disguise the program, the old
General Staff system carried on much as before. Even in official correspondence in the 1920s, the euphemism "leader's assistants" was often
forgotten, and Reichswehr officers would refer to "General Staff officers."

The training of General Staff officers was completely in the hands of T-
4, the Training Section of the Truppenamt, and was thus one of the chief
responsibilities of that department.[113] T-4 set up a comprehensive General
Staff course for the Reichswehr in 1922. Entry into this course via the Military District Examinations was extremely strict. In Military District 6 in
1922, out of 162 officers examined only 20 were selected for the General
Staff course.[114] Siegfried Westphal estimated that out of over 300 first lieu-

*Field radio station of the Fourth Division during the 1927 maneuvers.*

tenants examined every year in the 1920s, an average of only 32 to 36 officers were selected.[115]

Officers selected for General Staff training would enter into a four-year
program—three years devoted to academic course work and one year of
practical experience in troop duty.[116] In the first two years of the course,
academic instruction was carried out in the headquarters of the military
districts. From October to April, the General Staff candidate—normally a
junior captain—would attend fifty-three days of instruction at the military
district. In May there would be a staff ride of sixteen days, held in one of
the maneuver areas. From May to September, the student would serve
with a branch of the service other than his own.[117] General Staff students
were also required to pursue a program of study and reading when in
home garrison during October to April.[118] In the third year, as the student
was posted to troop duty, he would be assigned to serve as a trainee on
one of the higher staffs, such as infantry or cavalry divisional staffs. During the last year of the program, the candidate was posted to the Reichswehr Ministry in Berlin for a year of intensive academic instruction by
selected officers of T-4 and the army high command.[119] Only a fraction of
the small group of officers selected for the General Staff course would
complete the full four-year program and be admitted as full members of
the General Staff. Of the thirty or so officers who began the program,

about twenty would complete the first two or three years and then be weeded out with the classification "acceptable if needed." As few as ten officers a year were accepted for the final academic year in Berlin.[120]

The army was instructed to assign its best officers as instructors for the General Staff course in the military districts and in Berlin. Three experienced General Staff officers in each military district headquarters were to be assigned as instructors, freed of all duties in the summer so they could prepare for the fall and winter lecture program.[121] Two officers in the T-4 Section were assigned to full-time duty as Berlin instructors.[122] With twenty-one instructors in the military districts and two more in Berlin for an annual course enrollment of about three dozen students, the Reichswehr maintained an extremely favorable teacher-student ratio. The General Staff candidates were also carefully observed for character traits; the whole personality of each candidate was taken into account.[123] Thus the instructors were to become well acquainted with their students and to remember the impact their influence and example had upon them.[124] General Staff training was intended not only to create master tacticians but also to mold the character of the students. The officer accepted into the General Staff was to be "strong-willed, eager to take responsibility, calm under pressure and a troop leader."[125] As in von Moltke's day, the Reichswehr regarded the leading of troops, like the waging of war itself, to be an art—albeit a highly rational one—and certainly not a science.

The General Staff training of the Reichswehr emphasized higher level tactics and operations. The first academic year emphasized the reinforced rifle regiment, with its combined-arms tactics. The second academic year emphasized the division, and the third year in Berlin emphasized corps- and army-level tactics, including instruction on foreign armies and modern army-navy cooperation.[126] Like the Imperial General Staff course, the Reichswehr General Staff course included military history as a major subject. In the first academic year, there would be six hours of tactics per week followed by four classroom hours of military history. In the second year, military history and tactics would both be taught four hours per week.[127] In contrast to the old General Staff course, however, the importance of technology was to be emphasized in all Reichswehr General Staff studies. Course instructors were directed to emphasize technological developments in the German and foreign armies and encouraged to visit technical institutes with their students.[128] The new General Staff course contained no formal examinations. Students were regularly required to write military history papers and given tactical problems to solve. Grading was subjective. In dealing with tactical problems, instructors would review and discuss the student tactical solutions in seminars. Since the Germans treated each military problem as a unique situation, no "school solution" presenting the "correct answer" was imposed; rather, each student solution was examined and discussed on its own merits.[129]

The contrast between the German General Staff training of the 1920s and that of other countries is enormous. The British Army Staff College at Camberly provided a one-year course in the 1920s. During Bernard Montgomery's time as a student in 1920-21, it had returned to its "pre-war preoccupation with hunting and socializing." It provided "a gentlemanly introduction to staff duties," according to Montgomery's biographer, Nigel Hamilton.[130] The U.S. Army Command and General Staff School's course for most of the interwar period was also only one year's duration. Though the atmosphere was less social and more professional, General Omar Bradley, who attended the course in 1928-29, was highly critical of the whole instruction system: "The problems—and solutions—presented to us in the lectures were trite, predictable and often unrealistic. If you closely followed the undertones of the lectures, you could fairly easily predict what lay ahead and what to do."[131] In the Fort Leavenworth Staff School, then as now, tactical solutions were graded strictly according to their conformity with the official school solution, which was the "right" answer. Original, unconventional tactics were not encouraged in American General Staff training.[132]

In the Berlin year of the Reichswehr General Staff course, some lectures dealing with politics, economics, and international affairs were included in the curriculum. Late in the 1920s, a special program was set up called the Reinhardt courses, after their initiator, General Reinhardt. Some of the officers who had completed the full General Staff course were retained in Berlin and sent to take courses in history, politics, and economics at the University of Berlin.[133] Despite the Reinhardt courses and the lectures on politics and economics, the Reichswehr's General Staff course remained overwhelmingly military and practical in scope. A student's performance on divisional maneuvers was far more important than his performance in essentially civilian courses. The only nonmilitary subjects stressed in the course were foreign languages—and foreign language study took up more instruction time than all the civilian subjects put together.[134]

The emphasis on the practical military training of the General Staff, which concentrated on maneuvers and troop experience rather than theory, was in accord with the concepts of General von Seeckt: "I have nothing to say against theoretical training, and certainly nothing against practical training. Whoever would become master of his craft must have served as apprentice and journeyman; only a genius can bridge gaps in this sequence of instruction. Every man of action is an artist, and he must know the material with which, in which, and against which he works before he begins his task."[135] Von Seeckt's deemphasis of academic subjects in General Staff training, such as the politico-economic side of grand strategy,

*The Reichswehr stressed camouflage techniques. A motorized 77-mm gun during maneuvers of the Fourth Division, 1927.*

was explained by him in an incident he recounted from the 1914 campaign. In August 1914, when the German Army was approaching the Belgian frontier, the senior officers of the armies of the right flank were ordered to report to general headquarters for lectures on the "military-geographical description of Belgium." Von Seeckt and his senior assistant, Major Wetzell, were both exhausted from days of mobilization preparation and promptly fell asleep, missing the lectures. Von Seeckt recounted, "Well, we found our way to the very gates of Paris in spite of our ignorance of military geography, nor had I any special preparation for Serbia and Palestine afterwards."[136] Under von Seeckt, officer training would stick to military basics. The only exception was the advanced engineering-technical education program of the Reichswehr.

There was a second way an officer could enter the General Staff Corps. An officer who scored high in the Military District Examinations could be sent to a university for three or four years to earn a technical degree—usually in engineering. Upon obtaining his degree, the officer would usually be brought back to Berlin to serve in the Weapons Office. This was part of von Seeckt's program to emphasize the technological aspect of war in General Staff planning and training.[137] Although the officers who took this route were usually employed as the Reichswehr's technical experts, some of them also served successfully with troops. Lieutenant General Erich

Schneider, who received his engineering degree as a Reichswehr officer, served as an armored division commander in World War II.[138] Major General Dornberger was another famous officer who earned an engineering degree in the Reichswehr's General Staff program. He became a top rocket expert, first for Germany in World War II and then for the United States.[139]

CONCLUSION

The Reichswehr, building upon the Imperial Army's effectiveness as a training organization, created the best soldier, NCO, and officer training systems of its time. The Allied military leadership expressed admiration for the Reichswehr's programs. A study of the Reichswehr by the British General Staff said of the German NCO corps, "The army [is] assuming to an increasing extent the character of a body of potential military instructors ready for military expansion in time of war."[140] The Allies were so alarmed by the size and efficiency of the German NCO corps that the Council of Ambassadors actually protested to the German government, requesting that the Germans further limit the number of NCOs in the Reichswehr.[141] American observers of the Reichswehr consistently expressed admiration for the German military, especially the quality of the officer corps: "The German officer is distinctly a professional soldier. . . . All the officers from the highest grade to the lowest appeared to be very alert and efficient. . . . The reason for the high quality of the commissioned personnel of the German Army is very apparent when we consider that before the war the German regular commissioned personnel consisted of 60,000 and is now reduced to 4,000."[142]

Turning the Reichswehr's enlisted men into a large NCO corps offset the shortage of officers when the time came to rearm. The well-trained and carefully selected NCO corps played a greater role in the troop leadership of the German Army of the 1930s and 1940s than in other armies. In World War II, for example, the German corps and divisional headquarters contained far fewer officers but more NCOs than an American divisional or corps headquarters. Martin van Creveld pointed out, "Clearly American officers were employed on numerous tasks which, in the German Army, were carried out by officials, NCO's and enlisted men."[143] There is no indication that German headquarters were less efficient than American ones by their substitution of NCOs for officers. The Reichswehr's high standards for NCOs, including the senior NCOs in what was normally officers' training, appears to have been an effective policy.

Two major shortcomings affected the quality of the Reichswehr's officer corps and its training. The greater problem with Reichswehr officer training concerned the General Staff training program. Though effective, it was overly selective. When rearmament came in the 1930s, junior officer shortages could be eased by promoting NCOs, recalling reserve officers, and increasing the size of officer schools, but a shortage of trained General Staff officers was harder to remedy. In the 1930s, the small size of the General Staff corps was one of the most serious problems confronting the rapidly expanding German Army.[144]

The second major flaw was the Reichswehr's neglect of the economic-industrial aspects of modern war. World War I's vast expenditure of matériel clearly demonstrated the need for a group of officers who could carry out long-term industrial and procurement planning. The German Army even had an obvious model in the U.S. Army's Industrial College, founded in 1924. This school's one-year program, rated by van Creveld as "a smashing success," was centered on the study of procurement and national industrial mobilization.[145] German officers touring the United States visited the Army Industrial College, expressing admiration for the school and the quality of its education in their reports to the Truppenamt.[146] The Reichswehr took a step in this direction, creating a special staff under the army commander and appointing economic mobilization officers to every military district in 1925.[147] Like the General Staff program, however, this effort was much too small, and the Reichswehr never achieved a program like the American one. From the 1920s to the end of the Third Reich, military-industrial planning would remain one of the weakest links in German Army strategy.

The interwar German officer training system has been criticized for being too exclusively operational and tactical and engendering an officer corps of technocrats. As David Spires put it, "Officers whose efforts are limited to the small world of tactics and technology are in danger of isolating themselves and failing to appreciate the larger issues affecting their society."[148] Michael Geyer argued that the technically oriented interwar generation of German officers "never learned to evaluate operations within the context of a coherent strategy."[149] These criticisms beg the question of whether any special military training or course can produce skilled strategists. Although von Seeckt did insist that officers receive a firm grounding in the tactics and operations, to imply that the Reichswehr ignored strategy is inaccurate. Reichswehr General Staff training included lectures by civilian experts on political, international, and economic affairs,[150] and the Reinhardt courses allowed some officers to study politics and economics at the University of Berlin.[151]

It is difficult to reconstruct the strategic education of Reichswehr officers because much of it was carried out informally and not in any special "strategists' course." Von Seeckt's program of annual generals' staff rides was created as an educational tool and incorporated discussions of grand strategy. The annual General Staff winter war games, which lasted two months, included a great deal of political-international strategy.[152] Von Seeckt's insistence upon foreign language education for all officers and the official encouragement and funding of officers' travels to other nations demonstrates an awareness on von Seeckt's part that officers needed to possess a general education in international affairs.

The criticism that Reichswehr officers lacked education in strategy would be an attempt to explain, in hindsight, the poor strategic understanding of the Wehrmacht General Staff. The Reichswehr produced some highly competent strategists, men such as Ludwig Beck and Kurt von Hammerstein-Equord, but Hitler removed them. Perhaps a better explanation for the Army's strategic incompetence in World War II lies in Hitler's elimination of his military leaders from the realm of strategic decision making, not in any failure of Reichswehr officer training.

Hans von Seeckt set out to create an elite officer corps, capable of using the most up-to-date combined-arms tactics and of commanding troops using the most modern weaponry—even though Germany lacked both troops and weapons. Reichswehr training and officer selection met this goal, producing an officer corps comparable—even superior—to other officer corps. Despite its shortcomings—the small scale of the General Staff program and the lack of training in economic mobilization—the Reichswehr's officer training system built an effective foundation for an expandable force, creating a corps of leaders who could succeed on the modern battlefield under the most trying conditions.

# CHAPTER FIVE

# Developing Modern Weaponry

The Versailles Treaty forbade "the manufacture and importation into Germany of armored cars, tanks and all other similar constructions of war" (Article 169). "Importation into Germany of arms, munitions and war materiel of every kind shall be strictly prohibited"(Article 170). Poison gas manufacture was prohibited (Article 172), as was the possession of antiaircraft guns (Article 169). No military aircraft were allowed (Article 198), and aside from some heavy guns mounted in fortresses, the army was to possess no more than 204 77-mm guns and 84 105-mm guns. The army was also limited to only 792 heavy machine guns, 1,134 light machine guns, and 252 mortars.[1] The Interallied Military Control Commission, which came to consist of 337 officers and 654 soldiers, would be stationed in Germany to enforce the disarmament clauses of the Versailles Treaty. The commission would remain in Germany until 1927.[2]

The German government's policy from 1919 on was to revise and renegotiate the disarmament provisions of the Versailles Treaty; in this endeavor, it met some success. In the Boulogne Note of July 1920, the security police were allowed to acquire 150 armored cars and the Reichswehr 105 "armored personnel carriers," which were essentially armored cars.[3] The Paris Air Accords of 1926 lifted the Allies' strict limitations upon the German aircraft industry. But the process of revising the Versailles Treaty was a slow one. Aside from the antimilitary left wing of the Social Democratic party and the Communists, German politicians had no desire to see Germany disarmed and the nation left with nothing but an army that could serve as a border guard and internal security force. Thus from the day that the Versailles Treaty went into effect, it was the Reichswehr's policy to evade and violate the Treaty's disarmament provisions and to continue to develop and produce the whole range of modern weapons. The civilian political leaders knew of the Reichswehr's secret rearmament program and consistently supported it by assuring that camouflaged appropriations from the Reichstag were available for Reichswehr projects. Such moderate and democratic politicians as President Friedrich Ebert and Chancellor and Foreign Minister Gustav Stresemann were firm supporters of the secret rearmament program.[4]

German armaments manufacturers evaded the Versailles Treaty in several ways. One of the most effective means was to set up a foreign subsidiary and move armaments manufacture out of the country. This was done very effectively by Krupp. In 1921 Krupp acquired control of the Swedish Bofors Corporation and sent German arms design and production experts to Sweden to develop a variety of arms for the Reichswehr. Krupp also established a successful Dutch subsidiary, Siderius A.G., which stockpiled artillery and carried on Krupp's shipbuilding tradition.[5] The Rheinmetall Corporation bought control of Solothurn A.G. in Switzerland, a former watch manufacturer, and in the 1920s turned it into a production facility for machine guns.[6] The grandest scheme to move armaments development and manufacture out of Germany was the Reichswehr's program in Russia, which lasted from 1921 to 1933. Von Seeckt was the program's founder. As early as 1919 he put out feelers to a then-hostile Soviet Union through his Turkish friend Enver Pasha. In 1920-21 a special staff was formed by von Seeckt within the Intelligence Section of the Truppenamt, which was known as Special Group R (Sondergruppe R) and assigned the mission of negotiating joint arms production and establishing air and tank training centers in Russia. Von Seeckt appointed Colonel von der Lieth-Thomsen, the former Air Service chief of staff, as the General Staff's representative to the Soviet government in Moscow. The Russian connection established by von Seeckt would play a major role in the development of German aircraft, armored vehicles, and poison gas in the interwar period.[7]

In terms of weaponry, the disarmament provisions of the Versailles Treaty were both advantageous and disadvantageous for the Reichswehr's weapons development. The disadvantages were many. All new weapons had to be developed at home or overseas in great secrecy, and budget funds for rearmament had to be hidden. The tank prototype program of the 1920s progressed slowly because tank components had to be built by small groups of workers and designers, sworn to secrecy, building their weapons in clandestine workshops, so that neither the Interallied Military Control Commission nor its informants would find out. Since tanks could not be openly tested in Germany, they had to be shipped to Russia at great cost. When the weapons were tested at the Russian/German tank center at Kazan, the designers and builders could not be on the spot to observe deficiencies and rush the tanks back to the factory for immediate modifications.[8] There were nevertheless some genuine advantages for Germany from the Versailles Treaty's forced disarmament of the nation and the strict limitations upon the army's weaponry. Germany was not saddled with an enormous stockpile of obsolete weaponry, as were the Allies. A large proportion of the Allies' planes, tanks, guns, machine guns, and so forth, on inventory at the war's end were already outdated by 1918 standards, but with so much matériel on hand there was little possibility for the victorious powers to acquire new weaponry for a long time. Therefore, for years after the war, the Allies had to make their tactics fit the existing,

*The 105-mm LH/18 howitzer (10,600-meter range) was developed by the Reichs-wehr in the 1920s and used through 1945. (Author's collection)*

obsolete weaponry, whereas the German Army was free to develop its tactical ideas first and then create the weapons to fit the tactics.

The French Army had so many Renault light tanks left over at the end of the war that for more than a decade after, French tank tactics would be geared to this 1917 weapon. In the postwar U.S. Army, it was already recognized in 1920 that the 75-mm wartime fieldpiece was an unsuitable weapon, with its short-range flat trajectory and relatively small projectile. The U.S. Army's Artillery Board deemed that a 105-mm howitzer was necessary, but no satisfactory prototypes were produced until 1927. Even then, the army's stockpiles of 75-mm guns and ammunition were so large that it decided to make do with that weapon indefinitely. Not until 1940 did the U.S. Army adopt a modern 105-mm howitzer. Even then, there was resistance from the chief of ordnance, General C. M. Wesson, who wanted to retain the 75-mm gun because the United States had so many of them. He testified to Congress in 1940 that the 75-mm gun was "a splendid weapon" and argued that "France has not abandoned it."[9] The same thing happened to the U.S. Army with regard to tanks. Some excellent medium tank prototypes were developed in the early 1920s, notably by designer J. Walter Christie, but the army had enough tanks left over from the war and new tanks were not deemed urgently necessary. Consequently, the army did not acquire new tank models until the mid-1930s.[10]

In contrast, the German Army developed a whole range of modern guns in the 1920s, ready for mass production as soon as approval for full rearmament was given. For over two decades, the French and Americans trained with obsolete guns and tactics while Versailles forced the Germans to prepare for the next war. The French Army of 1940 contained a considerable amount of 1918 weaponry, while the German Army's weapons and tactics would be new.

General von Seeckt argued against maintaining large stockpiles of weapons. A small army with first-class weapons was superior to the French mass army: "The equipment of a large army with a new type of weapon is so enormously costly that no state undertakes the task unless compelled. The smaller the army, the easier it will be to equip with modern weapons, whereas the provision of a constant supply for armies of millions is an impossibility. . . . The accumulation of great reserve stocks is the most uneconomical process imaginable. It is also of doubtful military value, owing to the natural obsolescence of materiel."[11] Von Seeckt believed that "there is only one way to equip masses with weapons, and that is by fixing the type and at the same time arranging for mass production in case of need. The army is able, in cooperation with technical science, to establish the best type of weapon for the time being by constant study in the testing shops and on practice grounds."[12] This was the armaments philosophy fostered by von Seeckt and his successors in the high command. The Versailles Treaty was an inconvenience—but only that. It did not prevent the Reichswehr from developing any of the weapons it deemed tactically necessary. The German weapons developed in the 1920s were roughly equal to the best weaponry developed in the United States, Britain, and France. The German Army did not take any clear lead in overall weapons development, but neither did it fall behind in any major areas of technology.

The primary agencies for weapons development in the Reichswehr were the Truppenamt, particularly sections T-1 and T-2; the branch inspectorates; the Weapons Office; and the industrial concerns. The Truppenamt Operations and Organization sections were responsible for determining the overall needs of the army for weaponry with regard to military doctrine, strategic needs, and war plans. Each branch inspectorate was responsible for studying the tactical problems of its own arm and for developing concepts and requirements for weapons to fit the tactics. Each branch inspectorate had a corresponding specialist section within the Weapons Office that advised it on technical matters. For example, the Inspectorate of Motor Troops was called IN-6, and its corresponding section in the Weapons Office was WA-6. The branch inspectorate would set the general requirements for new weapons while the Weapons Office section, which contained the engineers and technical experts, would translate the requirements into exact technical specifications that included the weight, size, and range of the weapon. In some cases, as with the tank program, the Weapons Office would specify the exact model of gun to be mounted.[13]

The Weapons Office was responsible for drawing up development contracts and would normally go to two or three manufacturers with an order to develop prototypes. Weapons Office engineers would maintain constant contact with the contracting firm and with the branch inspectorates and Truppenamt during all stages of development. The Weapons Office would also offer technical suggestions for design modifications as the project progressed. When the prototype weapons were developed, the Weapons Office and branch inspectorate officers would conduct field tests. Tanks, poison gas, and aircraft were tested in Russia. Other vehicles, artillery, small arms, ammunition, engineer equipment and radios were all tested at army training areas and ranges within Germany. After trials between competing systems, the branch inspectorates and Weapons Office would decide upon the best weapon; the Truppenamt had the final word on adopting a weapon and on approving a production contract. During the 1920s, the army developed mostly prototype weapons that could hopefully, at a future date, be mass produced.[14]

The German system differed greatly from that of the British and Americans, who preferred to maintain their own ordnance design bureaus and weapons plants and build many of their own arms without outside civilian contractors. This system often worked well. In the interwar period, the U.S. army Ordnance Corps developed the excellent 105-mm howitzer and the M-1 Garand rifle. However, the Reichswehr's system guaranteed extensive design competition for every class of gun, plane, and vehicle. During the 1920s, Krupp and Rheinmetall, for example, competed intensively for every gun and heavy vehicle contract, thus maintaining first-rate armaments design teams. This system for assuring competition for weapons systems is one of the primary reasons German weapons designs were of such high quality in the interwar period.

General von Seeckt took a direct interest in seeing that the Weapons Office and Truppenamt worked together to produce improved weaponry. In January 1924 von Seeckt sent a reproving memo to all the branch inspectors and section chiefs in the Weapons Office: "Recent discussions have not had the desired success. . . . The High Command holds it as necessary that the chiefs of the departments and sections are continually educated in the continuing and newly-developed technologies and important technical-tactical questions."[15] Von Seeckt ordered that bimonthly seminars on weapons technology be conducted and that the department and section chiefs attend those seminars. Further memos from the same file refer to some of the seminar subjects that followed von Seeckt's order. In 1924, discussions were held on armored cars, tank technology, motorization, transport vehicles, gas warfare, mortars, new foreign rifle models, and American artillery development.[16] Reports on Weapons Office projects in progress were circulated to the T-1 and T-2 sections in the Truppenamt for comment.[17]

In the mid-1920s, the Weapons Office staff in Berlin consisted of sixty-four officers including two major generals, two colonels, and twelve lieutenant colonels. An additional twenty-one officers stationed at test ranges and arsenals were directly subordinated to the Weapons Office. Add the forty-eight officers normally stationed on the inspectorate staffs (excluding medical and veterinary officers), the twenty-three officers of T-1 and T-2 (some of whom spent considerable time reviewing armaments projects), and the officers stationed at inspectorate schools who carried out additional tests and equipment modifications and one has a significant percentage of a four-thousand-man officer corps engaged directly in weapons research and development.[18] In addition to these officers and institutions, the army used the Charlottenburg Polytechnic Institute, (Technische Hochschule) in Berlin as a cover organization for Reichswehr technical research, especially in ballistics and explosives.[19]

The German Army's doctrine of the war of maneuver became the chief design principle for Reichswehr weapons and equipment development in the 1920s. Weapons were to be more mobile than before and to possess high firepower. By the middle of the decade, the priorities would shift to emphasize development of vehicles for the Reichswehr's first comprehensive motorization program. At all times, the maintenance of German fortifications allowed by the Versailles Treaty and the development of equipment for trench warfare received the lowest priority for the development plan of the Weapons Office.[20]

The branch inspectorates and the Weapons Office felt no inhibitions about borrowing and adapting foreign design ideas for German weapons systems. Collecting information on foreign technology became a top priority for T-3, the Truppenamt's Intelligence Section. Most of the surviving intelligence files of the 1920s consist of information on and analyses of foreign weapons and vehicles. The United States, Britain, and France, as the most technologically advanced nations, received most of the attention. Information on foreign vehicles and weapons was collected from foreign publications and published as a series of booklets entitled *Technische Mitteilungen* (Technical Bulletins). German officers who visited the United States in the 1920s collected and brought back a considerable amount of technical data on American ordnance research with particular emphasis on new developments in explosives and ammunition, artillery development, and advances in vehicle technology.[21]

The Germans paid particular attention to the efficiency of the new French and British equipment in the French maneuvers of 1922 and 1923 and the British maneuvers of 1924 in reports that were circulated widely throughout the Reichswehr by T-3.[22] The *Militär Wochenblatt* reflected the technical emphasis of the Reichswehr; most issues contained a detailed technical evaluation of some foreign vehicle, aircraft, or cannon. Fritz Heigl, a former Austrian army captain, an automotive engineer active in the Austrian vehicle industry, and a university lecturer, was the German Army's best-known analyst of foreign tank and vehicle technology. He was one of the most prolific writers for the *Militär Wochenblatt* from the early 1920s to his death in the 1930s.[23] Heigl also published several books in the 1920s on foreign tank and vehicle technology that were widely distributed throughout the Reichswehr as officially endorsed texts.[24]

In the 1920s, the German Army was probably the best-informed army in the world in the field of understanding foreign tactics and technology. There was a strong motivation in the Truppenamt and the Weapons Office not to fall technically behind as the army had in the last war. Therefore, in addition to working out the original ideas of their own designers, officers at the Weapons Office felt no inhibitions in borrowing foreign technology, so that many features of American, British, and French inventions can be found in the Reichswehr weapons designs of the 1920s, especially in aircraft and tracked vehicles. The foreign technology that was incorporated into German weapons was rarely a direct copy of the original but rather a German modification and improvement of the design. The only foreign weapons system of the 1920s to be taken directly into Reichswehr service without modifications was the Skoda 7.5-cm Gebirgskanone (Mountain Gun) 15.[25]

INFANTRY WEAPONS

At the end of World War I, the German infantry company was as well equipped as any comparable Allied unit. With the 7.92-mm Model 98 Mauser rifle, the Germans possessed one of the best bolt-action rifles ever made. The Germans had developed the first true submachine gun, the Bergmann MP 18/1, a simple and efficient firearm; by the war's end, thirty thousand had been manufactured. The heavy Maxim 08 machine gun had proven its worth as the dominant weapon on the battlefield in World War I; and the lighter version of the heavy Maxim, the 08/15, served as the infantry's primary light machine gun. The 13-mm Mauser antitank rifle was the first true antitank weapon. Several thousand of these, which could pierce the light armor of the 1918 tanks, were issued to the infantry by the end of the war. The 76-mm light mortar had an approximate range of 1,200 meters. It had been redesigned and mounted on a carriage, so that it could fire on a flat trajectory like a light fieldpiece. The medium mortar,

Model 1916, was a 170-mm weapon with a range of approximately 1,100 meters that could also be mounted on a carriage.[26]

There were, of course, some reasons for dissatisfaction. A better anti-tank weapon than the single-shot, shoulder-fired 39-pound Mauser anti-tank rifle was needed. At 40 pounds, the Maxim 08/15 light machine gun was simply too heavy for the infantry, especially in a war of movement. On the other hand, all of the German weapons were at least efficient and reliable, which is more than can be said for some of the Allies' weapons (for example, the infamous French Chauchat light machine gun, one of the most unreliable military weapons ever built). With the German post-war infantry tactics built around the ten-to-twelve-man squad and the light machine gun, the replacement of the Maxim 08/15 became the chief weapons priority for the infantry branch inspectorate.

Throughout the 1920s, the Weapons Office and Infantry Inspectorate would evaluate the various light machine guns used by Germany in the war: In addition to the 08/15, the army used the Bergmann 15 A, the Dreyse MG 10, the Parabellum Model 1914, and the Danish Madsen gun, and test modifications of the wartime designs. In 1922 the Weapons Office wrote the specifications for a new light machine gun that, in accordance with the new tactics emphasizing the firepower of the forward units, would have as high a rate of fire as possible. Von Seeckt took a close interest in the tests, and in 1931 the Army selected the Dreyse MG 13 as its standard light machine gun.[27] The Dreyse MG 13, which saw some use in the Reichswehr in the 1920s, had a cyclic rate of 650 rounds per minute and a total weight of 23 pounds, a great improvement over the Maxim 08/15's weight of 40 pounds and cyclic rate of 450 rounds per minute.

In the period of rethinking the army's tactics right after the war, some revolutionary ideas for infantry armament cropped up in the Infantry Inspectorate and Weapons Office. In 1920 General Kurt Thorbeck, critic of the prewar General Staff's disregard of technology and president of the Rifle Testing Commission until his retirement in 1920, advocated reducing the rifle caliber from 7.92-mm to 6.0- or 6.5-mm.[28] In 1923 General von Taysen, inspector of infantry, requested the Weapons Office to develop an automatic rifle for the infantryman. The 98 Mauser, with its 9-pound weight and long barrel, was a superbly accurate weapon—but only in the hands of a trained marksman. If Germany went to war, it would need a weapon that was lighter and shorter than the 98 Mauser and simple enough for minimally trained conscripts to use. Von Taysen advocated a semiautomatic rifle with ballistics similar to the 98 Mauser and a magazine holding 20–30 rounds.[29] This technology would be realized twenty years later with the creation of the Gewehr 43 assault rifle. Von Taysen's ideas are the norm for infantry rifles today.

Von Taysen's advocacy in 1923 of an infantry semiautomatic assault rifle

*Side and front views of the 75-mm infantry cannon issued to the Reichswehr in 1928 and used until the end of World War II. (Author's collection)*

shows the quality of original tactical and technical thought coming from the branch inspectorates of that period. Unfortunately for the Germans, the assault rifle idea lay stillborn within the Weapons Office because of the stockpile effect. Despite its disarmament, Germany had large stocks of 98 Mausers, which equipped the army, police, and paramilitary groups and of which the army had several hundred thousand more hidden in storage sites throughout Germany. The existence of a large stockpile of these efficient weapons as well as a considerable sentimental attachment to the bolt-action rifle all acted against radically rearming the Reichswehr infantry.

## GAS WARFARE

The German Army ended World War I as the most expert practitioners of the art of gas warfare. Gas is one of the most technically and tactically difficult weapons to use in war. For gas to be effectively employed on the battlefield, the user must take into account the range, intelligence, and weapons data of the artilleryman as well as plan for meteorological and temperature conditions that affect gas dispersion. The user must achieve a correct mix of gases as well as time the salvo to create the rapid concentration of lethal gases that will surprise and cripple or kill the enemy. Postwar tactical studies by the Weapons Office showed that the gas warfare tactics developed by 1918 and the standard German chemical agents were extremely lethal and effective battlefield weapons.[30] There was no doubt within the Reichswehr that gas would continue to be a major weapon of war and that the army needed to violate the Versailles Treaty so it could continue the production and development of poison gases.

Within the Reichswehr's General Staff, the enthusiasm for gas warfare was certainly stronger than within the General Staffs of the victorious Allies. In 1923, in a seminar for Truppenamt officers, von Seeckt directed that the priority in gas warfare research be the uses of gas in a war of movement, particularly in gas-bomb attacks by aircraft. He assured the Truppenamt that money for gas research and production would be made available.[31] In 1924, when von Seeckt directed that in wartime only non-deadly gas, such as tear gas, would be used against enemy civilians, Joachim von Stülpnagel complained about the weakness of this policy in a letter to Majors Helmut Wilberg and Albrecht Kesselring, "Why only tear gas? If one is to carry out a decisive attack on civilian targets far behind the front. . . . Enemy propaganda will always say the Germans have employed gas bombs against civilians and no difference will be made between tear gas and deadly gas."[32]

The main problem of the Weapons Office was gas production. The major producer of poison gas in the war, IG Farben Company, was under close scrutiny by the Interallied Military Control Commission, and many gas factories were in the demilitarized Rhienland.[33] Dr. Hugo Stolzenberg, a leading chemist and poison gas expert, received financial support from the army to establish new plants for mustard, green-cross, and blue-cross gases. In 1923 Stolzenberg, on behalf of the Weapons Office, traveled to the USSR to find a suitable site for chemical-agent production. That same year, an agreement was concluded between the Reichswehr and the Soviet government to construct a gas factory in Trotsk on the lower Volga that would produce phosgene and mustard gas and that would have facilities to load one million artillery gas shells.[34] In 1925, however, financial problems and protests by Stolzenberg's competitor, IG Farben, caused the project to be abandoned. The Weapons Office, left with only a small output of gas in Germany, continued efforts to increase and improve the production and development of facilities for gas.

The Russian connection proved to be vital to the Reichswehr. Chemical agents could be produced and perfected in German laboratories, but in the USSR there was room for large-scale tests far from prying Allied eyes. In 1927 and 1928, guns and aircraft—along with twenty-eight German chemical experts, who carried out tests near the original Stoltzenberg factory on the Volga—were shipped to the USSR. The Soviets supplied much of the gas, notably mustard and diphosgene, and the Germans were able to practice bombardment and air delivery procedures.[35] Through the gas-warfare testing program in Russia and the support of gas production in Germany, the Weapons Office was able not only to keep the gas-warfare arm alive, but also to ensure that Germany entered World War II ahead of the Allies in that technology. Although the highly lethal nerve gas "Tabun" was developed by the German Army even before the start of World War II, it was not used.

COMMUNICATIONS

Maintaining communications with one's advancing troops was one of the major problems in conducting a war of maneuver. The breakdown in communications between the high command and the armies and corps in August and September 1914 has been posed as one of the main reasons the Schlieffen Plan failed.[36] The German wartime radios were bulky and only moderately efficient, yet they served well enough for defensive warfare with established headquarters and static trench lines. As soon as the Imperial Army went on the offensive, however, communications began breaking down. During the Caporetto offensive in October 1917, Captain Erwin Rommel, commanding three companies of the Württemberg

Mountain Battalion, had his signalers lay telephone lines during the advance so he could communicate with the regimental headquarters. Since telephone lines take time to emplace, Rommel was often out of effective communications—that is, separated from reliable artillery support.[37] If telephone communications were barely adequate for troops advancing at a footpace, they were certainly inadequate for the type of mobile war that von Seeckt envisioned.

The Inspectorate of Communications Troops, IN-7, and its corresponding Weapons Office section, WA-7, sponsored extensive radio research in the 1920s and laid the groundwork for an effective series of military radios. One of the most important engineering breakthroughs of the era, the use of ultra-short-wave frequency radios in the 5–15 megahertz range, was pioneered by German civilian firms. By 1927 the German radio industry was well ahead of foreign ones in the ultra-short-wave field.[38] The ultra-short-wave band was to prove effective for short-range communications by tank and infantry units. Mounting a radio in every tank was deemed a necessity by German armor expert Ernst Volckheim in 1924,[39] and the Weapons Office required that a radio mount be incorporated into every prototype tank of the 1920s. From the early 1920s on, the Reichswehr mounted various radio arrangements in army trucks for the regimental and divisional mobile headquarters. Armored troop carriers, commonly used as reconnaissance vehicles, normally carried radios. The Truppenamt Intelligence Section would analyze the effectiveness of British radio communications in the British maneuvers of 1924.[40]

By the early 1930s, IN-7 and the Weapons Office had developed a comprehensive program for a mobile army. Army-to-division communications would be carried out by a 100-watt radio with a range of 250 kilometers. Within the division, communication would be by 5-watt radio with a 50-kilometer range. For armored vehicles, a 20-watt ultra-short-wave radio with a 3–6 kilometer range was developed, while for the infantry, a portable 0.5-watt ultra-short-wave radio with a 5-kilometer voice range was developed. The latter weighed only 12 kilograms.[41]

The Reichswehr's radio development program was a successful one, partly because IN-7 and the Weapons Office carefully followed new civilian technological advances and quickly adapted them for military use. For example, the Enigma code machine was invented by a German, Arthur Schertius, in 1923; by 1926, it was in military service.[42] Although mounting radios in all armored vehicles seemed obvious to the Reichswehr in the 1920s, it was not obvious to the French. In the Battle for France in 1940, only a few French tanks were equipped with radios, forcing the French armored units to communicate by flags and flares as they fought German armored units—all of whose vehicles had radios.

The postwar German Army was allowed to retain a limited number of late-model light and medium guns as divisional artillery. The 1916 model 77-mm fieldpiece, made by Rheinmetall, became the standard divisional light gun. The 1916 model 105-mm howitzer, made by Krupp, was adopted as the divisional howitzer. Both guns were effective by the standards of the era and continued to give effective service up to World War II. The postwar tactics outlined in *Leadership and Battle* emphasized the importance of effective light guns for infantry support in the war of movement. The Truppenamt's recommended tables of organization for the infantry regiment in 1921 proposed that one battery of six infantry cannons be an integral part of every infantry regiment.[43] The light 77-mm fieldpiece of the Reichswehr was too heavy and unwieldy to serve as an effective infantry support weapon in World War I. Drawn by six horses and with large wooden wheels, it was difficult to maneuver through rough battlefield terrain, which was necessary to bring the gun close enough to the forward infantry units to provide direct fire on enemy strongpoints.

The infantry support gun, a small-caliber, light-weight cannon that could be maneuvered with the forward troops, was already a well-known concept. In World War I, the Imperial Army had used a short-barreled, lightened version of the 77-mm Krupp fieldpiece—the L/20. This weapon weighed 855 kilograms—too heavy to be easily manhandled about the battlefield. Other short-barreled field gun adaptations by Krupp and Rheinmetall weighed between 650 and 855 kilograms.[44] All the major combatants of World War I employed a variety of infantry guns, from the tripod-mounted 37-mm French light gun to the effective 76.2-mm Russian storm gun. In the 1920s, the Allies only experimented with infantry guns, whereas the Germans gave their development high priority.[45]

An excellent example of the tactical doctrine driving weapons design in the interwar period is the development of the 75-mm light infantry gun, one of the more innovative gun designs of the era, produced by Rheinmetall. Its development was initiated by the infantry and artillery inspectorates and the Weapons Office shortly after the end of World War I, and in 1927 it was adopted and put into production for the army. It remained in service to the end of World War II. Although the 75-mm light infantry gun was small, weighing only 400 kilograms, it still fired a 6-kilogram shell, almost as large as the shells fired by the 855-kilogram Krupp L/20. The Rheinmetall infantry gun had a short barrel that used a unique cannon breech system: The whole barrel pivoted down from the fixed breech and the gun was then loaded like a shotgun. The gun's carriage was a simple box trail, and it could be fitted with either pneumatic tires or wooden wheels. The maximum range of the 75-mm infantry gun was 3,375 meters, as compared with the 5,000–7,800 meter range of wartime infantry guns; but the former's range was considered more than adequate for a weapon intended for close, direct support fire. Its light weight and small base and wheel size made it easy for an infantry unit to manhandle around the battlefield in a war of maneuver.[46] The United States, Britain, France, and several smaller powers also developed infantry guns in the 1920s, but in size, firepower, and simplicity, the 75-mm Rheinmetall gun was the best of its era.

Because postwar German tactics emphasized the reinforced rifle regiment as the smallest unit capable of independent missions, the Inspectorate of Infantry saw the need for even heavier artillery to serve the needs of the infantry regiments. Research was carried out on heavy infantry guns in the 1920s. As a result, the Reichswehr adopted a 150-mm Rheinmetall infantry gun. This design incorporated a light-alloy carriage and trail, with a total weight of 1,550 kilograms. The maximum range was 4,700 meters and it commonly fired a 40-kilogram shell. The 150-mm gun (15-cm S IG 33) was the largest caliber gun ever to be classified by any nation as an infantry gun, but as one commentator noted, it was a "reliable and robust weapon."[47] The gun remained in service to 1945.

The Reichswehr's 105-mm howitzer was a wartime model with a maximum range of 7,600 meters, too limited for a war of maneuver.[48] In the late 1920s, a program to replace the divisional howitzer was initiated and the gun adopted was another Rheinmetall design: the 105-mm light field howitzer 18, a conventional split-trail gun with a maximum range of 10,600 meters and a standard high-explosive shell of 14.81 kilograms. This gun was used throughout World War II; in some countries, postwar models were in service long afterward.[49]

Krupp and Rheinmetall were the primary competitors for every cannon contract of the 1920s. The Rheinmetall Corporation's designs generally proved superior to Krupp's, which was a blow to Krupp's prewar dominance of artillery development. It was a favorable situation for the Weapons Office, which was able to pick, choose, and even combine the best technical developments of the two companies. For the heavy 100-mm gun developed between 1926 and 1930, the Weapons Office split the final production product between Krupp and Rheinmetall and created a Rheinmetall gun with a Krupp carriage. This combination produced a weapon with a maximum range of 18,300 meters, considerable even by modern standards.[50]

The antiaircraft development program of the 1920s was given high priority, for the Versailles Treaty had denied Germany antiaircraft cannon. A suitable light antiaircraft gun, the 20-mm antiaircraft gun (2-cm Flak 30), was designed by Rheinmetall in the late 1920s; it had a standard rate of fire of 120 rounds per minute and an anti-aircraft range of 299 meters– 2,000 meters. The 20-mm flak gun was also suitable as a ground weapon. It was adopted by the Reichswehr and saw extensive service in the navy, ground forces, and Luftwaffe (Air Force) in the first part of World War II.[51] The heavy antiaircraft gun research was less successful. In 1925 the army decided that 75 millimeters was the smallest practical caliber for a heavy antiaircraft gun; by the late 1920s, both Krupp and Rheinmetall had developed prototype 75-mm flak guns. The Krupp designers, working at the Krupp Bofors subsidiary in Sweden, however, developed an 88-mm flak gun around a 20-pound shell. The design was sent to Germany in 1931 and was developed into the famous 88-mm gun of World War II. In 1933 it was adopted by the army and put into production by Krupp.[52]

The artillery research of the 1920s provides a good example of how well the Reichswehr's research and development program worked. A majority of the guns used by Germany in World War II had been developed in the 1920s and generally gave satisfactory service. The only mediocre gun adopted in the interwar period was the 37-mm antitank gun. Neither the Truppenamt nor the Weapons Office saw it as the best solution, but by 1928 the army had decided that a standard antitank gun needed to be adopted quickly, and the 37-mm gun program was the most advanced solution developed.[53] For the most part, German artillery armament was admirably suited to Germany's tactical requirements for a war of movement. In keeping with the German tradition of tactical flexibility, future divisional artillery commanders would have available guns of assorted ranges and capabilities that could be applied to a wide variety of tactical situations.

ARMORED VEHICLES

During the war, German automotive designers had shown that they could design and build tanks equal to those of the Allied powers. Shortly after the war, the Germans sold the components of their most advanced tank, the LK II, to the Swedish Army. Its designer, Josef Vollmer, went to Sweden to assemble a modified version of the LK II that was armed with machine guns instead of cannons. These modified vehicles, known as Strv M/21s, went into service in 1920 as the first Swedish tanks.[54] The revolutionary uprisings of 1918-19 created a need for armored cars. The Erhardt Company, which had made armored cars during the war, built 20 armored cars in 1919 that were merely modifications of the 1917 model.[55] Krupp-Daimler's heavy truck chassis provided the basis for 40 armored cars built by Daimler. By January 1920, a total of 94 postwar German armored cars had been built; the Treaty of Versailles demanded that they be scrapped.[56] In 1920, however, the Boulogne Note was negotiated, in which the Allies allowed the German security police to possess 150 armored cars, each equipped with two machine guns; 50 of the most modern cars were retained by the police.

In 1921 a contract for 85 new armored cars was split among the Benz, Daimler, and Erhardt companies. Like most armored cars of the era, the Daimler and Erhardt vehicles were designed around an existing heavy truck frame. With four-wheel drive, 7–12 millimeters of armor, and speeds of 50–60 kilometers per hour, these vehicles were roughly comparable to other armored cars of the era.[57] One notable feature of all three armored car models was a steering wheel at both ends. With a second driver, the cars could reverse direction without turning. This particular feature would become standard on most German military armored cars of the 1930s and 1940s.

The Boulogne Note allowed the Reichswehr to possess 105 "armored troop carriers," so a variation of the Daimler armored car was produced. In 1922 the army contracted for 25 and modified 20 previously acquired armored cars. The mediocre cross-country capability of these vehicles, called the SD Kfz 3, meant they were not fully acceptable for wartime duty. They were nevertheless useful for training and successful as radio vehicles. In 1927 some would be modified to carry 20-watt middle-wave radios with a transmission range of 15 kilometers.[58]

In May 1925 the Weapons Office issued the specifications for Germany's first postwar tanks. Daimler, Krupp, and Rheinmetall were contracted to build two tanks each to the following specifications: a fully loaded weight of 16 tons, a top speed of 40 kilometers per hour, able to cross a 2-meter trench, able to negotiate a 1-meter-high obstacle, gas proofed, an engine of 260–280 horsepower, a mounted radio, and amphibious capability with a 4 kilometer per hour water speed. The tank would also mount a turret with a 75-mm gun and a machine-gun, as well as two other machine gun mounts, one of these in a second small turret in the tank's rear. The tank would have 14-mm of armor at all points and a crew of six: a commander, a driver, a radioman, two gunners, and a rear turret gunner.[59] The tank's cover name would be "large tractor" and Captain Pirner of the Weapons Office was appointed project officer for the program.

Between 1925 and 1929 Krupp, Daimler, and Rheinmetall all managed to develop modern tanks. The models had a similar shape and layout. The tanks met most of the specifications of the Weapons Office except that all were overweight—the Rheinmetall tank by the greatest factor (17,580 kilograms).[60] The large tractor models show some similarities with the British medium and heavy tanks of the mid-1920s. For example, the extra turret in the rear was normal for an era that considered heavy and medium tanks as breakthrough vehicles that needed all-around firepower. Lieutenant Ernst Volckheim, one of the few experienced German tank officers, concluded that tanks should be able to fire in all directions simultane-

*A later model Rheinmetall "heavy tractor." (Courtesy of U.S. Army Ordnance Museum, Aberdeen Proving Ground, Maryland)*

ously.[61] The Vickers Medium Mark III tanks of the 1920s had two machine-gun turrets in addition to the cannon turret.[62] Although the general shape of the large tractors was similar to the British Mark IIIs and the armor requirement the same as the Vickers Mark III, the large tractors were very different vehicles. The 75-mm gun made the large tractor one of the most heavily armed tanks of the 1920s. The British tanks of the late 1920s had 3-pounder (47-mm) guns. With 250-horsepower BMW engines, the 16.5-to-17.5-ton Rheinmetall and Krupp tanks were better engined than the British Vickers Medium Mark III, with its 180-horsepower engine for an 18.75-ton vehicle.[63]

The three German designs differed greatly with regard to the transmission, steering, and suspension designs. The Rheinmetall Corporation built one tank with a differential drive and newly patented steering system, the other tank with a clutch-drive system. All of the tanks used small bogie wheels, but arrangement of the wheels and suspensions varied.[64] To meet the amphibious requirement, each tank would be able to mount a propeller on the back that would be operated by the rear turret gunner.[65] The amphibious requirement is an example of borrowing the ideas of American tank designer Christie. In the early 1920s Christie built and successfully tested a fully amphibious, tracked, light-armored vehicle for the U.S. Marine Corps. The Christie vehicle was powered in the water by two large propellers, and according to the German Army journal *Technische Mitteilungen* (Technical Bulletins) on foreign tanks, it had "solved the problem of creating a battle-worthy amphibious tank."[66] Other German tank experts, like Heigl and Volckheim, were familiar with Christie's work and argued that amphibious tanks were a necessity.[67] After the excitement about Christie's experiments had died down and the Germans had carried out extensive field testing, the Weapons Office decided that it was not worth the extra trouble and expense of creating amphibious tanks and dropped the requirement in the early 1930s.

The six heavy tanks were test vehicles for the latest automotive technology; as such, they served their purpose well. The Rheinmetall, Daimler, and Krupp tanks were equal to—and, in armament, superior to—the tanks being tested in Britain, France, and the United States. If anything, the large tractors were overdesigned. The rear turret was unnecessary and inconvenient, for the engine compartment had to be built around it. The amphibious propeller system was also an unnecessary complication. The three companies learned from these mistakes. To be sure, the tank program enabled them to create competent tank design teams. For example, Professor Ferdinand Porsche, who would become Germany's leading tank designer, was the chief designer and supervisor of Daimler's large tractor program.[68] Lieutenant Colonel Oswald Lutz, who enthusiastically promoted the tank prototype program in the Inspectorate of Motor Troops, and Captain Pirner in the Weapons Office would also gain useful experience in tank design from the large tractors.

The next tank contract given to Krupp, Daimler, and Rheinmetall came as the large tractors were being completed. It was for a light tank, with the cover name "light tractor," which the Weapons Office wanted finished as soon as possible. In July 1928 the Weapons Office presented the specifications for the new tank to the three firms and, as with the large tractor, two prototypes were to be built by each company. Daimler fell out of the competition, so a total of four tanks were built. The light tanks were completed and ready for testing in about a year and a half, a much shorter development time than for the heavy tanks, owing to the improved atmosphere for weapons construction in Germany with the departure of the Interallied Military Control Commission in early 1927.

The Weapons Office wanted a vehicle with a multiuse chassis to serve as a tank and as an armored supply vehicle.[69] The light tank would be armed with a half-automatic 37-mm gun and a machine gun. The Weapons Office specified that the tank would carry 150 shells for the gun and 3,000 rounds for the machine gun. An average speed of 25–30 kilometers per hour was specified, with a cross-country speed of 20 kilometers per hour. The tank was to be maneuverable and to have enough armor protection to resist 13-mm bullets. It was to be able to cross a trench of 1.5 meters and have a range of 150 kilometers. The tank was to have a radio and, if possible, amphibious capability. The total weight was not to exceed 7.5 tons. Like the large tractors, the light tractors were to be gas proofed.[70]

*Rheinmetall model of the "light tractor," circa 1930. (Courtesy of U.S. Army Ordnance Museum, Aberdeen Proving Ground, Maryland)*

Whereas the heavy tractor was envisioned as an infantry support vehicle, the light tractor was seen as a "tank killer" armed with a high-velocity 37-mm gun. Like the heavy tractors, the light ones were state-of-the-art vehicles; however, they contained significant technological advances over the heavy tractors. The Rheinmetall vehicles were more advanced than Krupp's because they used a cletrac-drive system,[71] a controlled differential that was a step up from the braked-differential truck drive. The first tank to be designed with a cletrac drive was a Renault experimental light tank built only two years before, in 1926.[72] The Krupp tank and one of the

Rheinmetall tanks were built with several small double-bogie wheels, but one of the Rheinmetall tanks was built with four large bogie wheels and a Christie suspension, a robust and effective design that gave superior cross-country speed and performance.[73] An effective 100-horsepower Daimler truck engine powered the Rheinmetall tanks, whose only official drawback was that at 8.9 tons, they exceeded the official weight limits.

There are some similarities in design between light tractors and foreign tanks. The light tractors mounted their engines in the front and their turrets in the rear, as did the Vickers light tanks of the late 1920s.[74] But the German light tanks, with a 37-mm gun and a machine gun, were more heavily armed than the British tanks, which had just one heavy machine gun. The German light tanks were also twice the weight of the British vehicles, which weighed only 4.25–4.75 tons each. For a further difference, the British medium and light tanks of the era were riveted, whereas the German vehicles were welded. In their heavy armament and in their use of the cletrac drive, the German tank designs of the 1920s are closer to French than to British technology.[75]

The third tank model of the 1920s was a Krupp special design, which was not developed on an army contract but rather as a private venture with considerable encouragement from Lutz. From 1924 to 1927 Lutz worked as a section leader for vehicle development in the Weapons Office, and in 1928 he was assigned to the Inspectorate of Motor Troops. Ever since Christie's tank designs of the early 1920s, which allowed a tank to run on roads at high speeds on its road wheels and then, with the track attached, operate across country, German armor experts were excited by the possibility of an armored vehicle that could combine the road speed of an armored car with the terrain-crossing ability of a tank.[76] The vehicle, designed by Engineer O. Merker in the Krupp plant in Essen, was an especially complicated machine that carried four large auto-type wheels and a track system. The wheels could be lowered and the track system raised for road travel.

Six prototypes were completed in 1928. Each had a turret, a fully automatic 37-mm cannon in the turret as well as a light machine gun in the rear. Three tanks were built with a Benz 50-horsepower engine, and three with a 70-horsepower NAG engine. The whole vehicle weighed only 5.3 tons. The top wheeled speed was 46 kilometers per hour, and the top tracked speed was 23 kilometers per hour.[77] Lieutenant Colonel Lutz hoped for a tank that could switch from tracks to wheels in one minute, without the driver leaving the vehicle. He was asking for more than the technology of 1928 could produce. Although Merker passionately tried to develop a reliable vehicle, the wheel/track idea was a flop. According to Lutz, there were constant problems with the wheel/track drive system, and the vehicle was "difficult to control" in either mode.[78] Some vehicles

*Two views of the Austrian version of the wheel-tank chassis, early 1930s. An example of a wheel track tank similar to the Krupp prototype. (Courtesy of U.S. Army Ordnance Museum, Aberdeen Proving Ground, Maryland)*

were tested by the army at the Soviet testing ground at Kazan and rated as unsuccessful.[79] Although the German Army dropped the idea of wheel/ track tanks, Krupp sent the plans, Merker, and a construction team to the Landsverk Company in Sweden, a Krupp subsidiary, where the wheel/ track tank was further developed and in 1931 put into production as the Landsverk Model 30 tank. Krupp made its research and development investment back, for the tank sold well in the international market.[80]

The attempt to develop the wheel/track tank is another example of how hard the Germans were trying to keep up with, and surpass, foreign technology. A wheel/track tank was a popular concept at the time. The French developed a prototype armored vehicle in the early 1920s, a program that the Reichswehr followed with some interest.[81] The Austrian motor industry also experimented with the wheel/track vehicle. The Saurer Company produced prototypes in the early 1930s; in 1939, the Wehrmacht obtained a few production models from the Austrians to equip some armored units. The 1930s version of the vehicle, the SD Kfz 254, remained unsatisfactory, and the vehicles did not last long in service.[82]

Since the development problems of the Krupp wheel/track tank were already evident by 1928, Lutz and the staff of the Inspectorate of Motor Troops transferred their interest to six-to-eight-wheeled armored cars and half-tracked vehicles that would fulfill the combat reconnaissance role envisioned for the wheel/track tank.[83] An armored car development program was already under way, and from 1928 on it would receive considerable funding from the Reichswehr.[84]

The Reichswehr had never been satisfied with the poor cross-country mobility of the Daimler armored troop transport. Studies undertaken by the Inspectorate of Motor Troops in 1926-27 resulted in Weapons Office contracts for armored cars in 1927 awarded to Büssing, Daimler, and Magirus. The prototype armored cars were required to have a top speed of at least 65 kilometers per hour and be able to cross trenches 1.5 meters wide and to negotiate a 33-degree incline. As with the 1921 armored cars, these vehicles would be able to be driven from either end. The total weight of each tank was not to exceed 7.5 tons. The initial amphibious requirement was soon dropped.[85]

By 1928 each company had produced imaginative vehicles that surpassed the foreign armored car designs of the 1920s in cross-country capability. The Daimler project, led by Professor Ferdinand Porsche, produced a low-silhouette, 100-horsepower, fast, agile eight-wheeled vehicle, with four-by-four drive forward and backward and 13.5 millimeters of armor. The Magirus prototype was similar to the Daimler vehicle.[86] The Büssing vehicle, a ten-wheeled armored car, had good speed and cross-country performance, but problems with braking ten wheels made it dangerous at high speed. After tests, the Büssing vehicle was dropped, and the Reichswehr ordered additional Daimler and Magirus armored cars.[87] Rheinmetall built the turret system with a 37-mm cannon and one machine gun.[88] The multi-wheel armored car program convinced the Reichswehr of the value of eight-wheeled armored cars, and the Daimler, Magirus, and Büssing vehicles of the 1920s were the direct ancestors of the effective eight-wheeled armored car (the SD Kfz 231), which saw extensive service in World War II.

The development of half-track vehicles for the German Army came later during the army's motorization program. Prototypes of half-track carriers and armored cars began in 1930. In deciding upon half-tracks as a possible armored car solution in 1928, Lutz and the Inspectorate of Motor Troops were only approving a well-known technology. Simple half-tracks were improvised in World War I by mounting one or two small roller wheels to a truck chassis and attaching a track. This arrangement was first used by the Allies, but in 1918 a Benz-Bräuer light truck was adapted as a half-track by the Germans.[89] Germany's first true postwar half-track, in which the rear drive was all track and not an adaptation, was built in the mid-1920s by the Dürkopp Company, which redesigned a heavy truck model for a half-track. The Dürkopp half-track was intended as a heavy farm vehicle, but its practical design did not prevent the company from soon going broke.[90] Germany's other half-track producer was the Maffei Company, which produced the ZM 10 heavy truck. The ZM 10 had an extra drive wheel and two roller wheels that could be lowered; a track could then be attached around them and the rear wheels to create a heavy cross-country truck. The Maffei Company acquired much of the technology from France under a licensing arrangement in 1927; by 1930 it had a civilian half-track in production that could carry eight passengers or 1,000 kilograms of cargo. The Reichswehr and the Austrian Army quickly bought the vehicle. The Maffei Company continued to develop half-tracked vehicles for the Reichswehr and the Wehrmacht.[91]

The development of armored vehicles in the 1920s was due largely to the work of Oswald Lutz, a central figure in German armor development from 1924 to 1938. In 1924 Lutz, then a lieutenant colonel, was appointed to the Weapons Office as a section leader to oversee vehicle development. He was certainly the right man for the job. Lutz was technically minded and had spent his entire career in army transport, starting as a lieutenant with the Bavarian Army railroad troops and serving in the war as director of motor transport for the Sixth Army.[92] When Lutz arrived at Section 6 of the Weapons Office, he complained that nothing had been done to develop new armored cars since the 1921 models had been built.[93] He pushed his section into intensive study, which resulted in several weapons development programs. In 1928, when Lutz was transferred to the Inspectorate of Motor Troops, he continued to advocate new programs for armored vehicle development. The Weapons Office armor program also attracted the support of General von Seeckt, who visited Gustav Krupp in Essen for several days in November 1925, shortly after the first tank specifications were drawn up. There they discussed the tank program and the weapons research and development that Krupp had undertaken at the Bofors plant in Sweden.[94]


MOTOR VEHICLES

World War I saw the extensive use of motor vehicles in the German Army. In November 1918 the motor troops consisted of 2,000 officers, 100,000 men, 12,000 automobiles, 25,000 trucks, 3,200 ambulances, and 5,400 motorcycles.[95] If the Allied blockade had not severely limited German supplies of oil and rubber, the Germans would have built considerably more motor vehicles. At the conclusion of the war, the Allies possessed about 200,000 vehicles of all types.[96]

During the war, German industry had developed a wide range of vehicles suitable for the military. Heavy antiaircraft guns and 77-mm fieldpieces had been mounted on Erhardt and Daimler tanks and saw wide use. Many of the German medium and heavy trucks were efficient four-by-four vehicles. For several years after the war the Reichswehr was equipped with a wide variety of wartime vehicles. The 1918 Daimler KDI heavy truck, which mounted the 77-mm fieldpiece, remained in army service well into the 1930s.[97] Until the late 1920s, the commanders of the military districts had the authority to procure automobiles and trucks for their commands.

The economic problems Germany had in the early 1920s made any long-term motorization planning by the Reichswehr impractical. However, the growth of the German economy after 1923 coupled with an improvement in the motor industry's position and the lifting of Allied controls on the building of civilian tracked vehicles in late 1923 made the consideration of army motorization possible by 1925. In the economic boom following 1923, the number of vehicles in Germany increased dramatically. In 1925 there were 175,665 automobiles in use, as opposed to 100,340 in 1923. The number of trucks in 1925 grew to 80,363 from 51,736 in 1923. From 1923 to 1925, the number of motorcycles went from 54,389 to 161,508, and special vehicles (tractors, heavy movers, and so on) from 1,484 to 8,290.[98] In 1926 the army presented its first motorization program, which was less of a procurement plan than a statement of policy. The motorization program, which was constantly revised between 1926 and 1930, would attempt to assess the army's specific needs for motor vehicles and set uniform standards for procurement. The intention was to identify civilian production models that, with only a few modifications, could be readily accepted by the army. The central thrust of the program was to plan for a much-expanded army that would be largely motorized. The use of civilian vehicles would speed equipment of the army while keeping costs down.[99]

One part of the motorization program—the development of tracked, self-propelled artillery—was given high priority by General von Seeckt. In his commander's report of 1922, von Seeckt said of the guns mounted on the Erhardt trucks, "The present motorized batteries are not modern motorized artillery. . . . The cross-country performance is not acceptable."[100] In the priorities list of the Weapons Office published shortly after the motorization program was initiated, the development of improved motorized artillery was given high priority, just below tank develop-ment.[101] In accordance with the concept of using civilian technology, a light 25-horsepower Hanomag tracked tractor provided a mount for a 37-mm Rheinmetall antitank gun, and the larger, 50-horsepower tractor a mount for the 77-mm field gun. Tests in Russia proved these civilian/military vehicles to be efficient designs. Only a few, however, were bought by the army in the late 1920s due to budget restrictions.[102] A variety of tracked and wheeled civilian tractors were bought directly from civilian firms and used to motorize some engineer and artillery units.[103]

For the most part, the motorization program was the greatest failure of the Weapons Office and the Inspectorate of Motor Troops. The original concept of adapting civilian vehicles to army needs was sound, and that principle would form the basis for the U.S. Army's extremely successful motorization program.[104] One of Field Marshal von Hindenburg's favorite sayings was, "In war only the simple succeeds." What the Weapons Office and the Inspectorate of Motor Troops did was not simple. They soon came to approach army motor-vehicle procurement in the same way they produced weapons. By 1927-28, it was clear to the Weapons Office that all branches of the army could be motorized,[105] so the tactical needs of all the army branches were studied and a long list of vehicle needs presented to the motor industry along with detailed specifications for weight, cross-country mobility, and so on. Instead of studying the available civilian motor vehicles and picking a few robust and simple types for military use, which would have kept costs down and made maintenance easy, the army pressed the motor industry to develop a wide range of new vehicles.

In the 1920s, the army asked the motor industry to develop amphibious automobiles, trucks of various sizes with maximum cross-country performance, and special three-axled six-wheeled automobiles as staff cars. The Daimler, Horch, and Selve companies built some of the latter to army specifications in the 1920s. The result was an elegant and extremely expensive staff car with moderate cross-country capability.[106] In the late 1920s and early 1930s, the Reichswehr bought limited quantities of dozens of vehicle types from thirty-six different auto manufacturers.[107] All sorts of technically advanced vehicles were produced at high cost with no attempt at simplifying or standardizing. By constant research, tinkering, and testing, the Weapons Office showed its enthusiasm for motorization and its grasp of the latest technology, but the limited budget for vehicle procurement was squandered and the Wehrmacht in the 1930s would inherit a bewildering variety of vehicles and special projects that it could not standardize or make cost efficient. The Reichswehr motorization program is an example of a military organization that lost sight of the original plan and became overexcited by technology. The military had overreacted to Thorbeck's valid criticism that the pre-1914 army had ignored technology.

# CHAPTER SIX

# The Development of German Armor Doctrine

Under von Seeckt's command and in the late 1920s, the German Army made great progress in developing a comprehensive modern armor doctrine. The Truppenamt created a progressive tank doctrine in 1923 that emphasized the offensive qualities of the tank. Throughout the 1920s, many officers in the Truppenamt and in other branches actively studied and discussed tank tactics. From 1919 on, the *Militär Wochenblatt* was filled with articles by an assortment of German officers writing about tank technology and tactics. As with weapons development, many foreign ideas were studied and adopted, but even at this early date German Army officers developed their own original ideas. The three foundations of German armor theory in the 1920s were the army's experience with armor in World War I, foreign armor ideas and experience, and original concepts from within the Reichswehr.

EARLY ARMOR EXPERIENCE

In comparison with the grand Allied tank attacks at Cambrai, Amiens, and Soissons, and the dozens of other Allied tank attacks of 1917-18, the activities of Germany's own armored force tend to be overlooked. The Germans managed to form nine tank companies in 1918 and to create a tank school, tank headquarters (the equivalent of a brigade headquarters), and tank workshops—in all, a force of about twenty-five hundred men.[1] The German tank force would engage in twelve battles in 1918. The largest German battle, at Villers-Bretonneux on April 24, 1918, employed thirteen tanks. The German tank actions, like most of the British, French, and American tank battles of 1918, consisted of small tank detachments supporting infantry regiments in taking limited objectives.[2] The German Army's experiences with tank actions provided enough battle knowledge for it to draw some sound conclusions and create an early tank doctrine.

Initially, the German tank units were independent companies of five tanks each. This gave the German tank force a total of forty-five tanks by the summer of 1918, with a further forty-five tanks in reserve to replace damaged vehicles. By the autumn of 1918 the Germans realized that a five-tank company was too weak and reorganized their force into three tank battalions of three companies each. As the German-made light tanks reached the forces in 1919, the Germans planned to organize tank battalions of thirty light tanks, with ten tanks per company.[3] From their tank battles, the Germans learned that the tank was a good infantry support weapon. For example, in attacks on March 21, April 24, May 27, July 15, and August 31, 1918, the tank-supported German infantry regiments managed to take their objectives.[4] However, according to Ernst Volckheim, one of the German tank officers, the greatest tactical problem of the early tank corps was the lack of effective communications with the infantry and artillery.[5] In the confusion of battle on August 31 the Germans lost two tanks to their own artillery fire when they retired from the action and a nearby German battery thought it was subject to a British attack.[6]

From the failure of a German tank attack at Rheims on June 1, 1918, against a strong French defensive position that contained a deep trench system and rough ground before the lines, the Germans learned the importance of carefully selecting the terrain for an attack.[7] In the tank action of October 11, 1918, north of Cambrai, the Germans learned the value of the tank in the defense. In what Volckheim called the "most successful German tank battle," ten German tanks managed to plug a hole in the line and halt a British tank-led advance.[8] In 1918 the Germans even developed their own tank attack formations, which tended to be an advance in an irregular line, with each tank no more than 50 meters apart—close enough to signal by sight. The Germans had learned the value of "zig-zag driving," at Rheims, where they were confronted with a strong antitank defense.[9]

In the mobile campaign fought in Romania in 1916, the Germans learned the value of using their small armored-car force as a weapon for surprise attacks and deep penetration raids.[10] An attack by five German armored cars at Vadenji in 1916 cost the Romanians 450 dead and wounded; the Germans lost one armored car. The Germans were impressed by the success the Romanians had when they combined armored cars and cavalry in their attacks. Armored car use would be stressed in postwar German tactics.

Of course, the Germans learned more about fighting tanks than anyone else in World War I. When tanks first appeared, armor-piercing ammunition was distributed to German machine gunners, and infantry antitank weapons were developed such as the 13-mm Mauser antitank rifle and the Becker 20-mm antitank cannon.[11] The Germans built antitank obstacles and produced anti-tank mines. The 37-mm Skoda gun as well as the other small infantry guns used at the front had too low a muzzle velocity—130 meters per second—to be effective.[12] The Rheinmetall and Fischer com-

*Motor transport column carries mock tanks during maneuvers of Fourth Division near Naumberg, 1927.*

panies therefore created light 37-mm antitank guns that were introduced at the front in 1918.[13] The full-sized 77-mm field guns of the artillery were nevertheless the preferred antitank weapons, because all of the light antitank weapons were effective only at ranges of a few hundred yards or less. The heavier guns, on the other hand, could stop a tank at ranges of 1,000 meters or more. By 1918, mounting 57-mm or 77-mm cannons on trucks to create a mobile antitank force was seen as an ideal solution.[14]

The postwar battles of the German Freikorps in the Baltics show that German soldiers had absorbed a good deal of practical experience in armored and motorized warfare. When the Iron Division Freikorps fought the Bolsheviks in the Spring of 1919, it used armored cars and two armored trains extensively in a mobile campaign. In the successful German offense on Riga in May 1919, armored cars led part of the attack.[15] In another battle, the Iron Division assembled its armored cars and motorized an infantry battalion, moving 40 kilometers to successfully counterattack the Soviets.[16]

## ARMOR IN LEADERSHIP AND BATTLE

Although the Versailles provisions that forbade tank and armored car units were inconvenient to the German Army, they did not prevent the

Germans from studying armored warfare, writing about it, or even training for it. As mentioned in Chapter Five, the Interallied Military Control Commission could not keep the Germans from secretly developing modern tank technology. One did not need to be a tank enthusiast or a visionary military theorist in 1920 to realize that tanks and armored cars were going to play a major role in any future conflicts. The members of the German General Staff understood this, and in volume 2 of their primary doctrinal regulation, *Leadership and Battle*, they included a considerable section on the use of tanks and armored vehicles.[17]

Tank tactics and unit organization were firmly based on the German experience in World War I. The Truppenamt envisioned two types of battle tank: a light tank of 6–10 tons with a two-man crew armed with a heavy machine gun or a small-caliber cannon, and a heavy tank of 20 tons armed with a cannon and several machine guns.[18] Given the technology of the era, 20 kilometers was seen as the maximum advance that a tank could achieve in a day of battle.[19] The Truppenamt specified tank unit organizations up to regimental size. The heavy tanks would be organized into two-tank platoons. Two platoons would constitute a battery, which would be commanded by a captain with his own command tank. Three batteries and a support unit would constitute a section (*Abteilung*). A heavy tank regiment would be composed of three sections and a maintenance/supply unit. The light tanks were to be organized into five-tank platoons. A company would be composed of three platoons, with a tank for the commander, and a radio tank, and maintenance/supply staff. A battalion would be created from three companies and a regiment from several battalions and integral maintenance/supply formations.[20]

The Truppenamt took the view common to all major armies of the early 1920s and envisioned the tank as an all-purpose infantry support weapon in a war of movement. The heavy tank was not seen as particularly useful in a war of movement, but rather was to be used in breaking through a defended front, as in World War I.[21] Tanks were offensive weapons; indeed, it was not advised to use tanks in the defense.[22] The lessons of World War I were also combined with the traditional German teaching of seeking out the "decisive point": "The high command will employ tanks where they seek the decision. They must achieve surprise, be used in mass on a wide front and be employed in deep columns so that sufficient reserves can be brought into play."[23] In order to attain a deep penetration of the enemy front, *Leadership and Battle* advised using tanks in waves to maintain offensive momentum.[24] To reach the correct mass of tanks, every division in the front line was to employ at least one battalion of light tanks in an attack.[25] Using tanks in small numbers or on a narrow front was emphatically discouraged, for a small number of tanks would attract the concentrated fire of the defenders' entire antitank arsenal.

*Reichswehr armored car with a radio mount on a field exercise, circa
1924–1927.*

*Leadership and Battle* also placed considerable faith in the armored car
as an important weapon. Even though the armored car was restricted to
the road, it possessed speed and firepower and could be especially effective on the enemy's flanks and in his rear areas. In cooperation with cavalry, bicycle troops, motorized infantry, and artillery, the armored car was
described as "a primary weapon in the war of movement."[26] The use of
the armored car in reconnaissance, as an advanced guard and rear guard
weapon, was also emphasized.

ERNST VOLCKHEIM

In the 1920s the German Army officer corps contained a number of men
who significantly contributed to armor theory and equipment development. The most important of these early German armor tacticians and
theorists was Lieutenant Ernst Volckheim, one of only a few Reichswehr
officers who had practical experience in the German wartime tank
corps.[27]

Volckheim was assigned to the German tank corps in February 1918,
saw his first tank combat at Villers-Bretonneux in April 1918, and partook
of several more tank battles before he was badly wounded on October 11,

1918. As an officer in the army's First Heavy Tank Company, which was equipped with the German-made A7V tanks, Volckheim saw as much tank warfare as most of the experienced Allied tank officers. He was retained by the Reichswehr after the war as an officer of the motor transport troops. Volckheim's career as a tank theorist and tactician began in 1923, when he was assigned to the Reichswehr Ministry's Inspectorate for Motor Troops and then detailed to the weapons testing detachment at Döberitz. Promoted to first lieutenant in 1925, Volckheim was designated to teach armor and motorized tactics at the Infantry Officer School in Dresden. In the late 1920s, Volckheim served as an instructor of motorized troops. From 1923 on, Volckheim was exclusively engaged in the development of armored forces. He attended the German tank school at Kazan in Russia in 1932-33, and from 1937 to 1939 he was in charge of writing the tactical manuals for the panzer troops.[28]

Ernst Volckheim was a prolific writer on tanks and motorization. His first book on armor was a history of the German Tank Corps in action in 1918. Largely autobiographical, *German Tanks in the World War* (1923) was a vivid and well-written account of the German armored experience.[29] From 1923 to 1927, Volckheim produced no fewer than two dozen signed articles on armored war for the *Militär Wochenblatt*. The semiofficial weekly journal of the German Army was edited by General (retired) Konstantin von Altrock,[30] a progressive military theorist who included numerous German articles and translations of foreign articles on armored war in his journal throughout the 1920s. In 1924 and 1925, von Altrock issued a special monthly supplement called *The Tank* (Der Kampfwagen), an eight-page journal devoted to tanks, armored cars, and all aspects of army motorization; Lieutenant Volckheim wrote the lead article in every issue.

In 1924 Volckheim's *The Tank in Modern Warfare*, written as a basic text for armored warfare, was published. In it, Volckheim described the best-known light and heavy tank models: For a standard light tank example, he used the French Renault; for a heavy tank, the British Mark V. He provided detailed organization tables for light and heavy tank units based upon the Truppenamt's proposed unit organizations in *Leadership and Battle* and outlined a training plan for tank units. Most of the book, however, is taken up by a discussion of the tactical employment of tanks, antitank defense, and Volckheim's recommendation for a modern tank force.

Volckheim's books were favorably received throughout the army. *The Tank in Modern Warfare* was endorsed by the high command as a standard text on armored warfare. General von Altrock wrote a favorable review of Volckheim's *German Tanks in the World War*.[31] Some of Volckheim's early articles were reprinted in pamphlet form and issued throughout the army—for instance, a twelve-page pamphlet, *Tanks and*

*Anti-Tank Defense* (Der Kampfwagen und Abwehr dagegen), was re-printed in 1925 from a *Wissen und Wehr* article.[32]

Volckheim was not a grand theorist of warfare and his imagination, un-like J. F. C. Fuller's, did not run to visions of all-tank armies. Yet Volckheim was a sound tactician for his day, and as early as 1924 he produced some good original ideas on armored warfare. Volckheim disagreed with the of-ficial German doctrine, favoring light tanks, which in fact was the main-stream view of modern armies and tank theorists of the early 1920s. Volckheim argued that the only real advantage of a light tank was its higher speed and that higher speed was only useful in enabling a tank to move quickly through areas covered by artillery fire. The major advan-tage of a tank was its armament, not its speed. In a future war, when both sides had tanks, the tank with the heavier armament would be victorious in any tank-to-tank engagement. Therefore, Volckheim contended, the heavily gunned but slow medium tank would become the main armor weapon of the future. A 20-kilometer-per-hour cross-country speed would suffice for the medium tank. As for armament, Volckheim was ex-cited about French experiments at mounting 75-mm guns on tanks.[33] Volckheim in this case was an accurate predictor, and the more famous ar-mor theorists of the era were wrong. In World War II, the fast, lightly armed light tanks would play a minor role and the slower, heavily gunned medium tanks would dominate the battlefield. Armament, not speed, did become the most important ingredient of tank success, and it remains so to this day.

Volckheim was also the first armor theorist to emphasize the impor-tance of the tank as an antitank weapon. In *Tanks and Anti-Tank Defense*, a 1925 pamphlet, Volckheim stated that the first mission of the tank was the destruction of enemy tanks.[34] Volckheim again disagreed with *Leader-ship and Battle* and argued for a defensive role for tanks. The brigade or regiment on the defensive should hold its tanks in reserve for a counterat-tack against enemy tanks and troops who penetrated the defensive posi-tions.[35] Volckheim's emphasis upon the tank as an antitank weapon came directly from his unit's wartime experience.[36]

Like most officers of the 1920s, Volckheim believed that the tank was essentially an infantry support arm, like the artillery or the cavalry. The major tactical unit envisioned was the infantry division or regiment, which would be supported by a regiment or battalion of tanks and ar-mored cars. Most of Volckheim's writings of the 1920s dealt with the prac-tical tactical problems of infantry unit support. In the *Militär Wo-chenblatt* issues of 1924 and 1925, Volckheim presented a series of tactical problems and their solutions for the infantry regiment or battalion with tanks and armored cars in support and for the infantry unit facing ar-mored attacks. The problems were usually short and accompanied by maps. A suggested solution, in the form of an operations order for the theoretical commander, would follow in a later issue.[37] These problems and solutions were presented in the standard German form for officer school and General Staff tactical problems. As these problems and solutions were published at the same time that Volckheim was actively involved with the training of infantry and motor troops officers at Döberitz and Dresden, it may be surmised that Volckheim was publishing the actual problems and solutions being used in training at the time.

Because of its wartime experience, the German Army was more advanced in antitank tactics than the other armies of the day. In the 1920s Volckheim wrote many articles on antitank defense. In 1924 he outlined a regimental defense against an enemy tank force that emphasized putting outpost and reconnaissance troops well forward, establishing strongpoints with field guns and mortars in the direct fire mode along the likely avenues of approach for tanks, and maintaining a strong reserve of troops and tanks that could counterattack enemy armor that penetrated the outpost line. The field gun, Volckheim wrote, was an excellent antitank gun and the artillery should detail gun sections, camouflage them carefully, and avoid using them for fire support missions so that enemy counterbattery guns would be unlikely to find them.[38] This defensive system was a variation of World War I tactics. Replace the field guns and mortars of 1924 with antitank guns, and these tactics would be extremely effective in World War II.

In his writings of the 1920s, Volckheim shows that he was thoroughly familiar with foreign armored technology and tactical writings. No mere copyist, he criticized and rejected, borrowed and adapted, foreign ideas and tactics. Volckheim admired the French tank force for the high quality of its officers and much of its equipment, but he could not resist critiquing French doctrine and technology. The French heavy tank of 1925 was undermanned and the French tank exercises did not pay enough attention to artillery liaison, Volckheim commented.[39]

J. F. C. Fuller influenced Volckheim, as he did almost all of the armored theorists of the 1920s. During and after the war, Fuller had overseen the development of specialized armored vehicles for engineer support. Volckheim appreciated this idea and asserted that tank units, to be fully effective, needed to be accompanied by their own armored engineer units equipped with special vehicles that could lay bridges and demolish obstacles.[40] Volckheim also concurred with the British wartime practice of mounting radios in some tanks, a Fuller innovation, and argued that all tanks should have radios to be able to communicate not only with each other but also with infantry and artillery units.[41]

Volckheim was especially influenced by the technical developments of American J. Walter Christie. Volckheim was particularly impressed by the

Christie tanks of the early 1920s, which could run at high speed on road wheels and, with tracks attached, could operate cross-country. Volckheim saw this wheel/track combination as the solution to the medium tanks' short range and low speed. In the wheeled mode, the medium tank could replace the armored car. Although the armored car was fast, it was lightly armed, suitable only for reconnaissance. A tank in a wheeled mode, however, was almost as fast as an armored car and had the option of attacking enemy targets immediately with its heavy armament. Surprise and shock could be attained in a mobile war.[42] Christie's amphibious armored vehicle also excited Volckheim. He doubted that effective amphibious tanks could be built, but creating a tank with the ability to cross rivers on its own was militarily so important that further research was necessary in the field.[43] In urging the adoption of Christie's ideas, Volckheim was within the mainstream, but he deserves some credit for thinking through the tactical possibilities of such technology in detail.[44]

Ernst Volckheim is important to the evolution of the German armor force because he was the German Army's first serious writer on the subject. Volckheim, with the help of von Altrock, was able in a short period to develop an indigenous German literature on armored and mechanized warfare. In 1923, when Volckheim began writing, most of the articles on mechanized warfare in the *Militär Wochenblatt* were translations or summaries of foreign articles. By 1926 most of the articles on armor and mechanization were written by German officers. The publication of *The Tank* in 1924 initiated a wave of interest in armored warfare within the Reichswehr so that officers from the artillery, infantry, horse transport troops, and cavalry were contributing articles.[45] Some of the early contributors on armored tactics and equipment would become prolific writers on the subject. Lieutenant Wilhelm Brandt, a wartime officer who received an engineering degree after the war, started regularly contributing articles on the technical aspects of armored vehicles.[46] After Fritz Heigl, Brandt was the German Army's major writer on armor technology in the 1920s. In the 1940s, as an SS Obersturmbannführer, Brandt continued to write highly technical articles on armor for the *Militär Wochenblatt*.

IDEAS ABOUT ARMORED WARFARE IN THE TRUPPENAMT

In the 1920s, interest in armored warfare was not confined to the Inspectorate of Motor Troops and the Weapons Office. The Operations Section (T-1), the Organization Section (T-2), and the Training Section (T-4) were all involved in the study of armored warfare. In January 1927 a report from T-1 under Werner von Fritsch (later army chief) concluded, "Armored, quickly moving tanks most probably will become the operationally decisive offensive weapon. From an operational perspective this weapon will be most effective, if concentrated in independent units like tank brigades."[47] In June 1927, T-2 directed that all armored car units belonged to the motor troops.[48] This ensured that the armored car units would be controlled and trained by the army's most progressive armored warfare advocates, not placed at the mercy of the cavalry arm—in Germany, as in other countries, the most tactically reactionary of the army's branches. A conference on tank tactics and technology took place in the newly formed defense office, the Wehramt, in October 1927, with Major Kesselring from that section participating.[49] At the same time, T-4, under Colonel von Blomberg, was creating training schedules for tank regiments.[50]

These stages of evolution in armored warfare concepts helped flesh out the armored tactics and organization in *Leadership and Battle*. The 1923 manual provided for armored units up to regiments. In 1924 Volckheim outlined a basic training program. But von Fritsch, von Blomberg, and the Truppenamt differed from *Leadership and Battle* by treating tank units as operationally independent units instead of as infantry support weapons.

The Intelligence Section (T-3) of the Truppenamt did a thorough job of collecting and disseminating information on foreign armor tactics and technology. Starting in 1925 the Truppenamt published a biweekly collection of translations and summaries of articles from foreign sources.[51] American, Polish, French, British, and Soviet ideas on armored warfare were circulated.[52] The British and French maneuvers and tactical manuals were analyzed from articles, press reports, and the observation of German officers. T-3 contacted Volckheim for his analysis of foreign tanks and armor training.[53] Enough accurate, up-to-date information on French doctrine was assembled for T-3 to issue a booklet of over sixty pages covering all aspects of French doctrine; the booklet was used in training and maneuvers.[54] T-3 also published analyses of the French maneuvers of 1922 and 1923. The German officers who observed the 1922 maneuvers, the first major maneuvers since the war, were not impressed, for the French tactics lacked flexibility and revealed a preference for defensive, positional warfare.[55] In the French maneuvers of 1923, the Germans reviewed the problems of liaison and communications between all the combat arms, criticizing French methods and the French command set-up in their light division. The French, they averred, "had a poor understanding of the tactics of their own arms and of combined arms tactics."[56]

The French maneuver results caused the Germans to conclude that horses and mechanical units did not work well together. The cavalry, moreover, was obsolete as a strategic weapon owing to gas warfare; tank improvements would take its place.[57] The Germans praised the performance of the experimental French half-tracks and newer armored equipment, but on the tactical side, the Germans found that the Reichswehr training and tactics were superior.[58] The Germans expressed more admiration for British tactics shown during the maneuvers of 1924 and 1925 than they had for the French, but some of the British problems taught the Germans other lessons. Von Blomberg, who studied the British maneuvers because "the English are furthest along with motorization tests," drew the lesson that mixing motor columns and horse-drawn columns was impossible.[59] Reichswehr officers visiting the United States in the 1920s collected considerable information on U.S. Army motorization, tank equipment, and training. German army officers were encouraged to take three-month foreign tours in order to improve their fluency in foreign language—a special travel allowance was even paid. Officers completing such tours were expected to write full reports on their host country upon their return. From 1923 on, the United States was a favorite country for German officers to visit, not only because English was the most popular foreign language in the officer corps but also because the United States was far friendlier to Germans than other nations: They were allowed to travel freely, visit military installations, and collect unclassified information. Several dozen travel reports of the 1920s still exist in the German military archives; those covering America are by far the most detailed.

In the mid-1920s, Colonel von Boetticher, later to become a major general and military attaché to the United States, visited America and reported on artillery motorization.[60] Captain Speich in 1924 and retired general Schirmer in 1926 also reported on American motor vehicles and artillery tractors.[61] After viewing American tanks and talking with American officers, Schirmer reported that 40-ton tanks were too heavy for modern war, recommending 20-ton tanks as superior vehicles.[62] An extensive study of U.S. tanks was conducted during a 1928 trip by Major Radelmeier, later to become a panzer general, and Captain Austmann. The two Germans not only talked with many American officers but also were allowed to observe armored unit maneuvers at Fort Leonard Wood. Their report contains many photographs of new American equipment and vehicles.[63]

VON SEECKT ON ARMORED WARFARE

Hans von Seeckt was not a tank tactician or armored theorist, but from 1924 on, as the German Army was stabilized and the daily situation was no longer one of constant crisis, he pushed strongly for tank training and tactical development. In a secret order of August 1924, the army command ordered the military districts to ensure that in each unit and garrison, someone would be assigned as Armor Officer, responsible for practical troop training in armored warfare. The Inspectorate of Motor Troops was made responsible for following all armor developments and for assembling information and training material for distribution. The divisional officers from the motor battalions were also responsible for overseeing training.[64]

The job of the unit armor officer was not just another extra duty for motor officers. The high command ordered that the transfer of tank officers was to be avoided and that those who had served a term as tank officer could serve for a second tour of duty in that assignment. All appointments and transfers of armor officers were to be reported directly to the Inspectorate of Motor Troops. The armor officer's duties were (1) to hold classes for officers and NCOs as often as possible; (2) to distribute training materials to the troops; and (3) to serve as the commander's adviser in all matters pertaining to armored vehicles and to act during exercises as the commander of the mock tank units.[65]

Von Seeckt insisted that tanks were to be represented "in war games and maneuvers as often as possible" so that troops could learn to cooperate with them in attacks and practice antitank defense.[66] The units participating in divisional maneuvers in 1924 were ordered to build mock-ups of the light French Renault tanks and the British Mark V tanks. The primary training materials on armored warfare were specified as Ernst Volckheim's *The Tank in Modern Warfare* and his tactical problems in the *Militär Wochenblatt*; Fritz Heigl's instructional tables on foreign tanks, which were to be issued down to company level; and further materials such as pamphlets and article reprints issued by the Inspectorate of Motor Troops. The high command ordered that all branches of the army were to practice firing from moving armored vehicles—this meant the Reichswehr's armored troop transports—against both stationary and moving targets. Furthermore, all questions related to armored vehicle training were to be referred to the Inspectorate of Motor Troops.[67]

Yet another secret letter of instruction was issued by the army high command on October 6, 1924, and sent to each military district commander. The letter referred to a senior commanders' conference in March of that year. The instructions of the August letter were repeated, and each division involved in the autumn maneuvers was ordered to report to the Truppenamt's Training Section on the tactical lessons learned from operating with mock armored vehicles.[68]

In the annual *Remarks of the Army Chief*, distributed throughout the army, von Seeckt insisted in every year from 1920 to 1925 that more training be given in motorized and armored warfare. In every year but 1921, von Seeckt urged that combat troops practice tactical motor movement.[69] In his *Remarks* of 1923, von Seeckt initiated the program of building mock armored vehicles for training. All motor units were ordered to con-

*Early (bicycle-powered) version of the Reichswehr mock tank, early 1920s. (Courtesy of U.S. Army Ordnance Museum, Aberdeen Proving Ground, Maryland)*

struct wood-and-canvas mock tanks that could be mounted on vehicles in order to enhance the realism of the training.[70] In that same year, von Seeckt directed that the tactical representation of the most modern weapons, specifically tanks and aircraft, was to be given a much larger role in unit training.[71]

### OTHER GERMAN ARMOR THEORISTS

Oswald Lutz and Alfred von Vollard-Bockelberg, both senior officers in the Inspectorate of Motor Troops and the Weapons Office, played a major role in the development of German armored warfare theory in the 1920s. First as a section leader in the Weapons Office from 1924 to 1927 and then on the staff of the Inspectorate of Motor Troops from 1928 through 1935 (he became first commander of Panzer Troops in 1931), Lutz enthusiastically sponsored the study of armor. When Lutz first arrived at the Weapons Office, he energetically began to train his staff in armored warfare. A course was set up to teach the technical aspects of motor technology, but Lutz insisted that the tactical aspects of tanks and motor vehicles be included as well.[72] During 1925 Lutz's section completed several stud-

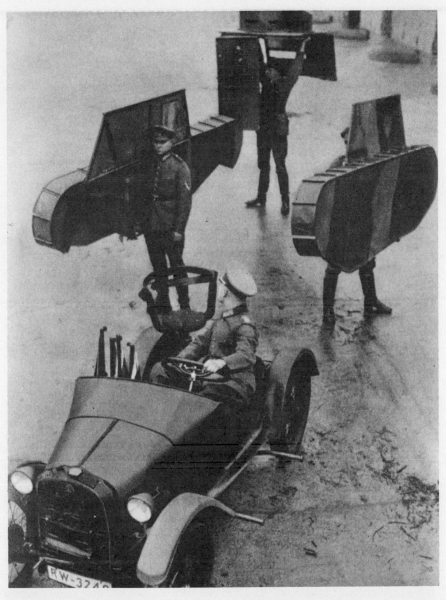

*Transport troops mount a mock tank on "Dixie" auto, late 1920s. (Courtesy of U.S. Army Ordnance Museum, Aberdeen Proving Ground, Maryland)*

ies on armored warfare, including the use of artillery tractors and half-tracks in World War I, the state of the German motor industry, and the latest foreign motor-vehicle developments. Captain Pirner, the Weapons Office armor specialist, wrote a study on modern tanks.[73]

From these studies, Lutz came to the conclusion in 1925-26 that two tanks were needed by the army: a medium one with heavy armor and weaponry and low speed to act as a battle tank, and a light one with light armor and weaponry and high speed whose first duty would be reconnaissance, but which could also carry out raids, general support, and long-range missions. The first German tank program would be designed around Lutz's armor concepts.

In 1926, when Colonel Alfred von Vollard-Bockelberg became inspector of motor troops, the small technical course for motor officers at Berlin-Moabit was transformed. In the early 1920s, the focus of the course had been motor technology and maintenance, but under von Vollard-Bockelberg's direction, the course by 1928 included the study of tank and motorized warfare tactics. The Inspectorate of Motor Troops' school would steadily evolve in a tactical studies direction, and when rearmament began it became the Panzer Troops School.[74] Von Vollard-Bockelberg was the first director of the motorization program. Under his direction, the first prototype panzer battalion was organized in 1927–1929. The Sixth Motor Battalion in Münster was converted into a unit of one motorcycle company, one armored car company, and one mock-tank company.[75] Von Vollard-Bockelberg coined the term "motorized fighting troops" to replace the more mundane "motor troops." Like Lutz, he supported every effort for motorization and armor study.

MISCONCEPTIONS ABOUT GERMAN ARMOR DEVELOPMENT

No aspect of Reichswehr history has suffered more from misinformation and faulty analysis than the early development of the German armor force. There is so much misinformation published about this subject that some corrections to the record are necessary. One relatively minor historical error concerning German armor development is in *Tanks of World War I*. Authors Peter Chamberlain and Chris Ellis asserted that the German tank units of that war "were ad hoc units composed of men drafted from artillery, engineer and signal battalions. They thus lacked the fighting spirit and self-esteem of the Allied tank men."[76] In fact, the German tank unit members in World War I were all volunteers, and many of them were drawn from the infantry as well.[77] Due to its small size, the German tank force may have been only minimally effective on the battlefield, but none of the German historians of early German armor—Volckheim,

Ludwig Ritter von Eimannsberger, Guderian, Nehring, and others—ever described the German tankers as lacking fighting spirit or self-esteem. Another common misconception—that the Germans merely copied British technology in their first tanks—has been dealt with in Chapter Five.

Yet another example of poor analysis can be found in Albert Seaton's *The German Army, 1933–45*, wherein Seaton argued that "in the early days, under von Seeckt, there had been no intention of developing the Kraftfahrtruppe [motor transport troops] as a main fighting arm. . . . [I]t was at first a resting place, a niche in which officers could be held on the active list."[78] In reply, notice that it was von Seeckt who turned tank training and development over to the Inspectorate of Motor Troops in 1924–25, thus setting the stage for that arm to evolve into the panzer force. In the immediate postwar era, the Reichswehr assigned its few experienced tank officers, such as Captain Thofehrn and Lieutenant Volckheim, to the motor transport troops—an indication that, from the beginning, the Reichswehr planned to create a tank force within that branch. As for the motor transport troops being a niche, von Tschischwitz, who commanded them in the early 1920s, was by 1927 appointed to command Group 1, one of the two Reichswehr field commands equivalent to an army. Other motor troop senior officers of the 1920s, such as von Vollard-Bockelberg and Lutz, reached top positions in the army. A better case can be made that, in the early 1920s, the Reichswehr assigned highly competent officers to the motor troops. The early days of the Reichswehr also saw junior officers such as Heinz Guderian and Ritter von Thoma assigned to the motor troops.

Unfortunately, in the mass of books written since World War II on the history of German armored development, three serious misconceptions have been so often repeated and popularized that they have become real obstacles to a sound understanding of German Army doctrine and organization in the interwar period: (1) that Heinz Guderian was virtually the sole creator of Germany's armored forces and doctrine; (2) that Guderian and other armor enthusiasts had to struggle against a reactionary high command and General Staff; and (3) that German armor doctrine was a direct development of ideas taken from British military theorists. There is some truth in all of these assertions. Guderian played a central role in the development of the panzer division in the 1930s; there were some reactionaries in the General Staff—as one might expect of any organization; and there was some influence on German armor doctrine by British tank theorists, notably General J. F. C. Fuller. Still, taken singly or in combination, each assertion created a skewed picture of German armor development.

The emphasis upon Heinz Guderian's role comes primarily from Guderian's autobiography, published in Germany in 1950 as *Erinnerungen eines Soldaten* and which since has undergone several printings, the latest in 1979.[79] Shortly afterward, an English-language edition of Guderian's memoirs appeared that was edited by Basil Liddell Hart. Liddell Hart also emphasized Guderian's role in *The German Generals Talk*, written in 1948. Both of these English-language books have gone through many print runs and remain popular. More attention has been paid to Guderian than to any other German general with the exception of Erwin Rommel. Not only has Guderian been the subject of English and German biographies,[80] but he has become virtually the only name that many military writers associate with pre–World War II German armor.

Guderian's beginning in mechanized warfare dates to 1922, when as a captain and General Staff Corps officer, he was assigned to the Inspectorate of Motor Troops. In Berlin, on the inspectorate staff, he wrote staff studies and learned something of the technical side of motorized warfare. He served as an instructor of tactics and military history in the Second Division from 1924 to 1927. He then returned to the Truppenamt, where he was again engaged in studying motor transport. In 1928 Guderian began teaching tank tactics at the motor transport technical course set up near Berlin. He continued studying and teaching tank tactics and in 1930 served as commander of a motorized battalion near Berlin. In 1931, when he became a lieutenant colonel, Guderian was assigned to serve as chief of staff of the Inspectorate of Motor Troops, at that time headed by Oswald Lutz. In 1934, when Lutz was appointed the first commander of panzer troops, Guderian again became his chief of staff. In 1935, while still a colonel, Guderian became the commander of one of Germany's first three panzer divisions. In 1938, when Lutz was relieved by Hitler, Guderian became chief of mobile troops. During World War II, Guderian served as a corps and army commander. In 1944 he became chief of the General Staff.[81]

If Guderian had been a modest man and never written a word about himself, he would have gone down in history as an excellent general, a first-rate tactician, and a man who played a central role in establishing and developing the first panzer divisions. But Guderian was far from modest. By his own account, he was the central figure in German tank development from the 1920s on. Echoes of this refrain are found in the accounts of Guderian's biographers and his many admirers.[82]

For example, Kenneth Macksey made much of Guderian's early articles on armor and motorized war:

As he [Guderian] read more deeply into his subject there began to appear profound conclusions drawn from his study of ancient and contemporary history. This led to the pursuit of a pastime which used to absorb the old Prussian General Staff—prodigious writing in military journals. Encouraged by General von Altrock, the Editor of the *Militär Wochenblatt*, he composed articles (some of them anonymous?) which crystallised his thoughts and his style and, at the same time, won him a reputation for clear exposition on controversial matters of immediate interest in the contemporary debate surrounding the reasons for Germany losing the last war. But it also won him enemies, for at this early stage the tank enthusiasts proposed converting the cavalry to mechanised divisions.[83]

As a matter of fact, Heinz Guderian wrote only five signed articles for the *Militär Wochenblatt* between 1922 and 1928, all of them mundane pieces, including "French Motorized Supply at Verdun" and "Reconnaissance and Security for Motor Marches."[84] Guderian's tactical articles tended to be short pieces of only a page or two, such as "Cavalry and Armored Cars"[85] and "Troops on Motor Vehicles and Air Defense."[86] Such articles were not revolutionary but rather typical expressions of contemporary tactics. In the 1920s, Guderian's "prodigious" military writing was actually rather meager, no match for either the sheer volume or the originality of Ernst Volckheim's. Guderian's major work on armored warfare was *Achtung! Panzer!* written in 1936-37. This work detailed the tactics and operations of the new panzer division in wartime. *Achtung! Panzer!* was indeed a brilliant and original book, but it was the product of a long evolution of armored thought that relied heavily on the work of previous armor theorists, most particularly the Austrian general (later German armor general) Ludwig Ritter von Eimannsberger, whose major book, *The Tank War* (Der Kampfwagenkrieg), was published in 1934 and gained a wide audience in the German Army.[87]

Even for an autobiography, Guderian's *Panzer Leader* goes in for too much self-aggrandizement. Volckheim, for example, receives passing mention in one sentence of the book.[88] Lutz is heartily praised—mostly for his support of Guderian's ideas after he became Lutz's chief of staff in 1931.[89] Other officers who contributed significantly to German armor development in the 1920s and 1930s, men like Pirner, Heigl, von Eimannsberger, von Vollard-Bockelberg, and the many officers who trained in the Kazan tank school, are glossed over or not mentioned at all in Guderian's account. The Guderian version of German armored development might best be contrasted with General Walther Nehring's *The History of the German Panzer Corps 1916 to 1945* (Die Geschichte der deutschen Panzerwaffe 1916 bis 1945), which carefully details the work of dozens of German officers who contributed to the development of German armor.

In short, the army high command's documented enthusiasm for motorization, the technical accomplishments of the Weapons Office in tank and vehicle design, the theoretical work of Volckheim and others, the motorization experiments of the Inspectorate of Motor Troops and the tank school in Kazan all combined with von Seeckt's doctrine of a war of maneuver and the emphasis upon combined-arms tactics provided a broad theoretical basis for the blitzkrieg of World War II. Thanks to the maneuvers of the 1920s, the German Army was well prepared to create a modern armored force with a sound combat doctrine when rearmament began in earnest in the 1930s. Although Guderian's role was important, he was by no means indispensable as the creator of the panzer troops. As the military historian Colonel Trevor N. Dupuy put it, "Guderian was undoubtedly the leader of the movement toward armor-warfare doctrine, but it is evident that there were a number of other young General Staff officers with comparable opinions and similar capability, who could readily have provided the leadership in his stead."[90]

The second major misconception—that Guderian and other tank enthusiasts had to struggle against a reactionary military establishment—is also based mainly upon Guderian's version of events. With regard to the early experiments using motorized troops in exercises, a program that Guderian helped plan between 1921 and 1924, he quoted Colonel von Natzmer, then inspector of motor transport troops, as ridiculing the idea of using motor troops in a combat role: "They're supposed to carry flour."[91] Guderian did not point out, however, that von Natzmer was thoroughly out of step with von Seeckt and the Truppenamt. In every yearly *Observations of the Chief of the Army Command* from 1920 to 1925, von Seeckt stressed the importance of motorized transport for combat troops. Exercises using motor troops in a combat role were praised by von Tschischwitz, von Natzmer's predecessor, and included in the *Observations of the Chief of the Army Command* of 1922.[92]

In many ways, Guderian was like Ludendorff: a brilliant man but an extremist and an egotist, with a personality that bordered on the fanatic. It is notable that Guderian was one of the few General Staff officers who supported Nazism with real enthusiasm. It was characteristic of him to represent any disagreement or even a lack of enthusiasm for his ideas as reflective of a reactionary military mind. Guderian expressed a hearty contempt for General Ludwig Beck, chief of the General Staff from 1935 to 1938, whom he characterized as hostile to ideas of modern mechanized war: "He [Beck] was a paralyzing element wherever he appeared. . . . [S]ignificant of his way of thought was his much-boosted method of fighting which he called 'delaying defense.' "[93] This is a crude caricature of a highly competent general who authored Army Regulation 300 (*Troop Leadership*) in 1933, the primary tactical manual of the German Army in World War II, and under whose direction the first three panzer divisions were created in 1935, the largest such force in the world of the time. The "delaying defense" that Guderian ridiculed was not Beck's creation—it had been the standard defensive doctrine since 1921.

This image of the military prophet struggling against great odds is attractive to military historians. Nevertheless, it does not fairly reflect the experience of Guderian or the German armor theorists in the 1920s and 1930s. The careers of German tank and motorization advocates prospered. Guderian received his first divisional command while still a colonel. There is no German parallel to Dwight Eisenhower's experience in 1920, when he was rebuked by the U.S. Army's chief of infantry after having advocated a stronger tank force for infantry divisions and then was threatened with a court-martial if he continued publishing in that vein.[94] Guderian complained of a "very vocal opposition" to armored units in 1936,[95] at the very moment the German Army was creating armored and motorized units faster than it could equip them.

The third popular misconception about the German armored force— that its doctrine came directly from the works of British theorists—finds its source in the writings of Basil H. Liddell Hart. In Liddell Hart's edition of Guderian's memoirs, Guderian is correctly translated as saying, "It was principally the books and articles of the Englishmen Fuller, Liddell Hart and [Gifford] Martel, that excited my interest and gave me food for thought. These far sighted soldiers were even then [1920s] trying to make of the tank something more than just an infantry support weapon. They envisaged it in relationship to the growing motorization of our age, and thus they became the pioneers of a new type of warfare on the largest scale."[96] Then, in the English edition, Liddell Hart edited out a brief tribute by Guderian to Fritz Heigl, inserting the following paragraph, which does not appear in Guderian's own German edition:

> I learned from them [Fuller, Liddell Hart, Martel] the concentration of armor, as employed in the battle of Cambrai. Further, it was Liddell Hart who emphasized the use of armored forces for long-range strokes, operations against the opposing army's communications, and also proposed a type of armored division combining Panzer and Panzer-infantry units. Deeply impressed by these ideas, I tried to develop them in a sense practicable for our own army. So I owe many suggestions of our further development to Captain Liddell Hart."[97]

Basil Liddell Hart wanted very much to be acknowledged as the father of the successful German blitzkrieg tactics and specifically claimed this upon several occasions.[98] Liddell Hart's claim through Guderian that he greatly influenced German armor theorists and tactics has been accepted uncritically by many military historians.[99] A careful examination of prewar German books, documents, and articles yields no evidence that Liddell Hart was widely known in the German Army or that he had any influence whatsoever upon German tactical thinking. Guderian did not cite Liddell Hart as a source in *Achtung! Panzer!* nor did von Eimannsberger, Heigl, or Volckheim ever cite Liddell Hart or show any familiarity with his ideas. The great practitioner of armored warfare, Field Marshal Rommel, had never heard of Liddell Hart before he read an article of his in late 1942.[100] Some short articles by Liddell Hart written for the London *Daily Telegraph* were translated in the General Staff's journal of foreign military news and in the *Militär Wochenblatt* in the 1920s, but so were hundreds of other articles by a wide variety of American, French, British, Italian, and Polish junior officers.[101] This would have been the German Army's only familiarity with Liddell Hart in the 1920s as its armor doctrine was evolving.

This is not to say that Guderian and other German officers were not familiar with British theorists. J. F. C. Fuller was well known and highly regarded by the German Army in the 1920s. Fuller's reputation was not made by the brilliance of his theories, but because Fuller, as chief of staff of the wartime British Tank Corps, had planned the mass tank attack at Cambrai in 1917 and drawn up Plan 1919, in which the Allies had planned to overrun the German Army that year with masses of tanks. Fuller's writings were useful to the Germans, not because they appreciated his grand theories of war—the Germans already had their own theorists in Clausewitz, von Moltke, von Schlieffen, and, in the 1920s, von Seeckt—but because of the solid practicality of most of Fuller's ideas. In the 1920s it was hard, practical experience that the German armor tacticians lacked and sought in Fuller's writings. Fuller's first major book, *Tanks in the Great War* (1920), contained much useful information—for instance, how the British had organized their tank units, dealt with vehicle maintenance and repair, developed tank tactics, and created special armored engineer and supply support. The book even included organizational charts, maps, and diagrams of tank battle formations, as well as an analysis of major tank engagements and the lessons that had been learned. It was the best basic tank textbook available in the 1920s, and that is how the Germans used it.[102]

Fuller's works became popular at an early date in Germany. His subsequent, numerous writings on armored warfare were quickly translated and published in the *Militär Wochenblatt* and other journals. In 1926 the General Staff's journal of foreign military news devoted three issues to excerpting Fuller's book, *The Reformation of War*.[103] Other foreign military theorists did not get this kind of treatment by the Reichswehr. Ernst Volckheim's *The Tank in Modern Warfare* shows a strong Fuller influence in Volckheim's advocacy of specialized armored engineers. Heinz Guderian cited Fuller and British armor theorist Martel, in *Achtung! Panzer!*

Ludwig Ritter von Eimannsberger used Fuller as a major source in *The Tank War*. Fuller's memoirs were even translated into German.[104]

Although Fuller's ideas definitely had an impact on German armor theorists, the Germans cannot rightly be called disciples of Fuller or of Martel. The German tactical writers were, in the main, critical readers who carefully chose concepts—Fuller's and others'—that seemed reasonable and practical and discarded the rest. For example, the German battlefield tank formations of the 1920s and 1930s are straight from Fuller, but none of the German armor tacticians took Fuller's concept of using masses of small (one- or two-man) "tankettes" seriously. And as early as 1924, Volckheim felt free to adopt some Fuller ideas while rejecting his enthusiasm for light, fast tanks.

# CHAPTER SEVEN

# Developing a Reichswehr Air Doctrine

In 1919 the Air Service (Luftsreitkräfte), like the General Staff, initiated a systematic program of studying the lessons of the war. On November 13, 1919, the Air Service Headquarters established a plan for analyzing the war experience to develop new manuals and regulations for the air arm. The work load was evenly distributed among a group of experienced flying officers, most with squadron command or General Staff experience. This initial program would examine three major aspects of army air support: (1) air unit organization; (2) combat tactics; and (3) technical developments affecting air power. Eighty-three officers were assigned to twenty-one subcommittees on these three topics. They would consider such subjects as supply organization of the Air Service, enemy technology, aerial weaponry, ground facilities, cooperation with ground forces, and a technical examination of all types of combat and support aircraft.[1]

The officers assigned to the study committees were primarily captains and first lieutenants. Despite their relatively junior rank, however, most of these officers were experienced commanders. Some, like Captains Kurt Student and Helmut Wilberg, had already been admitted to the General Staff Corps. Several, like Captain Hugo Sperrle, would become famous generals in World War II. Two weeks after the Air Service had initiated its program, General von Seeckt issued his directives for organizing the General Staff into committees for studying the war (see Chapter Two). Von Seeckt's order was passed on to the Air Service in December 1919, and additional study groups and committees were formed to provide a truly comprehensive picture of the war experience as a basis for outlining recommendations for improving air doctrine.[2] In some ways, the Air Service went beyond the requirements set by von Seeckt. Already the most technically oriented branch of the army, the Air Service set up a special committee to study the technical and industrial aspects of aerial warfare. This committee of thirty-one officers, generally men with technical experience or engineering degrees, was established on December 4, 1919.[3]

In late December 1919 another twenty-seven committees were formed to study specific organizational and tactical questions.[4] By the beginning of 1920, over 130 of the best Air Service officers were busy writing study papers or serving on committees. Many officers served on two or three of the committees set up in November and December 1919. The senior offi-

cers of the Air Service were directly involved in the work. Lieutenant
Colonel Wilhelm Siegert, Air Service chief of staff during the war, served
as the senior officer for more than twenty officers studying homeland defense.[5] The questions and problems dealt with by the officers illustrate
that by 1918 the German Air Service had become a highly sophisticated
force for army tactical support and home air defense. The tactical air support of the field army was the primary subject for the twenty-seven special study groups established on December 24, 1919. Five of these study
groups were devoted to reconnaissance and observation. Eight groups
were formed to study tactical support of ground troops and cooperation
between air and ground units.[6] Three committees were formed to study
air defense, including methods of combating enemy fighters and gaining
air superiority.[7] The remaining committees examined more specialized aspects of aerial warfare, including supply organization, air support in
mountain operations, and air operations over the ocean.[8]

More of the original study papers and committee discussion reports of
the Air Service have survived than those of the ground forces. Therefore,
it is easier to develop a more detailed picture of the Air Service's program
than of the ground forces' program.[9] For example, one of the major topics
of discussion for the Air Service in 1919-20 was the best organization for
army observation and support units. The tendency was to recommend
the adoption of balanced support groups of four squadrons: one squadron for observation and ground support, one squadron of twelve planes
for ground attack, one squadron for artillery observation, and one squadron of liaison aircraft.[10] Several study papers recommended that an air
squadron of four liaison aircraft, four observation aircraft, several "C" aircraft (heavily-armed two-seater observation and attack aircraft), and several ground attack aircraft be attached to each fighting division.[11] The necessity of organizing large divisional air squadrons incorporating support,
observation, and attack aircraft was the consensus of the experienced air
commanders.

The most striking feature of the Air Service's 1919-20 analysis of the
wartime operations is the general lack of interest in strategic air operations. Although Siegert was an expert on bombing operations, and
bomber commanders such as Captain Ernst Brandenburg, pour le mérite
commander of bombing raids against England, were available to study the
issue of bombing, neither the General Staff nor the Air Service established
any committees or study groups to deal with the subject. Only one paper
on strategic bombing was submitted, in 1920, to Truppenamt T-4 (Air Section), which coordinated the study effort after the dissolution of the Air
Service in May 1920, and it was the translation of an article by Italian Air
Force captain Amedeo Mecozzi.[12] Later in the 1920s the Reichswehr commissioned several studies on heavy bomber tactics and the wartime expe-

rience. One study summarizes attacks and subsequent damage inflicted upon Germany by the Allied strategic bombing campaign.[13] Another highly technical report of the mid-1920s was on bombing accuracy and bombing patterns of various types of bombs; it included Polish, French, Italian and U.S. data as well as many aerial strike photographs from the war.[14] Most of the surviving postwar studies on bombers, however, concern the tactical role of heavy bombers in supporting ground armies.[15]

In one postwar study, the British bombing attacks against German rail centers behind the Somme front in 1916 were discussed as an example of the effective use of heavy bombers.[16] The German bombing attacks against the French and British rail lines and supply centers in support of the 1918 Ludendorff offensives were discussed as another example of the successful utilization of the bomber force.[17] The use of slow, heavy bombers in direct tactical support of front line troops was ruled out, for heavy bomber losses had occurred when this was tried in 1918. All-metal armored ground-attack aircraft were deemed the most suitable for the specialized role of front-line support.[18] In the postwar German studies, heavy bombers were styled as army and army-group support weapons for use against military targets in the rear communications zone whose disruption would directly and immediately affect the fighting efficiency of troops on the front lines. The German Air Service, painfully aware of the failure of its 1917-18 strategic bombing campaign to inflict serious damage upon the enemy, had clearly decided in 1920-21 against strategic bombing of the enemy homeland as a serious military option. Although further study in the 1920s and 1930s slightly relaxed the German prejudice against strategic bombing, the early postwar attitude concerning strategic bombing remained prevalent. The Germans still saw a role for the heavy bomber force, but only as an army-led support weapon.

The German Air Service, superior to its opponents in fighter tactics during the war, considered ways to improve fighter unit organization and tactics in the next war. Erhard Milch, a future Luftwaffe field marshal and a World War I commander of both fighter and observation squadrons, served as the senior officer on the committee studying the battle for air supremacy.[19] In "The Struggle for Air Supremacy," a study written in January-February 1920, Milch emphasized that in a future war, fighter planes should have the top aircraft production priority, with second priority going to observation and support aircraft.[20]

In October 1920 a board of eleven wartime fighter unit commanders presented its recommendations for future fighter unit organization to Truppenamt T-4 (Air Section). The fighter organization committee was a particularly distinguished and experienced group, containing three pour le mérite fliers: First Lieutenant Bolle; Lieutenants Jakobs and Degelow; and future Luftwaffe generals, Captains Sperrle, Student, and Wilberg.[21]

The fighter unit committee recommended large fighter groups of six squadrons but unanimously agreed that using a wing of several groups as a tactical organization was impractical. Most of the board recommended a fighter group containing both one- and two-seater aircraft. After some debate and considerable disagreement, most of the board concluded that several fighter squadrons could be commanded in battle by one commander. For this type of complicated aerial coordination, however, improvements in air-to-air radio communication were necessary. The board made other recommendations unanimously: a squadron commander should fly with his men and not command from the ground, and fighter airfields should be as close as possible to the front lines.[22] Wartime experience had taught the Air Service that concentration and command of fighter forces was a primary tactical requirement for aerial victory.

VON SEECKT AND THE REICHSWEHR'S AIR FORCE

The Versailles Treaty ordered the Germans to disband their Air Service and prohibited Germany from having any military aviation whatsoever. This was a particularly hard blow to German military pride, because unlike the army, the Air Service was an effective fighting force to the very end and could honestly claim never to have been truly defeated in battle. On November 11, 1918, the German Air Service possessed 2,570 modern combat aircraft and 4,500 aircrew at the front. The total military aircraft inventory in November 1918 was probably close to the 15,000 aircraft that were turned over to the Allies as part of the peace process.[23]

Naturally, the German General Staff wanted to preserve such a superb weapon. General Hans von Seeckt, as the General Staff's representative to the Versailles Peace Conference, tried to secure for Germany permission to possess an air force of 1,800 aircraft and 10,000 personnel.[24] Von Seeckt, recognizing the importance of air power, found the denial of an air force to Germany one of the most unbearable aspects of the treaty.[25] He persistently tried to renegotiate the Versailles air provisions until in May 1920, under Allied pressure, the German Air Service was formally disbanded.[26] The Reichswehr then attempted to preserve an air force in the form of "police" air squadrons, equipped with military aircraft, which officially belonged to the German states. By 1920-21, however, even this small force was ordered to disband.[27]

Von Seeckt was regarded by the German air officers to be a strong advocate of military air power. He favored the development of military aviation as an independent branch of the armed forces, coequal with the army and navy.[28] Upon becoming chief of the army command, von Seeckt fought the Army Personnel Office to retain 180 flying officers for the Reichswehr, an action that many considered unnecessary for an army that was not allowed any aircraft.[29] Von Seeckt won that particular bureaucratic battle, ensuring that a carefully selected group of air officers was maintained within the Reichswehr to provide a foundation for the eventual resurgence of German air power. Von Seeckt created a small air staff within the Army Headquarters and prepared a small, secret air force for the Reichswehr complete with a training program for pilots and aircrew. All of this required the allocation of secret government funds and support, which he managed to obtain. In the words of General der Flieger Wilhelm Wimmer, "Seeckt used all of his influence and ability to protect his group of fliers against attacks all the way up to cabinet level."[30]

By March 1920, while the Air Service was being disbanded, von Seeckt was fashioning a shadow air force staff within the Truppenamt and Reichswehr Ministry Headquarters. The most important center for the shadow air force was the Air Organization Office, known as TA-L ("L" for "Luft"—"air") within the Truppenamt T-2 (Organization Section). TA-L was headed by recently promoted Major Helmut Wilberg. Officially, Wilberg was just another staff officer in the Organization Section; in reality, he was the primary officer responsible for air force planning and training, reporting directly to the chief of the Truppenamt.[31] Another flying officer was placed in Truppenamt T-3 (Intelligence Section) and was responsible for compiling information on foreign air forces. Several flying officers were assigned to the Weapons Office, where an Air Technical Office was created; it was responsible for aircraft development, testing, and procurement. In 1920 this office was headed by a technically minded General Staff officer and experienced flier, Captain Kurt Student.[32]

Throughout the 1920s, the shadow air force was well represented at the Reichswehr Ministry Headquarters. In 1927 Helmut Wilberg was on the staff of the chief of the Truppenamt, flying officers Major (later Field Marshal) Sperrle and Captain Reinicke manned the Air Organization Office in T-2, and Major von dem Hagen served as the air officer in T-3.[33] The strongest representation of the shadow air force in the Reichswehr Ministry was in the Weapons Office, where normally six of the approximately sixty assigned officers were airmen.[34] Like the Reichswehr itself, the shadow air force was a small but competently staffed organization for planning, training, and conducting research. Through the air staff, von Seeckt ensured that the framework was left in place around which a real air force could later be built.

Von Seeckt insisted that the Reichswehr, as a modern field army, was to be "air-minded." Therefore, a small air staff of usually three flying officers was assigned to each of the seven military district headquarters. They were to ensure that air tactics and technology were studied within the Reichswehr and that air power would be taken into account in all troop training. Simulated air attacks and aerial observation were developed by the military air staff as a normal part of command exercises and divisional maneuvers.[35] Von Seeckt ordered that the 180 flying officers be spread throughout the Reichswehr. The 1927 officers' roster, for example, reveals that officers with combat experience in the Air Service—indicated by the possession of the Imperial Army's pilot and observer badges in the officers' decorations rosters—were to be found in almost every regiment of the army. Flying officers operated under a dual chain of command, carrying out their normal military duties with their units but also subject to assignment and detachment for flying courses by the Reichswehr's shadow air command.[36]

The officers assigned to flying duties in the USSR were officially retired from the Reichswehr for the duration of their duty there, only to be readmitted to the army with their rank and previous promotion seniority upon their return.[37] The 1927 officers' roster shows that only 134 war-experienced flying officers were officially on duty with the Reichswehr that year, far too low a figure to account for the 180 flying officers brought into the Reichswehr in 1920, even accepting some attrition by death and retirement. The air training conducted in the USSR in the 1920s accounts for the low official figure. As many as 32 of the Reichswehr's experienced pilots served in Russia each year in the late 1920s.[38] The officers' rosters of the 1920s also indicate that a disproportionately large share of the experienced pilots were assigned to the Reichswehr's three small cavalry divisions, which were only 15 percent of the total Reichswehr strength. In 1927, a typical year, more than 20 percent of the fliers were assigned to the cavalry.[39] Since the cavalry divisions of the Reichswehr were "over-officered" in comparison with the rest of the army, the cavalry was probably used as a holding unit for flying officers, who could thus be detached more easily for service by the Air Organization Office.[40]

Although von Seeckt did cleverly build—and hide—a secret air corps, he cannot be counted among the contributors to Germany's air doctrine. He recognized the importance of a large air force as a major tactical weapon, part of a combined-arms force that could assist the ground armies in gaining the victory. This was a continuation of the views held by a majority of the General Staff in 1918. In his own writings, von Seeckt emphasized the importance of gaining air superiority by initially concentrating air attacks against enemy airfields.[41] Upon gaining air superiority, the air force would be diverted to major tactical targets, with top priority going to the disruption of the enemy's mobilization and supply centers.[42] Long-range aerial reconnaissance in support of the ground armies would remain a major mission of the air force.[43] At no time did von Seeckt express even the slightest interest in strategic air warfare or in the bombing of enemy cities.

Recognizing that he was neither an air tactician nor an air strategist, von Seeckt listened carefully to his air officers, respecting them enough to argue their positions to others. Captain Helmut Wilberg served as von Seeckt's air adviser in 1919 and drew up the plan for a postwar air force of eighteen hundred aircraft. Von Seeckt was impressed with Wilberg's work; he presented the plan, unaltered, to the Allied peace negotiators, urging its acceptance.[44]

In his visits to the Reichswehr's units and field exercises, von Seeckt constantly reminded the army's senior officers of the importance of taking air power into consideration. In his annual *Commander's Remarks to the Army*, von Seeckt devoted an entire section, usually two out of twenty pages, to air defense issues, along with sharp criticisms and recommendations for improvements.[45] In the 1923 report, he directed that aircraft be represented more often in army training and recommended the new tactical manual *Leadership and Battle* as a guide for simulating aircraft action.[46]

Hans von Seeckt's most important achievement in laying the foundation for a future air force was the militarization of civil aviation in the 1920s, which turned virtually the whole aircraft industry and civilian airlines into a military reserve force. Since Germany was denied a military air force, von Seeckt used his not-inconsiderable political skills to ensure that civil aviation would be directed by former military flying officers who would enthusiastically cooperate with the Reichswehr. After World War I the most important aviation post in Germany was director of the Aviation Branch in the Reich Transportation Ministry. Von Seeckt arranged for the post to go to Captain Ernst Brandenburg, one of Germany's top military aviators who had been a bomber-wing commander during the war. This appointment was accomplished only after some political outcry, for Brandenburg had led bombing missions against England and a strong foreign protest was expected.[47] Brandenburg held the post of director of the Aviation Branch from 1924 to 1933, working closely with von Seeckt to ensure the development of civil aviation along militarily favorable lines.[48]

Erhard Milch, another army captain and wartime squadron commander who had been accepted to the General Staff during the war, left the army in 1920 and entered civil aviation. He showed great aptitude and business sense for the airline industry. By 1924 he was one of the leaders of German civil aviation. In 1925 Ernst Brandenburg, who controlled government subsidies to civil aviation and who pushed a policy of airline consolidation, ruled that the two major civilian air companies in Germany—Junkers and Aero-Lloyd—were to merge into one large national airline: Deutsche Lufthansa.[49] Milch was devoted to civilian aviation but also to military aviation. His good friend and wartime commander was

Wilberg, with whom he maintained an extensive correspondence on military aviation in the 1920s.[50]

Former Air Service pilots came to dominate German civil aviation. Fritz Siebel, a wartime pilot officer and postwar aircraft manufacturer, received subsidies from Brandenburg's office to set up Sportflug GmbH (Sportflying LTD) in 1924. Ostensibly a civilian pilot-training school, Sportflug was actually a front for military pilot training. It would grow into a system of ten pilot schools spread throughout the Reich.[51] Other pilot schools and aircraft enterprises that were useful to the Reichswehr received government subsidies from the Transportation Ministry.[52] The directorate of civil aviation also sponsored aeronautical research programs at the request of the Reichswehr.[53] With Brandenburg, Milch, and other former officers holding key positions in Germany's aviation industry, German civil aviation in the 1920s was thoroughly militarized. Only in the Soviet Union could one say that civil aviation worked so closely with the military. Lufthansa became, in effect, a reserve air force. All of this stems from von Seeckt's astute judgment in recognizing the importance of civil aviation for the Reichswehr's air development and in securing Brandenburg's appointment as civil aviation director.

## HELMUT WILBERG AND THE CREATION
## OF A REICHSWEHR AIR DOCTRINE

During the 1920s and 1930s, Helmut Wilberg became the leading air theorist for the Reichswehr. As a captain and member of the General Staff Corps, Wilberg was appointed the first chief of the Air Organization Office in March 1920—a post he held until 1927.[54] The Air Organization Office served as the central agency for all Reichswehr aviation matters.[55] Wilberg's flying experience and wartime record were impressive. He was one of the first pilots in the German Army, having received the civil pilot's license number 26 in September 1910.[56] Before World War I, he served with the army's Aviation Inspectorate.[57] During the war, he commanded the air units in support of the First and Fourth German armies.[58] In the first half of the war, Wilberg served with General von Seeckt as the air staff officer for the Southern Army Group during the Macedonian campaign.[59] During 1919 he was on the staff of General Thomsen, chief of the Air Service, and then with the Prussian War Ministry, where he served as von Seeckt's air adviser for the Versailles negotiations as well.[60] According to historian Mathew Cooper, von Seeckt, particularly impressed by Wilberg's outline for a postwar German air force, appointed him the Truppenamt's air chief in 1919.[61] Thus, even though the position of chief of the Air Organization Office was not officially created until March 1920, Wilberg was already acting as the Truppenamt's air expert in 1919.

In 1919 and 1920, Wilberg served as chief editor for the study papers and committee reports produced by Air Service officers as part of the evaluation of the wartime lessons.[62] Wilberg also wrote special studies on tactical air power[63] and on the Air Service's supply system.[64] In the latter study, Wilberg admitted that the Allied aircraft industry was more efficient than the German but that until the end of the war, the German manufacturers and supply system had done a good job of getting replacement matériel to the front. He denied that the failure of the German offensive in 1918 was due to a shortage of aircraft. The only major supply shortage that caused some inconvenience that year was gasoline. Wilberg asserted that the major problem of the Air Service in 1918 was the shortage of pilots and personnel. The problem of replacing personnel losses became progressively worse throughout that year, and the situation was one of simply too few units and personnel compared with Allied air power. Still, according to Wilberg, the German Air Service remained a potent force right up to the armistice in November 1918.[65]

Wilberg came out of World War I as one of Germany's most highly regarded air tacticians. Described by General Freiherr von Bülow as an "energetic and clear-headed officer," Wilberg was appointed air commander for the Fourth Army in Flanders during the critical battles of 1917.[66] General Max Schwarte, in his 1922 history of the German Army in the war, described the performance of the Air Service in Flanders as the "high point of its organizational, technical and tactical development," singling out Wilberg's leadership for special praise.[67] In response to the British offensives, Wilberg reorganized thc Fourth Army's air units, seeking to create large tactical formations. During some periods in 1917-18, he had seventy squadrons under his command.[68] Wilberg was the first German air commander to organize and employ entire air groups in the ground attack role. He was regarded by the army as one of the pioneers of ground-support tactics.[69]

When Wilberg became chief of the Air Organization Office, one of his primary duties was to keep a file of former Air Service personnel and civil aviation installations, aircraft, and matériel that could be mobilized in time of war. Wilberg compiled the records of all the wartime pilots, observers, and aircrew, keeping in contact with them through the Ring deutscher Flieger, a Reichswehr-sponsored Air Service veterans association led by Colonel Siegert.[70] Wilberg's files, one of the most extensive surviving document collections of the Reichswehr, contain careful inventories of the air facilities, aircraft, and personnel available to the Reichswehr in time of emergency.[71]

Wilberg's mobilization preparations also led him to carry out a signifi-

cant amount of work in the field of industrial planning.[72] He was assisted
in this work by air industry executives, mostly former officers, whose
correspondence with him is evidence of the strong bonds within the Air
Service. Milch and Wilberg were wartime friends (Wilberg had given
Milch a squadron command) and Milch wrote regularly to Wilberg, detailing technical problems within the aircraft industry, as well as providing reports of Lufthansa's considerable experience with long-distance flights.[73]
Other companies also shared their information readily with the Air Organization Office.[74]

As the Reichswehr's leading air officer, Wilberg carried on the General
Staff tradition of regularly assigning special tactical and historical studies.
Some of the papers from Wilberg's tenure as chief of the Air Organization
Office include a detailed technical report on bombing patterns and accu-
racy,[75] a study of tactical air support in 1918,[76] and a study of night fighter
tactics.[77]

During his tenure as chief of the Air Organization Office, Wilberg edited
a series of tactical air manuals, distributing them to the Reichswehr air officers. In order to deceive the Interallied Military Control Commission,
the pamphlets—called "green mail" (*Grüne Post*) because they had green
covers—were usually entitled "Compilations from the Publications of
Foreign Air Forces." In reality, these documents represented the air doctrine of the Truppenamt. One copy, entitled "An Officer's Study of the Air
Weapon and Its Use," was essentially a manual for the organization and
employment of army-level tactical air support. Green mail was undated,
but internal evidence puts this publication in the 1925–1926 period.[78]
The manual contains a complete table for organization of tactical air support. Each division would have an observation squadron of nine aircraft
assigned to it, and each corps would have a small squadron of six long-
range reconnaissance aircraft and six artillery observation planes. The
army headquarters would have six long-range reconnaissance and six
night reconnaissance aircraft.[79]

The shadow air force manual specified that bomber, fighter, and
ground-support aircraft would be organized into brigades, or wings, of
two groups. Each group would consist of three squadrons. A brigade
would consist of ninety-four two-seater fighters; mixed brigades of one-
and two-seater fighters would have the same number of planes. Night
fighter brigades would have sixty aircraft, day bomber brigades sixty-
eight aircraft, and night bomber brigades thirty-eight aircraft.[80] The manual outlines the principles of army-level tactical air operations, including
an explanation of how division- and army-level reconnaissance would
work[81] and of the roles of fighters and bombers. Wilberg's wartime experience is evident in the manual. The role of the fighter is still primarily
bomber escort and air defense. The manual cautions against using fighters

in a deep penetration of enemy airspace because of the heavy losses that can be expected in an offensive air battle. Only when a decisive effect can be attained should fighters be sent deep into enemy territory.[82]

A strategic role as well as a tactical one is assigned to the bomber force: "The battle mission [of bombers] is to strike the enemy forces and his major sources of economic strength."[83] The strategic mission, however, is downplayed: "The primary mission of the bomber forces assigned to the field army is the battle against the enemy forces and their supply."[84] Concentrated bomber attacks against a few targets is preferred to striking numerous targets. German research into bombing rated the bomb load of a day bomber brigade at a medium range of 200–300 kilometers as 20 tons, that of a night bomber brigade as 36 tons.[85] The manual recommends that fighter bases be placed 20–40 kilometers from the front, and day bomber bases 40–60 kilometers from the front. Air installation layouts and recommended runway lengths are set out in detail.[86]

Essentially, this manual reflects a practical, balanced approach that emphasizes the tactical use of air power. It recalls the importance of organizing the air support units to meet the requirements of each specific mission and at all times, it stresses the creation of a proper mix of aircraft types.

The Reichswehr's primary tactical regulation, *Leadership and Battle with Combined Arms*, contains several sections on the use of air power. The air unit organization and battle tactics outlined in the regulation are the result of the Air Service studies written in 1919-20 and edited by Wilberg. Part 1 of *Leadership and Battle*, published in 1921, contains two sections on aerial reconnaissance and air support.[87] The importance of constant liaison between ground and air forces is highlighted throughout. Heavy bombers are recommended for tactical employment in the support of ground troops against enemy targets outside of artillery range. Since the Germans regarded the heavy bomber as vulnerable to enemy fighters, the tactical manual recommended that these weapons be used only at night.[88] Enemy rail centers and supply points are named as the most important heavy bomber targets.[89] The air power sections of *Leadership and Battle*, Part 1, reflect the experience of the Air Service of 1917-18, except for the view—possibly inserted by von Seeckt—that fighter planes should wage an offensive battle over enemy lines to gain air superiority.[90]

The second part of *Leadership and Battle*, published in 1923, contains even more (thirty-three pages) on air defense and air force tactics. Tactical air support for ground troops is still emphasized. The basic principles of fighter combat are presented in some detail. For example, the concentration of large fighter groups is recommended.[91] Pilots are reminded that superior altitude and direction (for example, flying out of the sun) are essential to a fighter's success.[92] Ground forces are advised to also bear in mind the enemy's air power. Extensive camouflage, constant changes of troop positions and other methods of passive air defense are described.[93] *Leadership and Battle* discusses every aspect of aerial warfare, from air support in the war of maneuver to air tactics when the army is on the defensive. The whole impression is of an air-minded army with a practical air doctrine. The German approach is even more striking when it is compared with the French Army's primary postwar tactical manual, *Regulation for the Tactical Employment of Large Forces* (published in 1921).[94] The Reichswehr's tactical manual devotes considerably more text and detail to the employment of tactical air forces than does the French manual, and the role of air power in war receives more emphasis in the German manual than in the French.

## THE STUDY OF FOREIGN AIR DOCTRINE

In the 1920s, the British, American, and Italian air doctrines evolved in a strikingly different fashion from that of the Reichswehr. The air doctrine of these Allied nations endorsed the ideas of the more radical strategic bombing theorists. The Royal Air Force (RAF) was the first to establish strategic bombing as a basic tenet of military air doctrine. In April 1918 the British cabinet, emotionally charged by the German bombing campaign against London—which the Germans would soon end—pushed an air law through Parliament transforming the Royal Flying Corps into the Royal Air Force, a military force equivalent to the British Army and Royal Navy. British politicians, including David Lloyd George and Winston Churchill, and such military leaders as Field Marshal Jan Smuts wanted to see Germany severely bombed from the air. In June 1918 General Hugh Trenchard of the RAF organized the Independent Air Force, a strategic bomber force with which he promised to paralyze German war production.[95] The British bombing campaign against Germany, like the German campaign against England, was a failure. The loss of 352 RAF bombers in the 1918 campaign probably cost the British more money than the damage that the whole British bombing campaign inflicted on the Germans.[96] Despite the dismal performance of the Independent Air Force, its commander, Trenchard, a true believer in strategic bombing, went on to become the postwar chief of the air staff until 1929.

Trenchard's personality dominated the RAF during its formative years, saddling the new service with a poorly conceived doctrine of aerial warfare. Trenchard had a grandiose vision of aerial warfare: He believed that a large strategic air force could win wars single-handedly[97] and that the

RAF would become a strategic offensive weapon. In 1922 he proposed that the RAF Home Force should consist of twenty-four day bomber squadrons, fifteen night bomber squadrons, and thirteen fighter squadrons, for a 3:1 bomber-to-fighter ratio.[98]

For Trenchard, attack was the best form of aerial warfare. This was in line with the wartime tradition of the RAF, which from 1916 to the end of the war had persisted in carrying the air war to the Germans regardless of losses. Trenchard's, and thus the RAF's, doctrine of offensive warfare was more akin to religious faith than systematic analysis of the wartime experience. In fact, the British air doctrine of World War I proved to be a bloodbath for British fliers. The British air losses against the Germans virtually equaled the total German air losses against all opponents.[99] Yet despite the horrendous casualty figures, neither Trenchard nor his staff were inclined to question the basis for the RAF's offensive air doctrine.

In the 1920s the RAF gained some practical experience bombing rebellious Iraqi and Afghan tribesmen into submission. From these small campaigns against primitive peoples with no means of air defense, grand military conclusions were drawn about the effects of bombing civilians, the effectiveness of the aircraft, and bombing accuracy.[100] Interestingly, no thorough scientific study was made by the postwar RAF about the effectiveness of their 1918 bombing campaign, even though that would have been a far firmer basis upon which to build an air doctrine.[101] Trenchard's legacy to the RAF would be his unshakable faith in the efficacy of strategic bombing. Even in the late 1930s, the RAF preferred to commit most of its resources to Bomber Command. However, in 1936-37, the government compelled the RAF to commit more resources to Fighter Command. This decision, contrary to the wishes of the majority of the air staff, would save Britain in 1940.[102]

While Trenchard was imbuing the RAF with his theories of strategic air warfare, many U.S. Army Air Corps officers were moving toward a similar position. In the first few years after World War I, the U.S. Army tended toward a balanced air doctrine. The 1923 Air Service Manual allowed for a strategic bombing campaign but placed most of its emphasis upon tactical air operations in support of ground forces.[103] By 1926, however, a major division of military doctrine had appeared within the Air Corps. In 1926 *TR 440-15: Fundamental Principles for the Employment of the Air Service*, issued by the director of the Air Service (soon to be the Air Corps), was the primary manual for the air arm. It reflected the tactical emphasis regarding aerial warfare taken by the 1923 manual.[104] However, the Air Service Tactical School's primary textbook, written by several officers and published in April 1926, nevertheless emphasized strategic bombing by an independent bomber force as a war-winning measure.[105] The Tactical School text, called *Employment of a Combined Air Force*, endorsed the

idea that destroying enemy morale and the will to resist was a primary aim
of war and that bombing attacks upon the enemy's civilian population at
the beginning of a war would be an effective means to ensure that aim.[106]
These two strains of thought coexisted within the U.S. Army Air Corps
until the outbreak of World War II.

Much of the swing toward a strategic role for air power in the U.S. military can be attributed to the influence of Brigadier General William Mitchell, tactical commander of the U.S. Air Service on the western front in
1918. During the war, Mitchell proved himself to be an able air commander and tactician when he orchestrated the effort of over seventeen
hundred aircraft in support of the American offensive at St. Mihiel; it was
the largest air armada yet seen.[107] After the war, Mitchell, who created
American tactical air doctrine, became more and more enthusiastic about
the possibilities of strategic bombardment. In 1920 he predicted that the
principle value of the air arm of the future would be in "hitting an enemy's nerve centers at the very beginning of the war so as to paralyze them
to the greatest extent possible."[108] Several years later, Mitchell remarked
that "I was sure that if the war lasted, air power would decide it."[109]

Mitchell was court-martialed by the army in 1925 for his vehement and
extreme criticism of the army and navy leadership in air policy. He resigned from the army in 1926. Both before and after his resignation, he
wrote numerous articles and books in which he expressed the opinion
that air power was decisive in modern war. In the period leading up to
World War II, Mitchell was viewed throughout the Army Air Corps as a
prophet and a martyr to the cause of air power.[110]

The most famous, and most extreme, of the post–World War I air power
theorists was the Italian officer Giulio Douhet. In his 1921 book, *The
Command of the Air* (revised in 1927), Douhet asserted that strategic
bombing was the most effective use of air power.[111] The heavily armed
and partially armored bombers "can always get the best of the faster pursuit plane."[112] As one of the principles of air warfare, he held that the
bomber would always get through and that there was no effective defense
that could be mounted against a large bomber force.[113] Douhet's primary
thesis was that air power, especially strategic bombers, was now the most
important single factor in warfare. Although *Command of the Air* was not
translated from the Italian until the late 1920s, its basic tenets seem to
have been known in the U.S. Army Air Corps and the RAF. In any case, for
the British and Americans, Douhet was more a promoter of the strategic
bombing ideas already popular in both forces than the originator of such
ideas.

For its part, the German shadow air force was fully informed of foreign
air theories and technical developments. Wilberg and members of the
Reichswehr's air staff put considerable effort into keeping up with foreign

technology. Starting in 1919 the Reichswehr air staff published a regular newsletter for Reichswehr officers entitled *Luftfahrtnachrichten* ("Air News"). The first issue, published in August 1919, provided data on all the major and minor air powers, particularly emphasizing technical information.[114] Another newsletter, the *Technical Air Report*, was published by the air officers in the Truppenamt; the first issue came out in 1920.[115] The Air Organization Office also subscribed to numerous foreign air journals, including the American *Air Service Journal*.[116]

The views of General Mitchell were well known in the Reichswehr. For example, a lecture on aerial technology given by Mitchell to the Flying Club of New York in 1920 was translated for the Reichswehr air newsletter of July 1, 1920.[117] Mitchell was respected by the Germans for his command of the tactical air support at St. Mihiel, so his major articles and lectures were often translated and published in the *Militär Wochenblatt*.[118] Hugh Trenchard's theories were also known to the Germans. Military commentator and former General Staff officer Hans Ritter discussed Trenchard's air theories in *The Air War* (1926).[119] In this book, Ritter was able to comment on the views of General Mitchell and General Fuller, even mentioning Professor Robert H. Goddard's rocket experiments—indicating just how closely foreign military developments were studied in Germany. Giulio Douhet, whose book was translated into German somewhat later, was also mentioned in the reports of the Reichswehr's Air Organization Office in the 1920s.[120]

The shadow air force maintained at least one officer assigned to T-3, the Truppenamt's Intelligence Section. The air intelligence officers of the 1920s painstakingly collected and analyzed information on foreign air forces and foreign air technology. One Air Intelligence Office file from 1926, several hundred pages long, contains up-to-date tables with a textual summary of the strength, organization, equipment, and deployment of all the major air forces in the world. An analysis of the major military aircraft models is also provided.[121] In addition to collecting foreign publications, the Air Intelligence Office also requested reports on foreign air forces from German officers who traveled overseas. In 1925 Major Wilberg traveled to the United States and then reported on his observations of the U.S. military.[122] Major von dem Hagen, senior air officer in the Truppenamt's Intelligence Section, visited the United States in 1928 and then wrote an extensive report on the U.S. Army Air Corps.[123]

Germany was forbidden by the Versailles Treaty to have military attachés. By the late 1920s, however, it became possible to attach Reichswehr officers to foreign armed forces. This became the Reichswehr's substitute for a formal attaché system. In 1929 the German Foreign Ministry was able to arrange for Captain Wolfram Freiherr von Richthofen to serve with the Italian Air Force for six months.[124] That same year, the Reichswehr arranged to send Captains

Warlimont and Speidel to the United States to attend American service schools. Warlimont was assigned to study ordnance and artillery; Speidel was attached to the Army Air Corps—the first German since the war to be attached to the U.S. Army.[125] Speidel was able to spend two-to-six weeks at the Air Corps Tactical School, Engineering School, Technical School, Primary and Advanced Flying Schools, as well as serving with observation, attack, bomber, and fighter squadrons. Speidel not only was able to send several boxes of manuals and books to the Air Organization Office, he also had the opportunity to fly several American Air Corps aircraft.[126]

Armed with a comprehensive body of information on foreign forces, ideas, and technology, the Reichswehr air officers were able to carry out a sound and critical analysis of foreign doctrines and capabilities. The claims of the strategic bombing theorists came in for special criticism. In the 1920s General Schwarte (retired) was a prolific military writer, one of a large group of retired generals who turned their attention to writing military history and commentary in the postwar era.[127] In 1928 Schwarte, impressed by the claims of the foreign strategic bombing enthusiasts, publicly lectured on strategic bombing theory, asserting that the German population and industries were helpless against the air forces of their hostile neighbors: France, Belgium, Czechoslovakia, and Poland. Schwarte insisted that these enemy nations possessed fourteen thousand brand-new planes—60 percent of them large bombers, each with a bomb capacity of 2,000 kilograms.[128] The Air Organization Office conducted a study of Schwarte's assertions, probably in response to inquiries by alarmed politicians, and concluded that his assessment of the enemy strategic bombing threat to Germany was wildly overstated. According to the Reichswehr air officers, France, Belgium, Czechoslovakia, and Poland together could not count more than sixty-three hundred aircraft—and even this figure was considered to be too high. Furthermore, this figure included all aircraft types, such as noncombatant primary trainers. A very high percentage of the foreign aircraft was also considered to be thoroughly obsolete. The Air Organization Office provided corrected numbers and percentages of aircraft by type; the largest percentage of bombers—light and heavy—belonged to the Polish Air Force, which had 30 percent of its force in bombers. As for bomb load, the Air Organization Office considered 1,000–1,500 kilograms to be the heaviest realistic bomb capacity—and that pertained to only a few of the largest aircraft.[129]

TRAINING REICHSWEHR AIRCREWS

In 1924, after the Reichswehr had reached its final treaty form, the Truppenamt's Air Organization Office set out to create a systematic pilot and aircrew training program. The creation of the Sportflug company in 1924, heavily subsidized by the Reich Transportation Ministry, established ten flying schools in Germany. This system of civilian flying schools, which went through several official names as camouflage from the Interallied Military Control Commission, provided the Reichswehr pilot officers and former members of the Air Service, many now part of a secret reserve force, with the opportunity for refresher courses and additional training.[130] To ensure that the curriculum met military needs, Wilberg and the air officers assigned to the Truppenamt were directly involved with these schools. Since the Interallied Military Control Commission was on the lookout for violations of the Versailles Treaty, the Reichswehr turned to gliding as a legal means of openly encouraging an interest in aviation among German youth, as well as to assist in the training of future pilots. The Rhône region of Germany became the world's most famous gliding center. Wilberg encouraged Reichswehr officers to take up the sport. Captain Kurt Student became an enthusiast and even General von Seeckt visited gliding contests.[131] Most historians of the Luftwaffe agree that the gliding program played a major role in stimulating interwar aviation interest and research.

The secret agreement between the Reichswehr and the Soviet armed forces arranged by von Seeckt as part of the Rapallo Treaty in 1922 was a decisive factor in building the foundation for a renewed German air force. For the Reichswehr, the most important of the secret agreements was the construction of a pilot school and aircraft testing center in Lipetsk, about 220 miles from Moscow.[132] The Reichswehr poured millions of marks into creating a modern air complex, with two runways, numerous hangars and repair shops, and all the paraphernalia of an air installation, including barracks and an officers' mess. The Reichswehr-supported civilian flying schools in Germany could provide basic single- and multi-engine pilot instruction. Training fighter pilots required modern combat aircraft, however, and there was no place in Germany where a fighter group could easily be hidden. The open spaces of the USSR and the Soviets' eager cooperation proved a practical solution. The Russians benefited greatly from the arrangement, for the Germans provided excellent training to their Red Air Force personnel.

The Reichswehr obtained fifty Fokker DXIII fighter planes from the German military's old friend Anthony Fokker. The DXIII, a single-seat biplane fighter, was one of the hottest combat aircraft of its day. First flown in 1924, it gained four world speed records in 1925.[133] The fifty aircraft and the Lipetsk installation were ready for the first student group in 1925. During its first year, Lipetsk provided a refresher course for wartime pilots; after 1925, the Reichswehr decided to change its training priority to new, inexperienced Reichswehr pilots. These young officers would first

*Fokker DXIII of the shadow Luftwaffe carrying out a ground attack exercise at Lipetsk, Russia, circa 1928. (Courtesy of U.S. Air Force Historical Research Agency, Maxwell Air Force Base, Alabama)*

be trained at the civilian flying schools in Germany; then, the best pilots would be chosen to attend the advanced training at Lipetsk. The fighter pilot course, held in the summer, lasted twenty-two weeks. The pilots worked their way up from solo flights to mock battles with whole squadrons. The Fokker DXIII's were equipped for bombing and the pilots were also trained in ground attacks.[134] In the years that the Lipetsk installation was open, 1925–1933, an average of two hundred to three hundred Germans were stationed there as students, instructors, ground staff, or test pi-

*Air officers send up balloons to represent aircraft during maneuvers of the Sixth Infantry and Third Cavalry divisions, circa 1924–1927.*

lots.[135] In addition to the Fokker DXIIIs, the pilots were able to fly a variety of aircraft, including old Fokker DVIIs and such modern aircraft as the Heinkel HD17, the Heinkel HD21, and the Albatros L69.[136]

From 1928 to 1931, an observer's program was added at Lipetsk.[137] The Reichswehr now had a fairly comprehensive aircrew training program. The fighter pilots were trained in most aspects of aerial warfare, including advanced fighter tactics, ground-attack training, and bombing practice. Instrument flying was also part of the program.[138] The observer program lasted eighteen weeks, with ninety flying days.[139] The observers also took part in tactical, live-fire artillery and ground exercises.[140]

The training program organized by Helmut Wilberg was able to get around most of the Versailles restrictions on pilot training. Since the Paris Air Accords of 1926 forbade the Reichswehr to train more than eight pilots a year, Wilberg created a program that trained forty officer candidates a year as civilian pilots before they officially entered the army. In a 1926 report, the Reichswehr Air Organization Office remarked on the high quality of applicants for the pilot program. So many applied for the forty places that a careful selection could be made.[141] By 1933 the comprehensive training program laid out in the mid-1920s had built a core force of about 500 well-trained aircrew in the army: 120 fighter pilots trained at Lipetsk, 100 observers trained at Lipetsk, another 100 observers trained at Brunswick, and 200 pilots trained as observer and reconnaissance pilots in civilian schools.[142] In addition to these, Lufthansa and the Commercial Flying School were available as a reserve force of bomber and transport pilots.[143]

## TRAINING THE AIR STAFF

With an aircrew training program in place and functioning, the Air Organization Office also instituted a program of staff training for air officers. In the mid-1920s, the Truppenamt reinstituted the traditional war games of the old General Staff. During the winter, the old General Staff had played out various scenarios with teams of officers competing against one another. The games lasted for days, concluding with a detailed critique. In November 1926 the Truppenamt arranged a series of updated war games to be held from January to March the following year in Berlin. The January war games would be specifically for the air officers, with Lieutenant Colonel von Fritsch, chief of operations in the Truppenamt, and Lieutenant Colonel Wilberg, chief of the Air Organization Office, acting as the senior officers. Thirty-two Reichswehr officers, almost all pilots, and six naval officers from military commands throughout the Reich were ordered to Berlin for the January games.[144] The war games for the whole Truppenamt in February and March also included a large degree of military air participation: Three of the fifteen officers on the directing staff and two or three experienced pilot officers were assigned to each team, which had between seventeen and twenty-five Reichswehr officers.[145]

A detailed picture of the air war games for senior staff officers comes from the papers of Reichswehr captain Martin Fiebig, one of seven Reichswehr air officers assigned as instructors and advisers to the Soviet Air Force in the mid-1920s.[146] In 1925-26, Captain Fiebig served as an adviser to the Moscow Academy for Air Commanders, a school for the senior Soviet air staff, where he lectured on air doctrine. In 1926 Fiebig organized a war game for Soviet air staff officers, pitting the USSR against Poland and Romania—a realistic scenario. Luckily, a copy of this game survives, complete with Fiebig's commentary and reports, providing a clear picture of Reichswehr air doctrine of the period and the types of problems discussed in the Truppenamt's January 1927 war games.[147] In his critique of how the Soviets handled the games, Fiebig asserted that one of the prime objectives of the air forces is to carry out an immediate surprise attack upon enemy forces in order to disrupt mobilization and movement plans.[148] Captain Fiebig discussed strategic air bombardment with the Soviet officers, instructing them that it was one of the options available in air warfare. In the game, however, Fiebig advised the officers not to attempt any strategic air offensive against either opponent, but rather to limit the Russian bomber force to attacking tactical targets such as enemy airfields. Strategic bombing campaigns could only be attempted by large, well-trained bomber forces equipped with the most modern aircraft. The weak Soviet bomber forces of the era would have little hope against a firm air defense.[149]

The Reichswehr air officers in 1926 seem somewhat more favorable toward strategic air bombardment than they had been in the immediate postwar period, but they remained, on the whole, cautious in their approach to strategic bombing. In the first major war games of the reconstituted Luftwaffe in 1934, General Walther Wever—newly appointed chief of the Luftwaffe General Staff, although he had no air experience—wanted to throw the German bomber force into a strategic air offensive against the French. Considering that the German bombers were, at the time, provisionally armed, slow JU-52s, all of the experienced Reichswehr airmen disputed this decision, saying that the German bomber force would be 80 percent destroyed by the French fighter forces in a strategic campaign.[150]

The war games of the 1920s and the lectures on aerial warfare in the regular Reichswehr General Staff course constituted about the only specialized staff training given to air officers in the Reichswehr era. Not until the mid-1930s would the Luftwaffe be able to create its own staff school. Still, the system of air war games at least gave the more senior air officers the opportunity to discuss the strategy of aerial warfare. In 1929 the most experienced fighter pilot instructors were assigned to write a comprehensive manual on fighter tactics. These officers produced a tactical and operational manual that was thoroughly up-to-date—for example, gun cameras were used as a primary tool in fighter tactics instruction.[151] The Reichswehr pilots not only produced the tactical manual, they also worked out a complete fighter training schedule and drew up regulations for formation flying, high-altitude flight, and bombing practice.[152] For an air force without a formal air staff college or an air force headquarters, the Reichswehr air officers in the 1920s managed to produce much superior staff work.

## TRAINING THE ARMY

By all accounts, the 180 air officers brought into the Reichswehr in 1920 were able to do an effective job making the army aviation-minded and capable of understanding air-ground coordination, air observation, and tactical ground support. Artillery officers and NCOs received extensive train-

*Crew mans Maxim 08/18 machine gun on antiaircraft mount during maneuvers of Seventh Infantry Division near Naumberg, 1927.*

ing in artillery spotting techniques and interpreting aerial photographs. After 1925, officer cadets at the artillery school at Jüteborg were taken on airplane flights for observation orientation.[153]

In 1926 the American military attaché to Germany observed the Reichswehr divisional maneuvers and later commented that

> The assumption of the presence of both friendly and hostile air forces was made in every maneuver witnessed during the year, which assumption the umpires never failed to bring home to the commanders of every grade by constantly giving them an assumed air situation—the presence of friendly or hostile observation, combat, artillery or bombing planes in the air overhead. . . . In any case, the first consideration of every officer and man throughout was concealment from overhead observation.[154]

Aerial observation was also simulated in the 1924 maneuvers: "An officer, specially marked and often an ex-aviator, was permitted to ride on a motorcycle unmolested through and around the opponents' line. Returning, he reported in writing to the umpire designated, the result of his supposed aerial flight—the umpire permitting so much or all of the report as would be in keeping with an actual aerial flight to be transmitted to the commander sending out the aviator."[155] In that year, the Reichswehr also increased maneuver realism by arranging for commercial aircraft to over-fly the maneuver areas at specified times in order to simulate enemy air observation.[156]

## DEVELOPING AIR TECHNOLOGY

In the Versailles Treaty, the Allies strove to permanently cripple the German aircraft industry as well as to disband the military air force. All German aircraft production was shut down by the Allies for six months in 1921 and the performance characteristics of German civilian aircraft were carefully limited until 1926, when these restrictions were lifted by the Paris Air Accords. Despite these problems, the German aircraft industry— which by 1918 was substantial—refused to die. Within Germany, aircraft manufacturers evaded the Allied control teams. Some aircraft manufacturers simply moved abroad for part of the 1920s. Junkers established factories in Sweden, the USSR, and Turkey; Fokker moved to Holland; Rohrbach set up a branch in Denmark; and Dornier built planes in Switzerland and Italy.[157] By the mid-1920s, the German aircraft industry was reestablished as a force in civilian air production, with companies such as Junkers, Rohrbach, Heinkel, Albatros, and Focke-Wulf manufacturing a variety of training, sport, and passenger aircraft within Germany.[158] Some of the German civil aircraft, such as the Junkers F-13 cargo and passenger plane—a derivative of the all-metal attack planes of 1918—were among the most popular civilian aircraft in the world in the 1920s.

The Reichswehr was strongly involved in aircraft research and development in the 1920s. With the organization of the Reichswehr's Weapons Office in 1920, a team of six technically minded pilots led by Captain Kurt Student were assigned to the air branch of the Weapons Office. This team was to develop military aircraft prototypes in conjunction with German manufacturers. Student sought out Ernst Heinkel, a brilliant aircraft designer, and provided him with secret Reichswehr contracts for light reconnaissance aircraft. The result, the Heinkel HD17, proved to be excellent. Heinkel went on to design numerous aircraft for the Reichswehr, aircraft that were good enough to be adopted by the air forces and navies of Japan, Sweden, and Finland.[159]

Between 1925 and 1933, the Weapons Office Air Section received an average of 10 million marks per year for aircraft research, testing, and equipment procurement.[160] The primary goal of the Air Section was simply to keep up with Allied air developments and to produce modern prototype aircraft that could be mass produced when the time for rearmament arrived. With the relatively small sum of money available, the Weapons Office Air Branch helped develop and tested a variety of military aircraft, from observation planes to bombers. By the late 1920s, test flying was becoming the central focus of the Lipetsk installation. Between 1929 and 1932, at least a dozen different aircraft models—usually two or three aircraft of each type—were put through trials there. A Focke-Wulf light reconnaissance craft was tested and pronounced unacceptable. Heinkel, Arado, and Junkers fighter designs were also tested, and Dornier and Rohrbach provided bomber prototypes.[161]

By the early 1930s, the Reichswehr's air research program had developed such aircraft as the Dornier 11 bomber, the Arado 64 and Heinkel 51 fighters, and the Heinkel 45 and 46 reconnaissance aircraft, which together would form the initial unit strength of the resurgent Luftwaffe of 1934-35. Although none of these aircraft was a spectacular advance in aerial technology, according to Luftwaffe historians Mathew Cooper and Hanfried Schliephake the aircraft produced by the Reichswehr's air program were fully comparable to their foreign military counterparts.[162] The Reichswehr's goal of keeping up with the military technological race was, therefore, effectively fulfilled by the shadow air staff of the 1920s.

CONCLUSION

In 1933-34, when rearmament of Germany began in earnest, the Reichswehr's air staff had already developed a comprehensive air doctrine that emphasized the tactical role of the air force in supporting the ground forces. Strategic bombing, while not ruled out, definitely had a lower priority than tactical air support. Even when the Luftwaffe was established as a separate branch of the armed forces, the overwhelming majority of officers had been trained to think of air power in terms of just one element of a combined-arms effort—and most of the Luftwaffe officers seem to have accepted that view.

In 1934 the newly created Air Ministry established a special staff under the command of Helmut Wilberg, now a general, to prepare the Luftwaffe's primary operations manual. The result—Luftwaffe Regulation 16, *The Conduct of Air Operations* (Luftkriegsführung)—issued in 1935, served as the primary expression of Luftwaffe battle doctrine into World War II.[163] Six major missions of the Luftwaffe were outlined in Regulation 16: (1) combat action to achieve and maintain air superiority; (2) combat and other action in support of ground troops; (3) combat and other action in support of the navy; (4) action to interdict routes of enemy communication and supply; (5) strategic operations against sources of enemy power; and (6) attacks against targets in cities—that is, centers of government administration and control.[164] Not only was strategic bombing allocated the barest priorities of the Luftwaffe's mission, but an injunction against terror raids upon cities was included in Regulation 16, although the Luftwaffe did reserve the right to carry out retaliatory strikes.[165]

Luftwaffe Regulation 16 generally expressed Wilberg's balanced approach to air doctrine. When the Luftwaffe was created, Wilberg as the Reichswehr's top air strategist was the obvious choice for the first Luftwaffe chief of staff.[166] Nevertheless, Wilberg was disqualified because he was partly of Jewish ancestry and, as a professional soldier, held politics and politicians in disdain. The Luftwaffe retained Wilberg anyway. He held several important posts, including commander of the War College in 1935 and chief of staff to the German forces sent to Spain in 1936. He retired with the rank of General der Flieger in 1938.[167]

The Luftwaffe's first chief of staff was General Walther Wever. Although he was one of the army's ablest officers, he was neither a pilot nor an air unit commander. Wever came into the Air Ministry in 1933 as an enthusiastic advocate of strategic bombing. He hoped to build a long-range bomber force, and one of his first projects was to initiate a program to develop a heavy four-engine strategic bomber, dubbed the "Ural Bomber."[168] Wever was certainly at odds with the views of most of the Luftwaffe's senior officers, who though inferior in rank were much more experienced in aerial warfare.[169] Most of the early Luftwaffe's senior officers—men such as Helmut Wilberg, Erhard Milch, Hans Jeschonnek, Kurt Student, Wilhelm Speidel, and Wolfram Freiherr von Richthofen—were fighter pilots or former fighter commanders. A strategic bombing theory that asserted that "the bomber always gets through" could not sit well with fighter pilots. In fact, the German Air Service's World War I experience had taught the men that the bombers often did not get through.

Other senior Luftwaffe officers, such as Paul Deichmann and Hugo Sperrle, were wartime air observers, and Karl Drum was a reconnaissance pilot. The background of most early Luftwaffe leaders ensured that the German Air Force would be inclined toward a tactical air doctrine. Only a few of the senior Luftwaffe officers in 1933–1935, like Fritz Lorenz, later General der Flieger, were bomber pilots. This contrasts greatly with the British and U.S. Air Forces, in which wartime bomber leaders like Trenchard and Mitchell and their followers tended to play a major role in air force leadership during the interwar period. The subsequent evolution of British and American air doctrine along strategic bombing lines was a natural consequence.

Upon General Wever's death in an air crash in 1936, the Luftwaffe reverted to its inclination toward tactical air support, so strongly implanted in the air arm since the end of World War I. The Ural Bomber program was quickly scrapped. Germany would go to war with the kind of air force that the Reichswehr of the early 1920s had envisioned.

CHAPTER EIGHT

# The Reichswehr as a Mature Military Force

By the mid-1920s the Reichswehr had become what von Seeckt wanted it to be: a superb cadre force with which to build a large, modern army. When von Seeckt resigned as army commander in 1926, the Reichswehr was a mature military force. An effective new system had been built upon the ruins of the old. Much of the best of the old system, such as the General Staff, had been retained, but the army had undergone a comprehensive reform. The tactical doctrine of the air and ground forces had been analyzed, and a modern doctrine created. Enlisted and officer training programs had been established that were much more thorough than the old army's, and they effectively prepared the Reichswehr to employ its new tactics. The army had become more technically oriented and had begun an armaments program to build weapons that were tailored to its tactical doctrine.

As a mature force, the Reichswehr would be in a position to think in the long term and begin preparations to fight a large-scale war. Even before von Seeckt left the army command, the Reichswehr had begun training in large-scale warfare through multidivisional maneuvers. The system was in place by which the Reichswehr could test its organization, equipment, and tactical ideas and then carry out further refinements. Von Seeckt's successors, his protégés, would prove to be firm adherents of his system and would continue to modernize the army along the lines laid down in the early 1920s. Military systems and ideas do not, however, exist in a vacuum; Germany's strategic situation played a major role in the evolution of the modern Reichswehr. The Reichswehr knew who Germany's enemies were and in what terrain and against which armies Germany might someday have to fight.

REICHSWEHR STRATEGY OF THE 1920S

When the Reichswehr was established in 1919, it faced a hopeless strategic situation. Not only did Germany face a civil war, but the Allies maintained large military forces on the Rhine, ready to move into Germany unless it accepted the Versailles Treaty.[1] After the treaty was accepted by

169

Germany, the Anglo-Saxon powers no longer posed a military or strategic threat to that nation. The Americans quickly withdrew their occupation forces and made a separate peace agreement. The British, busy with imperial problems, quickly demobilized, leaving only a token military occupation force. Germany, however, still faced four nations that it regarded as military and strategic threats: France, Belgium, Czechoslovakia, and Poland. Some of the German generals saw Bolshevik Russia as a threat, but von Seeckt would disregard their concern. As early as 1919 he began seeking some means of rapprochement with the Russians. Von Seeckt pulled the German troops out of the Baltic countries, where they were fighting Bolshevik troops, and initiated diplomatic feelers. Germany and Russia were both threatened by the Allies and by Poland. In 1919 both nations were outcasts. Their mutual enemies and their mutual predicament provided a basis for a political and military understanding.[2]

In 1922 the German-Soviet rapprochement was complete with the Rapallo Treaty, which established diplomatic and trade links between the two nations. At the urging of the Reichswehr, secret military cooperation began between the German and Russian armed forces, a cooperation that would become essential to both nations. The Germans would provide capital, technical expertise, and military training; the Russians would provide secret training bases and factory sites where the Germans would build armaments forbidden by the Versailles Treaty. It was a beneficial relationship for both powers.[3]

France, Belgium, Czechoslovakia, and Poland would remain Germany's military enemies for the whole interwar period. In the long term, France, with its large army, its industrial power, its position on the Rhine—and its implacable hostility toward Germany—was Germany's most dangerous enemy. The French built a ring of alliances surrounding Germany by providing military aid to Belgium, Czechoslovakia, and Poland. The Germans considered Belgium hostile, because that nation was a loyal French ally. In 1919-20 the Czechs were seen as a dangerous enemy that might invade Germany and grab territory.[4]

In the short term, Poland was the most dangerous threat to Germany. At the Versailles Peace Conference, a reborn Poland pressed claims on German territory. As a starting point, Poland demanded that the 1772 borders be restored. These borders omitted Silesia, so Poland demanded Silesia as well, plus Danzig, most of East Prussia, and part of Pomerania for good measure. At the conference Lloyd George remarked that "no one gave more trouble than the Poles."[5] Many of Poland's claims were granted by the Allies. Danzig was turned into a "free city," and Poznan, most of West Prussia, a bit of East Prussia, and Upper Silesia were all ceded to Poland. German territorial concessions amounted to 13 percent of its prewar territory and 12 percent of its prewar population—most of it to Poland.[6] In

1919 an undeclared war between the Freikorps and Polish forces broke out on the German-Polish border.[7] In 1921, during the plebiscite in Upper Silesia, fighting broke out again. In an election overseen by the Allies, 61 percent of the population voted to remain German, yet a disproportionate share of that territory was awarded to Poland by the Allies.[8]

In the west, the French occupied the Rhineland but the region remained German despite French attempts to foster separatist movements. Germany's territorial loss in the west amounted to ceding Alsace-Lorraine to France. The Germans had never really considered these provinces to be fully part of the empire, for Alsace-Lorraine had been granted limited self-government only in 1913; thus there was no bitterness in Germany over this loss. The eastern provinces, however, were another story. The Germans refused to reconcile themselves to the loss of territories that had been German for centuries, such as Danzig. Von Seeckt constantly expressed the view that Poland must some day be destroyed, a position that was universally held in the Reichswehr and expressed by the highest government officials.[9] In a 1922 memorandum to the government, von Seeckt asserted, "Poland's existence is intolerable, incompatible with the survival of Germany. It must disappear, and it will disappear through its own internal weakness and through Russia—with our assistance. . . . With Poland falls one of the strongest pillars of the Treaty of Versailles, the preponderance of France."[10]

With the exception of the Ruhr crisis of 1923, when the French Army occupied the Ruhr and other parts of western Germany, the primary objective of Reichswehr and government military planning was war with Poland. In the 1920s Poland had a peacetime army of 300,000 men, backed up by a reserve of 1.2 million men.[11] After 1923 France would be less likely to attack Germany, while the threat from Poland would intensify. Marshal Józef Pilsudski's seizure of power in Poland in 1926 heightened tensions, leading to a serious war scare in 1927.[12] Although Germany had no strategic options for offensive war, Polish hostility in particular pushed the Reichswehr to develop a defensive strategy.

Considering Germany's almost impossible strategic predicament in the 1920s, the Reichswehr, and especially von Seeckt, showed great ability in dealing with this situation. The policy of collaboration with the USSR, initiated by the Reichswehr but accepted by Germany's civilian leaders, was a brilliant strategic stroke for a defeated and isolated Germany. This military collaboration would play a pivotal role in rebuilding German military power and would provide as well a useful ally in case Poland attacked. German-Soviet accord was based firmly upon a Polish foundation: The Russians were as eager as the Germans to see Poland destroyed.[13] In its policy and dealings with the civilian government of the USSR, the Reichswehr leadership showed far greater imagination and political sophistication than the prewar and wartime General Staff.

## WAR PLANS

The crises of the early 1920s, the disorder within Germany, and the chaotic state of the early Reichswehr made any form of serious war planning impossible. Between 1919 and 1923, war plans of every type were generally improvised locally. For example, during the Czech war scare of 1919-20, plans were created by the local headquarters to defend East Saxony against an invasion. The small number of available troops, however—a single reinforced brigade and some artillery and motor units—could have little more than delayed a Czech attack.[14]

During the Ruhr crisis of 1923, Reichswehr Headquarters in Berlin made plans to resist the French if they moved out of the Ruhr toward Berlin. Even the Reichswehr plans can best be characterized as improvisations. Mobilization orders were drawn up, reserve units were created and trained, weapons were stockpiled, and plans were made to form a defensive line on the Weser River. National pride and credibility required resistance if the French kept advancing, but as von Seeckt informed Chancellor Cuno in May and the new chancellor, Gustav Stresemann, later that year, there was no hope of defeating the French or even of holding a defensive line.[15] While preparing for armed resistance, von Seeckt encouraged a diplomatic settlement of the crisis.

Although the primary Reichswehr strategy of the 1920s was to avoid war—it would, after all, have been impossible to win—the army was forced by circumstances to turn to long-range planning, with the creation of a cadre force that could provide a foundation for eventual large-scale rearmament. In 1922 von Seeckt informed the government that to follow Allied demands meant the end of the Reichswehr and its degeneration into nothing more than a border police force, resulting in a defenseless Germany.[16] The national government agreed. Accordingly, from 1922 on, the government consistently supported the Reichswehr's secret rearmament policies; the crisis of 1923 and the success of the German-Soviet collaboration only strengthened the government's resolve.[17]

The Reichswehr's long-term strategy rested on four programs: (1) creating an effective cadre army; (2) preparing a reserve force; (3) manufacturing a stockpile of arms for an enlarged army and preparing for industrial mobilization; and (4) helping train and equip the Soviet armed forces. All four programs were to some degree successful. The Germans were the most successful in creating an effective cadre army, the least successful in creating a reserve force. By implementing all these measures simultaneously and consistently from 1922 to the end of the Weimar Republic, the Reichswehr steadily increased its real military power, with a consequent increase in Germany's standing in European politics. The Reichswehr cannot be described as friendly to the Weimar Republic; in fact, the army was a state within a state. Still, the best of the German politicians (notably Stresemann), realizing that international prestige and influence rested largely upon military power, supported the Reichswehr's programs to increase its size and effectiveness. When, in late 1926, von Seeckt left the scene and General Wilhelm Heye took over the Reichswehr, and again, in 1928, when General Wilhelm Groener was appointed Reichswehr minister, military-civilian cooperation became stronger than before.[18]

Long-term strategic planning requires a stable government and a well-disciplined, reliable military force. Germany did not achieve political and economic stability until after the Ruhr crisis, in 1924. Now the Reichswehr could truly be described as a well-disciplined, well-organized, and well-trained force. In this first peaceful postcrisis year of the Weimar Republic, German war planning finally abandoned its previous, seemingly improvisational, techniques to become more thorough and realistic. In the mid-1920s, the Reichswehr entered its mature phase as a military force.

Although the Reichswehr's war plans were basically defensive in nature, its plans against Poland took the form of a mobile defense emphasizing the counterattack, because the Reichswehr believed in the supremacy of the offense and was influenced by Allied restrictions on permanent defenses. According to von Seeckt's post-1923 war plans against Poland, the German forces would concentrate and attempt to envelop in a large pincers movement any Polish army entering Germany.[19] The Battle of Tannenberg, where heavily outnumbered German forces succeeded in surrounding and destroying the invading Russian Second Army in 1914, was one of the Reichswehr's favorite military campaigns for study, chiefly because its lessons could be applied to a Polish invasion from the same direction. The Allies also pushed the Germans into a mobile defense when they denied Germany the right to fortify its eastern borders by allowing only a few obsolete German fortifications to be maintained near Königsberg in East Prussia.[20] If the Germans had been allowed to build border fortifications after 1919, large funds and a major military effort probably would have gone into building fortresses against the hated Poles. Germany could also have developed a "Maginot Line" approach to strategy and tactics. Eventually, the Germans did build several concrete bunkers and positions in East Prussia. These bunkers were more suited to supporting a mobile defense, however, and never resembled a French-style defensive line.[21]

Military planning against Poland in the 1920s revealed a clear movement toward a more offensive mentality. Some officers in the Truppenamt even saw von Seeckt's plan for a mobile Tannenberg-like battle on the Polish front as too cautious. Major General von Hasse, chief of the Truppenamt, believed the best military solution would be to attack Poland.[22] The winter war games in 1928 provided a pessimistic scenario, in which the Germans lost territory to a Polish attack.[23] On the other hand, group maneuvers held in East Prussia in the autumn of 1928 were successful—an invading Polish force was encircled and destroyed in a mobile campaign.[24] Also in 1928, the Truppenamt ordered a study, in conjunction with the navy, that considered an offensive against the Polish port of Gdynia in a war.[25] There was considerable debate among the Truppenamt and the naval officers working on the study. The majority concluded that such an attack was bound to be very costly.[26] Yet, in ordering such a study Reichswehr Headquarters revealed that it was considering a more offensive policy toward Poland.

In contrast, German military plans against the French remained almost completely defensive until the late 1930s. Germany had no territorial ambitions in the west aside from regaining control of the Saarland and Rhineland. It would have been suicidal for the Reichswehr to consider attacking the far larger and better-armed French Army. Therefore, all war plans involving France emphasized the mobile delaying battle, designed to slow a French advance and inflict maximum French casualties. The hope was that this strategy would buy the Germans time to defeat the Poles in the east and then turn to a diplomatic solution.[27]

MOBILIZATION PLANS

Serious long-term planning to create an enlarged and rearmed Reichswehr suitable for modern warfare began in 1924. The Truppenamt sections T-1 (Operations) and T-2 (Organization) were made responsible for creating a comprehensive mobilization plan. By late 1924 or early 1925, the first draft of an army enlargement plan—several hundred pages—was complete.[28] The 1924-25 mobilization plans followed Hans von Seeckt's 1919 concept of an elite, well-armed field army backed by lightly equipped, less-well-trained militia forces suitable for border defense. In the rear, a replacement army (Ersatzheer) would be created to train recruits and serve as an emergency reserve.

The plan provided for an army force the equivalent of thirty-five divisions. The Reichswehr's seven infantry divisions would be tripled to form twenty-one divisions. Of these, fourteen would be equipped with a heavy artillery regiment, a flak battalion, and a tank battalion. With the Reichswehr's three cavalry divisions, a field army of seventeen divisions would be created—a force capable of offensive operations. The seven more lightly armed of the expanded infantry divisions would assume a defensive posture for border defense and be bolstered by the equivalent of four lightly armed border militia (Grenzschutz) divisions. Within the homeland, an Ersatzheer would be formed, which with its sixty-three infantry battalions and twenty-one artillery battalions would be equivalent to seven divisions. These divisions, minimally equipped, would train replacements for the field army; the replacement army would not be considered for use in battle except in a dire emergency.

The 1924-25 mobilization plans provide equipment and organization tables for all the army units and give some insights into the Reichswehr's early studies of motorization. In 1924-25, the Reichswehr was essentially an infantry force, dependent upon horse and rail for supply and transport. The motorization of certain branches of the army, however, was given high priority. The flak artillery battalions were to be completely motorized; headquarters were motorized and most of the artillery and pioneer units were to be motorized. The signal units, in particular, would essentially become motorized, with 268 trucks and 87 automobiles assigned to that branch.[29] The infantry would receive additional motor support in the form of five new truck regiments assigned to the field forces.[30]

These 1924-25 plans also followed von Seeckt's concept of mobilizing by waves. The first wave would be the best-equipped and best-staffed force, able to quickly go on the offensive as the field army. The second wave, with substantially less equipment and fewer trained men, would mobilize at the same time as the field force and man border defense positions. The last wave, the replacement army, might be mobilized later than the first two waves. The 1924-25 plans served two purposes. First, they were the Reichswehr's war plan for emergency expansion in case of attack. Second, they were the basis of long-term strategic planning for army expansion.

World War I taught the Germans that planning for military mobilization also meant preparing for industrial mobilization. Because even the limited rearmament envisioned in the 1924-25 mobilization plans required considerable industrial preparation, a special section of the Weapons Office was created in 1924 to deal with industrial planning. Originally it was called the Supply Staff, and after 1929, the Economics Staff. The first three officers to serve on the Supply Staff were Major Erich Soldan, Major Rudolf Jansen, and Captain Herrmann von Hanneken. All would become generals and would remain within the General Staff as industrial and economics experts during the 1930s and 1940s. In 1927 Captain Ludwig Thomas was assigned to the Supply Staff, where he remained until 1943 as the General Staff's premier specialist in industrial-military planning.[31] In 1926, in each of the seven military districts, an economics officer was assigned. The economics officer was responsible for liaison with government and industry leaders and for preparation of industrial inventories and regional mobilization plans. The economics officers reported to the Supply Staff.[32] The relationship between the Reichswehr and industry was close, especially during the Ruhr crisis, when the major industrial concerns donated money for Reichswehr rearmament. From 1924 on, the relationship was systematized and formalized. In 1925, a group of industrial leaders, many of them involved in secret Reichswehr contracts, created the Statistical Society (STEGA), which became a liaison organization between the Reichswehr and industry.[33] With the establishment of the Supply Staff, the economics officers, and STEGA, an efficient system of military-industrial planning was in place by 1926.[34]

During the Ruhr crisis, a somewhat haphazard emergency rearmament program was created. With the 1924-25 mobilization plans for a framework, and the Supply Staff and STEGA established, it was now possible to begin planning a comprehensive, long-range rearmament program. Considerable progress had been made in the early and mid-1920s toward amassing a Reichswehr armaments reserve. In early 1927, General Heye, the Reichswehr commander, informed the government that the Reichswehr had secretly stockpiled a reserve of 350,000 rifles, 12,000 light and heavy machine guns, 400 trench mortars, 600 light fieldpieces and 75 heavy guns.[35]

Von Seeckt was dismissed as Reichswehr commander in October 1926 for initiating a political controversy: He had invited a Hohenzollern prince to attend the fall maneuvers. To ensure that his policies would be carried on, von Seeckt arranged for General Heye, chief of the Truppenamt and a supporter of von Seeckt's policies, to be appointed commander after him. This prevented General Walther Reinhardt, von Seeckt's greatest rival within the Reichswehr and a man who differed greatly with von Seeckt on strategy and tactics, from achieving command of the army. If Reinhardt had become commander, war planning, organizational concepts, and tactical doctrine would probably have evolved in an entirely different direction. Reinhardt favored defense over offense and preferred the traditional mass-army concepts over von Seeckt's doctrine of an elite, professional army. In any case, Heye continued to follow the doctrine and policy lines laid down by von Seeckt. Heye's successor, General Curt von Hammerstein-Equord, army commander from 1930 to 1934, also developed the Reichswehr in a manner consistent with von Seeckt's long-term goals. Neither commander made any major changes in the fundamental concepts of the 1924-25 mobilization plans. Those plans remained the basis for army mobilization and organization planning into the Third Reich.

However, there were numerous amendments and proposed amendments to the details of implementing these plans. Since the core of the plans was the tripling of the Reichswehr's seven infantry divisions, it became known as the Twenty-One Division Army plan. In 1925 the Weapons Office recommended increasing the cavalry divisions from three to five; this idea was rejected by the Truppenamt.[36] In 1927, when the Interallied Military Control Commission left Germany, giving the army more opportunity to arm and train, the Reichswehr prepared a plan to put part of the Twenty-One Division program into effect. In 1928 the government agreed to finance a program to equip and man an "emergency army" of sixteen divisions, known as the A-Army. Limited equipment and reserves to man the other units of the army were planned by 1932.[37] Largely due to financial restrictions caused by the worldwide Depression, the Reichswehr did not have the equipment for the Twenty-One Division force in 1932, only the armaments for the Sixteen-Division A-Army, which should have been ready by 1930. Thus in 1932 a second rearmament program was initiated to provide for the entire Twenty-One Division force, including a small air force of 150 planes, an armored unit of 55 tanks, and heavy flak artillery and antitank guns.[38]

## CREATING A RESERVE FORCE

After organizing an effective regular army, the Reichswehr's next priority—even more important than collecting a stockpile of modern armaments—was the creation of a trained reserve force. The Versailles Treaty's denial of conscription and its limiting of Germany to a small, long-term army meant that with every passing year the number of trained, fit men available as a reserve would decline. With a twelve-year enlistment period for the Reichswehr, by 1932 only 100,000 Germans between the ages of twenty and thirty-five would have had military training—and those would have little practical knowledge of aircraft, tanks, heavy artillery, and so on. The French had specifically intended the twelve-year service of the Reichswehr to make the building of a reserve force impossible, ensuring that the German Army would be a hollow shell, a force with no depth at all.[39] Therefore, creating a reserve force that was sufficiently well trained to serve as a defensive militia, that was equipped with a minimum of modern weaponry, and that was capable of acting as a disciplined force would be, perhaps, the Reichswehr's greatest single problem. Without a reserve force, even an elite ten-division Reichswehr would be hard pressed to rearm and expand in a short time.

In the chaotic period immediately after the war, a bewildering variety of militias sprang up throughout Germany. Some were backed by the Reichswehr and some organized by state and local governments. During

1919, volunteer border defense regiments were formed in Saxony to guard the Czech border. After a few months of existence, some of these volunteers entered the Reichswehr, some were formed into border police units, and others were transferred to a reserve force—the People's Militia (Volkswehr).[40] Various local militias were formed. In Saxony, a Home Defense Force (Heimatschutz) was formed and later disbanded.[41] In East Prussia, one of the most threatened regions of Germany, civilian militias (Einwohnerwehr) were formed, but the equipment and organization were minimal. Bavaria quickly organized militias after the war, and a national law of April 25, 1919, extended the militia system to all German towns. French general Nollet of the Interallied Military Control Commission estimated that one million men were enrolled in the postwar German citizen militias.[42] This estimate is probably a bit high, but such was the state of militia organization in the early Weimar Republic that today one can only guess at the numbers.

After 1919 most of the German militias were disbanded and ordered by the government to turn in their guns. Von Seeckt supported the disbandment and disarming of the militias because most had fallen away from any semblance of military command or control. Although many well-armed and competently officered Freikorps and nationalist organizations offered their services to the Reichswehr during the Ruhr crisis, von Seeckt, who remembered the Kapp Putsch and rightfully doubted the discipline of these groups, turned down their offers. The decision was made in 1923 that if the Reichswehr were to have a reserve force, it would be equipped and trained by the army and completely under its control. It was better to have a small, reliable reserve than a large one with its own political agenda.

The only militias that the Reichswehr consistently maintained were the Grenzschutz, border militia formations, organized along the eastern border of Germany. The serious threat of war with Poland made such measures necessary. In East Prussia, in August 1920, a local defense force (Ortswehr) was established that absorbed the local militias. The Prussian government supported the East Prussian militia, and a complicated system of local committees was created to administer the system.[43] The regular army doubted the competence and discipline of these militia forces and their light weaponry made them an inadequate force.[44] The Ortswehr system was officially dissolved in late 1920, but some units were retained and transformed into Grenzschutz.

Throughout the Weimar Republic, the Reichswehr would, with the cooperation of the Saxon and Prussian governments, maintain a significant Grenzschutz force. Although any clear numbers are difficult to obtain, the Reichswehr in 1930 did estimate that it could double the existing seven infantry divisions. On paper, the Grenzschutz force may have been as high as seventy thousand to eighty thousand strong.[45] Realistically, the Grenzschutz may not have had more than forty thousand effective strength.

The most efficient reserve force of the Reichswehr was the Security Police formed after World War I. This force was clearly a military one. The police lived in barracks, were led by former army NCOs and officers, and were recruited from the Freikorps and Provisional Reichswehr. The Security Police were given military training and armed with rifles, machine guns, and armored cars. The Allies, who recognized the military nature of the force, repeatedly demanded its dissolution. In the end, the Allies did allow its existence but insisted that it keep no more than thirty-two thousand men quartered in barracks. Since the police were watched less carefully than the army, it is estimated that the Security Police force in the 1920s numbered close to seventy thousand men.[46]

An excellent picture of the Security Police and their relationship to the Reichswehr is found in an unpublished history of the First Battalion, Sixty-fifth Infantry Regiment, written by a German officer about 1937 or 1938. This manuscript outlines in detail how the Versailles Treaty was evaded on a large scale by the Security Police in Bremen, home of the Sixteenth, and later Sixty-fifth, Infantry regiments.[47]

In Bremen, in the fall of 1919, the Security Police were formed from the soldiers of Freikorps Caspari, which had in turn been formed from the soldiers of the Seventy-fifth Infantry Regiment. Major Caspari, a professional army officer, was appointed commander of the Bremen Security Police, which initially consisted of twelve police companies, two technical companies, one armored car squadron, and one mounted company.[48] The Security Police were well motorized and provided with full military equipment, including light and heavy machine guns. The standard police firearm was the carbine model of the army's Model 98 Mauser rifle.

After the Allies protested, restrictions were placed upon police armament. The Bremen unit was allowed only three armored cars, a limited number of rifles and machine guns, and the military training of the Bremen Security Police was ordered to be stopped. By 1922 the police in Bremen had been reduced to nine hundred men, organized into twelve companies, one armored car platoon, and one mounted company. In order to please Allied inspectors, the steel helmets of the Security Police were hidden and caps were used instead. Army field kitchens, military communications equipment, and weapons and ammunition stockpiles were also hidden. The Security Police were still given basic military training—just more discreetly than before. After 1923, Security Police training was carried out in accordance with the standard military manuals of the Reichswehr.[49] Throughout the 1920s, the police engaged in small- and large-unit military exercises, including live-fire exercises. As a reserve

force, the Bremen Security Police were on eight hours' mobilization notice to man the border defense line in the west. When the time came to
expand the army in 1934-35, the Bremen Security Police alone were able
to contribute the equivalent of two to three battalions. With their high
standard of discipline and training, the Security Police were quickly incorporated into the army. The Security Police program was the Reichswehr's most effective means of rapidly expanding the army.

The Reichswehr possessed other trained reserve forces that could serve
as a cadre for new recruits or form the core of an expanded militia force in
an emergency. As mentioned in Chapter Seven, the Air Organization Office maintained a roster of Air Service veterans who could be recalled to
service. In addition, Lufthansa was created partly to serve as a reserve air
force and could quickly be turned into a military force in an emergency.

Immediately after the war, the army set up a demobilization organization, which was actually a system of registering young men and veterans
for possible service. The organization was large enough to alarm the Allies, who secured its dissolution in 1921.[50] The administrative side of registering veterans and young men was taken over more discreetly by pension centers. Von Seeckt also ensured that former officers were appointed
district commissioners, whose official duties were fairly vague but were
generally concerned with keeping military ideas alive through sports and
youth training. Gordon Craig calls the district commissioners "the first
beginnings of a corps of reserve officers of a frontier guard and even of a
later reserve army."[51]

Although Reichswehr enlisted men were supposed to serve for twelve
years and officers for twenty-five, a regular program of discharging soldiers and officers before the end of their terms of service was established.
This helped the Reichswehr build a reserve of well-trained soldiers and
officers whose reliability was undoubted. By 1926 the rate of enlisted dis-
charges per year rose from 13 percent to 25 percent.[52] Officers were also
allowed to leave the service and enroll in the reserve. Captain Kurt Hesse
left the Reichswehr in 1929 to become a civilian instructor for the army.
His personnel records show that he was placed on reserve status at that
time.[53]

In the 1920s considerable effort was put into reviving the Krümper System created by General Scharnhorst in the early nineteenth century. After
Prussia was defeated by Napoleon in 1807, the Prussian Army was, by
treaty, reduced to 42,000 men by the French. Scharnhorst circumvented
this restriction by enrolling large numbers of recruits in the army and giving them a short term of military training. By rotating the nation's youth
through a training course of only a few months, the Krümper System sup-
posedly created a reserve of 150,000 men by 1813, when Prussia again
went to war against France.[54] During the Ruhr crisis, the German govern-

ment allowed a revival of this system by approving the recruitment of so-
called labor troops by the Reichswehr. This labor service was actually a
cover for the short-term training of military volunteers, the Black Reichswehr. In 1923 tens of thousands of young men were enrolled and trained
by the Reichswehr. After 1923 the system was continued. A 1929 British
report stated that there were an estimated 7,000 extra men being trained
by the Reichswehr.[55]

The Black Reichswehr reservists were often organized into Grenzschutz formations. The system provided the advantages of a far higher degree of command and control over the reserves than existed in Freikorps
or nationalist organizations. Even in the Black Reichswehr, however, there
were severe discipline problems. Some members created their own secret
military courts, carrying out executions of Germans who denounced secret Reichswehr activities to the Allies or to the parties of the Left.[56] Despite the excesses of some Black Reichswehr members, there was a strong
sentiment for a national militia. For example, during the 1923 crisis, numerous students from the universities of Berlin, Jena, Leipzig, and Halle
volunteered for military training with the full approval of university au-
thorities.[57]

In 1928, under the leadership of Groener, the new Reichswehr minister,
the reserve system was reorganized. With the government's approval, the
secret reserve forces were placed under tighter control by the Reichswehr. A plan for creating and equipping a large reserve force was established under the heading of land defense (Landesschütz). The training of
Grenzschutz formations and short-term army volunteers continued as before.[58] General Groener became excited by the national militia sentiment
and in 1930 he discussed with the government the notion of building a
militia army on the Swiss model.[59] Groener wanted to openly revive the
Krümper System: 40,000 recruits would receive three months of basic
training every quarter—thereby building a Reichswehr reserve at the rate
of 160,000 men per year. The Groener plan was proposed at the 1932 disarmament conference and quickly rejected by the other nations.[60]

There was some discussion within the Reichswehr about the military
value of the Grenzschutz and Black Reichswehr formations. General Ernst
Köstring remarked that in 1927, when he commanded a cavalry regiment,
he possessed an illegal reserve arms cache that he had to hide from Allied
inspectors. The reserve arms stockpiles in the hands of Reichswehr regiments were rather small and, considering their limited military value,
Köstring wondered why the Allies even bothered. In order to fight a modern war, the Reichswehr needed "an enormous reserve of men and materiel"; a quarter-year's training for a few youths would scarcely render
them militarily useful.[61] General Erich von Manstein spent several years in
T-1 (Operations) in the 1920s and was actively involved in planning and

training for the reserve force. In his memoirs, he remarked that the Grenzschutz units were not only too lightly armed, but that the members were either too old or they were youths with only minimal training. The Grenzschutz was spread so thinly along the border, with twelve men per kilometer, and possessed so little transport, that their only purpose was "to deal with any Polish irregulars." Against an enemy's regular army, the Grenzschutz could, at very best, be used as a delaying force.[62] Von Manstein also argued that the poorly equipped reserve divisions that the Reichswehr planned to mobilize in an emergency would probably only "serve to swell the POW count of the enemy."[63] Another General Staff officer, Siegfried Westphal, thought it was a good idea to increase the size of the army by adding a limited number of short-term trainees, but during the 1923 crisis the number of Black Reichswehr effectives was so small—in Berlin, there were only one thousand troops available—that their military worth was minimal.[64]

In general, the Reichswehr officers who took part in training and planning for the reserve forces in the 1920s developed a low opinion of their military effectiveness. The Truppenamt officers, like von Manstein, were not opposed to creating a reserve force, but the consensus at Reichswehr Headquarters was that a force of men who had only three to four months of training would not amount to much on the battlefield. The Krümper System was fine for the simpler battlefield of 1813, but the complexity of modern war reduced the system's effectiveness. When rearmament came in 1934-35, the Reichswehr decided to build a reserve force of men who had served two to three years as recruits or conscripts. The reserve divisions of the 1930s would be equipped on a scale much closer to that of the regular army. Essentially, after trying the Krümper System, the Reichswehr returned to the pre–World War I concept that only men with two to three years of soldiering experience could make effective reservists.

The Reichswehr programs for maintaining reserve officer lists and for building an air force reserve were successful. The creation of the Security Police as an army reserve force was one of the most successful Reichswehr evasions of the Versailles Treaty. The addition of this well-trained and well-officered force would play a major role in the expansion of the German Army in the 1930s. The Black Reichswehr and Grenzschutz—the whole Landesschütz program in general—were Reichswehr failures. At best, these reserve forces of the 1920s and 1930s provided some additional security in case of a Polish attack. The only other advantage to Landesschütz is that by experimenting and failing to create an effective reserve system in the 1920s, the Reichswehr had the good luck to make its mistakes on a small scale before the time for large-scale expansion came.

## CORPS AND ARMY TRAINING

By 1925 the Reichswehr had been progressively trained from the bottom up. The army had started with company and battalion training and worked up to regimental and divisional training by 1923–25. In 1926 the Reichswehr had matured to the point that most of the army was put through multidivisional maneuvers that year. Two major maneuvers were held, one in each of the two group command areas (the ten Reichswehr divisions were divided into two group commands. Group 1 was East Prussia and eastern Germany, Group 2 commanded units in southern and western Germany).

The prewar German Army had long been world experts in using large-scale maneuvers to train soldiers and command staffs. The Reichswehr policy on maneuvers was to use divisional and group exercises as a means of testing new equipment and tactical ideas, as well as to train soldiers and officers. Every year the maneuvers were closely observed and critiqued, not only by the group commander and his staff but also by the army commander. President Hindenburg would show up in his field marshal's uniform to observe, and the Reichswehr minister would also be present. The presence of the president and the Reichswehr minister testify to the importance the maneuvers had in the eyes of the government.

In the late 1920s, the Reichswehr gained extensive practice planning, moving, and fighting with full-strength divisions and corps, using the maneuver results to adjust Reichswehr tactical doctrine. The group maneuvers were planned with care. While the scenarios ensured that a variety of tactical situations would be introduced, considerable free rein was also given to the commanders. The maneuvers were kept as realistic as possible by trained umpires. The American military attaché to Germany during the Weimar era, Colonel Truman Smith, referred to the umpire service in his report of divisional maneuvers in 1924:

> The umpire service was very thorough—each unit to the company had with it a reliable non-commissioned officer as an assistant umpire, who was trained in the work and could make local decisions. The larger units had officers up to and including general officers. . . . The umpires, in unison, made a map study of the ground and maneuver problems in Berlin previous to the maneuvers. . . . [T]he umpire service impressed one as being thorough, sufficient and efficient. Decisions were given with promptness and judgment.[65]

Smith spoke highly of the way the German maneuvers were managed, pointing out that the U.S. Army, by contrast, had no field manuals or pamphlets on umpiring and nothing resembling serious umpire training.[66]

*General von Seeckt (center) talks with President Hindenburg at the Reichswehr maneuvers of 1928. (From Friedrich von Rabenau,* Seeckt: Aus seinem Leben, 1918–1936 *[Leipzig: Hase-Koehler Verlag, 1941])*

Of the German Army's seven infantry divisions, four complete divisions and portions of two others took part in the 1926 maneuvers. Units from the three cavalry divisions supported the infantry and a complete cavalry brigade took part in the Group 1 maneuvers.[67] The American observer's report and a report printed in a Swiss Army journal noted the tactical innovations demonstrated by the Reichswehr in these maneuvers.[68] The maneuvers had nothing to do with the positional warfare of World War I. Tactical movement and maneuver were stressed. Combinations of highly mobile units were tried. In the Group 2 maneuvers of September 1926, an advance of the Fifth Infantry Division was led by cavalry units reinforced with artillery and extra machine guns teamed with a force of mock tanks.[69] Another innovation was the changed role of the cavalry. Although the cavalry was a disproportionately large part of the Reichswehr, only a few squadrons were employed in the Group 2 maneuvers, and these groups made no attempt to ride in mass but acted in small groups as a screening force, fighting dismounted whenever the enemy was engaged.[70] The artillery used smoke rounds to cover and support a tank attack at one point—an Allied technique from World War I that the Germans first used in this maneuver.[71] Another change from the World War I techniques was noted by the American observer. The German artillery carefully dispersed and camouflaged their guns, making enemy observation and counterbattery fire difficult, but also making battery command and massed fire more difficult for the artillery.[72]

The increased motorization of the Reichswehr was also noted. Lieutenant Colonel Boelcke, writing for the Swiss Army journal, remarked that the Reichswehr's motor troops performed with great efficiency.[73] The American observer remarked, "The troops were amply supplied with all kinds of motorized transportation," and he praised the motorization of the headquarters units, which used specially adapted trucks that were "efficient and practical." The American officer added, "For the first time since the war, large numbers of motorcycles were noted."[74] Armored units, as represented by the Reichswehr's armored car companies and mock-tank units, were regularly employed in 1926. Both opposing forces paid attention to tank defense, for numerous tank traps and obstacles were erected. The armored cars and mock tanks were employed primarily in reconnaissance and support missions.[75]

In the 1926 maneuvers, night attacks and river-crossing operations were carried out. A new tactic, using machine guns as indirect fire support—firing over the heads of their own advancing troops—was practiced.[76] In both 1926 maneuvers, the simulated use of aircraft in reconnaissance, observation, and ground-attack roles was stressed. The Reichswehr troops constantly used camouflage and dispersal as a passive form of air defense.[77] The Reichswehr's most interesting tactical development was at first perceived by the American observer to be poor tactical unit handling. The Germans did not worry about maintaining a continuous front. Instead, units advanced boldly ahead without regard for the troops on their flanks: "Battalions and companies within the battalion pushed forward and continued to push forward, regardless of whether there were troops on their right or left, until stopped by the enemy."[78] The American observer added,

At first the impression was given that these irregularities in the advance came from the fact that the troops were unaccustomed in maneuvers on a big scale and were due to errors in carrying out the intentions and orders of superiors. But later it was proved to be done by intent. The German regulations call for troops to push on in their own battle sectors and get a grip on all points of vantage, irrespective of what troops on their flanks are successful in accomplishing. At the

same time, there was always observed complete cooperation between adjacent units in all situations in which one unit found itself in
a position to facilitate the advance of a neighboring unit.[79]

It is doubtful that any of the Allied armies or the Soviet or Polish armies
could have demonstrated such tactical finesse on a division-level maneuver in 1926. The fitness of the men also made a favorable impression
upon the American observer. The German Army regularly practiced long
marches, since marching was still the normal method of moving infantry
in the 1920s. In the 1926 maneuvers, the infantry were required to make
long marches by day and night. Some battalions made marches of 45 kilometers before going into action. The American attaché remarked that the
German troops showed no lack of "pep" after these marches.[80]

The 1926 maneuvers demonstrated that the Reichswehr had successfully unlearned the trench warfare mentality of World War I and had begun to master the technique of conducting a mobile war with combined
arms. The Reichswehr would continue to have multidivisional group maneuvers for most of the Army every year into the 1930s. In fact, the fall
group maneuvers were the high point of the military training year for the
whole army. When the Nazi takeover came and the Reichswehr was transformed into the Wehrmacht, the schedule of divisional and group training
would intensify.

Army Headquarters maneuver reports of the 1920s indicate that the
Reichswehr commanders were generally pleased with the state of unit
training and with the tactics of maneuver warfare. Even so, changes in tactics were initiated after each maneuver. In 1927 the Third Cavalry Division reported the following to Army Headquarters after its divisional maneuvers: "A battle without tanks is obsolete. The means of giving orders
for units operating with tanks that is taught in the branch schools is unsatisfactory."[81] The Third Cavalry Division noted that the mock tanks were
generally held back, because of their poor cross-country capability. The
division recommended that the fast Hanomag vehicles be obtained as
mock-tank chassis, since these were the only vehicles available with the
cross-country capability suitable for cavalry maneuvers. The Third Cavalry Division also recommended that more armored car training areas be
established—all of this from a branch of service that gave up its lances
only a few months before.[82] It took a few years, but the cavalry branch
was finally changing its reactionary attitudes.

General Reinhardt, commander of Group 2, reported in 1927 that the
maneuvers of that year had shown the troops to have learned the importance of maneuvering quickly, but that the officers needed more technical
experience.[83] In 1927 the army command required that Group 2 maneuvers include an exercise using a motorized infantry regiment in conjunc-

*Test chassis of the "Krupp Tractor," the basis for the PZ 1 tank, which was tested in Russia circa 1932. (Courtesy of U.S. Army Ordnance Museum, Aberdeen Proving Ground, Maryland)*

tion with a cavalry division. After the maneuvers, Reinhardt recommended that the troops practice longer motor marches and that better cross-country vehicles be provided for motorized troops.[84]

The large-scale maneuvers of the late 1920s and early 1930s show a consistent trend toward improving equipment and motorization concepts.[85] In the group maneuvers, Reichswehr Headquarters stressed training in mobility, offensive tactics, maneuver, and envelopment. The performance of the motorized units and their equipment continued to improve. The American military attaché, commenting on the 1930 maneuvers, reported that the German vehicles were sturdy and the truck and motorcycle detachments had performed well.[86] The last group maneuvers of the Weimar Republic in 1932 featured a trial of a new organization for the infantry and cavalry divisions. One of the major changes was the establishment of a motorized reconnaissance battalion as a standard element of the divisional organization. The new reconnaissance battalion was a balanced organization consisting of a motorized headquarters, a signals platoon, an armored car platoon, an antitank platoon, a machine-gun troop, a bicycle company, and a cavalry troop.[87]

The Reichswehr gained considerable experience in the tactical and command problems of modern warfare with large units by conducting war games. Realizing the importance of communications in conducting a war of maneuver, the Truppenamt in April 1928 carried out a major communications exercise involving all of the divisions and group headquar-

*Infantry supports a simulated tank unit on maneuvers, circa 1926–1928. (Courtesy of U.S. Army Ordnance Museum, Aberdeen Proving Ground, Maryland)*

ters.[88] The Truppenamt also experimented with motorized warfare plans and tactics using war games. In the 1926-27 winter war games, which involved more than forty General Staff officers from Berlin and headquarters around the nation, the Truppenamt scenario provided for a red army of seven infantry divisions, a cavalry division, and a motorized infantry division against a blue army of three infantry divisions and one cavalry brigade reinforced by a motorized infantry division and a motorized infantry brigade.[89] In these games, both sides were provided with large air forces.

The organization of a motorized division as envisioned in 1926 was based on three motorized infantry regiments, each with a motorized signals section and motorized infantry cannon company (see Appendix). The divisional reconnaissance element was almost regimental size. It comprised a headquarters, two motorized antitank gun sections of three guns each, two armored car companies of twelve armored cars each, a motorcycle company, a bicycle battalion, and an infantry company mounted on halftracks. A divisional tank company was also assigned to the reconnaissance unit. This unit had more than enough firepower and mobility to conduct reconnaissance while acting as a highly mobile armor force, with more than thirty armored vehicles able to conduct a break-through operation.[90] The 1926 motorized division made extensive use of tracked prime movers for the artillery. Some guns were also mounted on half-tracks.[91] The supply columns also made extensive use of half-tracks, with half of the tonnage in the two supply battalions carried on those ve-hicles.

An important feature of the 1926-27 war games was devoting a major part of the play to aerial warfare. The attacking red force possessed an air force largely composed of heavy bombers. The defending blue army had a more balanced air force, with two fighter brigades, two night bomber brigades, a day bomber brigade, and a night fighter brigade. Although the air force had its own unified command, it would serve under the tactical direction of the army high command. Since the attacking red army had a large bomber force, the defending blue air force strongly emphasized flak units to meet this threat.[92]

The group maneuvers, the communications exercises, and the Trup-penamt's annual war games are all evidence that, by the late 1920s, the Reichswehr preferred to think of modern war in terms of conventional forces, maneuver, and motorization. In these games, there was little con-sideration given the use of militia forces or defense by such unconven-tional means as guerrilla warfare. Despite the attempts to create a viable militia force and Reichswehr minister Groener's interest in building a large national militia, the Truppenamt simply ignored militia forces when training its officers in strategy and tactics. The continuous-front trench warfare of World War I was also ignored in the war games. The 1926-27 scenario shows that the Truppenamt believed a future war would be de-cided by large, relatively mobile regular forces fighting a war of maneuver. By the mid-1920s, this is the only type of war for which the Reichswehr was training, in sharp contrast to the French, who still thought in terms of the continuous front, and the Americans and British, who seem during this period to have had no clear doctrine of large-scale war at all. The Ger-mans held a clear vision of the next war and trained for it single-mindedly.

This clarity and single-mindedness paid off in the high standard of training reached by the Reichswehr divisions. The American military atta-ché, who observed division-level maneuvers in 1924 reported "the army, according to our standards, to be above average in training, discipline and fighting efficiency; superior in orders, staff work and high command."[93] In 1926 the American attaché was the only foreign observer permitted to attend both the Group 1 and the Group 2 maneuvers. That year, he re-ported that "the German Army appears to have reached a very high de-gree of training, both of its officers and of its men."[94] Rather than laugh at the simulated tanks and guns of the Reichswehr, he saw it as a sensible way to train troops when funds were low and equipment unavailable; he recommended such innovations to the U.S. Army.[95]

As the Germans noticeably improved in training and in handling large bodies of troops using modern weaponry and tactics, the victorious Allies stagnated. The first multidivisional maneuvers by the French Army after the war took place in 1922. Only a few divisions of the large French Army took part and the performance of the French high command was criticized by the German observers. According to the Germans, the French Army Staff College showed "a notable preference for trench warfare."[96] The Germans reported that the French tactics were unimaginative and "by the book"—always a point of criticism to the German General Staff.[97] In 1924 the French Army committed a mere three divisions to large-scale maneuvers. That year, the German observers concluded that the French eighteen-month term of conscript service could not produce soldiers capable of carrying out modern combined-arms tactics.[98]

The British Army waited until 1924 before conducting its major postwar maneuvers. During those maneuvers, the London *Times* made an unfavorable comparison between the army of 1914 and the present force. The 1914 British Expeditionary Force (BEF), said the *Times*, was a third larger than the present force available in England, and the force ten years before had been in a far higher state of training and readiness.[99] The U.S. Army, in terms of training, had the worst record of all the major powers. Between World War I and 1941, it conducted no multidivisional maneuvers. The only place where American officers could even theoretically train for warfare with large units was in the war games of the one-year course at the Command and General Staff School at Fort Leavenworth. Truman Smith, who had observed the German Army in the 1920s, before attending the U.S. Army Staff College, described the Fort Leavenworth training as "archaic." It was an approach to war that viewed it as a "series of mathematical formulas."[100]

## THE EVOLUTION OF GERMANY'S ARMORED FORCES

Although the Reichswehr had made considerable progress developing its own armor doctrine, by the mid-1920s the evolution of the German armored force was—as in the case of the air force—closely tied to the testing and training program carried out in the USSR. The armor training program at Kazan was much smaller than the pilot training program at Lipetsk and lasted for only a short time—from 1929 to 1933. Still, it played an important role in the evolution of German armor doctrine, because it enabled the Germans to make a smooth transition from the mid-1920s,

*Troops train for chemical warfare during maneuvers of the Fourth Division, 1927.*

when the Reichswehr's armor theorists had absorbed the lessons of World War I, to the early 1930s, when the army would begin to build a major armored force. The armor training and testing program was therefore one of the most important of the Reichswehr's secret programs. Without the opportunity to conduct realistic, hands-on training in Russia, the Reichswehr would have embarked upon rearmament without current armor experience.

The German armored vehicle program had enjoyed high priority since 1925. In the spring of 1927 the Reichswehr achieved a major diplomatic success: the conclusion of an agreement with the Soviet government to open an armor training and testing center in Kazan, deep inside the USSR. The Germans had been eager to build such a center ever since the German/Russian military collaboration had begun in 1922, but suspicion on the part of the Soviets, as well as disagreement within the government and the Red Army, had led to Soviet foot-dragging.[101] General von Blomberg, chief of the Truppenamt, thought the delay in establishing the armor school serious enough to discuss the matter directly with Commissar for War Voroshilov in 1928, when Voroshilov visited Berlin and von

Blomberg inspected the German installations in the USSR.[102] The Kazan installation, like that of the shadow air force in Lipetsk, would consist of numerous modern workshops and facilities, along with comfortable quarters and a handsome officers' mess.[103] In Kazan, the Reichswehr had plenty of open terrain at its disposal, ideal for armored vehicle training and testing.[104]

The first training course at Kazan started in the spring of 1929; the delay in opening the school was due to the difficulty in shipping the finished German tank and armored car prototypes to the center.[105] The Kazan center, officially called the Heavy Vehicle Experimental and Test Station, was under the direction of the Inspectorate of Motor Troops.[106] The first commandant was Lieutenant Colonel Mahlbrandt, and the first chief of the Test Section was Major Pirner, the Weapons Office tank engineer.[107] The first course leader, in 1929, was Friedrich Kühn, who would go on to become commandant of the Panzer Troops School in 1940. The gunnery instructor was former First Lieutenant Baumgart, who would be brought back into the army in 1934. The engineering teacher was Engineer Walter from Krupp.[108] The armor course trained ten to eleven students per year.[109]

The course, which lasted approximately one year, began with a four-to-five-month program of technical and tactical instruction at the Motor Troops School near Berlin. In the Spring, the German officers would travel to Kazan to train with armored vehicles until the Fall. At Kazan, emphasis was placed on company and battalion armor operations.[110] The goal of the Armor School was to produce a cadre of fully qualified armor instructors for the Reichswehr. Each officer would gain proficiency in tank operation, tank gun marksmanship, tank maintenance, and radio operation. Tactical field exercises were a major part of the course.[111] The Armor School was organized into five departments: training, testing, technical-tests, supply, and administration.[112]

The foundation of the Kazan center coincided with the Red Army's establishment of its first mechanized regiments. In 1929 the Red Army organized the First Mechanized Regiment, a unit composed of a tank battalion, an armored car battalion, a motorized rifle battalion, and an artillery battery.[113] At the time, the Red Army possessed only two hundred tanks and armored cars, most of them obsolete.[114] Therefore, neither the Germans nor the Russians had more than a handful of armored vehicles for training when the Kazan center opened in 1929. The Soviets, however, were just beginning the large-scale manufacture of modern tanks that year, and both they and the Germans were aided by a British government decision of early 1930 to allow the sale of modern British tanks to the USSR. That year, the Soviets acquired fifteen Vickers Medium Mark II tanks, twenty-six Carden-Lloyd Mark VI machine-gun carriers, eight Carden-Lloyd tanks, and fifteen Vickers-Armstrong 6-ton tanks, among other vehicles.[115] The Reichswehr was thus able to evaluate some of the latest British armored vehicles.[116]

Although some Soviet officers took the armor course at Kazan, the majority of officers there were German.[117] Voroshilov referred to Kazan as a German school and preferred to train most of the Soviet armor officers at the new Red Army Armor Center at Voronezh.[118] The Reichswehr/Red Army relationship featured considerable distrust on both sides. The two leading Soviet tank commanders, Polyakov and Yeroshenko, nonetheless worked well with their German counterparts on technical and training matters.[119] The Reichswehr–Red Army exchange program was important to both sides. In 1926 thirteen Red Army officers were attached to the Reichswehr or attended exercises. In 1927 fourteen Red Army officers served with the Reichswehr. In those two years, thirty-nine Reichswehr officers were detached for duties with the Red Army.[120]

The armor center at Kazan, according to historian John Erickson, had three major functions: (1) to train officers; (2) to test German armored vehicle prototypes; and (3) to perform comparative tests on foreign armored vehicles.[121] Extensive Weapons Office files on the German armor testing program at Kazan are in the German military archives. There are few extant German documents, however, on the armor training program or foreign-weapons testing. Until the archives in the former Soviet Union are available for inspection, the primary sources on the Armor School at Kazan remain *Die Geschichte der Deutschen Panzerwaffe*, a history of German armor written by General Walther Nehring, and a former student of the armor course, and a collection of photographs of the school published in Walter Spielberger's history of Reichswehr motorization, *Die Motorisierung der deutschen Reichswehr*.[122]

Despite the shortage of documents, it is still possible to recreate part of the armor tactical curriculum as it was taught at Kazan in 1929. A tactical textbook, *Atlas to Leadership and Battle* (Atlas zu F.u.G.I.: Ein Anschauungs-Lehrbuch), written by Major Siebert of the Reichswehr and published in 1929, contains a comprehensive review of German armored unit tactics of the late 1920s.[123] Siebert's textbook is essentially a rendering of the standard, large-unit tactical doctrine of the Reichswehr, with many large-scale maps and diagrams and a commentary drawn from the tactical manuals. Armored warfare receives considerable attention. Tanks units are portrayed—along with air squadrons and heavy artillery regiments—as army-level support units to be employed in mass and at the decisive point.[124] Armored cars are represented as a cavalry weapon and the army cavalry units are portrayed as mixed units consisting of mounted squadrons, armored car units, motorized artillery and engineers, and bicycle or motorcycle infantry to be deployed for reconnaissance duties.[125]

Tank units could be attached to the cavalry to form a motorized task force if the cavalry needed heavy firepower to hold a position for the advancing infantry divisions.[126] The army's heavy tank units are portrayed as particularly suitable breakthrough weapons, leading the attack against enemy positions and then turning 90 degrees to roll up the enemy's flanks.[127] In a major offensive, the heavy tanks would lead, reducing enemy defenses and opening the way for light tanks, accompanied by infantry, to drive quickly into the enemy's rear.

Siebert recommended that the field army keep a significant tank reserve to be employed in support of the attacking forces as soon as they had advanced out of their supporting artillery.[128] When the army was on the defensive in a mobile war, the army tank units, supported by infantry and artillery, would be held in reserve as a counterattack force.[129] Tanks were also seen as an important antitank weapon should an enemy tank attack break through.[130] The tank forces were not always to be kept in mass. When attacking a city, Siebert recommended apportioning the tanks among the assaulting infantry units.[131] Throughout his text, he stressed the necessity for cooperation between the tank and motorized forces and the air force.

Taking Major Siebert's textbook as the standard Reichswehr tank doctrine of 1929, the German tactical understanding of armored warfare was not very different from the standard tank doctrine in other armies at that time. In 1929, as in World War I, the tank was seen primarily as an infantry support arm and as an offensive breakthrough weapon. The use of masses of more-mobile light tanks in the exploitation role was a tactic worked out by the Allied powers by the end of World War I. In this emphasis upon the tank as a counterattack and antitank weapon, we can see the German analysis of the World War I experience in facing Allied tanks. The use of armored vehicles as infantry support weapons in city fighting is a particularly German doctrine in 1929 and certainly stems from the extensive German experience from 1919 to 1923 using armored cars, and sometimes tanks, to quell internal urban revolts.[132]

By 1930 the Germans had at the Kazan armor center a total of ten German tanks (six large tractors and four light tractors) and several prototype armored cars from Daimler and Büssing.[133] Also by 1930 the Soviets had provided thirty Soviet-made tanks to the school for training purposes.[134] There were enough armored vehicles at Kazan to practice company and battalion maneuvers. Most important, the Germans had the opportunity to observe and participate in large-scale armored maneuvers with the Soviets in 1930.[135] In 1929 three German officers on the Red Army staff were involved in inspecting the new Russian armored units. That year officers from Reichswehr Headquarters, including General von Hammerstein-Equord, were able to observe the Soviet maneuvers.[136] In 1931 there were several joint exercises involving the Red Army armor units and the German officers at Kazan, who used Soviet equipment.[137] Thus from 1929 to 1931 the Reichswehr had access to the first major Soviet armor experiments as well as to the latest British equipment.

By the time the Kazan armor center was shut down in the summer of 1933, the Reichswehr had developed a cadre of more than fifty well-trained armor specialists. Between 1929 and 1932, thirty German officers had completed the armor course.[138] More than twenty Reichswehr officers had either taught the course or taken part in the armor prototype testing program in Russia. In addition, all the German firms involved in armored vehicle production—Daimler, Rheinmetall, Büssing, and Magirus—maintained staffs of engineers, workmen, and technicians at Kazan, creating a cadre of men experienced in the technical and supply side of armored warfare. An unknown number of Reichswehr civilian officials and NCOs were also involved in the Armor School. Theo Kretschmer, an officer in the Kazan course and later a major general, said that the course had made the participating officers "fully trained armor soldiers."[139] Kretschmer also remarked that the Kazan program brought the later development of German armor forces great advantages.[140] The Reichswehr possessed only a small group of armor specialists, but by the early 1930s it was probably as well trained as any other group of armor officers in the world. These officers not only had a thorough technical training, they also had been able to take part in relatively large-scale armored exercises with the Red Army. Many of the alumni of the armor center would become the German Army's leading armored warfare instructors of the 1930s and 1940s. The first three commanders of the Tank Gunnery School founded in 1934— Lieutenant Colonel Baumgart, Colonel Kraeber, and Lieutenant Colonel Bonatz—were all trained at Kazan.[141] Ernst Volckheim, another Kazan alumnus, would be in charge of writing armored warfare manuals in the 1930s.[142] Colonel von Radlmaier and Colonel Harpe, who served as commandants at Kazan, became commanders of the Panzer Troops School.[143] Other officers trained at Kazan went on to become important armor commanders, including General Nehring, a corps commander in World War II, and General Reinhardt, who commanded the Forty-first Panzer Corps in France in 1940.

The armor training and testing in the USSR helped influence Reichswehr concepts. By the late 1920s, these ideas could be more openly discussed, for it became clear that the Versailles armaments restrictions would not last. The Reichswehr became more open about discussing modernization. Reichswehr minister Groener was well informed on armor development. In a lecture given in 1929-30, he spoke of the need to develop heavier (up to 47-mm) antitank guns, the need to motorize antitank units, and the need to develop automatic weapons of 13–20-mm

*Von Seeckt's successor, General Heye (left), Reichswehr minister Dr. Gessler (center), and navy commander-in-chief Admiral Zenker (right) observe maneuvers of Sixth Infantry and Third Cavalry divisions in Westphalia, 1927.*

bore.[144] Groener, without mentioning the Reichswehr's testing program in the USSR, told his audience that 7.5-ton light tanks and 15-ton medium tanks were, in his view, the necessary tanks of the future for the support of the cavalry and infantry and also for carrying out independent operations.[145] These weapons were, of course, the tanks being tested in Russia at that time.

At the end of the 1920s, the major issue concerning armored forces was the role armor would play in motorizing the cavalry. Groener made it clear in his lecture of 1929–30 that the cavalry would be progressively motorized during the next decade.[146] Groener also pointed to the role of the tank, "Tanks will either be part of the cavalry's realm or they will fight as an independent branch."[147] With the decision to motorize the cavalry, it became more adept at using armored forces. Ernst Kabisch, a retired lieutenant general who wrote on military affairs for the *Kölnische Zeitung*, wrote Groener in October 1932 describing the fall maneuvers of that year. Kabisch explained that maneuvers had become quite different from those held just after the war, and that the cavalry in particular had undergone great changes. He described how the First Cavalry Division had attacked the Ninth Infantry Regiment with the support of a (simulated) tank battalion and attached infantry. This force made a breakthrough and deep penetration into the enemy's rear.[148]

The training in the USSR and the large-scale maneuvers in Germany gave the Reichswehr officers a noticeable confidence when they wrote of armor operations. By the early 1930s, Reichswehr cavalry officers were thinking in terms of large motorized armored formations. One of the most popular ideas was to turn the cavalry into light divisions—a combined cavalry and motorized division with strong armored elements.[149] In 1932–1934, Major Nehring, who had recently completed the Kazan armor course, was assigned by T-4 (Training Section) to outline "the tactics of the Panzer Brigade in the framework of the Cavalry Corps."[150]

## Conclusion

In *The Evolution of Blitzkrieg Tactics*, Robert Citino claimed that "the perceived challenge from Poland was the primary reason for the development of blitzkreig tactics" by the Reichswehr.[151] Although it is true that Poland was seen as a major threat, Citino overstated his thesis. There is no documentary evidence to show that the Germans specifically tailored their tactical doctrine to a Polish campaign. The divisions of Reichswehr Group 2, stationed in western Germany to combat a French attack, trained no differently from the divisions of Group 1, stationed along the Polish border. The Reichswehr's tactics of mobile warfare were considered just as valid against the more dangerous French as they were against the Poles. The only clear example of the Reichswehr establishing special units and tactics to fulfill a specific strategic situation was the organization of a battalion of the Seventh Infantry Regiment and some artillery units as a specially trained and equipped mountain battalion.[152] The mountain troops were stationed in Silesia, near the Czech border. Since Czechoslovakia was perceived as hostile, it made sense to maintain some special units trained to fight in that nation's mountainous terrain.

From the mid-1920s to the early 1930s, the German Army became increasingly proficient in the tactics of motorized, large-scale warfare. The most ironic aspect of the situation is that the small, lightly armed Reichswehr became the best-trained army in the world in carrying out large-scale operations. The decision to develop mobile, motorized tactics was taken shortly after World War I and sprang from German analysis of that war (see Chapter Two). The evolution of German tactics depended largely on the success of the maneuvers and war games in which the Germans tried out the new concepts. A momentum built up in German tactical doctrine. By the time the Reichswehr was a mature military force, the officer corps was convinced of the efficacy of mobile warfare. Even the cavalry, the most conservative branch of the army, was eager to motorize and mechanize. By the early 1930s it would have been very difficult to turn the German Army into a defensive force.

It is hard to criticize the Reichswehr high command for either its tactics or its political-strategic policies of the late 1920s. Given the almost impossible strategic situation that the Germans faced, the Reichswehr developed cautious long-term war plans and mobilization strategies that formed an effective basis for rearmament. The Reichswehr continued to develop von Seeckt's concepts of mobile warfare with clarity and single-mindedness. General Heye and General von Hammerstein-Equord carried on the best aspects of von Seeckt's tactical doctrine and training policies, improving the Reichswehr's relationship with the government. The only real failure of the Reichswehr in the 1920s was its program to create a significant reserve force. As a mature military force, however, the Reichswehr in its tactical doctrine and training, was already well on its way to learning the methods that proved so successful in World War II.

# CHAPTER NINE

# Epilogue

Most of the tactics used in the blitzkrieg of 1939 and 1940 sprang directly from those developed by von Seeckt and the General Staff committees after World War I and expressed in Army Regulation 487, *Leadership and Battle with Combined Arms*, published in 1921 and 1923. The German Army that marched into Poland in 1939 and France in 1940 closely resembled what the Reichswehr in the early 1920s had planned to become. The organization of the infantry divisions of 1939 had already been published—with almost no revision—in volume two of *Leadership and Battle*, published in 1923.[1]

The logic and tactics of Army Regulation 487 would continue to have a profound effect upon the German Army through the 1930s and World War II. In the early 1930s, rapid changes in technology had made parts of the regulation obsolete, so in 1931-32 a committee, chaired by General Ludwig von Beck, wrote a new army tactical doctrine manual, which was published in 1933 as Army Regulation 300, *Troop Leadership*.[2] Army Regulation 300 would endure as the official expression of army tactical doctrine until 1945. Von Beck is generally identified as the primary author of *Troop Leadership*, and many military historians have praised the tactics and philosophy of leadership he expressed in the regulation.[3] Much of the philosophy of command and tactics that General Beck is praised for so eloquently expressing in the introduction to *Troop Leadership* in 1933, however, is only a paraphrase of *Leadership and Battle*, edited in 1921 by the Truppenamt Training Section and signed by von Seeckt. Von Beck's writing style is clear and elegant, an improvement upon the style of *Leadership and Battle*, yet whole passages are lifted from the earlier document. For example, statements in *Troop Leadership* such as "The teachings of wartime command cannot be summarized in regulations"[4] are virtually the same words used in *Leadership and Battle*.[5] The emphasis *Troop Leadership* places upon the responsibility of the leader, the importance of the leader's conduct on the battlefield as an example to his troops, the necessity of being tactically flexible, the care to be given the soldiers, and the need for independent leadership and action at every level are all expressed in the earlier regulation.[6] The basic tactical principles of *Troop Leadership* are the same as those of *Leadership and Battle*: the importance of offense, of finding the point of decision (Schwerpunkt), of the use of the delaying battle to gain time for preparing offensive action, and so on.

The major difference between *Troop Leadership* and *Leadership and Battle* is that the former places greater emphasis on motorized warfare—as one might expect. *Troop Leadership*'s vision of motorized warfare is far grander than the tactical regulations of 1921 and 1923. *Troop Leadership* does not speak of panzer divisions, but rather of large "armored commands"—commands comprising tank regiments, motorized infantry, and other elements.[7] The concept of the large "light command"—motorized infantry mounted on cross-country vehicles and motorized artillery and support elements—is also outlined.[8] Despite the specific evolution of tactics found in *Troop Leadership*, the greater part of that regulation, down to the organization of the document itself, is drawn with minimal changes from *Leadership and Battle*.

The initial expansion and rearmament of the Reichswehr in 1933–34 worked out in general accordance with the expansion plans developed after 1928. Hitler would order expansion and rearmament to progress much faster—beyond the army's wildest dreams. Army expansion certainly went beyond what the Reichswehr thought possible.[9] The Führerheer concept, in which the small, professional army would provide the foundation for a far larger force, nevertheless proved its worth. From Hitler's accession to power on July 30, 1933, to the invasion of Poland on September 1, 1939, the 100,000-man Reichswehr, with its limited reserves, expanded into a total army strength of 3,737,104 men (including the field army and reserves of 2,741,064 men and the replacement army of 996,040).[10] The Luftwaffe grew from a base strength of a few hundred Reichswehr officers and NCOs into a force of 550,000 men.[11] Even with this enormous expansion, many of von Seeckt's plans from the 1920s were incorporated into the 1930s rearmament. For instance, a reserve was built out of former soldiers who had served their term as conscripts; by 1939 four "waves" of troops had been created. The first wave was the fully trained and equipped field army of fifty-one active divisions, fifteen of these armored and motorized. These divisions had a high proportion of regular officers and NCOs. A second wave of seventeen reserve infantry divisions had been formed by 1939, each division having 2,000 fewer soldiers, a small proportion of active personnel (6 percent), and less equipment than the first wave. The third wave consisted of older reservists, no active personnel, and a supply train of more horses than trucks. The third wave was formed into twenty Landesschütz divisions considered suitable only for defense. The fourth wave consisted of fourteen replacement army training divisions.[12] Thus in 1939 the German Army was in a position to go to war and mobilize afterward.

Maintenance of high officer standards was another important Reichswehr policy that was passed on to the expanded Wehrmacht of the 1930s. With an officer corps composing just 4 percent of the total force, the Reichswehr had just enough officers to be efficient. The rapid expansion of the army and Luftwaffe therefore created a serious officer shortage. Fifteen hundred Reichswehr senior NCOs were commissioned as officers. Eighteen hundred retired and reserve officers were recalled to duty, and twenty-five hundred officers were brought into the army from the Security Police.[13] The officer cadet program was expanded, but the educational qualifications were still maintained. Even though the percentage of officers in the army fell to below 2.5 percent, the full four-year officer training program of the 1920s was the same until 1937. Even then, when the officer course was shortened to two years, the strict requirements for commissioning were unchanged. By the time Germany went to war in 1939, the percentage of officers had risen to just below 3 percent of the total force.[14] Like the Reichswehr before it, the Wehrmacht learned to make do with fewer officers and to rely upon the professional NCO corps to provide lower-level leadership. From 1939 through World War II, it was normal to have master sergeants as platoon leaders. As was the case regarding officers, the expanded army did not lower its NCO standards and the Reichswehr-trained NCO remained the backbone of the army through World War II, one explanation for the strong small-unit cohesion in the German Army until the end of World War II.[15]

General Frido von Senger und Etterlin, renowned as one of the German Army's finest tacticians of World War II, credited von Seeckt's concepts of mobile warfare and the creation of an elite field force (the professional army) within the total force as providing the inspiration for the successful tactics of 1939–40. Summing up the 1940 campaign in France, von Senger und Etterlin commented,

> If one thinks over the war up to now, one will recollect the vision of the clever General von Seeckt, which was rejected as wrong by the military of his time. Seeckt conceived the future form of war as a struggle between small professional armies to which the elite of the combatant nation would rally: Stukas (dive bombers), Panzer troops, parachutists. By the side of this force, the popular army—comprising the bulk of the infantry—played only a subordinate role. In view of the present course of the war, Seeckt was right. Nobody could foresee that a skillful combination of modern weapons, untested as yet by the experience of war, would yield such swift results.[16]

Many of the specific tactics of the blitzkrieg were developed in the 1920s. In the maneuvers of that decade, the German Army—in contrast to the other Western armies—learned to ignore the continuous front.

Reichswehr units advanced rapidly without regard to their flanks (see Chapter Eight). General von Seeckt would have felt comfortable with the conduct of the Polish campaign. The Luftwaffe's tactics in September 1939 were straight from his vision of air warfare. The Germans first concentrated their combat aircraft against the Polish Air Force in order to gain air superiority. Once air superiority was gained the Luftwaffe concentrated half of its attacks upon disrupting Polish mobilization and used the remaining sorties for direct support of the ground forces.[17] One of the few important tactics used in World War II that was not developed by the Reichswehr in the 1920s was the use of the panzer division, whose organization was created by General Heinz Guderian in the mid-1930s. The panzer division was an original concept not because it was a force that contained a mass of tanks but because it combined tanks, infantry, artillery, pioneers, and support troops into one well-balanced and self-sufficient mobile force. The panzer division was effective precisely because it was a combined-arms force that used all of its weapons, not just the tanks, with maximum effectiveness.

Even though the panzer division was Guderian's creation in 1935, it was less a quantum leap than a natural evolution from the army's tactics in the 1920s. The use of combined arms was the central tactical principle of the Reichswehr. In the 1920s, both the officer cadet training and the General Staff training set up by von Seeckt would stress attachment to other arms and a sound familiarity and competence in the tactics and weaponry of all branches of the army (see Chapter Four). Von Seeckt emphasized the combined-arms approach to the point of directing that infantry officers become qualified to command a cannon section. Coming from a background where combined arms were heavily emphasized, it was more natural for the Germans to create a division that combined tanks with other arms than it was for the British and French, whose military traditions did not stress cooperation among the different branches and whose armor theorists stressed tanks more than other arms.

Dominick Graham, who fought the Germans in North Africa, believes the key to understanding German tactical superiority in North Africa in 1941-42 was the German doctrine of combined arms. The Germans maneuvered and fought so that all arms—guns, tanks, and motorized infantry—could render each other effective support. The British defeats in Africa up to El Alamein were, in Graham's analysis, due to poor British tactics that operated the tanks far from infantry and gun support. Until late 1942 the British were generally unable to employ the different arms as an effective team in the manner of the Germans.[18] Graham also refuted the idea that the Germans were successful because they had adopted the mobile tactics of the prewar British armor theorists. He states that one of the tactical mistakes of the British Army was to follow the ideas of these theorists, who emphasized the dispersal of armored forces. The German tactics were precisely the opposite; they normally concentrated their mobile forces more tightly than the British with the result that the British were regularly outfought.[19]

The remarkable German victory over the British and French armies in 1940 cannot be explained by any German superiority of weaponry or numbers. At the start of the German offensive on May 10, 1940, the opposing sides were almost equal in the number and quality of their weaponry. The Germans had 136 divisions opposing 94 French divisions, 10 British divisions, 22 Belgian divisions, and 10 Dutch divisions—a total of 136 Allied divisions—on the northeastern front.[20] The British and French armies had a total of 22 armored and motorized divisions against the same number of German panzer and motorized divisions.[21] The Allies could even claim tank superiority in 1940, with approximately 3,000 tanks opposing 2,200–2,800 German tanks.[22] More than half of the German tanks were the light Mark I and Mark II tanks—only 627 Mark III and Mark IV battle tanks were available.[23] On the other hand, the French Army possessed the most heavily gunned, well-armored tanks. It had 1,800 heavy tanks, such as the Souma with the 47-mm gun and the Char B tank with heavy armor, a 75-mm hull gun, and a 47-mm turret gun—possibly the best tank anywhere in 1940.[24] Furthermore, the French Army had 11,200 guns in 1940 to Germany's 7,710. This superiority was offset, however, by France's weak flak arm, which possessed only 1,500 guns of all types. The Germans, on the other hand, had 2,600 of the superb, 88-mm flak guns and 6,700 light flak guns.[25]

Given the approximate parity of both sides in 1940 with regard to troops, armored divisions, and equipment, the explanation for the dramatic German victory in 1940 can be found in two factors: superior tactics and superior training. The clear German superiority in both of these areas began with the Reichswehr of the 1920s and continued into World War II. The best means to illustrate this is to compare the interwar British and French armies with the Reichswehr.

In the interwar period, the British Army seems to have had some vague notion that the next war might be something like 1918. After World War I, the infantry tactics were rewritten to include the experience of 1918, but beyond that the army's senior commanders showed little interest in preparing for the next major war. Some large maneuvers were held in the 1920s, and there were some important experiments with mechanized forces, but the objectives of the senior officers were to garrison the colonies, deal with Ireland, and simply maintain the force in a time of low budgets.[26] The British Army produced a considerable amount of tactical thought in this period. Men like Fuller, Liddell Hart, Martel, and others were busy writing about mechanized warfare, but theoretical work could not replace training.[27] Field Marshal Montgomery commented on the state of the British Expeditionary Force in 1939: "In the years preceding the outbreak of war no large-scale exercises with troops had been held in England for some time. Indeed, the Regular Army was unfit to take part in a realistic exercise."[28] Montgomery also asserted that due to lack of training, there "was a total lack of any common policy or tactical doctrine throughout the BEF, when differences arose these differences remained, and there was no firm grip from the top."[29] The British Army had gotten out of the habit of large-scale maneuvers. Between September 1939 and May 1940, the BEF in France not only did not hold multidivisional maneuvers, it also did not conduct staff war games or communications exercises.[30] When Montgomery began training his Third Division in a series of division exercises, it was considered a rare and revolutionary event. Even General Alan Brooke, the corps commander, would say that these exercises were "an eye-opener."[31]

The French Army, in contrast to the British, did have a clear body of tactical doctrine. Unfortunately for the French, their tactics for large-scale warfare were essentially frozen in the year 1918. The most influential officer in the French Army in the interwar period was Marshal Philippe Pétain, who was appointed vice president of the Army Council (the president of the council was the minister of war) in 1920. As vice president, he was the most important officer in the army: He would command the French armies in war. From this position (which he held until 1931), Pétain promoted his policy of the power of the defense.[32] One aspect of Pétain's thought was the importance of fortified positions; out of this doctrine came the Maginot Line, begun in 1926.[33] Many officers, in particular Marshal Ferdinand Foch, urged a more offensive attitude for army tactical doctrine.[34] Some officers—for example, Charles de Gaulle—would advocate mobile tactics in the 1930s, but such ideas would be countered by defense-minded men such as General Narcisse Chauvineau, who wrote numerous articles on military matters and a book (published in 1939) asserting that sustained power and mobility were mutually exclusive. He supported France's tactics of the continuous front and the Maginot Line.[35]

The state of training in the French Army in the interwar period was even more critical than the state of tactical doctrine. As I have already noted, only a small part of the French Army took part in multidivisional maneuvers in the 1920s. Training became worse in 1927-28, when the term of conscript service was reduced to one year.[36] This meant that conscripts were given six months of basic training and then spent six months with a field unit, often doing service in a fortress on the Maginot Line.[37] The one-year service period was just enough time to train a soldier to effectively man a fortress, but not enough time to train him in the complexities of maneuver warfare. Even when military service was lengthened in the late 1930s and new armament was provided to the army, the few field maneuvers that took place still concentrated on static, defensive tactics.[38] Between September 1939 and May 1940, the French high command would make no effort to provide any large-unit training for the Army. Rather than train, the French Army spent the first eight and a half months of World War II in garrison and in fortresses.[39]

The training factor alone would have proven decisive in 1940. Thanks to the Reichswehr's excellent training program and the German Army's unrelenting emphasis on multidivisional maneuvers, a typical German Army captain or major in 1940 would have participated in more multi-divisional maneuvers than the average British or French general. The quality of German training would also account for the consistent battle-field superiority demonstrated by the German Army throughout World War II. Colonel Trevor Dupuy calculated that the German Army main-tained a 20–30 percent combat-effectiveness superiority over the Western Allies in 1943-44.[40] Training can only be truly successful, however, if it is based upon a clear doctrine and tactical system. This brings us back to the vision of warfare outlined in 1919-20 by General von Seeckt and the Ger-man General Staff. In contrast to other armies, the German Army alone carried out a systematic analysis of the lessons of World War I. Of the ma-jor powers, Germany alone would correctly predict the course of future warfare and the tactics that would be successful. From this beginning in the early 1920s, the German Army cultivated the training program that created the conditions for victory in 1939 and 1940.

# Proposed Reichswehr Tables of Organization and Equipment from the 1920s

## Organization of a Reichswehr Infantry Division as Specified by the Versailles Treaty, 1919

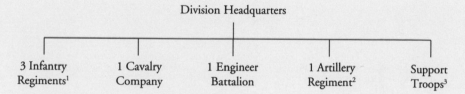

Division Headquarters

| 3 Infantry Regiments[1] | 1 Cavalry Company | 1 Engineer Battalion | 1 Artillery Regiment[2] | Support Troops[3] |

*Source:* Adapted from *Heeresdienstvorschrift* 487, *Führung und Gefecht der verbundenen Waffen* (Berlin: Verlag Offene Worte, 1921, 1923, 1925).

[1]Each regiment has 3 battalions.
[2]3 battalions, each with 1 medium battery and 2 light batteries; 1 of the 9 batteries is motorized.
[3]Medical battalion, signals battalion, truck battalion, wagon battalion.

## Organization of a Reichswehr Cavalry Division as Specified by the Versailles Treaty, 1919

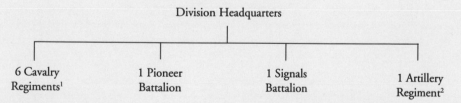

Division Headquarters

| 6 Cavalry Regiments[1] | 1 Pioneer Battalion | 1 Signals Battalion | 1 Artillery Regiment[2] |

*Source:* Adapted from *Heeresdienstvorschrift* 487, *Führung und Gefecht der verbundenen Waffen* (Berlin: Verlag Offene Worte, 1921, 1923, 1925).

[1]Each regiment has 4 cavalry companies, 1 signals platoon, and 1 machine-gun company.
[2]3 horse-drawn light gun batteries.

## Organization of a "Modern Infantry Division" as Specified by Army Regulation 487, 1923

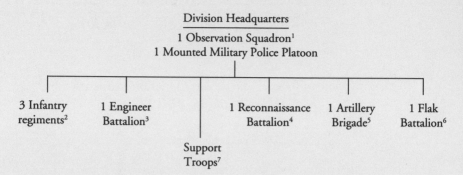

Division Headquarters

1 Observation Squadron[1]
1 Mounted Military Police Platoon

3 Infantry regiments[2]    1 Engineer Battalion[3]    1 Reconnaissance Battalion[4]    1 Artillery Brigade[5]    1 Flak Battalion[6]

Support Troops[7]

*Source:* Adapted from *Heeresdienstvorschrift* 487, *Führung und Gefecht der verbundenen Waffen* (Berlin: Verlag Offene Worte, 1921, 1923, 1925).

[1] 12 aircraft.
[2] Each regiment has 3 battalions and a 6-gun artillery battery.
[3] 1 bridge company, 1 pioneer company.
[4] 2 cavalry companies, 1 bicycle company, 1 armored car company.
[5] 2 artillery regiments. The first regiment has 3 battalions; each battalion has 1 medium and 1 heavy battery. The second regiment has 1 motorized battalion of 3 medium batteries, 1 battalion of motorized antitank guns, and 1 battalion of light guns.
[6] 1 motorized heavy battery, 2 motorized light batteries.
[7] Signals battalion, medical battalion, truck battalion, wagon battalion, veterinary detail.

## Organization of a "Modern Cavalry Division" as Specified by Army Regulation 487, 1923

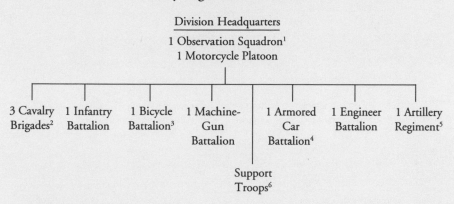

Division Headquarters

1 Observation Squadron[1]
1 Motorcycle Platoon

| 3 Cavalry Brigades[2] | 1 Infantry Battalion | 1 Bicycle Battalion[3] | 1 Machine-Gun Battalion | 1 Armored Car Battalion[4] | 1 Engineer Battalion | 1 Artillery Regiment[5] |

Support Troops[6]

*Source:* Adapted from *Heeresdienstvorschrift* 487, *Führung und Gefecht der verbundenen Waffen* (Berlin: Verlag Offene Worte, 1921, 1923, 1925).

[1] 12 aircraft.
[2] 2 regiments per brigade. Each regiment has 4 companies, 1 machine-gun company, and a 2-gun artillery section.
[3] 3 bicycle companies, 2 motorized 3-gun antitank batteries.
[4] 12 armored cars.
[5] 1 battalion with 3 light horse batteries; 1 motorized battalion with 2 medium howitzer batteries and 1 antitank battery; 1 motorized flak battalion with 1 heavy and 2 light batteries.
[6] Medical battalion, truck battalion, wagon battalion, veterinary detail.

## Organization of an Air Division as Specified by the Truppenamt Air Section Manual, c. 1925

Fighter Brigade 4
Two 2-seater fighter groups, each with three 15-plane squadrons.

Mixed Fighter Brigade 2
One 2-seater fighter group with three 15-plane squadrons, plus one 1-seater fighter group with three 15-plane squadrons.

Night Fighter Brigade 7
Two night fighter groups, each with three 10-plane squadrons.

Day Bomber Brigade 5
Two day bomber groups, each with three 11-plane squadrons.

Night Bomber Brigade 2
Two bomber groups, each with three 6-plane squadrons.

## Organization of a Motorized Division during the Reichswehr Winter War Games, 1926-27

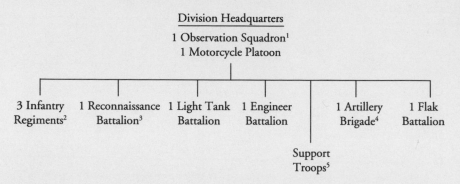

Division Headquarters

1 Observation Squadron[1]
1 Motorcycle Platoon

| 3 Infantry Regiments[2] | 1 Reconnaissance Battalion[3] | 1 Light Tank Battalion | 1 Engineer Battalion | | 1 Artillery Brigade[4] | 1 Flak Battalion |

Support Troops[5]

*Source:* Truppenamt T-4, War Games, 1926-27, File RH 2/2822, Bundesarchiv/Militärarchiv, Freiberg im Breisgau.

[1]6 aircraft
[2]Each regiment has 3 truck-carried battalions, 1 signals company, and 1 truck-mounted battery of 6 guns.
[3]2 armored car companies of 12 vehicles each, 1 light tank company, 1 motorcycle company, 1 bicycle battalion, 1 halftrack infantry company, 2 motorized antitank batteries.
[4]The first regiment has 2 motorized battalions, each with 2 medium and 1 heavy batteries. The second regiment has 1 motorized battalion of 2 medium and 1 heavy batteries, plus 1 battalion of 3 motorized antitank gun batteries.
[5]Truck regiment of 2 battalions, medical battalion, signals battalion, military police company, supply battalion.

## Organization of a Motorized Brigade during the Reichswehr Winter War Games, 1926-27

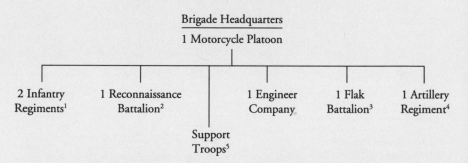

Brigade Headquarters

1 Motorcycle Platoon

| 2 Infantry Regiments[1] | 1 Reconnaissance Battalion[2] | | 1 Engineer Company | 1 Flak Battalion[3] | 1 Artillery Regiment[4] |

Support Troops[5]

*Source:* Truppenamt T-4, War Games, 1926-27, File RH 2/2822, Bundesarchiv/Militärarchiv, Freiberg im Breisgau.

[1]Each regiment has 3 motorized battalions and 1 motorized 6-gun artillery battery.
[2]Armored car company (12 vehicles), motorcycle company, motorized infantry company, and antitank gun section.
[3]2 gun batteries, 1 searchlight battery.
[4]2 motorized battalions, each with two 105-mm batteries and a heavy howitzer battery.
[5]Truck regiment of 2 battalions, medical detachment, signals company, military police detachment.

# NOTES

## CHAPTER ONE. THE LESSONS OF WORLD WAR I

1. For an overview of the Schlieffen Plan's operation, see Corelli Barnett, *The Swordbearers* (London: Eyre and Spottiswoode, 1963), 13–106.
2. Jehuda L. Wallach, *The Dogma of the Battle of Annihilation* (Westport, Conn.: Greenwood Press, 1986), 213–219.
3. Col. Gen. Wilhelm Groener, *Das Testament des Grafen Schlieffen* (Berlin: E. Mittler und Sohn, 1927), and *Der Feldherr wider Willen: Operative Studien über den Weltkrieg* (Berlin: E. Mittler und Sohn, 1931), especially 6–9.
4. Walter Görlitz, *History of the German General Staff, 1657–1945* (New York: Praeger, 1953), 170.
5. Hans Meier-Welcker, *Seeckt* (Frankfurt am Main: Bernard und Graefe Verlag, 1967), 76.
6. Anthony Livesey, *Great Battles of World War I* (New York: Macmillan, 1989), 77.
7. Col. Max Bauer, *Der Grosse Krieg in Feld und Heimat* (Tübingen: Osiander Verlag, 1921), 103–104.
8. Barnett, *Swordbearers*, 302.
9. Görlitz, *History of the German General Staff*, 195.
10. Ibid., 103.
11. Col. Gen. Wilhelm Groener, *Lebenserinnerungen: Jugend, Generalstab, Weltkrieg* (Göttingen: Vandenhoeck und Ruprecht, 1957), 429–431.
12. Wetzell to von Seeckt, July 24, 1919, U.S. National Archives, Washington, D.C. (hereafter NA), Von Seeckt Papers, File M-132, Roll 20, Item 90.
13. Deutsche Reichstag, *Die Ursachen des deutschen Zusammenbruchs im Jahre 1918*, 8 vols. (Berlin: Deutsche Verlagsgesellschaft für Politik und Geschichte, 1928).
14. Ibid., 6:323–337.
15. Gordon Craig, *The Politics of the Prussian Army, 1640–1945* (Oxford: Clarendon Press, 1955), 337–338.
16. Bruce Gudmundson, *Stormtroop Tactics: Innovation in the German Army, 1914–1918* (New York: Praeger, 1989), 21–22.
17. Barnett, *Swordbearers*, 40.
18. Gudmundson, *Stormtroop Tactics*, 25; and Wallach, *Battle of Annihilation*, 79.
19. Gudmundson, *Stormtroop Tactics*, 25.
20. Barnett, *Swordbearers*, 41.
21. Quoted in Martin van Creveld, *Command in War* (Cambridge, Mass: Harvard University Press, 1985), 170.
22. Alfred Knox, *With the Russian Army, 1914–1917* (New York: Arno Press, 1971), 283–284; and Norman Stone, *The Eastern Front, 1914–1917* (New York: Charles Scribner's Sons, 1975), 135 and 142–143.

23. For a full account of this battle, see Capt. C. R. Kutz, *War on Wheels* (London: John Lane, 1941), Chapter 7.

24. U.S. Army Cavalry School, *Cavalry Combat* (Harrisburg, Penn.: U.S. Cavalry Association, 1937), 254–258.

25. Gudmundson, *Stormtroop Tactics*, 113–121, contains an outline of Bruchmüller's methods and the attack on Riga.

26. For a history and detailed description of stormtroop tactics, see Timothy Lupfer, *The Dynamics of Doctrine: The Changes in German Tactical Doctrine during the First World War*, Leavenworth Paper 4 (Fort Leavenworth, Kans.: U.S. Army Command and General Staff College Press, July 1981); and Gudmundson, *Stormtroop Tactics*.

27. For diagrams as well as a description of German infantry organization and tactics of 1918, see John A. English, *On Infantry* (New York: Praeger, 1981), 20–21.

28. Rod Paschall, *The Defeat of Imperial Germany, 1917–1918* (Chapel Hill, N.C.: Algonquin, 1989), 101.

29. Ibid., 124. For a detailed analysis of the German counterattack at Cambrai, see William Moore, *A Wood Called Bourlon* (London: Leo Cooper, 1988); and David Chandler, "Cambrai: The German Counterattack," in *Tanks and Weapons of World War I*, ed. Bernard Fitzsimons (London: Phoebus, 1973), 122–128.

30. Paschall, *Defeat of Imperial Germany*, 141.

31. The final evolution of the German defensive tactics as endorsed by the high command is outlined in two pamphlets and reproduced in Field Marshal Erich von Ludendorff, ed., *Urkunden der Obersten Heeresleitung über ihre Tätigkeit, 1916/18* (Berlin: E. Mittler und Sohn, 1920), especially "Allgemeines über Stellungbau" (August 10, 1918), 594–604, and "Die Abwehr im Stellungskrieg," 604–640.

32. Barnett, *Swordbearers*, 208; and Paschall, *Defeat of Imperial Germany*, 46–48.

33. Barnett, *Swordbearers*, 298–299.

34. Görlitz, *History of the German General Staff*, 10.

35. Karl Demeter, *Das Deutsche Offizierkorps in Gesellschaft und Staat, 1650–1945* (Frankfurt am Main: Bernard und Graefe Verlag, 1962), 89.

36. Martin van Creveld, *The Training of Officers* (New York: Free Press, 1990), 27.

37. See ibid., 21–28, for a detailed outline of the prewar Kriegsakademie course.

38. Gudmundson, *Stormtroop Tactics*, 22–23.

39. Königlich-Preussisches Kriegsministerium, *Verordnung über die Ausbildung der Truppen für den Felddienst und über die grösseren Truppenübungen* (Berlin: Königliche Hofdruckerei, June 1870).

40. Ernst Jünger, *The Storm of Steel* (London: Chatto and Windus, 1929), 31, 64, and 120.

41. Holger Herwig, "The Dynamics of Necessity: German Military Policy during the First World War," in *Military Effectiveness*, vol. 1, ed. Allan Millett and Williamson Murray (Boston: Allen and Unwin, 1988), 101.

42. Gen. Erich von Ludendorff, *Ludendorff's Own Story*, vol. 2 (New York: Harper and Brothers, 1919), 206. Six thousand artillery officers and NCOs were sent to special courses in new tactics in 1917-18. See Gudmundson, *Stormtroop Tactics*, 161–162.

43. Herwig, "Dynamics of Necessity," 101.

44. Jünger, *Storm of Steel*, 240.

45. Ludendorff, *Ludendorff's Own Story*, vol. 2:209. On the scope of infantry training, see Paschall, *Defeat of Imperial Germany*, 113.

46. Oberste Heeresleitung, *Kompagnie-Ausbildungsplan während einer Ruhezeit bis zu 14 Tagen*, 2d ed. (Berlin: Reichsdruckerei, 1918).

47. Chef des Generalstabes des Feldheeres, *Nahkampfmittel*, Part 3 (Berlin: Reichsdruckerei, January 1917).

48. Georg Neumann, *Die Deutschen Luftstreitkräfte im Weltkriege* (Berlin: E. Mittler und Sohn, 1921), 268–269.

49. Richard Hallion, *Rise of the Fighter Aircraft, 1914–1918* (Annapolis, Md.: Nautical and Aviation Publishing Company of America, 1984), 72.

50. Ibid., 72–73 and 160–161.

51. Gen. Charles de Gaulle, *The Army of the Future* (London: Hutchinson, 1940), 47.

52. A German Army manual—Kriegsministerium, *Anhaltspunkte für den Unterricht bei der Truppe über Luftfahrzeuge und deren Bekämpfung* (Berlin: Reichsdruckerei, March 1913)—provides a good outline of prewar air doctrine. The primary air missions are given as reconnaissance, liaison, and artillery spotting. Bombing is also mentioned as a mission, but only once. Clearly, bombing is a secondary mission of the Zeppelin airships.

53. Walter Musciano, *Eagles of the Black Cross* (New York: Ivan Obolensky, 1965), 106.

54. John Morrow, *German Air Power in World War I* (Lincoln: University of Nebraska Press, 1982), 91.

55. David Divine, *The Broken Wing: A Study in the British Exercise of Air Power* (London: Hutchinson, 1966), 140–141.

56. Olaf Groehler, *Geschichte des Luftkrieges 1910 bis 1980* (Berlin: Militärverlag der Deutschen Demokratischen Republik, 1981), 58.

57. William Mitchell, *Memoirs of World War I* (New York: Random House, 1960), 306; originally published in *Liberty Magazine* in 1926. See also Kommandierender General der Luftstreitkräfte, *Weisungen für den Einsatz und die Verwendung von Fliegerverbänden innerhalb einer Armee* (N.p.: Generalstab des Feldheeres, May 1917), paragraphs 104–106.

58. Hallion, *Fighter Aircraft*, 131.

59. Ibid., 131–132. On the Junkers J-1 and Junkers CL1, see Bryan Philpott, *The Encyclopedia of German Military Aircraft* (London: Bison, 1981), 53–54.

60. Groehler, *Geschichte des Luftkrieges*, 92.

61. Kommandierender General der Luftstreitkräfte, *Hinweise für die Führung einer Fliegerabteilung in der Angriffsschlacht und im Bewegungskrieg* (N.p.: Generalstab des Feldheeres, February 1918).

62. Luftstreitkräfte, Ausbildungsvorschrift der Infanterie Kommandos, January 1918, Bundesarchiv/Militärarchiv, Freiburg im Breisgau, Germany (hereafter BA/MA), PH 17/98.

63. Reichsarchiv Abteilung B, Luftstreitkräfte Study, April 2, 1926, BA/MA, RH 2/2195. For an account of the German air support plan for the spring 1918 offensive, see pp. 6–19.

64. Divine, *Broken Wing*, 103.

65. Morrow, *German Air Power*, 116–117.

66. Raymond Fredette, *Sky on Fire: The First Battle of Britain, 1917–1918, and the Birth of the Royal Air Force* (New York: Holt, Rinehart, and Winston, 1966), Appendix, 263.

67. Groehler, *Geschichte des Luftkrieges*, 74.

68. Ibid., 85.

69. Fredette, *Sky on Fire*, 196.

70. Report of Major Freiherr von Bülow, quoted in ibid., 196.

71. For an account of the British strategy, see Joachim Kuropka, "Die britische Luftkriegskonzeption gegen Deutschland im Ersten Weltkrieg," *Militärgeschichtliche Mitteilungen* 27 (1980): especially 12–18.

72. Luftstreitkräfte, Bericht Hauptmann Hoth an Kommandierender der General der Luftstreitkräfte, August 7, 1918, BA/MA, PH 17/96.

73. For German flak defense in World War I, see Neumann, *Die Deutschen Luftstreitkräfte*, 275–286.

74. See Groehler, *Geschichte des Luftkrieges*, 81–85, for a good survey of the German air defense in World War I.

75. Divine, *Broken Wing*, 142–143.

76. Air Organization Office, Letter by Truppenamt Luftreferant 4.2.27 on Losses in the German Home Area to Enemy Bombers, February 4, 1927, BA/MA, RH 12-1/53.

77. Divine, *Broken Wing*, 143.

78. Richard Suchenwirth, *The Development of the German Air Force, 1919–1939*, USAF Historical Study 160 (New York: Arno Press, 1968), 2.

79. *All the World's Aircraft, 1919* (London: Jane's, 1919), 291–293. Written before the war ended, it singled out the Fokker D-7 for special praise, especially for its design. Of the German equipment to be handed over to the Allies in the 1918 armistice agreement, the Fokker D-7 was the only piece specified by model; see Kenneth Munson, *Aircraft of World War I* (Garden City, N.Y.: Doubleday, 1977), 93. Richard Hallion called the D-7 the "finest single-seat fighter produced during the war" (see Hallion, *Rise of the Fighter Aircraft, 1914–1918* [Baltimore: Nautical and Aviation Publishing Company of America, 1984], 152).

80. Mitchell, *Memoirs of World War I*, 268.

81. According to Paschall, the military leaders of World War I were generally competent and innovative men faced with an impossible problem. (*Defeat of Imperial Germany*, Chapter 9). This view contrasts with Basil H. Liddell Hart's scathing criticism of many of these same leaders in *The Real War, 1914–1918* (Boston: Little, Brown, 1930).

82. Ian Hogg, "Bolimow and the First Gas Attack," in Fitzsimons, ed., *Tanks and Weapons of World War I*, 17–21.

83. Ibid., 21.

84. A study of wartime gas tactics is contained in a German paper from the 1920s in NA, German Army Records, File T-78, Roll 18, File H 15/208.

85. Ibid.

86. Holt Manufacturing Company, "The Caterpillar Track-Type Tractor in the World War," ca. 1919, 15 pages, U.S. Army Museum, Aberdeen Proving Ground (a brief history of the Holt tractor before and in the early stages of the war).

87. On French tanks, see Richard M. Ogorkiewicz, "The French Tank Force," in Fitzsimons, ed., *Tanks and Weapons of World War I*, 95–101. On British tanks, see B. T. White, *British Tanks and Fighting Vehicles, 1914–1945* (Shepperton, Surrey: Ian Allan, 1970); and Peter Chamberlain and Chris Ellis, *Tanks of World War I: British and German* (London: Arms and Armour Press, 1969). J. F. C. Fuller, *Tanks in the Great War* (London: John Murray, 1920), is a very useful source on early tank history.

88. Fritz Heigl, *Taschenbuch der Tanks*, Vol. 3: *Der Panzerkampf*, ed. G. P. von Zezschwitz (Munich: J. F. Lehmanns Verlag, 1938), 6–8. Of forty-nine tanks,

only fourteen were able to support the attack. Of these, five were lost to artillery fire.

89. Ibid., 10–17.
90. Ludendorff, *Ludendorff's Own Story*, 2:101.
91. Chamberlain and Ellis, *Tanks of World War I*, 60.
92. Ludendorff, *Ludendorff's Own Story*, 2:204.
93. Ibid.
94. On technical data for the A7V, see Chamberlain and Ellis, *Tanks of World War I*, 59–64 and 76–77.
95. Ibid., 69–70 and 76–77.
96. Ibid., 63, 67, and 70.
97. On the German Tank Corps of World War I, see Ernst Volckheim, *Deutsche Kampfwagen Greifen An!: Erlebnisse eines Kampfwagenführers an der Westfront, 1918* (Berlin: E. Mittler und Sohn, 1937).
98. Paschall, *Defeat of Imperial Germany*, 115.
99. Liddell Hart, *Real War*, 429–438.
100. Bryan Perrett, *A History of Blitzkrieg* (New York: Stein and Day, 1983), 41.
101. Richard M. Ogorkiewicz, *Armoured Forces* (New York: Arco, 1975), 147.
102. Ibid., 172.
103. Lt. Gen. a. D. W. von Balck, *Entwicklung der Taktik im Weltkriege* (Berlin: Verlag von R. Eisenschmidt, 1922), 138.
104. Ibid., 174.
105. Lt. Gen. Max Schwarte, *Die Technik im Zukunftskriege* (Berlin: Verlag Offene Worte, 1923), 190.
106. Reichstag Committee, "Untersuchungsausschuss des Deutschen Reichstages, 1919–1928," in *Die Ursachen des Deutschen Zusammenbruches im Jahre 1918*, vol. 3 (Berlin: Deutsche Verlagsgesellschaft für Politik und Geschichte, 1928), 81.
107. Ibid., 82–86.
108. See Jean Hallade, "Big Bertha Bombards Paris," in Fitzsimons, ed., *Tanks and Weapons of World War I*, 141–147, for details on the Paris Guns.
109. Fuller, *Tanks in the Great War*, 171.
110. Colonel Thorbeck, *The Technical and Tactical Lessons of the World War*, Reports of the German Army Inspectorates, April 12, 1920, BA/MA, RH 12-2/94.
111. Ibid., 2–5.
112. Ibid., 16–17.
113. Ibid., 21.
114. Trevor N. Dupuy, *A Genius for War: The German Army and General Staff, 1807–1945* (Englewood Cliffs, N.J.: Prentice-Hall, 1977), 177–178.

CHAPTER TWO.  VON SEECKT AND RETHINKING WARFARE

1. The best general biography of von Seeckt is Meier-Welcker, *Seeckt*. Lt. Gen. Friedrich von Rabenau put together *Aus meinem Leben, 1866–1918* (Leipzig: Hase-Koehler Verlag, 1938) from von Seeckt's papers and also wrote *Seeckt: Aus seinem Leben, 1918–1936* (Leipzig: Hase-Koehler Verlag, 1941). They are useful works but suffer the disadvantage of having been written in the 1930s, so that von Seeckt appears more sympathetic to the Nazis than he actually was.
2. Meier-Welcker, *Seeckt*, 42.

3. Ibid., 43.
4. Ibid., 44.
5. Ibid., 49–55. See also Liddell Hart, *Real War*, 131–132.
6. Liddell Hart, *Real War*, 132–134.
7. Meier-Welcker, *Seeckt*, Chapter 5.
8. On the Romanian campaign and von Seeckt, see ibid., 85–113.
9. Von Seeckt, *Aus meinem Leben*, 308–309.
10. Hans von Seeckt to Joachim von Winterfeldt, August 4, 1916. NA, Von Seeckt Papers, File M-132, Item 90.
11. Quoted in Eberhard Kaulbach, "Generaloberst Hans von Seeckt—Zur Persönlichkeit und zur Leistung," *Wehrwissenschaftliche Rundschau* 16, 11 (1966): 673.
12. Von Seeckt, *Aus meinem Leben*, 624.
13. Hans von Seeckt, "Nachlass von Seeckt," a commentary by von Seeckt on "Bemerkungen zu Grundsätze für die Führung der Abwehrschlacht im Stellungskrieg" issued by the Oberste Heeresleitung, October 31, 1917, BA/MA, N 62/10.
14. Gen. Ernst Köstring, *Der militärische Mittler zwischen dem Deutschen Reich und der Sowjetunion, 1921–1941*, ed. Hermann Teske (Frankfurt am Main: E. Mittler Verlag, 1966), 31.
15. Hans von Seeckt to his wife, February 13, 1919, BA/MA, N 62/12.
16. Görlitz, *History of the German General Staff*, 231.
17. Meier-Welcker, *Seeckt*, Chapter 9.
18. Ibid., 217–232.
19. Waldemar Erfurth, *Die Geschichte des deutschen Generalstabes von 1918 bis 1945*, 2d ed. (Göttingen: Masterschmidt Verlag, 1960), 51.
20. Hans von Seeckt, Report to the Army High Command, February 18, 1919, NA, Von Seeckt Papers, File M-132, Roll 21, Item 110.
21. Hans von Seeckt to Lt. Gen. Wilhelm Groener, Proposal for Twenty-Four Division Army, February 18, 1919, NA, Von Seeckt Papers, File M-132, Roll 21, Item 110, 3.
22. Ibid.
23. Ibid.
24. Ibid., 4–5.
25. Hans von Seeckt, *Thoughts of a Soldier*, trans. Gilbert Waterhouse (London: Ernest Benn, 1930), 17.
26. Ibid., 54–55.
27. Ibid., 62–63.
28. Ibid., 65.
29. Ibid., 62.
30. Meier-Welcker, *Seeckt*, 222.
31. Von Seeckt, *Thoughts of a Soldier*, 61–62.
32. Ibid., 83.
33. Ibid., 103–104.
34. Ibid., 104.
35. Ibid., 98–99.
36. Ibid., 84–85.
37. Ibid., 11.
38. Ibid.
39. Von Seeckt to von Winterfeldt, August 4, 1916, 2.
40. Ibid., 1.
41. Hans von Seeckt to Lt. Gen. Wilhelm Groener, February 17, 1919, NA, Von Seeckt Papers, File M-132, Roll 25, Item 126.

42. Von Seeckt, *Thoughts of a Soldier*, 59.

43. On Maercker's position, see Harold Gordon, *The Reichswehr and the German Republic, 1919–1926* (Port Washington, N.Y.: Kennikat Press, 1957), 67. On the Reinhardt–von Seeckt disagreement, see Erfurth, *Die Geschichte des deutschen Generalstabes*, 59–61.

44. Hans von Seeckt to the War Ministry, early 1919, NA, Von Seeckt Papers, File M-132, Roll 25, Item 120.

45. F. L. Carsten, *The Reichswehr and Politics, 1918–1933* (Oxford: Clarendon Press, 1966), 55–56; also Lt. Gen. Wilhelm Groener to Hans von Seeckt, August 24, 1924, NA, Von Seeckt Papers, File M-132, Roll 25, Item 111.

46. Meier-Welcker, *Seeckt*, 203. Harold Gordon pointed out that "in contrast to many 'front officers,' the General Staff officers, by and large, represented the moderate point of view within the army" (see Gordon, *Reichswehr and the German Republic*, 68).

47. Rudolf Absolom, ed., *Die Wehrmacht im Dritten Reich*, vol. 1 (Boppard am Rhein: Harald Boldt Verlag, 1969), 25–26.

48. Barton Whaley, *Covert German Rearmament, 1919–1939: Deception and Misperception* (Frederick, Md.: University Publications of America, 1984), 134–135.

49. Whaley, *Covert German Rearmament*, 137.

50. Craig, *Politics of the Prussian Army*, 362–363.

51. "Die Neuorganisation des Reichswehrministeriums für das Heer," *Militär Wochenblatt* 51 (October 25, 1919).

52. Erfurth, *Die Geschichte des deutschen Generalstabes*, 52–58.

53. Von Rabenau, *Seeckt: Aus seinem Leben*, 193.

54. Ibid., 194.

55. Truppenamt T-4, "Ausbildung der als Führergehilfen in Aussicht genommenen Offiziere," July 31, 1922, BA/MA, 12-21/94. In this official document, the first page uses the official terminology, "zu Gehilfen der höheren Truppenführung." On page 2, the writers start referring to "Generalstaboffiziere."

56. Figures for the size of the various sections come from Reichswehrministerium, Heeres-Personal-Amt, *Rangliste des Deutschen Reichsheeres* (Berlin: E. Mittler und Sohn, 1924–1928).

57. Erich von Manstein served in T-1 in the 1920s; he provided a detailed view of that section's work in von Manstein, *Aus einem Soldatenleben, 1887–1939* (Bonn: Athenäum Verlag, 1958), 105–129. Rainer Wohlfeil outlined the high command organization and various changes in the 1920s in Wohlfeil, "Heer und Republik," in *Handbuch zur deutschen Militärgeschichte, 1648–1939*, vol. 6 (Frankfurt am Main: Bernard und Graefe Verlag, 1970), 312–316. See also Gordon, *Reichswehr and the German Republic*, 175–190.

58. Hans von Seeckt to Truppenamt et al., December 1, 1919, BA/MA, RH 2/2275.

59. Ibid.

60. Ibid.

61. On Captain Wegener, see Volckheim, *Deutsche Kampfwagen Greifen An!* Chapters 3 and 4.

62. Figures for the number of officers normally assigned to the Wehrministerium are taken from the Reichswehrministerium's *Rangliste des Deutschen Reichsheeres* (1924).

63. Truppenamt T-4 [Training Section] to Truppenamt et al., December 1, 1919, BA/MA, RH 2/2275, 2.

64. Chef der Heeresleitung an Truppenamt T-4 [Training Section], July 7, 1920, BA/MA, RH 2/2275.

65. Weapons Office, signed by "Kraehe," December 24, 1919, BA/MA, RH 2/2275.

66. This effort by the Air Service is examined in Chapter 7 of this volume.

67. Hans von Seeckt, "Bearbeitung der Kriegserfahrungen," Directive of December 1, 1919, BA/MA, RH 2/2275, 33–38.

68. Brian Bond, *Liddell Hart: A Study of His Military Thought* (London: Cassell, 1977), 25–27. See also Basil H. Liddell Hart, *The Memoirs of Captain Liddell Hart*, vol. 1 (London: Cassell, 1965), 42–43.

69. Liddell Hart, *Memoirs*, 1:49.

70. Ibid.

71. Truppenamt T-4 [Training Section], "Grundsätze für die Durchführung des hinhaltenden Gefechts," December 10, 1920, BA/MA, RH 2/2275 T-4, 187–193. Cf. *Heeresdienstvorschrift* 487, *Führung und Gefecht der verbundenen Waffen* (Berlin: Verlag Offene Worte, 1921, 1923, 1925), Part 1, 226–228.

72. *Heeresdienstvorschrift* 487, Parts 1 and 2. The Reichswehr commonly abbreviated this regulation as FuG.

73. Ibid., Part 1, 3.

74. Ibid.

75. Ibid., 9.

76. Ibid., 10.

77. Ibid., 140.

78. Ibid., 156.

79. Ibid., 131.

80. Ibid., 34–36.

81. Ibid., 145.

82. *Heeresdienstvorschrift* 487, Part 2. See Chapter 12 on aircraft and Chapter 13 on tanks.

83. *Heeresdienstvorschrift* 487, Part 1, 47.

84. Ibid., 12.

85. The most important of these were Reichswehr Heeresleitung, "Die Abwehr im Stellungskrieg" (September 20, 1918); "Die Angriff im Stellungskrieg" (January 1, 1918); "Ausbildungsvorschrift für die Fusstruppen im Kriege" (January 1918); "Der Sturmangriff" (September 1917).

86. *Heeresdienstvorschrift* 467, *Ausbildungsvorschrift für Fahrtruppen* (Berlin: Heeresleitung, 1923), 70–71.

87. Ibid., 71.

88. Ibid., 9.

89. In 1925, Heft I of *Heeresdienstvorschrift* 487, *Führung und Gefecht der verbundenen Waffen* was issued. This is also primarily composed of excerpts from Army Regulation 487, with numerous illustrations, maps, and diagrams as well as sections on basic map reading and the giving of orders.

90. *F.H. Felddienst: Handbuch für Unterführer aller Waffen* (Berlin: Verlag Offene Worte, 1924), 7–9.

91. Whaley, *Covert German Rearmament*, 134.

92. Ibid., 135. The complete tables of organization and equipment were specified by Reichswehr Heeresleitung, *Stärkenachweisung der Kommandobehörden und Truppen des Reichsheeres* (Berlin: Reichswehrministerium, 1928).

93. *Heeresdienstvorschrift* 487 p. 270, compares the Versailles-imposed divisions with the proposed divisions.

94. On the formation of the triangular division, see S. J. Lewis, *Forgotten Le-

*gions: German Army Infantry Policy, 1918–1941* (New York: Praeger, 1985), 8–10. The Reichswehr in the postwar period would keep the title "Brigade," but the unit was an administrative one only, encompassing all the infantry regiments in a division. The brigade had no tactical or command function in the Reichswehr.

95. A rifle company contained 3 officers and 161 men; a machine-gun company contained 4 officers and 126 men; a battalion, complete with headquarters, contained 18 officers and officials and 658 men. See Wohlfeil, "Heer und Republik," 320.

96. Ibid.

97. *Heeresdienstvorschrift* 487, Part 2, 270.

98. Ibid.

99. Ibid., 271.

100. Whaley, *Covert German Rearmament*, 134.

101. Averages are obtained from the Reichswehrministerium's *Rangliste des Deutschen Reichsheeres* from 1924 to 1928. The *Rangliste* provides a fairly accurate listing of all German commands, staffs, and unit headquarters.

102. Martin van Creveld, *Fighting Power* (Westport, Conn.: Greenwood Press, 1982), 49–50.

103. Ibid., 52–53.

104. Van Creveld, *Fighting Power*; and Dupuy, *Genius for War*, 1–5 and 253–255.

105. British Army General Staff, *Handbook of the German Army, 1928*, ed. E. T. Humphreys (London: War Office, 1928), 59–60.

106. Herbert Molloy Mason, *The Rise of the Luftwaffe* (New York: Ballantine, 1973), 73–74.

107. See the British Army's *Handbook of the German Army, 1928*, 59. See also Gordon, *Reichswehr and the German Republic*, 202–206, for an excellent overview of the German NCO system.

108. Van Creveld, *Fighting Power*, 122.

109. Französische Truppenführung, *Vorschrift für die taktische Verwendung der grossen Verbände* [translation of a 1921 French operations manual] (Berlin: Verlag Offene Worte, 1937), especially 84–85.

110. Ibid., 130.

111. Ibid., 146–147.

112. Ibid., 149.

113. Ibid., 87.

114. Ibid., 13–17. The commission that composed the French manual consisted of eleven generals, three colonels, one lieutenant colonel, and one major. General Georges was the chairman.

115. Van Creveld, *Fighting Power*, Chapters 4 and 5.

116. Albrecht Kesselring, *The Memoirs of Field Marshal Kesselring* (Novato, Calif.: Presidio Press, 1989), 20.


CHAPTER THREE.  DEBATE WITHIN THE REICHSWEHR

1. Van Creveld, *Fighting Power*, 134.

2. Erfurth, *Die Geschichte des deutschen Generalstabes*, 148.

3. Ibid.

4. Wallach, *Dogma of the Battle of Annihilation*, 210.

5. Ibid., Chapter 12. For a comprehensive list of Schlieffen School works, see ibid., 224–225.

6. Martin Kitchen, "Traditions of German Strategic Thought," *International History Review*, 1, 2 (April 1979): 172–173.

7. Von Seeckt, after his retirement, wrote a short book about von Moltke entitled *Moltke: Ein Vorbild* (Berlin: Verlag für Kulterpolitik, 1930).

8. Record of Conversation with General Groener, 1919, NA, German Army Records, File T-78, Roll 25, Item 111. See also Carsten, *Reichswehr and Politics*, 56–57.

9. Col. Gen. Wilhelm Groener to Hans von Seeckt, Letters and Replies, September-October 1919, NA, German Army Records, File T-78, Roll 25, Item 112. See also Craig, *Politics of the Prussian Army*, 383.

10. Cited in Carsten, *Reichswehr and Politics*, 30.

11. Edward Bennett, *German Rearmament and the West, 1932–1933* (Princeton, N.J.: Princeton University Press, 1979), 17.

12. Herbert Rosinski, *The German Army* (London: Praeger, 1966), 218–219.

13. Ibid., 301.

14. Ibid.

15. Görlitz, *History of the German General Staff*, 216; and Craig, *Politics of the Prussian Army*, 366.

16. Maj. Gen. Friedrich von Mantey to Friedrich von Rabenay, June 12, 1939, BA/MA, 62/7.

17. Carsten, *Reichswehr and Politics*, 107.

18. Quoted in ibid., 106 and 213. On von Stülpnagel's criticism of von Seeckt, see Friedrich von Rabenau, Commentary on Hans von Seeckt/Joachim von Stülpnagel Relationship, Letter Exchange, BA/MA, N 62/7, Part 1, 8.

19. Erfurth, in *Die Geschichte des deutschen Generalstabes*, disagreed with the view that von Seeckt was unsupportive of technical innovation. See ibid., 145, on von Seeckt's support of motorization, new weapons, and technical education for officers.

20. Gen. M. Faber du Faur, *Macht und Ohnmacht* (Hamburg: H. E. Günther Verlag, 1953), 125–126 and 155–156.

21. Von Seeckt's ability as a general was attested even by his foes, namely General von Luttwitz and Lieutenant Commander Ehrhardt. See Harold Gordon, "The Character of Hans von Seeckt," *Military Affairs* 20 (1956): 97.

22. Ibid., 101.

23. Gen. Guenther Blumentritt, *Von Rundstedt: The Soldier and the Man* (London: Odhams Press, 1952), 25.

24. Franz von Papen, *Memoirs*, trans. Brian Connell (London: André Deutsch, 1952), 117.

25. Gordon, *Reichswehr and the German Republic*, 444–445.

26. Walter Reinhardt was born March 24, 1872, in Württemberg, commissioned in the Württemberg Army in 1892, entered the General Staff Corps in 1900, and served in command and staff positions from 1900 to 1914. He served most of the war on the western front. He was chief of staff to the XIII Army Corps in 1915; commanded the 118th Infantry Regiment at Verdun in 1916; was chief of staff to the XVII Army Corps at the Somme, 1916; was chief of staff to the Eleventh Army; was chief of staff to the Seventh Army at the western front in 1917; was Prussian war minister in November 1918; was chief of army command in 1919; was Fifth Division commander from 1920–1924; was Second Group commander from 1924–1925; retired in 1927. He died August 8, 1930. See Gen. d.

Inf. Walter Reinhardt, *Wehrkraft und Wehrwille*, ed. Lt. Gen. Ernst Reinhardt (Berlin: E. Mittler und Sohn, 1932), 1–26.

27. Ibid.

28. Rosinski, *German Army*, 218–219.

29. Reinhardt, *Wehrkraft und Wehrwille*, 63–65.

30. Ibid., 71–73.

31. Ibid., 100.

32. Ibid., 103–104.

33. Ibid., 152–153.

34. Ibid., 167.

35. Von Seeckt's attempts to hold on to the traditional General Staff were attacked, as was von Seeckt's elite army concept. See Reinhardt, *Wehrkraft und Wehrwille*, 51–52 and 167.

36. Hermann von Kuhl was born in 1856; received a Ph.D. in 1878. He was a General Staff officer. He was chief of staff in 1914 of the First Army during the advance into France; he served in senior staff positions on the western front. He retired in 1919 and died in 1944. As a former member of General Staff Intelligence, von Kuhl was an expert on the French Army. See Hans Meier-Welcker, "General der Infanterie a.D. Dr. Hermann v. Kuhl," *Wehrwissenschaftliche Rundschau*, 6, 11 (1956): 595–610.

37. See ibid., 604–610, for a bibliography of von Kuhl's writings.

38. Ibid., 601.

39. Ibid., 600.

40. Ibid., 603.

41. Faber du Faur, *Macht und Ohnmacht*, 77 and 196. See also Rosinski, *German Army*, 172 and 219.

42. George Soldan, "Bewegungskrieg oder Stellungskrieg?" *Militär Wochenblatt* 35 (1926).

43. "Feldherr und Masse," *Militär Wochenblatt* 19 (1925).

44. General von Taysen, "Die französische Infanterie," *Militär Wochenblatt* 20 (1922).

45. Franz von Gaertner, *Die Reichswehr in der Weimarer Republik: Erlebte Geschichte* (Darmstadt: Fundus Verlag, 1969), 86.

46. On Ernst Jünger and his books, see Johannes Volmert, *Ernst Jünger: In Stahlgewittern* (Munich: Wilhelm Fink Verlag, 1985).

47. Jünger, *Storm of Steel*, 202, and *Copse 125* (London: Chatto and Windus, 1930), 81–83.

48. Jünger, *Storm of Steel*, 316.

49. Jünger, *Copse 125*, 190–191.

50. Ernst Jünger was born in 1895 in Heidelberg. After completing his Abitur in 1914, he enlisted in the army. In November 1915 he was commissioned a lieutenant; from 1917 to 1918 he was company commander on the western front in the Seventy-Third Regiment. He was wounded more than ten times. From 1919 to 1923, he served in the Freikorps and then in the Sixteenth Infantry Regiment as a lieutenant. He resigned from the Reichswehr in August 1923. For more biographical information, see Military Records of Ernst Jünger, BA/MA.

51. Volmert, *Jünger*, 12.

52. Ernst Jünger, "Die Ausbildungsvorschrift für die Infanterie," *Militär Wochenblatt* 3 (1923).

53. Wetzell was promoted to lieutenant general in 1926. He served as von Seeckt's chief staff assistant in 1914–1915.

54. Maj. Gen. Georg Wetzell, "Die alte Armee und die junge Generation," *Militär Wochenblatt* 2 (1925).

55. Kurt Hesse was born in Kiel in 1894. He was an officer cadet in Grenadier Regiment Five in 1913; a lieutenant in 1914; and a first lieutenant in 1917. He was commander of the First Machine Gun Company of Grenadier Regiment Five on the western front. He was wounded five times. In the Reichswehr, he served in the Ninth Cavalry Regiment from 1923 to 1925. He was promoted to captain in 1925. He performed regimental and staff duties for the Second Infantry Regiment from 1925 to 1928. He resigned from the army in 1929. He had received a doctorate in 1925. From 1929 on, he lectured at the Cavalry and Military School. He served in the reserves and was recalled to service in 1941. He joined the SA (Sturmabteilungen-Stormtroopers) in 1933.

56. Some of Kurt Hesse's works are *Der Feldherr Psychologos: Ein Suchen nach dem Führer der deutschen Zukunft* (Berlin: E. Mittler und Sohn, 1922); *Der Triumph des Militarismus* (1923); *Von der nahen Ära der "Jungen Armee"* (Berlin: E. Mittler und Sohn, 1924). His articles in the *Militär Wochenblatt* include "Worte an Ernst Jünger," 19 (1924); "Über dem Sturm," 18 (1924); "Die psychologische Schule," 10 (1922); "Über subjektive Darstellung," 27 (1919).

57. Hesse, "Worte an Ernst Jünger."

58. Hesse, *Der Feldherr Psychologos*, 180.

59. Ibid., 195.

60. Hesse, "Die psychologische Schule," 182–184.

61. Friedrich von Rabenau was born in Berlin in 1884; he received his Abitur in 1903. He was commissioned in 1904 and admitted to the General Staff in 1914. He served various General Staff positions from 1914 to 1918; was assigned to Truppenamt T-4 in 1923; was promoted to major in 1923; served in T-1 from 1924 to 1926; was promoted to major general in 1934. He received his Ph.D. from Breslau University in 1935. He was chief of Army Archives in 1937; commander of the Seventy-Third Infantry Division in 1939; and retired as general of artillery in 1943. He concluded his theological studies in 1943 and became a Lutheran minister in January 1944. Arrested for complicity in the anti-Hitler plot in July 1944, he was murdered by the Nazis, probably in Flossenbürg Concentration Camp, on April 11, 1945. His works include *Die alte Armee und die junge Generation* (Berlin: E. Mittler und Sohn, 1925); "Der Wegbereitere," in *Hundert Jahre preussisch-deutscher Generalstab*, ed. General von Cochenhausen (Berlin: E. Mittler und Sohn, 1933); *Operative Entschlüsse gegen eine Anzahl überlegener Gegner* (Berlin: E. Mittler und Sohn, 1935); editor, Hans von Seeckt, *Aus meinem Leben* (1938); *Seeckt: Aus seinem Leben* (1940); *Vom Sinn des Soldatentums. Die innere Kraft von Führung und Truppe* (n.p., 1940). Information from Von Rabenau Papers, BA/MA, N 62.

62. Von Rabenau, *Die alte Armee und die junge Generation*.

63. Ibid., 7.

64. Ibid., 9.

65. Von Rabenau, *Operative Entschlüsse gegen eine Anzahl überlegenen Gegner*.

66. Wetzell, "Die alte Armee und die junge Generation."

67. General von Taysen, "Entspricht die heutige Kampfweise unsere Infanterie der Leistungsfähigkeit eines kurz ausgebildeten Massenheeres?" secret memo of March 19, 1924, BA/MA, 12-2/94, 221–239), especially 12.

68. Von Seeckt, *Thoughts of a Soldier*, 125–126.

69. Major Benary, "Um Hesse," *Militär Wochenblatt* 5 (1925).

70. War Minister of Saxony, Verordnungsblatt des GK XIX A. K., April 23, 1919, Militärarchiv der DDR (hereafter MA/DDR), R. 11 41 12/1, 50. Volunteer border guard units were to be formed from short-term volunteers, and companies and regiments were authorized to set up training courses for these units.

71. Defense Plan for Freiwilliger Grenzer BN 6, June 21, 1919, MA/DDR R 11 41 12/1, 88–89; and Orders from Grenzer BN 6, June 18, 1919, ibid., 91.

72. Gordon, *Reichswehr and the German Republic*, 255–256.

73. Ibid., 257.

74. Joachim Fritz Constantin von Stülpnagel was born in 1880. Commissioned in 1898, he was appointed to the General Staff in 1909. During World War I, he served as a General Staff officer at the divisional and army levels. He served with the Army High Command Operations Section from 1918 to 1919. From 1920 to 1926, he served with the Reichswehr Ministry, Truppenamt. Promoted to lieutenant colonel in 1922, he served as a section leader in the Operations Section. He was promoted to major general in 1928 and lieutenant general in 1929. He became Third Division Commander in 1929, and in 1931 commander of the Reserve Forces with a promotion to general of infantry. Information from BA/MA, N5.

75. Lt. Col. Joachim von Stülpnagel, "The War of the Future," March 18, 1924, BA/MA, N/5–20, T-1, 24.

76. Ibid., 27.

77. Ibid., 28–30.

78. Ibid., 34–36.

79. Gordon, *Reichswehr and the German Republic*, 255.

80. See von Manstein, *Aus einem Soldatenleben*, 120–122, on his service as a Truppenamt officer organizing and training such units. The irregular border guard units were, in his opinion, not too effective against regular troops. At best, they could only act to delay them.

81. Truppenamt, Study on Volkskrieg, BA/MA, RH 2/2901, 94–95.

82. Truppenamt T-1, "Denkschrift über die Ziele und Wege der nächsten Jahre für unsere Kriegsvorbereitungen," August 14, 1925, NA, German Army Records, File T-78, Roll 441, Folder H1/663.

83. Gen. Erich von Ludendorff, *The Coming War* (London: Faber and Faber, 1931), 110–134.

84. Gen. Erich von Ludendorff, *The Nation at War* (London: Hutchinson, 1936), 140–141.

85. On Ludendorff's military thought, see Jehuda L. Wallach, *Kriegstheorien. Ihre Entwicklung im 19. und 20. Jahrhundert* (Frankfurt: Bernard und Graefe Verlag, 1972), 184–193.

86. Kriegsgeschichtliche Forschungsamt, Reichsarchiv, "Denkschrift: Fremde Heere am Rhein, 1918–1930," ca. 1930, MA/DDR, W-10/52143, 1–2.

87. Kriegsgeschichtliche Forschungsamt, Reichsarchiv, *Volkskrieg*, ed. Archivrat Liesner, 1930, MA/DDR, W10/50203. This work is several hundred pages.

88. Ibid., 14–19.

89. Ibid., 25–26.

90. Ibid., 20–23.

91. See Wallach, *Dogma of the Battle of Annihilation*, Chapter 8.

92. Kitchen, "The Traditions of German Strategic Thought," 163–190.

93. Barry Rosen, *The Sources of Military Doctrine* (Ithaca, N.Y.: Cornell University Press, 1984), 215.

CHAPTER FOUR.  TRAINING THE REICHSWEHR

1.  Maj. a.D. Karl Deuringer, "Die Niederwerfung der Räteherrschaft in Bayern, 1919," monograph of the Kriegsgeschichtlichen Forschungsamt, 1930s, MA/DDR, W-10/52136, 151.

2.  Adolf Reinicke, *Das Reichsheer, 1921–1934* (Osnabrück: Biblio Verlag, 1969), 11. On the 1920 fighting, see also Walter Görlitz, *Model: Strategie der Defensive* (Wiesbaden: Limes Verlag, 1975), 29–30. Model's battalion lost two officers and twelve men killed, as well as one hundred wounded.

3.  Major von Stockhausen, *Erfahrungen über Bekämpfung innerer Unruhen*, 1919, MA/DDR, R 11.41.20/5.

4.  Saxony maintained its War Ministry until 1920, and the records of the Saxon Army, which became part of the Reichswehr, are preserved in the Military Archives of the German Democratic Republic in Potsdam. See Records of Freiw. Grenzer BN 2, Letter of June 4, 1919, MA/DDR R 11 41 21/4 on setting up machine-gun courses.

5.  As noted earlier, the Führerheer concept was first outlined by von Seeckt in a message to the army. See Wohlfeil, "Heer und Republik," 207–209.

6.  German regimental histories of the Reichswehr period normally record the intensive work of 1920–1921 to create a comfortable garrison environment. "Geschichte des I/J-R. 65," ca. 1936/37, Crerar Collection, Royal Military College of Canada, Kingston, Ontario, outlines the renovations done in the barracks of the Sixteenth Infantry Regiment and notes the importance of creating a pleasant environment (see 5–6). This manuscript also contains photos of well-furnished soldier club rooms. See also *United States Military Intelligence*, Vol. 23–26, *Weekly Summaries*, ed. Richard D. Challener (New York: Garland Publishing, 1978) (hereafter Challener, ed., *Weekly Summaries*),, 7–8, for a description of Reichswehr barracks and living conditions.

7.  Challener, ed., *Weekly Summaries*, Report of June 10, 1927, 8–9.

8.  Hermann Teske, "Analyse eines Reichswehr-Regiments," *Wehrwissenschaftliche Rundschau*, 12, 5 (1962): 256.

9.  Ibid.

10.  Ibid.

11.  W. Behrens and Dietrich Kuehn, *Geschichte des Reiter-Regiments I*, Vol. 1: 1919–1939 (Cologne/Weidenbach: Kameradschaft ehem. RR1, 1962), 12.

12.  Wohlfeil, "Heer und Republik," 184.

13.  Gordon, *Reichswehr and the German Republic*, 69.

14.  Ibid., 169.

15.  A comparison can be made between the Reichswehr and another professional army of the 1920s: the U.S. Army. In this era, enlistments to the U.S. Army lagged, and commanders complained of the poor quality of recruits. See Robert Griffith, "Quality, Not Quantity: The Volunteer Army during the Depression," *Military Affairs*, 43 (1979): 171–177.

16.  In 1927 the army had 136 troop garrisons, 11 major training areas, and numerous arsenals, depots, and so on scattered throughout Germany. Information from Reichswehrministerium, *Rangliste des Deutschen Reichsheeres, 1927*.

17.  Gordon, *Reichswehr and the German Republic*, 175.

18.  Hans Meier-Welcker, "Der Weg zum Offizier im Reichsheer der Weimarer Republik," *Militärgeschichtliche Mitteilungen* 19 (1976): 150–152.

19.  Ibid., 150.

20.  British Army General Staff, *Handbook of the German Army, 1928*, 208.

21. Gerd Stolz and Eberhard Grieser, *Geschichte des Kavallerie-Regiments 5 "Feldmarshall v. Mackensen"* (Munich: Schild Verlag, 1975), 20.

22. Ibid., 43.

23. Ibid., 19. On the Reichswehr cavalry training of this era, see Dietrich von Choltitz, *Soldat unter Soldaten* (Zurich: Europa Verlag, 1951), 26–30. Choltitz described the importance of hunting and sport riding for the cavalry. The infantry, motor troops, and artillery were all much more progressive than the cavalry. Hasso von Manteuffel, a junior officer in the Third Cavalry Regiment, saw no real modernization of tactics and equipment until 1926. See Donald Brownlow, *Panzer Baron: The Military Exploits of General Hasso von Manteuffel* (North Quincy, Mass.: Christopher Publishing House, 1975), 44–45. Siegfried Westphal (later a general) recalled that as a junior cavalry officer in the early 1920s, he took part in numerous practice saber charges. (see Westphal, *Erinnerungen* [Mainz: Hasse und Koehler Verlag, 1975], 28).

24. Richard Challener, ed., "Winter Training in the German Army," *Weekly Summaries*, Report of June 10, 1927.

25. Ibid., 2.

26. Ibid., 3.

27. Ibid.

28. Ibid., 5–6.

29. Von Gaertner, *Die Reichswehr in der Weimarer Republik*, 83.

30. See Meier-Welcker, *Seeckt*. Meier-Welcker carefully documented von Seeckt's movements. For example, see his record of von Seeckt's visits in 1922 on 326–327, 330–335, and 343.

31. The battalions of the Sixteenth Regiment, for example, were regularly visited by the group and division commanders, who came specifically to observe training. See "Geschichte des I/J-R. 65," 9–15.

32. Von Seeckt letter of January 1, 1921, quoted in Demeter, *Das Deutsche Offizierkorps*, 300.

33. "Geschichte des I/J-R. 65," 9–11.

34. Ibid., 13.

35. Ibid., 14.

36. Ibid., 15.

37. Hans von Seeckt, *Bemerkungen des Chefs der Heeresleitung, 1920*, January 7, 1921, BA/MA, RH 2/2963, 1.

38. Ibid., 2–3.

39. Ibid.

40. Hans von Seeckt, *Bemerkungen des Chefs der Heeresleitung, 1922*, December 20, 1922, BA/MA, RH 2/2987, 4–7.

41. Ibid., 11.

42. Ibid., 13.

43. Hans von Seeckt, *Bemerkungen des Chefs der Heeresleitung, 1921*, December 28, 1921, BA/MA, RH 2/69, 5.

44. Hans von Seeckt, *Bemerkungen des Chefs der Heeresleitung, 1923*, BA/MA, RH 2/107, 4.

45. Ibid., 5.

46. Hans von Seeckt, *Bemerkungen des Chefs der Heeresleitung, 1925*, BA/MA, RH 2/70, 2.

47. Hans von Seeckt, *Bemerkungen des Chefs der Heeresleitung, 1924*, November 17, 1924, BA/MA, RH 2/70.

48. Von Seeckt, *Bemerkungen des Chefs der Heeresleitung, 1920*, 3.

49. Gordon, *Reichswehr and the German Republic*, 208–209.

50. Behrens and Kuehn, *Geschichte des Reiter-Regiments I*, 17.
51. Görlitz, *Model: Strategie der Defensive*, 37.
52. Figures from British Army General Staff, *Handbook of the German Army, 1928*, 59–60.
53. Ibid., 59.
54. Gordon, *Reichswehr and the German Republic*, 203–204.
55. Sächsische Ministerium für Militärwesen, Letter of Instruction, June 30, 1919, MA/DDR, R 11 41 22/7.
56. British Army General Staff, *Handbook of the German Army, 1928*, 292.
57. Two excellent studies of the social make-up and education of the German officer corps are Demeter's *Das Deutsche Offizierkorps* and Hans Hubert Hofmann, ed., *Das Deutsche Offizierkorps, 1866–1960* (Boppard am Rhein: Harald Bolt Verlag, 1980).
58. Absolom, *Die Wehrmacht im Dritten Reich*, 1:18.
59. On the creation of the security forces, see Craig, *Politics of the Prussian Army*, 404–405. On the addition of ex-NCOs to officer ranks in 1919, see Demeter, *Das Deutsche Offizierkorps*, 49–51.
60. In 1927 the Reichswehr officer corps consisted of 3 generals, 14 lieutenant generals, 25 major generals, 105 colonels, 190 lieutenant colonels, 380 majors, 1,122 captains, 653 first lieutenants, and 1,305 second lieutenants—a total of 3,797 officers. There were also 210 military officials of officer rank who completed the total of 4,000 officers. For figures, see British Army General Staff, *Handbook of the German Army, 1928*, 56 and 60–61. The Reichswehr also contained 293 medical officers and 200 veterinary officers, who were not counted as part of the 4,000 total (see the *Handbook*, 57).
61. Hofmann, *Das deutsche Offizierkorps* , 233.
62. Craig, *Politics of the Prussian Army*, 393–394.
63. Carsten, *Reichswehr and Politics*, 217.
64. Hans von Seeckt to All Branch Schools, Letter of November 8, 1924, BA/MA, RH 12-2/22. On von Seeckt's view of "supply exceeding the demand" in the officer corps, see Demeter, *Das Deutsche Offizierkorps*, 103.
65. Inspek. 1, *Entwurf: Lehrordnung für die Waffenschulen*, 1920, BA/MA, RH 12-2/54, 99.
66. Demeter, *Das Deutsche Offizierkorps*, 57.
67. See Reinicke, *Das Reichsheer*, 140–141.
68. Wohlfeil, "Heer und Republik," 338.
69. On the signal corps instruction, see Reinicke, *Das Reichsheer*, 198.
70. Wohlfeil, "Heer und Republik," 336.
71. Ibid., 337.
72. Rainer Wohlfeil and Hans Dollinger, *Die Deutsche Reichswehr* (Frankfurt am Main: Bernard und Graefe Verlag, 1972), 127.
73. Von Gaertner, *Die Reichswehr in der Weimarer Republik*, 107.
74. Ibid., 106–107. See also Reinicke, *Das Reichsheer*, 308–309.
75. Meier-Welcker, "Der Weg zum Offizier," 147–180. Another detailed description of the Reichswehr officer training program is found in David N. Spires, *Image and Reality: The Making of the German Officer, 1921–1933* (Westport, Conn.: Greenwood Press, 1984).
76. Meier-Welcker, "Der Weg zum Offizier," 148.
77. Ibid., 149.
78. Ibid., 157.
79. Ibid., 159.
80. Ibid.

81. Ibid., 160.
82. Ibid., 161.
83. Ibid., 165.
84. Ibid., 166–167.
85. Inspek. 1, *Entwurf: Lehrordnung für die Waffenschulen*, 4.
86. Ibid., 10.
87. Ibid., 9.
88. Ibid., 33.
89. Ibid.
90. Meier-Welcker, "Der Weg zum Offizier," 166.
91. Ibid., 165–166.
92. See Behrens and Kuehn, *Geschichte des Reiter-Regiments I*, 17–18, for a good outline of regimental-level training in the Reichswehr.
93. Hans Georg Model, *Der deutsche Generalstabsoffizier. Seine Auswahl und Ausbildung in Reichswehr, Wehrmacht und Bundeswehr* (Frankfurt am Main: Bernard und Graefe Verlag, 1968), 25–26.
94. Ibid.
95. Von Gaertner, *Die Reichswehr in der Weimarer Republik*, 101.
96. See Model, *Der deutsche Generalstabsoffizier*, 28. See also Westphal, *Erinnerungen*, 36.
97. An example of the Military District Examinations is found in the Crerar Collection of the Royal Military College of Canada, Kingston, Ontario: *Die Wehrkreis-Prüfung 1932, 11. Jahrgang* (Berlin: Verlag Offene Worte, 1932); see 84–89 for the language examinations.
98. Model, *Der deutsche Generalstabsoffizier*, 31. Model also provides examples of test problems from 1921 to 1932, 29–31.
99. Gordon, *Reichswehr and the German Republic*, 300.
100. Model, *Der deutsche Generalstabsoffizier*, 26.
101. Ludwig von der Leyen was born in 1885 in Berlin and commissioned in 1904. He was one of the most influential of the interwar infantry tacticians of the Reichswehr. A member of the General Staff, von der Leyen saw extensive combat and staff service in World War I. From 1922 to 1925, he served on the Training Section of the Truppenamt and was active in editing tactical manuals. From 1928–1930, he taught tactics at the Infantry School. Promoted to Major General in 1936. He commanded the Twelfth Infantry Division from 1939 to 1940. In 1940, he was promoted to general of infantry. From Ludwig von der Leyen, "Nachlass Ludwig von der Leyen," BA/MA, N 154.
102. Capt. Ludwig von der Leyen, *Taktische Aufgaben und Lösungen im Rahmen des verstärkten Infanterie Regiments*, 2d ed. (Berlin: Verlag Offene Worte, 1923).
103. Capt. Ludwig von der Leyen, *Von Zusammenwirken der Waffen* (Berlin: Verlag Offene Worte, 1925).
104. Von der Leyen, *Taktische Aufgaben und Lösungen*.
105. Ibid., 1.
106. Ibid.
107. The 1932 Military District Examinations had problems in the Tactical Section on attack, reconnaissance, and defense.
108. See Erwin Rommel, *Attacks!*, *[Infanterie Greift An!]*, trans. J. R. Driscoll (Vienna, Va.: Athena Press, 1979; reprint of 1936 edition), v. See also Martin Blumensen, "Rommel," in *Hitler's Generals*, ed. Corelli Barnett (New York: Grove Weidenfeld, 1989), 296–297.
109. For an example, see Lt. Kurt Hesse, Report of Lt. Kurt Hesse's Trip to

South America and the USA in 1924–1925, BA/MA, RH 2/182, 144–145, 177–182, 183–184 ff.

110. See von Manstein, *Aus einem Soldatenleben*, 92–93, concerning his visit to Spain; and Westphal, *Erinnerungen*, 35.

111. Gordon, *Reichswehr and the German Republic*, 302.

112. Quoted in Erfurth, *Die Geschichte des deutschen Generalstabes*, 144.

113. The best overview of General Staff training in the Reichswehr is in Model's *Der deutsche Generalstabsoffizier*.

114. Carsten, *Reichswehr and Politics*, 209.

115. Westphal, *Erinnerungen*, 36.

116. Truppenamt T-4 [Training Section], "Ausbildung der als Führergehilfen in Aussicht genommen Offiziere," July 31, 1922, BA/MA, RH 12-21/94.

117. Ibid., 13.

118. Ibid.

119. Ibid., 2.

120. Gordon, *Reichswehr and the German Republic*, 301; and Westphal, *Erinnerungen*, 36.

121. Truppenamt T-4 [Training Section], "Ausbildung der als Führergehilfen in Aussicht genommenen Offiziere," 2.

122. Ibid.

123. Ibid., 1.

124. Ibid., 3.

125. Ibid., 1.

126. Ibid., 5.

127. Ibid., 14–15.

128. Ibid., 3.

129. Model, *Der deutsche Generalstabsoffizier*, 43–44.

130. Nigel Hamilton, *Monty: The Making of a General, 1887–1942* (London: Hamish Hamilton, 1981), 151.

131. Gen. Omar Bradley and Clay Blair, *A General's Life* (New York: Simon and Schuster, 1983), 60.

132. See ibid., 60–61.

133. Van Creveld, *Training of Officers*, 32.

134. Ibid.

135. Von Seeckt, *Thoughts of a Soldier*, 125.

136. Ibid.

137. Reinicke, *Das Reichsheer*, 312.

138. Ibid.

139. Ibid.

140. British Army General Staff, *Handbook of the German Army, 1928*, 59–60.

141. Ibid., 60.

142. Challener, ed., "Report of November 27–December 10, 1926," *Weekly Summaries*, 3–4.

143. Van Creveld, *Fighting Power*, 52–53.

144. Rosinski, *German Army*, 293–294.

145. Van Creveld, *Training of Officers*, 64.

146. See Capt. Kurt Hesse's Report on U.S. Military Power, February 1925, BA/MA, RH 2/1820, 177–182. Hesse reported that the U.S. Army had made an excellent study of the economics of war.

147. Ernst W. Hansen, *Reichswehr und Industrie, Rüstungswirtschaftliche Zusammenarbeit und wirtschaftliche Mobilmachungsvorbereitungen 1923–1932*,

Militärgeschichtliche Studien 24 (Boppard am Rhein: Harald Boldt Verlag, 1978), 64–69 and 71–72.

148. Spires, *Image and Reality*, 54.

149. Michael Geyer, "German Strategy in the Age of Machine Warfare, 1914–1945," in *Makers of Modern Strategy*, ed. P. Paret (Princeton, N.J.: Princeton University Press, 1986), 572.

150. Van Creveld, *Training of Officers*, 29.

151. Ibid., 32. See also Spires, *Image and Reality*, 52.

152. See "Operatives Kriegsspiel 1926/27," November 1926, BA/MA, RH 2/2822, 1–56.

CHAPTER FIVE:  DEVELOPING MODERN WEAPONRY

1. See Table 3 in Whaley, *Covert German Rearmament*, 137.

2. For the organization of the Interallied Military Control Commission, see Michael Salewski, *Entwaffnung und Militärkontrolle in Deutschland 1919–1927*, Schriften des Forschungsinstitutes der Deutschen Gesellschaft für Auswärtige Politik 24 (Munich: R. Oldenbourg Verlag, 1966), 48–49. Salewski's work is the best general work on the Control Commission and its role in reinforcing German disarmament.

3. Whaley, *Covert German Rearmament*, 30–31.

4. Hans Gatzke provided evidence for Stresemann's involvement with secret rearmament. See his *Stresemann and the Rearmament of Germany* (Baltimore: Johns Hopkins University Press, 1954). In February 1923 President Ebert signed a secret accord with von Seeckt and Prussian Chief Minister Severing to secure support for the formation of secret paramilitary forces (see Lionel Kochan, *Russia and the Weimar Republic* [Cambridge: Bowes and Bowes, 1954], 69).

5. Whaley, *Covert German Rearmament*, 10–11. See also William Manchester, *The Arms of Krupp* (Boston: Little, Brown, 1968), 388–396.

6. Ian Hogg and John Weeks, *Military Small Arms of the Twentieth Century* (Northfield, Ill.: Digest, 1973), 5.41.

7. John Erickson, *The Soviet High Command: A Military-Political History, 1918–1941* (Boulder, Colo.: Westview Press, 1984), is the most detailed account of Reichswehr–Red Army cooperation. See also Helm Speidel, "Reichswehr und Rote Armee," *Vierteljahrsheft für Zeitgeschichte*, 1, 1 (January 1953).

8. On the disadvantages of the Versailles Treaty for the tank program, see Walter J. Spielberger, *Die Motorisierung der deutschen Reichswehr, 1920–1935* (Stuttgart: Motorbuch Verlag, 1979), 299 and 315–316.

9. Janice McKenney, "More Bang for the Buck in the Interwar Army: The 105-mm Howitzer," *Military Affairs* 42, (1978): 80–86.

10. See George Hofmann, "The Demise of the U.S. Tank Corps and Medium Tank Development Program," *Military Affairs* 37 (1973): 20–25.

11. Von Seeckt, *Thoughts of a Soldier*, 65–66.

12. Ibid., 66.

13. The "light tractor" would be built around the 37-mm Tak L/45 gun. See Spielberger, *Die Motorisierung der deutschen Reichswehr*, 317.

14. An excellent overview of the work and organization of the Weapons Office was written by a former Weapons Office officer: Erich Schneider, "Waffenentwicklung; Erfahrungen im deutschen Heereswaffenamt," *Wehrwissenschaftliche Rundschau* 3 (1953): 24–35.

15. Hans von Seeckt to Waffenamt and Inspektionen, January 21, 1924, BA/MA, RH 12-2-21.

16. Ibid.

17. Joachim von Stülpnagel, T-1 Operations, to Waffenamt, March 29, 1924, File on the Heavy Machine-Gun Tests, BA/MA, RH 12-2/150. Von Stülpnagel commented that perhaps the 20-mm Becker cannon might be easier to produce than other weapons.

18. Figures derived from the Reichswehrministerium, *Rangliste des deutschen Reichsheeres*, 1924, 1925, and 1927.

19. Gordon, *Reichswehr and the German Republic*, 186.

20. See Heereswaffenamt File H 15/85, 1928 NA, German Army Records, File T-78, Roll 178. General Ludwig, chief of the Weapons Office, set the research and development priorities for 1928. The highest priority for the pioneers Inspectorate was the development of motorized bridge units. Fortresses were given a low priority. In IN-6 (motor troops), the priorities were the development of motorized antitank guns and trucks with good cross-country mobility. The development of armored cars and tanks was also a high priority.

21. See "Reisebericht von Oberst von Boetticher," 1920s, BA/MA, RH 2/1820, Appendix 1; "Reisebericht Hauptmann Speich" (1924), ibid.; "Reisebericht von Gen. Lt. a. D. Schirmer" (1926), ibid.; "Reiseberichte Maj. Radelmaier, Hauptmann Austmann," 1929, BA/MA, RH 2/2198; "Reiseberichte von Maj. Radelmeier," 1929, BA/MA, RH 2/1822; and "Reisebericht Oberstleutnante Becker und Zimmerle," 1928, BA/MA, RH 2/1823.

22. See T-3, "Die französischen Herbstmanöver, 1922," August 11, 1923, BA/MA, RH 2/1547; T-3, "Die französischen Herbstmanöver, 1923," July 10, 1924, ibid.; "Bemerkungen zu den englischen Manövern, 1924," December 1, 1924, BA/MA, RH 2/1603.

23. A sampling of Fritz Heigl's articles in the *Militär Wochenblatt* include "Der neue englische Vickers-Tank," 44 (1925); "Der Char 2 C," 22 (1924); "Der Stand der Tankfrage im tschechoslowakischen Heere," 36 (1925); "Neue Tanks," 45 (1926); and "Neue Tanktypen," 17 (1925).

24. Fritz Heigl's early books on armor that were used as Reichswehr textbooks: *Taschenbuch der Tanks* (Munich: J. F. Lehmanns Verlag, 1926) and *Die schweren französischen Tanks. Die italienischen Tanks* (Berlin: Verlag von R. Eisenschmidt, 1925). He also created instructional charts on tanks—*Tank-Unterrichtstafeln: Der englische Tank Mark "D"*; *Der englische "Medium Mark D" Kampfwagen*; *Der schwere italienische Tank "Tipo 2000 Fiat"*; *Der leichte italienische Tank Fiat "Tipo 3000–1926"*; and *Der französische Tank "Char Léger-1925"*.

25. Ian Hogg, *German Artillery of World War II* (New York: Hippocrene, 1975), 30.

26. For information on small arms, see Hogg and Weeks, *Military Small Arms of the Twentieth Century*. On the German light and medium mortars, see James Hicks, *German Weapons—Uniforms—Insignia: 1841–1918* (La Canada, Calif.: Hicks and Son, 1958), 47–50 and 64–71.

27. Lewis, *Forgotten Legions*, 21–22.

28. Ibid., 20.

29. Ibid., 22–23.

30. Waffenamt, Study of Thirty-Four Gas Attacks against the U.S. Army in France in 1918, 1920s, NA, German Army Records, File T-78, File 181. The German war records were compared with the published American records of E. W. Spencer, "The History of Gas Attacks upon the American Expeditionary Forces during the World War." The Weapons Office editor of this study went into detail

concerning the tactical plans of the German gas attacks and cited several gas attacks as "schoolbook examples," where proper use of gas mixes, timing, salvo plan, and meteorology by the Germans caused hundreds of U.S. casualties in some attacks.

31. Hans von Seeckt, Lecture on Gas Warfare, BA/MA, RH 2/2207, File HL 27 1923 1A.

32. Maj. Helmut Wilberg to Heeresleitung Staff, Letter Explaining Von Seeckt's Directive of April 2, 1924, BA/MA, 2/2207; Joachim von Stülpnagel to Wilberg, March 24, 1924, with copy to Maj. Albrecht Kesselring, March 24, 1924, ibid.

33. Rolf Dieter Müller, "World Power Status through the Use of Poison Gas? German Preparations for Chemical Warfare, 1919–1945," in *The German Military in the Age of Total War*, ed. Wilhelm Deist (Leamington Spa, Eng.: Berk, 1985), 173.

34. Ibid., 174.

35. Ibid., 177–178. See also an agreement made between Chemische Fabrik, Stoltzenberg, and Junkers Luftverkehr for the testing and production of aerial gas bombs in BA/MA, RH 2/2207, a mid-1920s document.

36. Van Creveld, *Command in War*, 154–155.

37. See Rommel, *Attacks!* 209–233.

38. Rudolf Lusar, *Die deutschen Waffen und Geheimwaffen des 2 Weltkrieges und ihre Entwicklung* (Munich: J. F. Lehmanns Verlag, 1962), 198.

39. Ernst Volckheim, *Der Kampfwagen in der heutigen Kriegführung* (Berlin: E. Mittler und Sohn, 1924), 85–86.

40. T-3, "Bemerkungen zu den englischen Manövern 1924," December 1, 1924, BA/MA, RH 2/1603, 3–4, 10.

41. Reinicke, *Das Reichsheer*, 196.

42. Kenneth Macksey, *Technology in War* (London: Arms and Armour Press, 1986), 108.

43. *Heeresdienstvorschrift* 487, part 2, 270.

44. Franz Kosar, *Infanteriegeschütze und rückstossfreie Leichtgeschütze, 1915–1978* (Stuttgart: Motorbuch Verlag, 1979), 31–39 and 162.

45. For an overview of infantry guns, see ibid.

46. Hogg, *German Artillery of World War II*, 18–21. See also Kosar, *Infanteriegeschütze*, 162.

47. Hogg, *German Artillery of World War II*, 26; on the gun's specifications, see 26–30.

48. Ibid., 45.

49. Ibid., 45–47.

50. Ibid., 57–63.

51. Ibid., 144–145. See also Lusar, *Die deutschen Waffen und Geheimwaffen*, p. 176.

52. *Die deutschen Waffen und Geheimwaffen*, 162.

53. Report from Waffenamt signed [Chief] Ludwig, 1928, NA, German Army Records, File T-78, Roll 178, File H 15/85, 1928.

54. Ogorkiewicz, *Armoured Forces*, 273. Vollmer would end up designing tanks in Czechoslovakia in the 1920s and 1930s. He was a primary designer for the Czech tanks that the Wehrmacht absorbed in 1939 (see Whaley, *Covert German Rearmament*, 31).

55. Werner Oswald, *Kraftfahrzeuge und Panzer der Reichswehr, Wehrmacht und Bundeswehr* (Stuttgart: Motorbuch Verlag, 1970), 30–33.

56. Spielberger, *Die Motorisierung der deutschen Reichswehr*, 194.

57. For full technical data and diagrams of the Erhardt, Daimler, and Benz

Schupo-Sonderwagen 21, see Schmitt, *Strassenpanzerwagen: Die Sonderwagen der Schutzpolizei* (Berlin: R. Eisenschmidt Verlag, 1925). See also Spielberger, *Die Motorisierung der deutschen Reichswehr*, 194–210.

58. Spielberger, *Die Motorisierung der deutschen Reichswehr*, 209–210.

59. Beschreibung Grosse Traktor, Letter of February 24, 1927, BA/MA, RH 8/V 2669. See also Spielberger, *Die Motorisierung der deutschen Reichswehr*, 281–283.

60. *Beschreibungsbuch Grosstraktor* BA/MA, RH 8/v833.

61. Ernst Volckheim, "Kampfwagenbewaffnung," *Militär Wochenblatt* 5 (1924).

62. White, *British Tanks and Fighting Vehicles*, 45.

63. See ibid. on British medium tanks. See *Beschreibungsbuch Grosstraktor*, BA/MA, RH 8/v883, for data on Rheinmetall and Krupp Grosstraktors.

64. For a detailed, technical analysis, see Spielberger, *Die Motorisierung der deutschen Reichswehr*, 283–284.

65. For a photo of the Daimler-Benz propeller system, see ibid., 292.

66. *Technische Mitteilungen*, Vol. 2, *Die Kampfwagen fremder Heere* (Berlin: Verlag R. Eisenschmidt, 1926), 76–80.

67. See Volckheim, *Der Kampfwagen in der heutigen Kriegführung*, 83. See also Schwarte, who comments on foreign amphibious tank experiments in *Die Technik im Zukunftskriege*, 194.

68. Walter J. Spielberger and Uwe Feist, *Sonderpanzer* (Fullbrook, Calif.: Aero, 1968), 22.

69. Spielberger, *Die Motorisierung der deutschen Reichswehr*, 317–318.

70. Ibid., 317–319.

71. Richard M. Ogorkiewicz, *Design and Development of Fighting Vehicles* (Garden City, N.Y.: Doubleday, 1968), 112. "Cletrac" stood for "Cleveland tractor," the first model built with a controlled-differential drive; the technology was developed in the United States in 1916 and patented in 1918. See also Spielberger, *Die Motorisierung der deutschen Reichswehr*, 319.

72. Ogorkiewicz, *Design and Development of Fighting Vehicles*, 112.

73. Spielberger, *Die Motorisierung der deutschen Reichswehr*, diagram, 319.

74. White, *British Tanks and Fighting Vehicles*, 47.

75. Kenneth Macksey, *The Tank Pioneers* (New York: Jane's, 1981), over-stresses the idea that German tank technology was primarily copied from foreign designs and ideas. He asserts that the LK II was a copy of a British whippet, that the light tractor resembled the Vickers Medium Mark III, and that the large tractor incorporated ideas built into the British Independent tank (ibid., 118). These statements are true only in the most superficial sense. The German tank designs were technically very different.

76. On the wheel/track tank, see Ernst Volckheim, "Raupen oder Räder-raupen—Antrieb bei Kampfwagen," *Der Kampfwagen* 3 (December 1924), and *Der Kampfwagen in der heutigen Kriegführung*, 82–83.

77. Spielberger, *Die Motorisierung der deutschen Reichswehr*, 275–281.

78. On Oswald Lutz's role in the wheel/track tank, see his notes on "Entwicklung der Panzertruppe, 1925–1929," BA/MA, N 107/3, 9–11.

79. Ibid., 11.

80. Spielberger, *Die Motorisierung der deutschen Reichswehr*, 281.

81. See *Technische Mitteilungen*, Vol. 2: *Die Kampfwagen fremder Heere*, 35–37.

82. F. M. von Senger und Etterlin, *Die deutschen Panzer: 1926–1945* (Munich: J. F. Lehmanns Verlag, 1959), 176.

83. Lt. Col. Oswald Lutz, Notes on Development of the Panzertruppe, 1925–1929, BA/MA, N 107/3, 10.

84. The 1929 Reichswehr budget would contain 36 million marks for the development of four armored car prototypes, as well as additional appropriations for thirty-two other armored cars. See Spielberger, *Die Motorisierung der deutschen Reichswehr*, 228.

85. Ibid., 227.

86. Ibid., 228; see also Werner Oswald, *Kraftfahrzeuge und Panzer*, 217.

87. Spielberger, *Die Motorisierung der deutschen Reichswehr*, 228.

88. Ibid., 237.

89. Oswald, *Kraftfahrzeuge und Panzer*, 24.

90. Ibid., 182. See also Spielberger, *Die Motorisierung der deutschen Reichswehr*, 157.

91. Spielberger, *Die Motorisierung der deutschen Reichswehr*, 145–151.

92. Oswald Lutz was born November 6, 1876, in Ohringen and died February 26, 1944, in Munich. He was educated at the Gymnasium in Munich; commissioned a second lieutenant in the Bavarian Army in 1896; promoted to major in 1917, colonel in 1928, and major general in 1931. See BA/MA, N 107 and N 107/1.

93. Lutz, Notes on Development of the Panzertruppe, 18.

94. Meier-Welcker, *Seeckt*, 485.

95. Heinz Guderian, "Kraftfahrkampftruppen," *Militär-wissenschaftliche Rundschau* 1 (1936): 55.

96. Oswald, *Kraftfahrzeuge und Panzer*, 13.

97. Ibid., 20.

98. *Militär Wochenblatt* 27 (1926).

99. A good overview of the motorization program is provided by John Milsom, *German Military Transport of World War II* (New York: Hippocrene, 1975), Chapters 1 and 2; and Spielberger, *Die Motorisierung der deutschen Reichswehr*. See also Adolf von Schell, "Grundlagen der Motorisierung und ihre Entwicklung im Zweiten Weltkrieg," *Wehrwissenschaftliche Rundschau*, 13, 3 (1963): 210–229.

100. Chef der Heeresleitung, "Bemerkungen," December 20, 1922, BA/MA, RH 2/2987, 19.

101. Waffenamt Procurement Priority List II, January 6, 1927, BA/MA, RH 2/2200.

102. Spielberger, *Die Motorisierung der deutschen Reichswehr*, 177–181.

103. Ibid., 142–145 and 178.

104. Daniel Beaver, "Politics and Policy: The War Department Motorization and Standardization Program for Wheeled Transport Vehicles, 1920–1940," *Military Affairs*, 47 (1983): 101–108.

105. Spielberger, *Die Motorisierung der deutschen Reichswehr*, 45–48.

106. Ibid., 32–41.

107. Milsom, *German Military Transport*, 10.

CHAPTER SIX. THE DEVELOPMENT OF GERMAN ARMOR DOCTRINE

1. Ernst Volckheim wrote a good short history of the World War I German tank force: "Die deutsche Panzerwaffe," in *Die Deutsche Wehrmacht*, ed. Georg Wetzell (Berlin: E. Mittler und Sohn, 1939), 293–338.

2. Fritz Heigl, *Taschenbuch der Tanks*, Vol. 3: *Der Panzerkampf*, 9–116, analyzed all the Allied tank actions of 1917–18.

3. Volckheim, "Die deutsche Panzerwaffe," 298–299.

4. For a detailed review of each German tank action in World War I, see Heigl, *Taschenbuch der Tanks*, 3:121–150.

5. Volckheim, "Die deutsche Panzerwaffe," 308–309.

6. Heigl, *Taschenbuch der Tanks*, Nol. 3:147.

7. Ibid., 134–137.

8. Ibid., 150–153; and Volckheim, "Die deutsche Panzerwaffe," 306.

9. Volckheim, "Die deutsche Panzerwaffe," 310–311.

10. Heigl, *Taschenbuch der Tanks*, 3:158–159.

11. Ibid., 200–201.

12. Ibid., 190–191.

13. Ibid., 207.

14. Volckheim, "Die deutsche Panzerwaffe," 313.

15. Maj. Josef Bischoff, *Die Letzte Front: Geschichte der Eisernen Division im Baltikum, 1919* (Berlin: Schützen Verlag, 1935), 102–103.

16. Ibid., 108–109; on the organization of the Iron Division, see especially 263–264.

17. *Heeresdienstvorschrift* 487, Part 2, 42–69. The officers appointed to the General Staff to study tanks in 1919 were Major Thümmel, Captain Wegener, and Captain von Eickstädt. These three men probably wrote the section on tanks for *Leadership and Battle*. See Hans von Seeckt, Letter of December 1, 1919, BA/MA, RH 2/2275, 35.

18. *Heeresdienstvorschrift* 487, Part 2, para. 525.

19. Ibid., para. 524.

20. Ibid., para. 525.

21. Ibid., para. 533–534.

22. Ibid., para. 551.

23. Ibid., para. 535.

24. Ibid., para. 548.

25. Ibid., para. 536.

26. Ibid., para. 565.

27. Ernst Volckheim was born in Prussia in 1898. He joined the army as a volunteer in 1915 and was commissioned as a lieutenant in 1916; in 1917 he served as a commander of a machine-gun company. Information from Volckheim's official military record in BA/MA, Personnel File of Ernst Volckheim. The only other officer in the Reichswehr in the late 1920s who possessed the wartime Tank Corps badge was Major Thofehrn. See Reichswehrministerium, *Rangliste des Deutschen Reichsheeres*, 1927, 132.

28. Volckheim served as an armored regiment commander in the war and, as a colonel, he was chief of the Armor School in 1941 (BA/MA, Volckheim's personnel file).

29. Ernst Volckheim, *Die deutschen Kampfwagen im Weltkriege* (Berlin: E. Mittler und Sohn, 1923). A later edition was published as *Deutsche Kampfwagen Greifen An!*

30. Konstantin von Altrock was born in 1861 in Breslau. He was commissioned in 1881; appointed to the General Staff in 1901; and promoted to major general in 1914. He commanded the Sixtieth Infantry Brigade in 1914–1915; was promoted to lieutenant general in 1917; commanded the Twenty-Eighth Reserve Division in 1918; and retired in 1919. Von Altrock had a varied career. Before World War I, he commanded a battalion and a regiment and held several positions on the General Staff. Information from BA/MA, von Altrock's Personnel File.

31. Gen. Konstantin von Altrock, Review of Ernst Volckheim's *Die deutschen Kampfwagen im Weltkriege, Militär Wochenblatt* 28 (1923).

32. Ernst Volckheim, *Der Kampfwagen und Abwehr dagegen* (Berlin: E. Mittler und Sohn, 1925). This pamphlet is in the military library of the First Battalion, Sixteenth Infantry Regiment, Bremen, Germany.

33. Volckheim, *Der Kampfwagen in der heutigen Kriegführung*, 89–90.

34. Volckheim, *Kampfwagen und Abwehr dagegen*, 9.

35. Volckheim, *Der Kampfwagen in der heutigen Kriegführung*, 45, 57–58, and 61–72.

36. Volckheim describes this first tank combat in history in Chapter 8 of *Deutsche Kampfwagen Greifen An!*

37. For typical Volckheim problems published in *Militär Wochenblatt*, see "über Kampfwagenabwehr im Bewegungskrieg" 3 (1924) and "Kampfwagenverwendung im Bewegungskrieg," 10 (1924), 28 (1925), and 38 (1925).

38. Volckheim, *Der Kampfwagen in der heutigen Kriegführung*, 55–71. See also Volckheim, *Kampfwagen und Abwehr dagegen*.

39. Ernst Volckheim, "Verwendung französischer Kampfwagen im Gefecht," in *Der Kampfwagen* (February–May 1925).

40. Volckheim, *Der Kampfwagen in der heutigen Kriegführung*, 86–88.

41. Ibid., 85–86.

42. Ibid., 82–83.

43. Ibid., 83.

44. Ernst Volckheim, "Raupen oder Räderantrieb bei Kampfwagen," *Militär Wochenblatt* 5 (1924).

45. Some of the articles in the 1926 *Militär Wochenblatt* include artillery Lieutenant Ohnesorge, "Kraftantrieb und leichte Artillerie der Zukunft," 23; horse transport Lieutenant Gallwitz, "Infanteriegeschütz und Kampfwagenabwehr," 14; infantry First Lieutenant von Horn, "Kampfwagen und Strassenpanzer bei der russischen Manöver," 23; cavalry First Lieutenant Mügge, "Verständigung des Kampfwagenkommandant mit Fahrer und Schützen," 4; and Lieutenant Gesterding, "Kampfwagenabwehr," 31.

46. Some of Wilhelm Brandt's early articles for the *Militär Wochenblatt* are "Der leichte Kampfwagen," 12 (1924); "Gasschutz in Kampfwagen," 17 (1924); "Der Lärm in Kampfwagen," 31 (1925).

47. Quoted in Geyer, "German Strategy in the Age of Machine Warfare," 559.

48. T-2 to All Major Commands, June 9, 1927, BA/MA, RH 2/2200.

49. Wehramt to Truppenamt Sections, Memo, "Discussion of Tank Technology," October 25, 1927, BA/MA, RH 2/2200.

50. Geyer, "German Strategy in the Age of Machine Warfare," 559.

51. *Kriegs- und militärorganisatorische Gedanken und Nachrichten aus dem Auslande*, a biweekly journal established in 1925, was published openly—officially by T-2, but actually by T-3. The army did not wish to draw too much attention to the Intelligence Section.

52. Some short pieces by Basil Liddell Hart—for example, from the London *Daily Telegraph*—were translated at this time, along with many other articles on armor. See T-2, *Kriegs- und militärorganisatorische Gedanken* 16 (August 1926); 14 (July 1926); and 8 (April 1926). Such booklets as *Kampfwagen und Heeresmotorisierung 1924/1925* (Berlin: Verlag R. Eisenschmidt 1926) contained collections of articles on foreign armor and motorization.

53. Army Commander to Military District Commanders and Truppenamt Sections, Letter on Tank Training in the Army, August 1924, BA/MA, RH 12-2/51. Lieutenant Volckheim's name appears at the top of the letter, which he drafted.

54. T-3, *Merkblatt über französische Truppenführung und Taktik*, October 1927, MA/DDR, R 01 70/10, 14, on armor. It replaced the *Merkblatt* of November 1, 1926.

55. T-3, *Die französischen Herbstmanöver, 1922*, August 11, 1923, BA/MA, RH 2/1547.

56. Ibid.; T-3, *Die französischen Herbstmanöver, 1923*, July 10, 1924, BA/MA, RH 2/1547, 12–13.

57. T-3, *Die französischen Herbstmanöver, 1923*, 19.

58. Ibid., 23–24.

59. Colonel Werner von Blomberg, T-3, *Bemerkungen zu den englischen Manövern, 1924*, December 1, 1924, BA/MA, RH 2/1603; and von Blomberg to Chef der Heeresleitung, May 29, 1926, BA/MA, RH 2/2195. Von Blomberg argued that civilian trucks ought to be built to army specifications so that they could be commandeered in time of war. The British trucks had impressed the Germans as much as the most modern tanks.

60. Colonel von Boetticher, Report on Artillery Motorization in the U.S., BA/MA, RH 2/1820.

61. Captain Speich, Travel Report of December 30, 1924, ibid., and General (Ret.) Schirmer, Travel Report of October 21, 1926, ibid.

62. Schirmer, Travel Report of October 21, 1926, 288.

63. Major Radelmeier and Captain Austmann, Travel Report on American Visit, January 31, 1929, BA/MA, RH 2/1822.

64. See BA/MA, RH 12-2/51, August 1924, 13–17.

65. Ibid.

66. Ibid.

67. Ibid.

68. High Command, Letter of October 6, 1924, BA/MA, RH 12-1/21, 73, 74.

69. Hans von Seeckt, *Bemerkungen des Chefs der Heeresleitung*, 1920, BA/MA, RH 2/2963, 14; BA/MA, RH 2/2987, 1922, 10; BA/MA, RH 2/101, 1923, 6; BA/MA, RH 2/70, 1924, 22; BA/MA, RH 2/70, 1925, 21.

70. Hans von Seeckt, *Bemerkungen des Chefs der Heeresleitung, 1923*, BA/MA, RH 2/101, para. 15.

71. Ibid.

72. Oswald Lutz, *Nachlass*, BA/MA N 107/3.

73. Ibid.

74. Walther Nehring, *Die Geschichte der deutschen Panzerwaffe 1916 bis 1945* (Berlin: Propyläen Verlag, 1974), 110–111.

75. Ibid., 55.

76. Chamberlain and Ellis, *Tanks of World War I*, 66.

77. Volckheim, *Deutsche Kampfwagen Greifen An!* 1–3.

78. Albert Seaton, *The German Army, 1933–45* (London: Weidenfeld and Nicolson, 1982), 61.

79. Heinz Guderian, *Erinnerungen eines Soldaten* (Heidelberg: K. Vowinckel Verlag, 1950).

80. See Karl Walde, *Guderian* (Frankfurt am Main: Verlag Ullstein, 1976), and Kenneth Macksey, *Guderian, Panzer General* (London: MacDonald and James, 1975).

81. Biographical details taken from Heinz Guderian, *Panzer Leader*, ed. Basil H. Liddell Hart (New York: Ballantine, 1957).

82. The emphasis upon Guderian as the "Creator of the blitzkrieg" is expounded by his biographer Kenneth Macksey in *Guderian, Panzer General*; Barry Posen in *The Sources of Military Doctrine* (Ithaca, N.Y.: Cornell University

Press, 1984), 208–209; Len Deighton in *Blitzkrieg* (London: Triad/Grafton, 1981), 168–171; Charles Messenger in *The Art of Blitzkrieg* (London: Jan Allan, 1976), 79 and 81; Michael Howard in *The Causes of Wars*, 2d ed. (Cambridge, Mass.: Harvard University Press, 1983), 201; and Field Marshal Lord Carver in *The Apostles of Mobility* (London: Weidenfeld and Nicolson, 1979), 55–59.

83. Macksey, *Guderian*, 43.

84. See Heinz Guderian's articles in *Der Kampfwagen*: "Die Lebensader Verduns," 4 (1925); "Strassenpanzerkraftwagen und ihre Abwehr," 1 (1924); "Aufklärung und Sicherung bei Kraftwagenmärschen," 2 (1924); and "Kavallerie und Strassenpanzerkraftwagen," 5 (1925). See also Guderian, "Truppen auf Kraftwagen und Fliegerabwehr," *Militär Wochenblatt* 12 (1924).

85. Guderian, "Kavallerie und Strassenpanzerkraftwagen."

86. Guderian, "Truppen auf Kraftwagen und Fliegerabwehr."

87. Heinz Guderian, *Achtung! Panzer!* (Stuttgart: Union Deutsche Verlagsgesellschaft, 1937); Ludwig Ritter von Eimannsberger, *Der Kampfwagenkrieg* (Munich: J. F. Lehmanns Verlag, 1934).

88. Guderian, *Panzer Leader*, 9.

89. Ibid., 14–15.

90. Dupuy, *Genius for War*, 256.

91. Guderian, *Panzer Leader*, 11.

92. On von Seeckt's reports, see *Bemerkungen des Chefs der Heeresleitung*, 1920, BA/MA, RH 2/2963; 1921, BA/MA, RH 2/69; 1922, BA/MA, RH 2/2987; 1923, BA/MA, RH 2/101; and 1924 and 1925, BA/MA, RH 2/70.

93. Guderian, *Panzer Leader*, 22.

94. Dale Wilson, *Treat 'em Rough! The Birth of American Armor, 1917–1920* (Novato, Calif.: Presidio Press, 1990), 215–216.

95. Guderian, *Panzer Leader*, 27.

96. Ibid., 10.

97. Ibid., 10.

98. See Liddell Hart, *Memoirs*, 1:200. For a thorough discussion of how Liddell Hart actually revised the historical record in order to enhance his claims to having created the Blitzkrieg, see John J. Mearsheimer, *Liddell Hart and the Weight of History* (Ithaca, N.Y.: Cornell University Press, 1988), 164–217.

99. See Posen, *Sources of Military Doctrine*, 208–209; Brian Bond, *Liddell Hart*, 215–216; Larry Addington, *The Blitzkrieg Era and the German General Staff, 1865–1941* (New Brunswick, N.J.: Rutgers University Press, 1971), 32–33; Messenger, *Art of Blitzkrieg*, 52 and 81; Robert O'Neill, "Doctrine and Training in the German Army, 1919–1939," in *The Theory and Practice of War*, ed. Michael Howard (London: Cassell, 1965), 164; and Howard, *Causes of Wars*, 201.

100. The only mention of Liddell Hart by Rommel was after an article he read in June 1942. See Rommel, *The Rommel Papers*, trans. Paul Findlay and ed. Basil H. Liddell Hart (New York: Harcourt, Brace, 1953), 203.

101. Some of the Liddell Hart articles translated or summarized in the *Militär Wochenblatt* in the 1920s were "Der Nächste Grosse Krieg," 30 (1924), taken from an article in the *Royal Engineers' Journal*; "Vom künftigen Kriege," 9 (1925), a review of Liddell Hart's *Paris or the Future War*; an article on army motorization quoted *Paris or the Future War*, 3 (1926); "Kampfwagen und Kavallerie" quoted Liddell Hart's report on British maneuvers. Examples of other foreign articles translated in the *Militär Wochenblatt* are: "Die Entwicklung der Kampfwagen," from the U.S. Army's *Infantry Journal*; "Kraftwagen Programm in Russland," 24 (1926), from Russian sources; and "Kampfwagen in Morocco," 28 (1926), from the French press.

238 Notes to Pages 142–147

102. A 204–page study from the 1920s by T-3 uses Fuller as the main source. See T-3, *Die Tanks im Weltkrieg*, 1920s, BA/MA, RH 8/v1745.

103. See T-2, *Kriegs- und militärorganisatorische Gedanken und Nachrichten aus dem Auslande* 2, 9, 10, 11 (May-June 1926).

104. Gen. J. F. C. Fuller, *Erinnerungen eines freimütigen Soldaten* (Berlin: Rowohlt, 1932).

CHAPTER SEVEN. DEVELOPING A REICHSWEHR
AIR DOCTRINE

1. Flugmeisterei, Letter of November 13, 1919, BA/MA, RH 2/2275, 21–26.
2. Waffenamt, Letter of December 24, 1919, BA/MA, RH 2/2275, 85.
3. Flugmeisterei, Abteilung II, Letter of December 4, 1919, BA/MA, RH 2/2275, 38–40.
4. Waffenamt, Letter of December 24, 1919, BA/MA, RH 2/2275, 85–87.
5. Anlage II zu Idflieg B, November 13, 1919, BA/MA, RH 2/2275, 26.
6. Waffenamt, Letter of December 24, 1919, BA/MA, RH 2/2275, 85–87.
7. Ibid.
8. Ibid.
9. BA/MA, RH 2/2275, contains about twenty such reports.
10. Flugmeisterei, Report of June 1920, BA/MA, RH 2/2275, 150–153.
11. For a typical report, see Report of Major Streccius, July 30, 1920, BA/MA, RH 2/2275, 171–174.
12. Translation of Capt. Amedeo Mecozzi, Italian Air Force, "Long-Range Bomber Operations during the War," BA/MA, RH 2/2275, 446–471.
13. TA-L [Air Organization Office, T-2] Letter of February 4, 1927, BA/MA, RH 12-1/53.
14. Report by R. Spies, mid-1920s, BA/MA, RH 2/2187.
15. See Reichsarchiv Abt. B, Ref. Luftstreitkräfte, Study of April 2, 1926, BA/MA, RH 2/2195, 30 pages. This is a study of the 1918 air battle that concentrates on the tactical role of bombers.
16. Report by Captain Hoth to T-2 (Air), May 3, 1924, ibid., 253.
17. Ibid., 254–255.
18. Ibid., 259.
19. Waffenamt, Letter of December 24, 1919, BA/MA, RH 2/2275, 86.
20. D. J. C. Irving, *The Rise and Fall of the Luftwaffe: The Life of Luftwaffe Marshal Erhard Milch* (London: Weidenfeld and Nicolson, 1973), 14 and 344.
21. Fighter Organization Committee, "Ergebniss der Diskussion—Vorträge über Luftkampführung," October 13, 1920, BA/MA, RH 2/2275, 162–163.
22. Ibid.
23. Bryan Philpott, *History of the German Air Force* (New York: Gallery, 1986), 58.
24. Groehler, *Geschichte des Luftkrieges*, 138.
25. Hans von Seeckt, Speech in Hamburg, "Der Friedensvertrag und die Wehrmacht," February 20, 1920, NA, Von Seeckt Papers, File M-132, Roll 25, Item 110.
26. Hanfried Schliephake, *The Birth of the Luftwaffe* (Chicago: Henry Regnery, 1972), 12.
27. Ibid. See also Irving, *Rise and Fall of the Luftwaffe*, 11–12, for an account of Erhard Milch's service with the "air police."
28. Von Rabenau, *Seeckt: Aus seinem Leben*, 529.

29. Suchenwirth, *Development of the German Air Force*, 5.
30. Ibid.
31. Ibid., 6.
32. Ibid.
33. Reichswehrministerium, *Rangliste des Deutschen Reichsheeres*, 1927.
34. Ibid. In 1927, Capt. (later Col. Gen.) Kurt Student, Major Steinkopf-Hartig, Captain Pirner, Captain (later General der Flieger) Volkman, Captain Seldner, and Capt. (later Lt. Gen.) Fritz Lorenz were the fliers assigned to the Weapons Office.
35. Suchenwirth, *Development of the German Air Force*, 7.
36. TA-L, Letter of November 23, 1926, BA/MA, RH 12-1/15. Orders were issued assigning twenty-nine air officers to pilot refresher courses lasting from six to nine months. Regimental commanders were to comply without hesitation to such orders by the army commander.
37. Karl-Heinz Völker, *Die Entwicklung der militärischen Luftfahrt in Deutschland, 1920–1933*, (Stuttgart: Deutsche Verlags-Anstalt, 1962), 142.
38. Ibid.
39. The 1927 figures were 33 of 134 listed fliers in the cavalry—24.62 percent. See Reichswehrministerium, *Rangliste des Deutschen Reichsheeres*, 1927.
40. There is clear evidence that some units of the Reichswehr—notably ambulance companies—were used as official cover for officers on special duty. Ernst Volckheim, the German Army's tank expert, was officially assigned to the Second Ambulance Company for most of the 1920s. Volckheim's personnel file, however, which is not open to the public, stated that he was detached to the Reichswehr Ministry for training and weapons testing; no mention is made of the Second Ambulance Company.
41. Von Seeckt, *Thoughts of a Soldier*, 61.
42. Ibid., 62.
43. Ibid., 84.
44. Mathew Cooper, *The German Air Force, 1922–1945: An Anatomy of Failure* (London: Jane's, 1981), 379.
45. See Von Seeckt, *Bemerkungen des Chefs der Heeresleitung 1923*, NA, Von Seeckt papers, File M-132, Roll 25, Item 133, 6–7, for von Seeckt's comments on air defense.
46. Ibid., 4, para. 15.
47. Von Rabenau, *Seeckt: Aus seinem Leben*, 530.
48. Ibid.
49. Irving, *Rise and Fall of the Luftwaffe*, 12–16.
50. On the Milch-Wilberg wartime relationship, see Ibid. Some of the Milch-Wilberg correspondence is in BA/MA, RH 2/2187.
51. Mason, *Rise of the Luftwaffe*, 123.
52. See Völker, *Die Entwicklung der militärischen Luftfahrt in Deutschland*, especially 145–157. Völker's work is the best account available of the Reichswehr's secret air force. Völker named many other former military fliers who were important in civil aviation, including Major Keller (ret.) and former navy lieutenant von Gronau, who worked in the Transportation Ministry (see ibid., 145), as well as former navy flier Gotthard Sachsenberg, who ran several aviation companies after the war (see ibid., 152–153).
53. Absolom, *Die Wehrmacht im Dritten Reich*, 1:68–74. Absolom listed all the civilian air agencies that worked with the Reichswehr, including companies that carried out research, such as Messgeräte-Baykow GmbH, which conducted important work in the development of direction-finding equipment.

54. Wilberg was succeeded as chief of the Air Organization Office by a series of exceptionally able officers: Lt. Col. Wilhelm Wimmer, Maj. Hugo Sperrle, and Maj. Hellmuth Felmy. See Suchenwirth, *Development of the German Air Force*, 17.

55. Ibid., 17.

56. See Rolf Roeingh, *Wegbereiter der Luftfahrt* (Berlin: Deutscher Archiv-Verlag, 1938), xxiii.

57. Maj. Gen. Hermann Franke, *Handbuch der neuzeitlichen Wehrwissenschaften*, Vol. 2: *Die Luftwaffe* (Berlin: Verlag von Walter de Gruyter, 1939), 443.

58. Ibid., 239.

59. Ibid., 443.

60. Völker, *Die Entwicklung der militärischen Luftfahrt*, 127.

61. Cooper, *German Air Force*, 379.

62. Order of December 24, 1919, BA/MA, RH 2/2275, 32–33. Wilberg's signature is on the order, which directed certain officers to write evaluations of their wartime experiences.

63. Helmut Wilberg, Anlage II, zur ID flieg B. NR., November 13, 1919, BA/MA, RH 2/2275, 25.

64. Helmut Wilberg, Denkschrift of February 8, 1922, BA/MA, RH 2/2275, 384–385.

65. Ibid.

66. Peter Supf, *Das Buch der deutschen Fluggeschichte*, vol. 2 (Berlin: Verlagsanstalt Hermann Klemm, 1935), 294.

67. Max Schwarte, ed. *Der grosse Krieg, 1914–1918*, vol. 4 (Berlin: E. Mittler und Sohn, 1922), 603.

68. Irving, *Rise and Fall of the Luftwaffe*, 8–9.

69. Supf, *Das Buch der deutschen Fluggeschichte*, 295.

70. Mason, *Rise of the Luftwaffe*, 108.

71. Files on "Ziviles Flugwesen," March 1921–August 1923, BA/MA, RH 2198; "Werkzeuge, Maschinen usw. zur Verfügung des Reichswehrministeriums," 1920s, BA/MA, RH 2/2191.

72. Lt. Col. Helmut Wilberg, Report on the German Air Industry, Its Prospects for Rapid Growth and Production, and Its Requirements for Production Subsidies and Research Facilities, 1926, BA/MA, RH 2/2187, 25–47.

73. Erhard Milch, Direktion Lufthansa, to Helmut Wilberg, April 4, 1927, BA/MA, RH 2/2187.

74. Albatros Company, Report on Technical Developments in Increasing Aircraft Speed, March 5, 1927, BA/MA, RH 2/2187.

75. R. Spies, Report Using Polish, French, American and Italian Data, mid-1920s, BA/MA, RH 2/2187.

76. Reichsarchiv, Historical Study of Air Operations in 1918, April 2, 1926, BA/MA, RH 2/2195, 30 pages.

77. Hans von Fichte, "Erfahrungsberichte-Nachtjäger," May 22, 1928, BA/MA, RH 2273.

78. "Studie eines Offiziers über die Fliegerwaffe und ihre Verwendung," a manual published by the army circa 1925. In author's collection.

79. Ibid., 4.

80. Ibid., 5.

81. Ibid., 8–10.

82. Ibid., 10–11.

83. Ibid., 11.

84. Ibid.

85. Ibid.
86. Ibid., 14–15.
87. *Heeresdienstvorschrift* 487, Part 1, 38–44 and 58–63.
88. Ibid., 41.
89. Ibid., 42.
90. Ibid., 43.
91. *Heeresdienstvorschrift* 487, Part 2, 12.
92. Ibid.
93. Ibid., 35–42.
94. The German Army translated and published the French manual as Französische Truppenführung, *Vorschrift für die taktische Verwendung der grossen Verbände* (Berlin: Verlag Offene Worte, 1937).
95. A good overview is found in Divine's *Broken Wing*. On the political strategy behind the strategic bombing campaign, see Kuropka, "Die britische Luftkriegskonzeption gegen Deutschland im Ersten Weltkrieg," 7–24.
96. Divine, *Broken Wing*, 142–143. A Handley Page bomber cost 6,000 pounds, and a DH-4 cost 1,400 pounds in 1918. Divine estimates that the Independent Air Force can only claim a share in the less than 600,000 pounds of damage the Germans suffered from bombing from June to November 1918.
97. Ibid., 163–164.
98. Ibid., 165.
99. Exact figures are hard to obtain. Olaf Groehler, in *Geschichte des Luftkrieges 1910 bis 1980*, 96, gives the figure of 6,300 German air deaths as opposed to 6,166 British aircrew dead and 5,500 French dead. Russian, Belgian, Italian, and American casualty figures are not given, and the French numbers are probably too low. A reasonable estimate is that the heavily outnumbered German Air Service shot down its enemies with a 1:3 loss ratio.
100. Divine, *Broken Wing*, 162.
101. Ibid.
102. David MacIsaac, "Voices from the Central Blue: The Air Power Theorists," in *Makers of Modern Strategy*, ed. P. Paret (Princeton, N.J.: Princeton University Press, 1986), 624–647.
103. Thomas Greer, *The Development of Air Doctrine in the Army Air Arm, 1917–1941*, USAF Historical Study 89 (Maxwell Air Force Base, Ala.: Air University Press, 1955), 38.
104. Ibid., 40.
105. Ibid., 40–41.
106. Ibid., 41.
107. Greer, *Development of Air Doctrine*, 5.
108. Ibid., 9.
109. Ibid., 13.
110. For an example of the favorable manner in which Mitchell and his theories were seen in the United States, see Edward Warner, "Douhet, Mitchell, Seversky: Theories of Air Warfare," in *Makers of Modern Strategy*, ed. Edward Earle (Princeton, N.J.: Princeton University Press, 1943), 485–503.
111. Giulio Douhet, *The Command of the Air*, (New York: Arno Press, 1972; reprint of 1927 rev. edition), 34–35.
112. Ibid., 44.
113. Ibid., 55.
114. *Luftfahrtnachrichten* 1, August 1919, BA/MA, RH 2/2277.
115. Ibid., 471–480 and 503.
116. Weapons Office, Letter of May 12, 1920, ibid. See also Weapons Office,

Letter of October 22, 1919, ibid., 23, which asks T-3 to subscribe to seventeen additional foreign journals. See also ibid., 230–240, for the German journals on file.

117. General [William] Mitchell, Translation of Lecture on Aerial Technology, July 1, 1920, BA/MA, RH 2/2277, 471–480.

118. An article on Mitchell's ship-bombing experiments appears in *Militär Wochenblatt*, 19 (1921). *Militär Wochenblatt*, 32 and 47 (1925) feature translations of articles that Mitchell wrote for the *Saturday Evening Post*.

119. Capt. Hans Ritter, *Der Luftkrieg* (Berlin: F. Koehler Verlag, 1926), 189–190.

120. Maj. Hellmuth Felmy to Capt. Wolfram Frieherr von Richtofen, 1929, requesting a report on the thought of Douhet, who is described as "well-known and followed carefully in the magazines," MA/DDR, R 06 10/4, 305.

121. TA-L, Referat VI, "Militärische Faktoren für die Bewertung der modernen Luftmächte," April 9, 1926, BA/MA, RH 2/2279.

122. Maj. Helmut Wilberg, Reisebericht, 1925–1926, BA/MA, RH 2/1820, 199.

123. Major von dem Hagen, Reisebericht, November 1928, BA/MA, RH 2/1822.

124. See MA/DDR, R 06 10/4.

125. Ibid., 138–141.

126. Captain Speidel, Reports of 1929, ibid., 145–158.

127. Max Schwarte's works include *Die militärischen Lehren des grossen Krieges* (Berlin: Verlag Offene Worte, 1920); *Die Technik im Weltkriege* (Berlin: Verlag Offene Worte, 1920); *Die Technik im Zukunftskriege* (Berlin: Verlag Offene Worte, 1923); and *Kriegslehren im Beispiel aus dem Weltkrieg* (Berlin: Verlag Offene Worte, 1925).

128. Gen. a.D. Schwarte, Vortrag, 1928, BA/MA, RH 12-1/53, 51–58.

129. T-2 (Luft), Letter of September 26, 1928, BA/MA, RH 12-1/53, 49.

130. Völker, *Die Entwicklung der militärischen Luftfahrt*, 137–138.

131. Cooper, *German Air Force*, 383.

132. An overview of this construction at Lipetsk from 1924 to 1933 is found in Mason's *Rise of the Luftwaffe*, 140–156.

133. Michael Taylor, *Warplanes of the World: 1918–1939* (New York: Charles Scribner's Sons, 1981), 171.

134. Schliephake, *Birth of the Luftwaffe*, 18.

135. Völker, *Die Entwicklung der militärischen Luftfahrt*, 141–142.

136. Schliephake, *Birth of the Luftwaffe*, 17–19.

137. Völker, *Die Entwicklung der militärischen Luftfahrt*, 140.

138. Betr. Ausbildungslehrgang L 1927, November 30, 1926, BA/MA, RH 2/2299.

139. Ibid., 43.

140. Schliephake, *Birth of the Luftwaffe*, 18.

141. TA-L, Report of August 30, 1926, BA/MA, RH 12-1/15, 111.

142. Karl-Heinz Völker, *Die deutsche Luftwaffe, 1933–1939* (Stuttgart: Deutsche Verlags-Anstalt, 1967), 16.

143. Cooper, *German Air Force*, 385.

144. T-1, Letter of November 1926, BA/MA, RH 12-1/15, 112.

145. Ibid., 112–113.

146. Manfred Zeidler, "Luftkriegsdenken und Offiziersausbildung an der Moskauer Zukovskij Akademie im Jahre 1926," *Militärgeschichtliche Mitteilungen*, 27 (1980): 127–174.

147. Ibid. Fiebig's war games and reports are on 140–157.

148. Ibid., 154.

149. Ibid., 153–154.

150. Suchenwirth, *Development of the German Air Force*, 172–173.

151. Ibid., 28.

152. Ibid., 27–28.

153. Reinicke, *Das Reichsheer*, 375.

154. Challener, ed., *Weekly Summaries*, Report of November 27–December 10, 1926, 6.

155. Challener, ed., *Weekly Summaries*, Report of November 1–November 14, 1924, 10432–10433.

156. Ibid.

157. Karl Ries, *The Luftwaffe: A Photographic Record, 1919–1945* (London: B. T. Batsford, 1987), 9.

158. See Erich Meyer, ed., *Deutsche Kraftfahrzeug-Typenschau: Luftfahrzeuge und Luftfahrzeugmotoren 1926* (Dresden: Verlag Deutsche Motor, 1926), for a catalog of German civil aircraft types in production.

159. On the early Reichswehr-Heinkel relationship, see Mason, *Rise of the Luftwaffe*, 101–102 and 135–138. Ernst Heinkel's account of his early Reichswehr contracts is in his autobiography, *Stürmisches Leben* (Stuttgart: Mundus Verlag, 1953), 119–135. Performance data on early Heinkel aircraft can be found in Taylor, *Warplanes of the World: 1918–1939*, 165–166.

160. Suchenwirth, *Development of the German Air Force*, 18.

161. Schliephake, *Birth of the Luftwaffe*, 19–21.

162. Cooper, *German Air Force*, 2; and Schliephake, *Birth of the Luftwaffe*, 28.

163. P. Deichmann, *German Air Force Operations in Support of the Army*, USAF Historical Study 163 (Maxwell Air Force Base, Ala.: Air University Press, 1962), 9.

164. Ibid., 9–10.

165. Suchenwirth, *Development of the German Air Force*, 170.

166. Mason, *Rise of the Luftwaffe*, 160–161; and Suchenwirth, *Development of the German Air Force*, 239.

167. Suchenwirth, *Development of the German Air Force*, 239.

168. Mason, *Rise of the Luftwaffe*, 180.

169. See Suchenwirth, *Development of the German Air Force*, 172–173.

CHAPTER EIGHT. THE REICHSWEHR
AS A MATURE MILITARY FORCE

1. A strategic overview was provided by General Groener to the government in June 1919. Groener saw the German military situation as hopeless and recommended that the government accept the Versailles Treaty. See "Denkschrift des Ersten Generalquartiermeisters, Gen. Lt. Groener über die Lage am 17. Juni 1919," MA/DDR, W 10/52141.

2. There are numerous accounts of the German-Soviet relationship of the 1919–1922 period. See Craig, *Politics of the Prussian Army*, 408–415; Carsten, *Reichswehr and Politics*, 68–71 and 136–147; and Gaines Post, Jr., *The Civil-Military Fabric of Weimar Foreign Policy* (Princeton, N.J.: Princeton University Press, 1973), 110–114.

3. Post, *Civil-Military Fabric of Weimar Foreign Policy*, 110–129.

4. Intelligence reports of 1919 reckoned the Czech Army at 243,000 soldiers. Skoda was said to be building 1,200 new cannons for the Czech Army, and the two Czech divisions near Königgrätz were seen as a threat to Silesia. See Ministe-

rium für Militärwesen, Saxony (Nachrichtenstelle Dresden), to Freiwilliger Grenzer Regiments, Intelligence Report of May 26, 1919, MA/DDR, R 11 41 20/7, 38–41 and 41–43. See also Freiwilliger Grenzer Rgt. 3, Daily and Weekly Intelligence Reports, "Aufklärungstätigkeit an der Sächsischen-Böhmischen Grenze," April–September 1919, MA/DDR, R 11 41 30/4.

5. Robert Citino, *The Evolution of Blitzkrieg Tactics: Germany Defends Itself against Poland, 1918–1933* (Westport, Conn.: Greenwood Press, 1987), 7.

6. Ibid., 5.

7. Ibid., 13.

8. Wohlfeil and Dollinger, *Die Deutsche Reichswehr*, 204.

9. The German foreign minister, in a memorandum to the Reich chancellor in 1922, stated that restoring the German-Russian border was an aim of German foreign policy—in other words, the destruction of Poland. Quoted in John Wheeler-Bennett, *The Nemesis of Power*, 2d ed. (London: Macmillan, 1964), 133–137.

10. Von Seeckt, "Deutschlands Stellung zum russischen Problem," Memo of September 1922, quoted in Carsten, *Reichswehr and Politics*, 140.

11. Hans Roos, "Die militärpolitische Lage und Planung Polens gegenüber Deutschland vor 1939," *Wehrwissenschaftliche Rundschau* 7, 4 (1957): 183.

12. Oskar Reile, *Die deutsche Abwehr im Osten, 1921–1945* (Munich: Verlag Welsermühl, 1969), 68–69.

13. The best account of German/Soviet military cooperation in the 1920s from the Soviet viewpoint is Erickson, *Soviet High Command*, especially Chapters 6 and 9.

14. Freiwilliger Grenzer Rgt. 3, Defense Plan for East Saxony, 1919, MA/DDR, R 11 41 30/8, 1–3. See also Freiwilliger Grenzer Batt. 6, Defense Plan of June 21, 1919, MA/DDR, R 11 41 12/1, 88–91. This plan recommended sabotage, retreat, and delaying tactics against the superior Czech forces.

15. Gordon, *Reichswehr and the German Republic*, 254–256.

16. Hans von Seeckt to Chancellor Josef Wirth, June 10, 1922, reproduced in Wohlfeil and Dollinger, *Die Deutsche Reichswehr*, 95.

17. Even Gustav Stresemann, the chancellor and foreign minister who worked to lower tensions with the Allied powers, supported the Reichswehr's secret rearmament programs. See Gatzke, *Stresemann and the Rearmament of Germany*, 39, 50–55, 61, 80–88, and 91–92.

18. Wilhelm Deist, *The Wehrmacht and German Rearmament* (London: Macmillan, 1981), 9–17.

19. On von Seeckt's war plans against Poland, see Notes to Dr. Ziegler on Von Seeckt's War Plans, April 30, 1942, NA, Von Seeckt Papers, File M-132, Roll 7. See also Lieutenant General Lieber to Maj. Friedrich von Rabenau, September 26, 1938, BA/MA, N 62/12, 18.

20. Citino, *Evolution of Blitzkrieg Tactics*, 66–69.

21. Ibid., 68–70.

22. Lieber to von Rabenau, September 26, 1938, 18.

23. Citino, *Evolution of Blitzkrieg Tactics*, 147–150.

24. Ibid., 173–180.

25. Ibid., 158.

26. Ibid., 163.

27. On German war plans against France, see Charles Burdick, "Die deutschen militärischen Planungen gegenüber Frankreich, 1933–1938," *Wehrwissenschaftliche Rundschau*, 6, 12 (1956): 678–681. See also Notes to Dr. Ziegler on Von Seeckt's War Plans, April 30, 1942.

28. See German Army Enlargement Plan, 1924-25, NA, Von Seeckt Papers, File M-132, Roll 430.

29. Ibid.

30. Ibid.

31. On the history of the Supply Staff, see Georg Thomas, *Geschichte der deutschen Wehr- und Rüstungswirtschaft (1918–1943/45)*, vol. 14 in *Schriften des Bundesarchivs*, ed. Wolfgang Birkenfeld (Boppard am Rhein: Harald Boldt Verlag, 1966), 53–57.

32. Ibid., 56–57.

33. Hansen, *Reichswehr und Industrie, Rüstungswirtschaftlicher Zusammenarbeit und wirtschaftliche Mobilmachungsvorbereitungen*, 1923–1932, 82–85.

34. Ibid., 82–86.

35. Carsten, *Reichswehr and Politics*, 221.

36. Post, *Civil-Military Fabric of Weimar Foreign Policy*, 194.

37. Ibid., 194–199.

38. Burkhart Müller-Hillebrand, *Das Heer 1933–1945, Entwicklung des organisatorischen Aufbaues*, vol. 1 (Darmstadt: E. Mittler und Sohn, 1954), 18–20.

39. Challener, ed., *Weekly Summaries*, Report of March 8–March 21, 1924, 10108.

40. Chief of Staff of the District Command to the Staff of Freiwilliger Grenzer BN 3, July 10, 1919, MA/DDR, R 11 41 31/8. See also Reports from Freiwilliger Grenzer BN 3, July 14, 1919, and August 21, 1919, ibid.

41. Memo of Military District Command Saxony, "Bildung von Freiwilligen-Verbänden während und nach der Demobilmachung des Feldheeres," 1919, MA/DDR, R 02 20 25.

42. Citino, *Evolution of Blitzkrieg Tactics*, 21.

43. Ibid., 24–25.

44. Ibid., 26.

45. Craig, in *Politics of the Prussian Army*, estimated that 50,000–80,000 men were trained in the "Black Reichswehr." Posen, in *Sources of Military Doctrine*, 185, estimated that the Reichswehr had 150,000 reserve soldiers. If one subtracts the approximately 70,000 Security Police from the figure, one arrives at 80,000. These estimates, however, all seem high, a reflection of "paper strength."

46. Craig, *Politics of the Prussian Army*, 405.

47. "Geschichte des I/J-R. 65," Part 3.

48. Ibid.

49. Ibid.

50. Craig, *Politics of the Prussian Army*, 401 and passim.

51. Ibid., 401.

52. Görlitz, *History of the German General Staff*, 225.

53. BA/MA, Personnel File of Kurt Hesse.

54. Bennett, *German Rearmament and the West*, 15.

55. Quoted in Craig, *Politics of the Prussian Army*, 405.

56. Wheeler-Bennett, *Nemesis of Power*, 92–93.

57. Craig, *Politics of the Prussian Army*, 402.

58. See Bennett, *German Rearmament and the West*, 17–18. See also Absolom, *Die Wehrmacht im Dritten Reich*, 1:35–39.

59. Bennett, *German Rearmament and the West*, 40.

60. Ibid., 40–41.

61. HermannTeske, ed., *General Ernst Köstring* (Frankfurt am Main: Mittler, 1966), 39.

62. Von Manstein, *Aus einem Soldatenleben*, 121.

63. Ibid., 112.

64. Westphal, *Erinnerungen*, 34.

65. Challener, ed., *Weekly Summaries*, Report of November 1–November 14, 1924, 10432.

66. Truman Smith, "The Papers of Truman Smith," U.S. Army War College, Carlisle Barracks, Pennsylvania, 68.

67. Challener, ed., *Weekly Summaries*, Report of November 27–December 10, 1926, 2.

68. Ibid. See also Lt. Col. S. Boelcke (ret.), "Die süddeutschen Reichsheermanöver, 1926," *Schweizerische Monatsschrift für Offiziere aller Waffen*, 38, 11 (November 1926): 360–367.

69. Boelcke, "Die süddeutschen Reichsheermanöver, 1926," 362.

70. Ibid., 363.

71. Ibid., 364.

72. Challener, ed., *Weekly Summaries*, Report of November 27–December 10, 1926, 6.

73. Boelcke, "Die süddeutschen Reichsheermanöver 1926," 364.

74. Challener, ed., *Weekly Summaries*, Report of November 27–December 10, 1926, 10.

75. Ibid., 7.

76. Ibid.

77. Ibid., 6.

78. Ibid.

79. Ibid.

80. Ibid., 10.

81. Third Cavalry Division to Infantry Inspectorate, Report of November 3, 1927, BA/MA, RH 12-2/100.

82. Ibid.

83. General Walter Reinhardt to T-4 Truppenamt, Erfahrungsbericht, November 11, 1927, BA/MA, RH 12-2/100.

84. Ibid., 3.

85. Citino, *Evolution of Blitzkrieg Tactics*, 173–191, reviews the Reichswehr maneuvers of 1927–1932.

86. Ibid., 184–185.

87. Ibid., 185.

88. Report of Communications Exercise, April 18, 1928, BA/MA, RH 12-2/95, 24 pages.

89. Operatives Kriegsspiel 1926/27, November 1926, BA/MA, RH 2/2822, 1–3.

90. Ibid., 10–11.

91. Ibid.

92. Ibid., 2–3.

93. Challener, ed., *Weekly Summaries*, Report of November 1–November 14, 1924, 10432.

94. Challener, ed., *Weekly Summaries*, Report of November 27–December 10, 1926, 2.

95. Ibid., 5.

96. T-3 Truppenamt, "Die französischen Herbstmanöver, 1922," September 11, 1923, BA/MA, RH 2/1547, 9.

97. Ibid.

98. T-3 Truppenamt, "Die französischen Herbstmanöver, 1924" December 10, 1924, BA/MA, RH 2/1547, 11.

99. Challener, *Weekly Summaries*, Report of May 17–May 30, 1924, 10213–10214.

100. Smith, "The Papers of Truman Smith," 54.

101. Erickson, *Soviet High Command*, 256–258.

102. Ibid., 257–258.

103. In *Die Motorisierung der deutschen Reichswehr*, 262–274, Walter Spielberger provides photographs of the Kazan installation.

104. Ibid.

105. John Milsom, *Russian Tanks, 1900–1970* (Harrisburg, Penn.: Stackpole, 1971), 30.

106. Spielberger, *Die Motorisierung der deutschen Reichswehr*, 274.

107. Milsom, *Russian Tanks*, 31–33.

108. Walter Nehring, *Die Geschichte der deutschen Panzerwaffe*, Appendix I, 12.

109. Ibid., for a complete student and faculty roster covering 1929 to 1932.

110. Ibid., 9–10.

111. Ibid., 10.

112. Erickson, *Soviet High Command*, 269.

113. Milsom, *Russian Tanks*, 30.

114. Ibid.

115. Milsom, *Russian Tanks*, 34.

116. Ibid.

117. Ibid., 33.

118. Ibid., 35. See also Erickson, *Soviet High Command*, 257.

119. Milsom, *Russian Tanks*, 32–33.

120. Erickson, *Soviet High Command*, 258.

121. Ibid., 269.

122. See Spielberger, *Die Motorisierung der deutschen Reichswehr*, Chapter 7.

123. Major Siebert, *Atlas zu F.u.G.I.: Ein Anschauungs-Lehrbuch* (Berlin: Verlag Offene Worte, 1929).

124. Ibid., 3–4.

125. Ibid., 16–17 and 20–21.

126. Ibid., 23.

127. Ibid., 48.

128. Ibid., 52.

129. Ibid., 56.

130. Ibid., 59.

131. Ibid., 63.

132. See Spielberger, *Die Motorisierung der deutschen Reichswehr*, 11, for a photograph of a captured British Mark V tank being used by German forces against Communist insurrectionists in Berlin in 1919. See page 14 for photographs of an A7V tank being used by government troops against Communists in 1919.

133. Ibid., 227–229, 234, and 237.

134. Milsom, *Russian Tanks*, 34.

135. Nehring, *Die Geschichte der deutschen Panzerwaffe*, Appendix I, 9–10.

136. Erickson, *Soviet High Command*, 271.

137. Milsom, *Russian Tanks*, 35.

138. Nehring, *Die Geschichte der deutschen Panzerwaffe*, Appendix I, 12.

139. Quoted by Nehring, ibid., Appendix I, 10.

140. Ibid.

141. Ibid., 112.

142. Ibid.

143. Ibid, 114.

144. Gen. Wilhelm Groener, Lecture to Deutschen Gesellschaft, "Gedanken über die Entwicklung des Kriegswesens," 1929-30, MA/DDR, NF 15/533.

145. Ibid.

146. Ibid.

147. Ibid.

148. Lt. Gen. Ernst Kabisch to Gen. Wilhelm Groener, October 10, 1932, MA/DDR NF 15/533.

149. Nehring, *Die Geschichte der deutschen Panzerwaffe*, 64–66.

150. Ibid., 76.

151. Citino, *The Evolution of Blitzkrieg Tactics*, xii.

152. Bernhard Kranz, *Geschichte der Hirschberger Jäger 1920 bis 1945* (Düsseldorf: Diederichs, 1975), 13–14.


CHAPTER NINE. EPILOGUE

1. *Heeresdienstvorschrift* 487, Part 2, 270.

2. Addington, *Blitzkrieg Era and the German General Staff*, 36.

3. Robert O'Neill, "Fritsch, Beck, and the Führer," in *Hitler's Generals*, ed. Corelli Barnett (London: Weidenfeld and Nicolson, 1989), 27, describes Army Regulation 300 as "one of the most renowned of German military publications. . . . [It gained Beck] a great reputation for the clarity of his ideas and expressions." Addington, *Blitzkrieg Era and the German General Staff*, 36, says, "*Troop Command* preserved the best facets of the old pre-1914 doctrine and drew sound lessons from the experiences of World War I, its reasoning foreshadowed a good understanding of the future role of armor." Martin van Creveld regarded the philosophy and tactics of Army Regulation 300 highly, devoting Chapters 4, 5, and 11 of *Fighting Power* to analysis of its leadership philosophy and tactics.

4. *Heeresdienstvorschrift* 300, *Truppenführung*, Part 1, para. 4.

5. *Heeresdienstvorschrift* 487, Part 1, para. 5.

6. Compare the introduction to *Heeresdienstvorschrift* 300, Part 1, 1–15, with *Heeresdienstvorschrift* 487, Part 1, 1–15.

7. *Heeresdienstvorschrift* 300, Part 2, para. 746.

8. Ibid., para. 749.

9. See Müller-Hillebrand, *Das Heer 1933–1945*, 17–22.

10. Van Creveld, *Fighting Power*, 152.

11. Ferdinand Otto Miksche, *Vom Kriegsbild* (Stuttgart: Seewald Verlag, 1976), 138–139.

12. See Miksche, *Vom Kriegsbild*, 138–139; and Müller-Hillebrand, *Das Heer 1933–1945*, 70–72.

13. Lewis, *Forgotten Legions*, 36.

14. Van Creveld, *Fighting Power*, 138–139.

15. Ibid., 121–124.

16. Quoted in Wallach, *Dogma of the Battle of Annihilation*, 233.

17. Groehler, *Geschichte des Luftkrieges*, 221 and 226–227.

18. Shelford Bidwell and Dominick Graham, *Fire Power: British Army Weapons and Theories of War, 1904–1945* (London: George Allen and Unwin, 1982), 224–226, 228–229, and 232–233.

19. Ibid., 233.
20. Alistair Horne, *To Lose a Battle: France, 1940* (New York: Penguin, 1969), 217.
21. Miksche, *Vom Kriegsbild*, 149.
22. Horne, *To Lose a Battle*, 218.
23. Ibid.
24. Ibid.
25. Ibid., 219–220.
26. A good general history of the British Army in this period is Brian Bond, *British Military Policy between the Two World Wars* (Oxford: Clarendon Press, 1980).
27. A good overview of British tactical thinkers of the interwar period is Robert Larsen, *The British Army and the Theory of Armored Warfare, 1918–1940* (Newark: University of Delaware Press, 1984).
28. Bernard Montgomery, *The Memoirs of Field Marshal Montgomery* (New York: Signet, 1958), 43.
29. Ibid., 49.
30. Ibid., 49.
31. Hamilton, *Monty*, 343.
32. Richard Griffiths, *Pétain: A Biography of Marshal Philippe Pétain of Vichy* (Garden City, N.Y.: Doubleday, 1972), 102.
33. Ibid.
34. Ibid., 130–131.
35. Alvin Coox, "General Narcisse Chauvineau: False Apostle of Prewar French Military Doctrine," *Military Affairs* 37 (1973): 16.
36. Aapad Kovacs, "French Military Legislation in the Third Republic, 1871–1940," *Military Affairs*, 13 (1949): 12.
37. Ibid., 12–13.
38. Griffiths, *Pétain*, 132.
39. Horne, *To Lose a Battle*, 136–141.
40. Dupuy, *Genius for War*, 253–255.

# SELECTED BIBLIOGRAPHY

## PRIMARY SOURCES

### U.S. NATIONAL ARCHIVES, WASHINGTON, D.C.

*German Army Records, File T-78 (microfilm)*

Roll 7,      General Staff, Study on development of General Staff After the First World War, 1939.

Roll 29,     General Staff, Study on Morale of German Troops, September–November 1918.

Roll 33,     Wehrkreis Stuttgart, Military Library Inventory, 1923.

Roll 123,    General Staff, Contains "Der Sturmangriff" by von Brandis, 1917.

Roll 152,    Weapons Office, Descriptions of Foreign Equipment.

Roll 153,    Weapons Office, Files on Weapons Tested and Under Development.

Roll 177,    Weapons Office, Files on Weapons Testing, 1932/1933.

Roll 178,    Weapons Office, Weapons Development and Supply, 1920s.

Roll 179,    Weapons Office, Russian-German Cooperation, 1930.

Roll 180,    Weapons Office/Wehrwirtschaft, Planning Papers on Economic Aspects of War, Late 1920s.

Roll 181,    Truppenamt, Strength Studies, 1926–1937.

Roll 201,    Air Office, General Staff, Study on Training and Leadership of Luftwaffe, 1934.

Roll 202,    Truppenamt T-4, Freikorps and Black Reichswehr Training, 1924.

Roll 203,    General Staff, World War I Documents on Training Storm Battalions.

Roll 278,    Chief of Truppenamt, Training Plans, 1926–1928.

Roll 280,    Truppenamt, Grenzschutz and Militia, 1927–1931.

Roll 285,    Von Seeckt Papers From 1926.

Roll 370,    General Staff, Lt. Col. Jodl, Tactical Lessons for General Staff Exams, 1920s.

Roll 392,    Truppenamt Mobilization Appendixes, 1928–1940.

Roll 429,    Allied Military Control Commission.

Roll 430,    Truppenamt T-1/T-2, Mobilization Plans for a Twenty-One Division Army, 1924–1925.

Roll 441,    Truppenamt T-1, Army Expansion, 1925.

*Von Seeckt Papers, File M-132 (microfilm)*

Roll 1,      Military Correspondence, 1915–1926, and Personal Correspondence, 1919–1926.

Roll 15,     Letters to Von Seeckt from Various Persons, 1919–1928.

Roll 18,     Letters to Von Seeckt from Senior Officers, 1915–1936.

Roll 19,     Letters to Von Seeckt from Senior Officers, 1915–1936.

Roll 20,   World War I Battle Reports; Memoranda to Versailles Committee.
Roll 21,   Correspondence Relating to Groener, Versailles, and Other Matters.
Roll 24,   1920 Study on "Germany and Russia," 1920.
Roll 25,   World War I Battle Maps and Memos on Military Matters, 1919–1926.


MILITÄRARCHIV DER DEUTSCHEN DEMOKRATISCHEN
REPUBLIK, POTSDAM

*Microfilm Files*

Roll NF 14/255,  Von Rabenau Papers; Von Seeckt on Ottoman Staff Chief.
Roll NF 15/533,  Reichswehr Minister, Letters and Reports, Late 1920s and early
                 1930s.


*Archival Files*

Doc. R 01 70/10,   Truppenamt T-3, Pamphlet on French Command and Tactics,
                   1927.
Doc. R 02 20/25,   Saxon War Ministry, Formation and Training of Volunteer
                   Units, 1919.
Doc. R 06 10/4,    Inspektionen der Waffenschulen, Late 1920s and Early 1930s.
Doc. R 11 41 10/3, Saxon War Ministry and Freiwilliger Grenzer Regt. 1, 1919–
                   1920.
Doc. R 11 41 12/1, Freiwilliger Grenzer BN 6, Defense Plans, 1919.
Doc. R 11 41 20/5, Freiwilliger Grenzer Regt. 2, Grenzschutz Units, 1919.
Doc. R 11 41 20/7, Freiwilliger Grenzer Regt. 2, Staff Files.
Doc. R 11 41 21/4, Intelligence Files on Czechs, 1919.
Doc. R 11 41 22/7, Ministerium für Militärwesen, Sachsen, Troop Training, 1919.
Doc. R 11 41 30/4, Freiwilliger Grenzer Regt. 3, Intelligence.
Doc. R 11 41 31/8, Saxon War Ministry, Training the Volkswehr, 1919; Files on
                   Freiwilliger Grenzer BN 3; Volkswehr Roster, July–October
                   1919.
Doc. W 10/50203,   Reichsarchiv Historical Study on Volkskrieg, 1930s.
Doc. W 10/52110,   German Intelligence Files, 1920s.
Doc. W 10/52127,   German Intelligence.
Doc. W 10/52136,   Maj. a.D. Karl Deuringer, "Die Niederwerfung der Räteherr-
                   schaft in Bayern, 1919," Monograph of the Kriegsgeschicht-
                   liche Forschungsamt, 1930s.
Doc. W 10/52139,   Reichsarchiv Historical Study, 1930s.
Doc. W 10/52141,   Gen. Groener's Report on Strategic Situation, 1919.
Doc. W 10/52143,   Reichsarchiv Historical Study, Ca. 1930.


BUNDESARCHIV/MILITÄRARCHIV, FREIBURG IM BREISGAU

*Archival Files*

Doc. N 5,    Nachlass Joachim Fritz Constantin von Stülpnagel.
Doc. N 33,   Nachlass Werner von Fritsch.
Doc. N 62,   Nachlass Friedrich von Rabenau.

Doc. N 107,              Nachlass Oswald Lutz.
Doc. N 107/1,            Nachlass Oswald Lutz.
Doc. N 107/3,            Nachlass Oswald Lutz: Notes on the Development of the Armor Force, 1925–1929.
Doc. N 154,              Nachlass Ludwig von der Leyen.
Doc. N 179,              Nachlass Erhard Milch.
Doc. PH 17/19,           Air Service, Tactical Manual for Ground Support, 1918.
Doc. PH 17/55,           Reichsarchiv, Historical Study on American Air Service, 1925.
Doc. PH 17/96,           Air Service Files, 1918.
Doc. PH 17/98,           Air Service, Training Plan for Aircraft in Ground Support, 1918.
Doc. RH 2/69,            Army Commander's Report, 1921.
Doc. RH 2/70,            Army Commander's Report, 1925.
Doc. RH 2/94,            Truppenamt Correspondence File.
Doc. RH 2/101,           Army Commander's Report, 1923.
Doc. RH 2/1547,          Truppenamt T-3, Report on French Maneuvers, 1923 and 1924.
Doc. RH 2/1603,          Truppenamt T-3, Report on British Army, 1925.
Doc. RH 2/1820,          Truppenamt T-3, Officers' Reports on Foreign Visits.
Doc. RH 2/1822,          Truppenamt T-3.
Doc. RH 2/1823,          Truppenamt T-3, Officers' Reports on Foreign Visits.
Doc. RH 2/2187,          Air Organization Office Correspondence File.
Doc. RH 2/2191,          Weapons Office File, 1920s.
Doc. RH 2/2195,          Reichsarchiv Historical Study on Air Tactics, 1918; Assorted Studies and Correspondence, 1926.
Doc. RH 2/2197,          Air Organization Office.
Doc. RH 2/2198,          Air Organization Office, Mobilization Information, Early 1920s.
Doc. RH 2/2200,          Weapons Office, Rearmament Programs.
Doc. RH 2/2206,          Weapons Office, Report on Foreign Equipment, 1925.
Doc. RH 2/2207,          Air Organization Office, Correspondence, 1919–1921.
Doc. RH 2/2273,          Air Organization Office.
Doc. RH 2/2275,          Air Organization Office, Tactical Studies.
Doc. RH 2/2277,          Commanders' Reports, Artillery Inspectorate, 1926.
Doc. RH 2/2279,          Air Organization Office, Study of Foreign Air Forces, 1926.
Doc. RH 2/2291,          Weapons Office, German Programs in Russia.
Doc. RH 2/2299,          Air Organization Office, Assorted Files and Studies, 1920s.
Doc. RH 2/2822,          Truppenamt T-4, War Games, 1926–1927.
Doc. RH 2/2901,          Air Office, Mobilization Information, 1920s; Tactical Studies.
Doc. RH 2/2963,          Army Commander's Report, 1920.
Doc. RH 2/2987,          Army Commander's Report, 1922.
Doc. RH 8/v 883,         Weapons Office, Inspection 6, Vehicle Development.
Doc. RH 8/v1745,         Weapons Office, "Die Tanks im Weltkrieg," 1920s.
Doc. RH 8/v2669,         Weapons Office, Data on Large Tractor, 1927.
Doc. RH 8/v2670,         Weapons Office, Correspondence with Krupp, 1925–1927.
Doc. RH 8/v2673,         Weapons Office, Data on Light Tractor, 1930.
Doc. RH 8/v2674,         Weapons Office, Correspondence with Krupp, 1931/1932.
Doc. RH 12-1/15,         Truppenamt T-4, Officer Training, 1920s.
Doc. RH 12-1/53,         Air Organization Office, Includes Tactical Studies, 1920s.
Doc. RH 12-2/21,         Army Commander, Correspondence, 1924–1925.

Doc. RH 12-2/22,    Army Commander, Correspondence with Weapons Office, 1919–1926.
Doc. RH 12-2/51,    Truppenamt T-3, Reports and Correspondence on Foreign Armies.
Doc. RH 12-2/54,    Heeresinspektionen and T-4 Files, Officer Training, 1920s.
Doc. RH 12-2/66,    Infantry Inspectorate, Reports, 1920s.
Doc. RH 12-2/94,    Army Commander Correspondence, Reports from Inspectorates, 1920–1927.
Doc. RH 12-2/95,    Truppenamt T-4, Wehrkreisprüfung, 1928; Winter Exercises 1928/1929.
Doc. RH 12-2/100,    Infantry Inspectorate, Reports, 1924–1935.
Doc. RH 12-2/101,    Reports from Branch Schools, Beginning in 1925.
Doc. RH 12-2/150,    Weapons Office, Reports on Weapons Tests, 1918–1924.

*Personnel Files*

Konstantin von Altrock
Wilhelm Brandt
Kurt Hesse
Ernst Jünger
Friedrich von Taysen
Ernst Volckheim

## MANUSCRIPTS

"Geschichte des I/J-R. 65." Ca. 1936-37. Crerar Collection, Royal Military College of Canada, Kingston, Ontario.
Holt Manufacturing Company. "The Caterpillar Track-Type Tractor in the World War." Ca. 1919. U.S. Army Museum, Aberdeen Proving Ground, Aberdeen, Maryland.
Smith, Truman. "The Papers of Truman Smith." U.S. Army War College Library, Carlisle Barracks, Pennsylvania.

## GERMAN OFFICIAL DOCUMENTS

Brandis, Cordt von. *Der Sturmangriff: Kriegserfahrungen eines Frontoffiziers.* Berlin: Chef des Generalstabes, September 15, 1917.
Chef des Generalstabes des Feldheeres. *Nahkampfmittel.* Vol. 3. Berlin: Reichsdruckerei, 1917.
Heeresdienstvorschrift 487. *Führung und Gefecht der verbundenen Waffen.* Berlin: Verlag Offene Worte, 1921, 1923, 1925.
*F.H. Felddienst: Handbuch für Unterführer aller Waffen.* Berlin: Verlag Offene Worte, 1924.
Französische Truppenführung. *Vorschrift für die taktische Verwendung der grossen Verbände.* Berlin: Verlag Offene Worte, 1937.
German Army. "Studie eines Offiziers über die Fliegerwaffe und ihre Verwendung." Ca. 1925.
*Heeresdienstvorschrift* 300. *Truppenführung.* Part 1 (1933); Part 2 (1934).

*Heeresdienstvorschrift* 467. *Ausbildungsvorschrift für Fahrtruppen*. Berlin: High Command, 1923.

*Heeresdienstvorschrift* 472. *Ausbildungsvorschrift für die Kraftfahrtruppe*. 1924.

Imperial Army. *Anhaltspunkte für den Unterricht bei der Truppe über Luftfahrzeuge und deren Bekämpfung*. Berlin: Reichsdruckerei, March 1913.

*Kampfwagen und Heeresmotorisierung 1924/1925*. Berlin: R. Eisenschmidt Verlag, 1926.

Kommandierender General der Luftstreitkräfte. *Weisungen für den Einsatz und die Verwendung von Fliegerverbänden innerhalb einer Armee*. N.p.: Generalstab des Feldheeres, May 1917.

Königlich- Preussisches Kriegsministerium. *Verordnung über die Ausbildung der Truppen für den Felddienst und über die grösseren Truppenübungen*. Berlin: Königliche Hofdruckerei, June 1870.

Ludendorff, Field Marshal Erich von. *Urkunden der Obersten Heeresleitung über ihre Tätigkeit, 1916/18*. Berlin: E. Mittler und Sohn, 1920.

*Luftwaffedienstvorschrift* 10. *Die Aufgaben des Kampffliegers*. 1934-35.

*Militärische Aufgaben-Sammlung*. Berlin: Verlag Offene Worte, 1922–1924.

Oberste Heeresleitung. *Kompagnie-Ausbildungsplan während einer Ruhezeit bis zu 14 Tagen*. 2d ed. Berlin: Reichsdruckerei, 1918.

Reichstag Committee Untersuchungsausschusses des Deutschen Reichstages, 1919–1928. *Die Ursachen des Deutschen Zusammenbruches im Jahre 1918*, Vols. 3 and 6. Berlin: Deutsche Verlagsgesellschaft für Politik und Geschichte, 1928.

Reichswehrministerium Heeresleitung. *Stärkenachweisung der Kommandobehörden und Truppen des Reichsheeres*. Berlin: Reichswehrministerium, 1928.

Reichswehrministerium Heeres-Personal-Amt. *Rangliste des Deutschen Reichsheeres*. Berlin: E. Mittler und Sohn, 1924–1928.

Taktische Aufgaben im Rahmen des verstärkten Inf-Regiments. Berlin: Verlag Offene Worte, 1923.

*Die Wehrkreis-Prüfung 1932, 11 Jahrgang*. Berlin: Verlag Offene Worte, 1932.

## SECONDARY SOURCES

### BOOKS AND ARTICLES PUBLISHED BEFORE WORLD WAR II

Adam, Generalmajor Wilhelm. "Die Fahrtruppe." In *Die Deutsche Wehrmacht*, ed. Gen. Georg Wetzell, 413–442. Berlin: E. Mittler und Sohn, 1939.

Balck, Lt. Gen. a.D. W. von. *Entwicklung der Taktik im Weltkriege*. Berlin: Verlag R. Eisenschmidt, 1922.

Bauer, Col. Max. *Der Grosse Krieg in Feld und Heimat*. Tübingen: Osiander Verlag, 1921.

Baur, Lt. Col. Hugo. "Eisenbahntruppen." In *Die Deutsche Wehrmacht*, ed. Gen. Georg Wetzell, 443–462. Berlin: E. Mittler und Sohn, 1939.

Bernhardi, Freiherr von. *Vom Kriege der Zukunft. Nach den Erfahrungen des Weltkrieges*. Berlin: E. Mittler und Sohn, 1920.

Bischoff, Maj. Josef. *Die Letzte Front: Geschichte der Eisernen Division im Baltikum, 1919*. Berlin: Schützen Verlag, 1935.

Boelcke, Lt. Col. S. "Die Süddeutschen Reichsheermanöver, 1926." In *Schweizerische Monatschrift für Offiziere aller Waffen* 38, 11 (Nov. 1926): 360–367.

British Army General Staff. *Handbook of the German Army, 1928.* Ed. E. T. Humphreys. London: War Office, 1928.

————. *Infantry Training.* Vol. 2. London: His Majesty's Stationery Office, 1926.

Challener, Richard D., ed. *United States Military Intelligence.* Vols. 23–26. New York: Garland, 1978.

De Gaulle, Charles. *The Army of the Future.* London: Hutchinson, 1940.

Deutsches Reichsarchiv. *Der Weltkrieg, 1914 bis 1918.* 14 vols. Berlin: E. Mittler und Sohn, 1925–1940.

Douhet, Giulio. *The Command of the Air.* New York: Arno Press, 1972; reprint of 1927 rev. edition.

Eimannsberger, Ludwig Ritter von. *Der Kampfwagenkrieg.* Munich: J. F. Lehmanns Verlag, 1934.

Falkenhayn, Gen. Erich von. *General Headquarters 1914–1916 and Its Critical Decisions.* London: Hutchinson, 1919.

Franke, Maj. Gen. Hermann. *Handbuch der neuzeitlichen Wehrwissenschaften.* Vol. 2: *Die Luftwaffe.* Berlin: Verlag von Walter de Gruyter, 1939.

Fuller, J. F. C. *On Future Warfare.* London: Sifton Press, 1928.

————. *The Reformation of War.* New York: Dutton, 1923.

————. *Tanks in the Great War.* London: John Murray, 1920.

————. *Tanks in the Great War, 1914–1918.* New York: Dutton, 1920.

Grey, C. G. *Jane's All the World's Aircraft: 1919.* London: David and Charles, 1969; reprint of 1919 edition.

Groener, Col. Gen. Wilhelm. *Der Feldherr wider Willen.* Berlin: E. Mittler und Sohn, 1931.

————. *Das Testament des Grafen Schlieffens.* Berlin: E. Mittler und Sohn, 1927.

Guderian, Heinz. *Achtung! Panzer!* Stuttgart: Union Deutsche Verlagsgesellschaft, 1937.

Heigl, Fritz. *Die schweren französischen Tanks. Die italienischen Tanks.* Berlin: Verlag R. Eisenschmidt, 1925.

————. *Taschenbuch der Tanks.* Munich: J. F. Lehmanns Verlag, 1926.

————. *Taschenbuch der Tanks.* Vol 3: *Der Panzerkampf.* Ed. Panzerreg. Cpt. G. P. von Zezschwitz. Munich: J. F. Lehmanns Verlag, 1938.

Hesse, Kurt. *Der Feldherr Psychologos: Ein suchen nach dem Führer der deutschen Zukunft.* Berlin: E. Mittler und Sohn, 1922.

————. *Von der nahen Ära der "Jungen Armee."* Berlin: E. Mittler und Sohn, 1925.

Hoeppner, Gen. der Kavallerie Ernst. *Deutschlands Krieg in der Luft. Ein Rückblick auf die Entwicklung und die Leistungen unserer Heeres-Luftstreitkräfte im Weltkriege.* Leipzig: Koehler und Amelang Verlag, 1921.

Jünger, Ernst. *Copse 125.* London: Chatto and Windus, 1930.

————. *The Storm of Steel.* London: Chatto and Windus, 1929.

Kabisch, Lt. Gen. Ernst. *Gegen englische Panzerdrachen.* Stuttgart: Loewes Verlag, 1938.

*Die Kampfwagen fremder Heere.* Vol 2: *Technische Mitteilungen über Kampfwagen und Strassenpanzerwagen.* Berlin: Verlag von R. Eisenschmidt, 1926.

Kruger, Engineer R. "Tanks in the World War." Trans. Capt. William Lucas, Jr., *Infantry Journal* 22 (October 1923): 402–411.

Kutz, Capt. C. R. *War on Wheels.* London: John Lane, 1941.

Leeb, Gen. der Artillerie Wilhelm Ritter von. "Die Abwehr." *Militärwissenschaftliche Rundschau* 2 (1937): 13–144, 154–188, 278–363.

————. *Die Abwehr.* Berlin: E. Mittler und Sohn, 1938.

Leyen, Capt. Ludwig von der. *Taktische Aufgaben und Lösungen im Rahmen des verstärkten Infanterie Regiments*. 2d ed. Berlin: Verlag Offene Worte, 1925.
————. *Vom Zusammenwirken der Waffen*. Berlin: Verlag Offene Worte, 1925.
Liddell Hart, Basil H. *The British Way in Warfare*. New York: Macmillan, 1933.
————. "The Development of the 'New Model Army.'" *Army Quarterly* 9 (1924): 37–50.
————. *Europe in Arms*. New York: Random House, 1937.
————. "The 'Man in the Dark' Theory of Infantry Tactics and the 'Expanding Torrent' System of Attack." *RUSI Journal* 66 (1921): 1–22.
————. *The Real War, 1914–1918*. Boston: Little, Brown, 1930.
————. *The Remaking of Modern Armies*. Boston: Little, Brown, 1928.
————. "A Science of Infantry Tactics," *Royal Engineers Journal* 33 (1921): 169–182, 215–233.
————. "Suggestions on the Future Development of the Combat Unit—The Tank as a Weapon of Infantry." *RUSI Journal* 64 (1919): 660–666.
————. "The Ten Commandments of the Combat Unit—Suggestions on Its Theory and Training." *RUSI Journal* 64 (1919): 288–293.
Ludendorff, Gen. Erich von. *The Coming War*. London: Faber and Faber, 1931.
————. *Ludendorff's Own Story*. Vols. 1 and 2. New York: Harper and Brothers, 1919.
————. *The Nation at War [Der Totale Krieg]*. London: Hutchinson, 1936.
————. *Der Totale Krieg*. Munich: Ludendorffs Verlag, 1935.
Martel, Lt. Col. G. *In the Wake of the Tank*. London: Sifton Praed, 1931.
Mehler, Colonel. *Der Soldat der Zukunft*. Berlin: Verlag Offene Worte, 1931.
Melville, Cecil. *The Russian Face of Germany*. London: Wishart, 1932.
Mertens, Carl. *Reichswehr und Landesverteidigung*. Wiesbaden: n.p., 1927.
Meyer, Erich, ed. *Deutsche Kraftfahrzeug-Typenschau: Luftfahrzeuge und Luftfahrzeugmotoren 1926*. Dresden: Verlag Deutsche Motor, 1926.
Miksche, Ferdinand Otto. *Attack: A Study of Blitzkrieg Tactics*. New York: Random House, 1942.
Mitchell, William. *Memoirs of World War I*. New York: Random House, 1960; originally published in *Liberty Magazine* in 1926.
Neumann, Georg. *Die Deutschen Luftstreitkräfte im Weltkriege*. Berlin: E. Mittler Verlag, 1921.
Poseck, Mar von. "Die Kavallerie." In *Die Deutsche Wehrmacht*, ed. Gen. Georg Wetzell, 250–292. Berlin: E. Mittler und Sohn, 1939.
Rabenau, Friedrich von. *Die alte Armee und die junge Generation*. Berlin: E. Mittler und Sohn, 1925.
————. *Operative Entschlüsse gegen eine Anzahl überlegener Gegner*. Berlin: E. Mittler und Sohn, 1935.
————. *Seeckt: Aus seinem Leben, 1918–1936*. Leipzig: Hase-Koehler Verlag, 1941.
Reinhardt, Inf. Gen. Walther. *Wehrkraft und Wehrwille*. Ed. Lt. Gen. Ernst Reinhardt. Berlin: E. Mittler und Sohn, 1932.
Ritter, Capt. Hans. *Der Luftkrieg*. Berlin: F. Koehler Verlag, 1926.
————. *Der Zukunftskrieg und seine Waffen*. Leipzig: F. Koehler Verlag, 1924.
Roeingh, Rolf. *Wegbereiter der Luftfahrt*. Berlin: Deutscher Archiv-Verlag, 1938.
Rommel, Erwin. *Attacks! [Infanterie Greift An!]*. Trans. J. R. Driscoll. Vienna, Va.: Athena Press,1979; reprint of 1936 edition.
Schleicher, K. von. "Der deutsche Wehrgedanke." *Illustrierte Zeitung* 27, 7 (1932).
Schlieffen, Alfred von. *Cannae*. Berlin: E. Mittler und Sohn, 1936.

Schmitt. *Strassenpanzerwagen: Die Sonderwagen der Schutzpolizei*. Berlin: Verlag R. Eisenschmidt, 1925.

Schrott, Col. Ludwig. *Die Vorbereitung auf die Wehrkreisprüfung*. Berlin: E. Mittler und Sohn, 1929.

Schwab, Otto. *Ingenieur und Soldat*. Berlin: E. Mittler und Sohn, 192[?].

Schwarte, Max. *Kriegslehren im Beispiel aus dem Weltkrieg*. Berlin: Verlag Offene Worte, 1925.

———. *Die militärischen Lehren des grossen Krieges*. Berlin: Verlag Offene Worte, 1920.

———. *Die Technik im Weltkriege*. Berlin: Verlag Offene Worte, 1920.

———. *Die Technik im Zukunftskriege*. Berlin: Verlag Offene Worte, 1923.

Schwarte, Max, ed. *Der grosse Krieg, 1914–1918*. Vols. 1–10. Berlin: E. Mittler & Sohn, 1922–1923.

Seeckt, Hans von. "The Army of the Future." *Living Age* (November 1929): 288–294.

———. *Aus meinem Leben, 1866–1917*. Ed. Lt. Gen. Friedrich von Rabenau. Leipzig: Hase-Koehler Verlag, 1938.

———. *The Future of the German Empire*. Trans. Oakley Williams. London: Thornton Butterworth, 1930.

———. *Gedanken eines Soldaten*. Berlin: Verlag für Kulturpolitik, 1928.

———. *Moltke: Ein Vorbild*. Berlin: Verlag für Kulturpolitik, 1930.

———. "Neuzeitliche Kavallerie." *Militär Wochenblatt* 6 (1927).

———. *Die Reichswehr*. Leipzig: R. Kittler Verlag, 1933.

———. *Thoughts of a Soldier*. Trans. Gilbert Waterhouse. London: Ernest Benn, 1930.

———. "Die Willenskraft des Feldherrn." *Militär Wochenblatt* 1 (1936).

Siebert, Major. *Atlas zu F.u.G.I.: Ein Anschauungs-Lehrbuch*. Berlin: Verlag Offene Worte, 1929.

Soldan, Georg. *Der Mensch und die Schlacht der Zukunft*. Oldenburg: Gerhard Stalling, 1925.

Supf, Peter. *Das Buch der deutschen Fluggeschichte*. Vol. 2. Berlin: Verlagsanstalt Hermann Klemm, 1935.

Thomsen, Lt. Gen. Hermann. "Die Luftwaffe vor und im Weltkriege." In *Die Deutsche Wehrmacht*, ed. Gen. Georg Wetzell, 487–522. Berlin: E. Mittler und Sohn, 1939.

Tschischwitz, General von. *Manöver und grössere Truppenübungen*. Berlin: Verlag R. Eisenschmidt, 1930.

U.S. Army Cavalry School. *Cavalry Combat*. Harrisburg, Penn.: U.S. Cavalry Association, 1937.

Volckheim, Ernst. *Deutsche Kampfwagen Greifen An!: Erlebnisse eines Kampfwagenführers an der Westfront 1918*. Berlin: E. Mittler und Sohn, 1937.

———. *Die deutschen Kampfwagen im Weltkriege*. Berlin: E. Mittler und Sohn, 1923.

———. "Die deutsche Panzerwaffe." In *Die Deutsche Wehrmacht*, ed. Gen. Georg Wetzell, 293–338. Berlin: E. Mittler und Sohn, 1939.

———. *Der Kampfwagen in der heutigen Kriegführung*. Berlin: E. Mittler und Sohn, 1924.

———. *Kampfwagen und Abwehr dagegen*. Berlin: E. Mittler und Sohn, 1925.

———. "Uber die Waffen des Zukunftskrieges." *Militär Wochenblatt* 39 (1926).

Wachenfeld, Gen. der Flieger Edmund. "Die Luftwaffe nach dem Weltkriege." In *Die Deutsche Wehrmacht*, ed. Gen. Georg Wetzell, 528–557. Berlin: E. Mittler und Sohn, 1939.

Warner, Edward. "Douhet, Mitchell, Seversky: Theories of Air Warfare." In *Makers of Modern Strategy*, ed. Edward Earle, 485–503. Princeton, N.J.: Princeton University Press, 1943.


BOOKS AND ARTICLES PUBLISHED AFTER WORLD WAR II

Absolom, Rudolf, ed. *Die Wehrmacht im Dritten Reich*. Vol. 1. Boppard: Harald Boldt Verlag, 1969.
Addington, Larry. *The Blitzkrieg Era and the German General Staff, 1865–1941*. New Brunswick, N.J.: Rutgers University Press, 1971.
Alfoldi, Laslo. "The Hutier Legend." *Parameters* 5, 2 (1976).
Andronikow, I. G., and W. G. Mostowenko, *Die roten Panzer: Geschichte der sowjetischen Panzertruppen, 1920–1960*. Ed. and trans. F. M. von Senger und Etterlin. Munich: J. F. Lehmanns Verlag, 1963.
Atkinson, James. "Liddell Hart and Warfare of the Future." *Military Affairs* 30 (1966): 161–163.
Balck, Hermann. *Ordnung im Chaos: Erinnerungen, 1893–1948*. Osnabrück: Biblio Verlag, 1980.
Barnett, Corelli. *The Swordbearers*. London: Eyre and Spottiswoode, 1963.
Barnett, Corelli, ed. *Hitler's Generals*. New York: Grove Weidenfeld, 1989.
Baumbach, Werner. *The Life and Death of the Luftwaffe*. New York: Ballantine, 1967.
Beaver, Daniel. "Politics and Policy: The War Department Motorization and Standardization Program for Wheeled Transport Vehicles, 1920–1940." *Military Affairs* 47 (1983): 101–108.
Behrens, W., and Dietrich Kuehn, eds. *Geschichte des Reiter-Regiments* I, Vol. 1: *1919–1939*. Cologne/Weidenpach: Kameradschaft ehem. RR1,1962.
Bennett, Edward. *German Rearmament and the West, 1932–1933*. Princeton, N.J.: Princeton University Press, 1979.
Benoist-Mechin, T. *Auf dem Weg zur Macht, 1925–1937*. Oldenburg: G. Stalling Verlag, 1965.
Bidwell, Shelford, and Dominick Graham. *Fire Power: British Army Weapons and Theories of War, 1904–1945*. London: George Allen and Unwin, 1982.
Birkenfeld, W. *Geschichte der deutschen Wehr- und Rüstungswirtschaft, 1918–1945*. Boppard am Rhein: Harald Boldt Verlag, 1966.
Blumentritt, Gen. Guenther. *Von Rundstedt: The Soldier and the Man*. London: Odhams Press, 1952.
Bond, Brian. *British Military Policy between the Two World Wars*. Oxford: Clarendon Press, 1980.
———. *Liddell Hart: A Study of His Military Thought*. London: Cassell, 1977.
Bond, Brian, and Williamson Murray. "The British Armed Forces, 1918–1939." In *Military Effectiveness*, vol. 2, ed. Allan Millett and Williamson Murray, 98–131. Boston: Allen and Unwin, 1988.
Bradley, Gen. Omar, and Clay Blair. *A General's Life*. New York: Simon and Schuster, 1983.
Brownlow, Donald. *Panzer Baron: The Military Exploits of General Hasso von Manteuffel*. North Quincy, Mass.: Christopher Publishing House, 1975.
Burdick, Charles. "Die deutschen militärischen Planungen gegenüber Frankreich, 1933–1938." *Wehrwissenschaftliche Rundschau* 6, 12 (1956): 678–681.

Carr, Edward. *German-Soviet Relations between the Two World Wars, 1919–1939*. Baltimore: Johns Hopkins University Press, 1951.

Carsten, F. L. *The Reichswehr and Politics, 1918–1933*. Oxford: Clarendon Press, 1966.

———. "The Reichswehr and the Red Army, 1920–1933." *Journal of the Royal Service Institutions* 3 (1963): 248–255.

Carver, Field Marshal Lord Michael. *The Apostles of Mobility*. London: Weidenfeld and Nicolson, 1979.

———. "False Dawn: Tanks at Cambrai." In *Tanks and Weapons of World War I*, ed. Bernard Fitzsimons, 129–131. London: Phoebus, 1973.

Chamberlain, Peter, and Chris Ellis. *Pictorial History of Tanks of the World, 1915–1945*. New York: Galahad, 1972.

———. *Tanks of World War I: British and German*. London: Arms and Armour Press, 1969.

Chandler, David. "Cambrai: The German Counterattack." In *Tanks and Weapons of World War I*, ed. Bernard Fitzsimons, 122–128. London: Phoebus, 1973.

Chaney, Otto. *Zhukov*. Norman: University of Oklahoma Press, 1971.

Choltitz, Dietrich von. *Soldat unter Soldaten*. Zurich: Europa Verlag, 1951.

Citino, Robert. *The Evolution of Blitzkrieg Tactics: Germany Defends Itself against Poland, 1918–1933*. Westport, Conn.: Greenwood Press, 1987.

Cook, Don. *Charles de Gaulle: A Biography*. New York: G.P. Putnam's Sons, 1983.

Cooper, Mathew. *The German Air Force, 1922–1945: An Anatomy of Failure*. London: Jane's, 1981.

———. *The German Army, 1933–1945*. London: MacDonald and James, 1978.

Coox, Alvin. "General Narcisse Chauvineau: False Apostle of Prewar French Military Doctrine." *Military Affairs* 37 (1973): 15–19.

———. "Military Effectiveness of Armed Forces in the Interwar Period, 1919–1941: A Review." In *Military Effectiveness*, vol. 2, ed. Allan Millett and Williamson Murray, 256–270. Boston: Allen and Unwin, 1988.

Craig, Gordon. *The Politics of the Prussian Army, 1640–1945*. Oxford: Clarendon Press, 1955.

Creveld, Martin van. *Command in War*. Cambridge, Mass.: Harvard University Press, 1985.

———. *Fighting Power*. Westport, Conn.: Greenwood Press, 1982.

———. *The Training of Officers*. New York: Free Press, 1990.

Cross, Robin. *The Bombers*. New York: Macmillan, 1987.

De Gaulle, Charles. *Lettres, notes et cornets, vol. II: 1919–juin 1940*. Paris: Plon, 1980.

Deichmann, P. *German Air Force Operations in Support of the Army*. USAF Historical Study 163. Maxwell Air Force Base, Ala.: Air University Press, 1962.

Deighton, Len. *Blitzkrieg*. London: Triad/Grafton, 1981.

Deist, Wilhelm. *The Wehrmacht and German Rearmament*. London: Macmillan, 1981.

Demeter, Karl. *Das Deutsche Offizierkorps in Gesellschaft und Staat, 1650–1945*. Frankfurt am Main: Bernard und Graefe Verlag, 1962.

Dinardo, R. L., and Austin Bay. "The First Modern Tank: Gunther Burstyn and His Motorgeschütz." *Military Affairs* 50 (1986): 12–15.

Divine, David. *The Broken Wing: A Study in the British Exercise of Air Power*. London: Hutchinson, 1966.

Dorst, Klaus, and Wolfgang Wünsche. *Der Erste Weltkrieg*. Berlin: Militärverlag der Deutschen Demokratischen Republik, 1989.

Doughty, Robert. "The French Armed Forces, 1918–1940." In *Military Effectiveness*, vol. 2, ed. Allan Millett and Williamson Murray, 39–69. Boston: Allen and Unwin, 1988.

Dupuy, Trevor N. *The Evolution of Weapons and Warfare*. New York: Da Capo Press, 1984.

————. *A Genius for War: The German Army and General Staff, 1807–1945*. Englewood Cliffs, N.J.: Prentice-Hall, 1977.

Dyck, Harvey. *Weimar Germany and Soviet Russia, 1926–1933: A Study in Diplomatic Instability*. London/Toronto: Chatto and Windus, 1966.

English, John A. *On Infantry*. New York: Praeger, 1981.

Erfurth, Waldemar. *Die Geschichte des deutschen Generalstabes von 1918 bis 1945*. 2d ed. Göttingen: Masterschmidt Verlag, 1960.

Erickson, John. *The Soviet High Command: A Military-Political History, 1918–1941*. Boulder, Colo.: Westview Press, 1984.

Eudin, Zenia, and Harold Fisher. *Soviet Russia and the West, 1920–1927*. Stanford, Calif.: Stanford University Press, 1957.

Faber du Faur, Gen. M. *Macht und Ohnmacht*. Hamburg: H. E. Günther Verlag, 1953.

Förster, Gerhard. *Totaler Krieg und Blitzkrieg*. Militärhistorische Studien 10. Berlin: Deutscher Militärverlag, 1967.

Franks, Norman. *Aircraft versus Aircraft*. New York: Crescent, 1986.

Fredette, Raymond. *The Sky on Fire: The First Battle of Britain, 1917–1918, and the Birth of the Royal Air Force*. New York: Holt, Rinehart, and Winston, 1966.

Gaertner, Franz von. *Die Reichswehr in der Weimarer Republik: Erlebte Geschichte*. Darmstadt: Fundus Verlag, 1969.

Gatzke, Hans W. "Russo-German Military Collaboration during the Weimar Republic." *American Historical Review* 63 (1958): 565–597.

————. *Stresemann and the Rearmament of Germany*. Baltimore: Johns Hopkins University Press, 1954.

Geyer, Michael. *Aufrüstung oder Sicherheit—Die Reichswehr in der Krise der Machtpolitik, 1924–1936*. Wiesbaden: Franz Steiner Verlag, 1980.

————. "German Strategy in the Age of Machine Warfare, 1914–1945." In *Makers of Modern Strategy*, ed. P. Paret, 527–597. Princeton, N.J.: Princeton University Press, 1986.

————. "Der zur Organisation erhobene Burgfrieden." In *Militär und Militarismus in der Weimarer Republik*, ed. Klaus-Jürgen Müller and Eckardt Opitz, 15–100. Düsseldorf: Droste Verlag, 1978.

————. "Die Wehrmacht der Deutschen Republik ist die Reichswehr. Bemerkungen zur neueren Literatur." *Militärgeschichtliche Mitteilungen* 14 (1973): 152–199.

Gibson, Irving M. "Maginot and Liddell Hart: The Doctrine of Defense." In *Makers of Modern Strategy*, ed. Edward Earle, 365–387. Princeton, N.J.: Princeton University Press, 1941.

Gilbert, Martin. *The Atlas of the First World War*. London: Dorset Press, 1970.

Gordon, Harold. "The Character of Hans von Seeckt." *Military Affairs* 20 (1956): 94–101.

————. *The Reichswehr and the German Republic, 1919–1926*. Port Washington, N.Y.: Kennikat Press, 1957.

Görlitz, Walter. *Model: Strategie der Defensive*. Wiesbaden: Limes Verlag, 1975.

Görlitz, Walter, ed. *The Memoirs of Field Marshal Keitel*. Trans. David Irving. New York: Stein and Day, 1966.

Greenhous, Brereton. "Evolution of a Close Ground-Support Role for Aircraft in World War I." *Military Affairs* 39 (1975): 22–28.

Greer, Thomas. "Air Arm Doctrinal Roots, 1917–1918." *Military Affairs* 20 (1956): 202–216.

———. *The Development of Air Doctrine in the Army Air Arm, 1917–1941.* USAF Historical Study 89. Maxwell Air Force Base, Ala.: Air University Press, 1955.

Griffith, Robert. "Quality, Not Quantity: The Volunteer Army during the Depression." *Military Affairs* 43 (1979): 171–177.

Griffiths, Richard. *Pétain: A Biography of Marshal Philippe Pétain of Vichy.* Garden City, N.Y.: Doubleday, 1972.

Groehler, Olaf. *Geschichte des Luftkrieges 1910 bis 1980.* Berlin: Militärverlag der Deutschen Demokratischen Republik, 1981.

Groener, Col. Gen. Wilhelm. *Lebenserinnerungen: Jugend, Generalstab, Weltkrieg.* Göttingen: Vandenhoeck und Ruprecht, 1957.

Groener-Geyer, Dorothea. *General Groener: Soldat und Staatsmann.* Frankfurt am Main: Societäts Verlag, 1954.

Guderian, Heinz. *Erinnerungen eines Soldaten.* Heidelberg: K. Vowinckel Verlag, 1950.

———. *Panzer Leader [Erinnerungen eines Soldaten].* Ed. Basil H. Liddell Hart. New York: Ballantine, 1957.

Gudmundson, Bruce. *Stormtroop Tactics: Innovation in the German Army, 1914–1918.* New York: Praeger, 1989.

Guske, Claus. *Das Politische Denken des Generals von Seeckt.* Historische Studien 122. Lübeck/Hamburg: Matthiesen Verlag, 1971.

Haeussler, Helmut. *General Wilhelm Groener and the Imperial German Army.* Madison: University of Wisconsin Press, 1962.

Hallade, Jean. "Big Bertha Bombards Paris." In *Tanks and Weapons of World War I*, ed. Bernard Fitzsimons, 141–147. London: Phoebus, 1973.

Hallgarten, George F. W. "General Hans von Seeckt and Russia, 1920–1922." *Journal of Modern History* 21 (1949): 28–34.

Hallion, Richard. *Rise of the Fighter Aircraft, 1914–1918.* Annapolis, Md.: Nautical and Aviation Publishing Company of America, 1984.

Hamilton, Nigel. *Monty: The Making of a General, 1887–1942.* London: Hamish Hamilton, 1981.

Hansen, Ernst W. *Reichswehr und Industrie, Rüstungswirtschaftliche Zusammenarbeit und wirtschaftliche Mobilmachungsvorbereitungen, 1923–1932.* Militärgeschichtliche Studien 24. Boppard am Rhein: Harald Boldt Verlag, 1978.

Harper, Lt. Gen. G. M. *Notes on Infantry Tactics and Training.* London: Sifton, Praed, 1921; reprint of a 1918 pamphlet.

Hegener, Henri. *Fokker—The Man and the Aircraft.* Letchworth, Eng.: Harleyford, 1961.

Heinkel, Ernst. *Stürmisches Leben.* Stuttgart: Mundus Verlag, 1953.

Hermann, Hans Carl. *Deutsche Militärgeschichte: Eine Einführung.* Frankfurt am Main: Bernard und Graefe Verlag, 1968.

Herwig, Holger. "The Dynamics of Necessity: German Military Policy during the First World War," in *Military Effectiveness*, vol. 1, ed. Allan Millett and Williamson Murray, 80–115. Boston: Allen and Unwin, 1988.

Hicks, James. *German Weapons—Uniforms—Insignia: 1841–1918.* La Canada, Calif.: Hicks and Son, 1958.

Higham, Robin. *Armed Forces in Peacetime. Britain, 1918–1940: A Case Study*. Hamden, Conn.: Archon Books, 1962.

———. "The Dangerously Neglected—The British Military Intellectuals, 1918–1939." *Military Affairs* 30 (1966): 73–87.

Hilger, Gustav, and Alfred Meyer. *The Incompatible Allies*. New York: Macmillan, 1953.

Hofmann, George. "The Demise of the U.S. Tank Corps and Medium Tank Development Program." *Military Affairs* 37 (1973): 20–25.

Hofmann, Hans Hubert, ed. *Das deutsche Offizierkorps, 1866–1960*. Boppard am Rhein: Harald Boldt Verlag, 1980.

Hogg, Ian. *Armour in Conflict: The Design and Tactics of Armoured Fighting Vehicles*. New York: Jane's, 1980.

———. "Bolimov and the First Gas Attack." In *Tanks and Weapons of World War I*, ed. Bernard Fitzsimons, 17–21. London: Phoebus, 1973.

———. *German Artillery of World War II*. New York: Hippocrene, 1975.

Hogg, Ian, and John Weeks. *Military Small Arms of the Twentieth Century*. Northfield, Ill.: Digest, 1973.

Homze, Edward L. *Arming the Luftwaffe: The Reich Air Ministry and the German Aircraft Industry, 1919–39*. Lincoln: University of Nebraska Press, 1976.

———. "The Continental Experience." In *Air Power and Warfare*, ed. Alfred Hurley and Robert Ehrhart, 36–49. Washington, DC: Office of USAF History, 1979.

Horne, Alistair. *To Lose a Battle: France, 1940*. New York: Penguin, 1969.

Howard, Michael. *The Causes of Wars*. 2d ed. Cambridge, Mass.: Harvard University Press, 1983.

Hürten, Heinz. "Das Wehrkreiskommando VI in den Wirren des Frühjahres 1920." *Militärgeschichtliche Mitteilungen* 15 (1974): 127–156.

Irving, D. J. C. *The Rise and Fall of the Luftwaffe: The Life of Luftwaffe Marshal Erhard Milch*. London: Weidenfeld and Nicolson, 1973.

Kahn, David. *Hitler's Spies: German Military Intelligence in World War II*. New York: Collier, 1978.

Kaulbach, Eberhard. "Generaloberst Hans von Seeckt—Zur Persönlichkeit und zur Leistung." *Wehrwissenschaftliche Rundschau* 16, 11 (1966): 666–681.

Keitel, Wilhelm. *The Memoirs of Field Marshal Keitel*. Ed. Walter Görlitz. London: William Kimber, 1965.

Kemp, Anthony. *The Maginot Line*. New York: Military Heritage Press, 1988.

Kennedy, Paul. "Britain in the First World War." In *Military Effectiveness*, vol. 1, ed. Allan Millett and Williamson Murray, 31–79. Boston: Allen and Unwin, 1988.

———. "Military Effectiveness in the First World War." In *Military Effectiveness*, vol. 1, ed. Allan Millett and Williamson Murray, 329–350. Boston: Allen and Unwin, 1988.

Kennett, Lee. *The First Air War, 1914–1918*. New York: Free Press, 1991.

Kesselring, Albrecht. *The Memoirs of Field Marshal Kesselring*. Novato, Calif.: Presidio Press, 1989.

Killen, John. *The Luftwaffe: A History*. London: Muller, 1967.

Kitchen, Martin. "The Traditions of German Strategic Thought." *International History Review* 1, 2 (April 1979): 163–190.

Knox, Alfred. *With the Russian Army, 1914–1917*. New York: Arno Press, 1971.

Kochan, Lionel. *Russia and the Weimar Republic*. Cambridge: Bowes and Bowes, 1954.

Kosar, Franz. *Infanteriegeschütze und rückstossfreie Leichtgeschütze, 1915–1978*. Stuttgart: Motorbuch Verlag, 1979.

————. *Panzerabwehrkanonen, 1916–1977*. Stuttgart: Motorbuch Verlag, 1980.

Köstring, Gen. Ernst. *Der militärische Mittler zwischen dem Deutschen Reich und der Sowjetunion 1921–1941*. Ed. Hermann Teske. Frankfurt am Main: E. S. Mittler Verlag, 1966.

Kovacs, Aapad. "French Military Legislation in the Third Republic, 1871–1940." *Military Affairs* 13 (1949): 1–13.

Kranz, Bernhard. *Geschichte der Hirschberger Jäger 1920 bis 1945*. Düsseldorf: Diedrichs, 1975.

Kuropka, Joachim. "Die britische Luftkriegskonzeption gegen Deutschland im Ersten Weltkrieg." *Militärgeschichtliche Mitteilungen* 27 (1980): 7–25.

Lacouture, Jean. *De Gaulle*. New York: New American Library, 1966.

————. *De Gaulle: le rebelle*. Vol. 1. Paris: Editions du Seuil, 1984.

La Gorce, Paul-Marie de. *The French Army: A Military-Political History*. trans. Kenneth Douglas. New York: George Braziller, 1963.

Larson, Robert. *The British Army and the Theory of Armored Warfare, 1918–1940*. Newark: University of Delaware Press, 1984.

Lewis, S. J. *Forgotten Legions: German Army Infantry Policy, 1918–1941*. New York: Praeger, 1985.

Liddell Hart, Basil H. *Dynamic Defence*. London: Faber and Faber, 1940.

————. *Memoirs of Captain Liddell Hart*. 2 vols. London: Cassell, 1965.

————. *Strategy*. 2d. ed. London: Faber and Faber, 1967.

Liddell Hart, Basil H., ed. *The German Generals Talk*. New York: Quill, 1979.

Linke, Horst G. *Deutsch-sowjetische Beziehungen bis Rapallo. Abhandlungen des Bundesinstituts für ostwissenschaftliche und internationale Studien* 22. Cologne: Verlag Wissenschaft und Politik, 1970.

Livesey, Anthony. *Great Battles of World War I*. New York: Macmillan, 1989.

Lupfer, Timothy. *The Dynamics of Doctrine: The Changes in German Tactical Doctrine during the First World War*. Leavenworth Papers 4. Fort Leavenworth, Kans.: U.S. Army Command and General Staff College Press, July 1981.

Lusar, Rudolf. *Die deutschen Waffen und Geheimwaffen des 2 Weltkrieges und ihre Entwicklung*. Munich: J. F. Lehmanns Verlag, 1962.

Luvaas, Jay. *The Education of an Army: British Military Thought, 1915–1940*. Chicago: University of Chicago Press, 1964.

Maass, Bruno. "Vorgeschichte der Spitzengliederung der frühen deutschen Luftwaffe 1920–1933." *Wehrwissenschaftliche Rundschau* 7, no. 9 (1957): 505–522.

MacIsaac, David. "Voices from the Central Blue: The Air Power Theorists." In *Makers of Modern Strategy*, ed. P. Paret, 624–647. Princeton, N.J.: Princeton University Press, 1986.

McKenney, Janice. "More Bang for the Buck in the Interwar Army: The 105-mm Howitzer." *Military Affairs* 42 (1978): 80–86.

Macksey, Kenneth. *Guderian, Panzer General*. London: MacDonald and James, 1975.

————. *The Tank Pioneers*. New York: Jane's, 1981.

————. *Tank Warfare*. New York: Stein and Day, 1972.

————. *Technology in War*. London: Arms and Armour Press, 1986.

Maier, Klaus. "Total War and German Air Doctrine before the Second World War." In *The German Military in the Age of Total War*, ed. Wilhelm Deist, 210–219. Leamington Spa, Eng.: Berg, 1985.

Manchester, William. *The Arms of Krupp*. Boston: Little, Brown, 1968.

Manstein, Erich von. *Aus einem Soldatenleben, 1887–1939*. Bonn: Athenäum Verlag, 1958.

Marshall, S. L. A. *Blitzkrieg: Its History, Strategy, and Challenge to America*. New York: William Morrow, 1940.

Marwedel, Ulrich. *Carl von Clausewitz: Persönlichkeit und Wirkungsgeschichte seiner Werken bis 1918*. Militärgeschichtliche Studien 25. Boppard am Rhein: Harald Boldt Verlag, 1978.

Mason, Herbert Molloy. *The Rise of the Luftwaffe*. New York: Ballantine, 1973.

Mearsheimer, John J. *Liddell Hart and the Weight of History*. Ithaca, N.Y.: Cornell University Press, 1988.

Meier-Welcker, Hans. "General der Infanterie a.D. Dr. Hermann v. Kuhl." *Wehrwissenschaftliche Rundschau* 6, 11 (1956): 595–610.

———. *Seeckt*. Frankfurt am Main: Bernard und Graefe Verlag, 1967.

———. "Seeckt in der Kritik." *Wehrwissenschaftliche Rundschau* 19, no. 5 (1969): 265–284.

———. "Seeckt über die Chefstellung im Generalstab." *Wehrwissenschaftliche Rundschau* 17, no. 1 (1967): 15–21.

———. *Untersuchungen zur Geschichte des Offizierkorps. Anciennität und Beförderung nach Leistung*. Beiträge zur Militärund Kriegsgeschichte 4. Stuttgart: Deutsche Verlags-Anstalt, 1962.

———. "Der Weg zum Offizier im Reichsheer der Weimarer Republik." *Militärgeschichtliche Mitteilungen* 19 (1976): 147–180.

Messenger, Charles. *The Art of Blitzkrieg*. London: Jan Allan, 1976.

Messerschmidt, Manfred. "Aussenpolitik und Kriegsvorbereitung." Vol. 1 in *Das Deutsche Reich und der Zweite Weltkrieg*. Stuttgart: Deutsche Verlags-Anstalt, 1979.

———. "German Military Effectiveness between 1919 and 1939." In *Military Effectiveness*, vol. 2, ed. Allan Millett and Williamson Murray, 218–254. Boston: Allen and Unwin, 1988.

Miksche, Ferdinand Otto. *Vom Kriegsbild*. Stuttgart: Seewald Verlag, 1976.

Militärgeschichtliches Forschungsamt. *Handbuch zur deutschen Militärgeschichte, 1648–1939*. Vol. 7. Ed. Michael Salewski, Herbert Schottelius, Gustav-Adolf Caspar, Rolf Güth, Karl Köhler, and Karl-Heinz Hummel. Munich: Bernard und Graefe Verlag, 1978.

Milsom, John. *German Military Transport of World War II*. New York: Hippocrene, 1975.

———. *Russian Tanks, 1900–1970*. Harrisburg, Penn.: Stackpole, 1971.

Model, Hans Georg. *Der deutsche Generalstabsoffizier. Seine Auswahl und Ausbildung in Reichswehr, Wehrmacht und Bundeswehr*. Frankfurt am Main: Bernard und Graefe Verlag, 1968.

Montgomery, Bernard. *The Memoirs of Field Marshal Montgomery*. New York: Signet, 1958.

Moore, William. *A Wood Called Bourlon*. London: Leo Cooper, 1988.

Morgan, J. H. *Assize of Arms: The Disarmament of Germany and Her Rearmament (1919–1939)*. New York: Oxford University Press, 1946.

Morrow, John. *German Air Power in World War I*. Lincoln: University of Nebraska Press, 1982.

Mueller, Gordon. "Rapallo Reexamined: A New Look at Germany's Secret Military Collaboration with Russia in 1922." *Military Affairs* 40 (1976): 109–116.

Müller, Klaus-Jürgen. *Ludwig Beck—Studien und Dokumente zu seinem politischen und militärischen Denken*. Boppard am Rhein: Harald Boldt Verlag, 1978.

Müller, Rolf Dieter. *Das Tor zur Weltmacht*. Militärgeschichtliche Studien 32. Boppard am Rhein: Harald Boldt Verlag, 1984.

———. "World Power Status through the Use of Poison Gas? German Preparations for Chemical Warfare, 1919–1945." In *The German Military in the Age of Total War*, ed. Wilhelm Deist, 171–209. Leamington Spa, Eng.: Berk, 1985.

Müller-Hillebrand, Burkhart. *Das Heer, 1933–1945, Entwicklung des organisatorischen Aufbaues*. Vol. 1. Darmstadt: E. Mittler und Sohn, 1954.

Munson, Kenneth. *Aircraft of World War I*. Garden City, N.Y.: Doubleday, 1977.

Murray, Williamson. "British and German Air Doctrine between the Wars." *Air University Review* 31, 3 (March-April 1980).

———. *Strategy for Defeat: The Luftwaffe, 1933–1945*. Maxwell Air Force Base, Ala.: Air University Press, 1983.

Musciano, Walter. *Eagles of the Black Cross*. New York: Ivan Obolensky, 1965.

Nehring, Walther. *Die Geschichte der deutschen Panzerwaffe 1916 bis 1945*. Berlin: Propyläen Verlag, 1974.

Nenninger, T. "The Experimental Mechanized Forces." *Armor Magazine* (May-June 1969): 33–39.

Nuss, Karl. *Militär und Wiederaufrüstung in der Weimarer Republik*. Berlin: Militärverlag der Deutschen Demokratischen Republik, 1977.

Ogorkiewicz, Richard M. *Armoured Forces*. New York: Arco, 1975.

———. *Design and Development of Fighting Vehicles*. Garden City, N.Y.: Doubleday, 1968.

———. "The French Tank Force." In *Tanks and Weapons of World War I*, ed. Bernard Fitzsimons, 95–101. London: Phoebus, 1973.

O'Neill, Robert. "Doctrine and Training in the German Army, 1919–1939." In *The Theory and Practice of War*, ed. Michael Howard. London: Cassell, 1965.

Oswald, Werner. *Kraftfahrzeuge und Panzer der Reichswehr, Wehrmacht und Bundeswehr*. Stuttgart: Motorbuch Verlag, 1970.

Otto, H. *Schlieffen und der Generalstab, 1890–1905*. Berlin: Deutscher Militärverlag, 1966.

Paget, R. T. *Manstein: His Campaigns and His Trial*. London: Collins, 1951.

Papen, Franz von. *Memoirs*. trans. Brian Connell. London: André Deutsch, 1952.

Paschall, Rod. *The Defeat of Imperial Germany, 1917–1918*. Chapel Hill, N.C.: Algonquin, 1989.

Perrett, Bryan. *A History of Blitzkrieg*. New York: Stein and Day, 1983.

———. *Knights of the Black Cross*. New York: St. Martin's Press, 1986.

Philpott, Bryan. *The Encyclopedia of German Military Aircraft*. London: Bison, 1981.

———. *History of the German Air Force*. New York: Gallery, 1986.

Pitt, Barrie. "Germany 1918: New Strategy, New Tactics." In *The History of the First World War*, 8 vols., ed. Peter Young. London: BPC, 1971.

Porch, Douglas. "The French Army in the First World War." In *Military Effectiveness*, vol. 1, ed. Allan Millett and Williamson Murray, 190–228. Boston: Allen and Unwin, 1988.

Posen, Barry. *The Sources of Military Doctrine*. Ithaca, N.Y.: Cornell University Press, 1984.

Post, Gaines, Jr. *The Civil-Military Fabric of Weimar Foreign Policy*. Princeton, N.J.: Princeton University Press, 1973.

Probert, H. A. *The Rise and Fall of the German Air Force, 1933–1945*. London: Arms and Armour Press, 1983.

Rahn, Werner. *Reichsmarine und Landesverteidigung, 1919–1928. Konzeption und Führung der Marine in der Weimarer Republik.* Munich: Bernard und Graefe Verlag, 1976.

Reid, Brian. "Colonel J. F. C. Fuller and the Revival of Classical Military Thinking in Britain, 1918–1926." *Military Affairs* 49 (1985): 192–197.

Reile, Oskar. *Die deutsche Abwehr im Osten, 1921–1945.* Munich: Verlag Welsermühl, 1969.

Reinicke, Adolf. *Das Reichsheer, 1921–1934.* Osnabrück: Biblio Verlag, 1986.

Ries, Karl. *The Luftwaffe: A Photographic Record, 1919–1945.* London: B. T. Batsford, 1987.

Ritter, Gerhard. *The Schlieffen Plan.* London: O. Wolff, 1958.

———. *The Sword and the Scepter.* Vol. 3. Coral Gables, Fla: University of Miami Press, 1972.

Rolak, Bruno J. "Fathers of the Blitzkrieg." *Military Review* 5 (1969): 73–76.

Rommel, Erwin. *The Rommel Papers.* trans. Paul Findlay and ed. Basil H. Liddell Hart. New York: Harcourt, Brace, 1953.

Roos, Hans. "Die Militärpolitische Lage und Planung Polens gegenüber Deutschland vor 1939." *Wehrwissenschaftliche Rundschau* 7, 4 (1957): 177–191.

Rosinski, Herbert. *The German Army.* London: Praeger, 1966.

Salewski, Michael. *Entwaffnung und Militärkontrolle in Deutschland, 1919–1927.* Schriften des Forschungsinstitutes der Deutschen Gesellschaft für Auswärtige Politik 24. Munich: R. Oldenbourg Verlag, 1966.

Schell, Adolf von. "Grundlagen der Motorisierung und ihre Entwicklung im Zweiten Weltkrieg." *Wehrwissenschaftliche Rundschau* 13, 3 (1963): 210–229.

Schliephake, Hanfried. *The Birth of the Luftwaffe.* Shepperton, Surrey: R. Oldenbourg, 1971.

Schmidt-Richberg, Wiegand. *Die Generalstäbe in Deutschland, 1871–1945.* Beiträge zur Militär- und Kriegsgeschichte 3. Stuttgart: Deutsche Verlags-Anstalt, 1962.

Schneider, Erich. "Waffenentwicklung, Erfahrungen in deutschen Heereswaffenamt." *Wehrwissenschaftliche Rundschau* 3. (1953): 24–35.

Schramm, Wilhelm Ritter von. "Generaloberst Beck und der Durchbruch zu einer neuen deutschen Wehrtheorie." *Aus Politik und Zeitgeschichte* 8 (1968).

Schüddekopf, Otto-Ernst. *Das Heer und die Republik.* Hannover: Norddeutsche Verlagsanstalt, 1955.

Seaton, Albert. *The German Army, 1933–45.* London: Weidenfeld and Nicolson, 1982.

Senff, Hubertus. "Die Entwicklung der Panzerwaffe im deutschen Heer zwischen den beiden Weltkriegen." *Wehrwissenschaftliche Rundschau* 19, 8 (1969): 432–451, and 9 (1969): 525–531.

Senger und Etterlin, F. M. von. *Die deutschen Panzer: 1926–1945.* Munich: J. F. Lehmanns Verlag, 1959.

———. *Die Kampfpanzer von 1916–1966.* Munich: J. F. Lehmanns Verlag, 1966.

———. *Die Panzergrenadiere.* Munich: J. F. Lehmanns Verlag, 1961.

Smith, Arthur. "The German General Staff and Russia, 1919–1926." *Soviet Studies* 8 (October 1956): 125–133.

Speidel, Helm. "Reichswehr und Rote Armee." *Vierteljahrsheft für Zeitgeschichte* 1, 1 (Jan. 1953).

Speidel, Wilhelm. "The Reichswehr's Illegal Air Force Command and Its Secret Collaboration with Soviet Russia before 1933." In *World War II German Military Studies,* vol. 23, ed. Donald Detwiler, 1–151. New York: Garland, 1979.

Spielberger, Walter J. *Die Motorisierung der deutschen Reichswehr, 1920–1935.* Stuttgart: Motorbuch Verlag, 1979.

Spielberger, Walter J., and Uwe Feist. *Sonderpanzer*. Fullbrook, Calif.: Aero, 1968.

Spires, David N. *Image and Reality: The Making of the German Officer, 1921–1933*. Westport, Conn.: Greenwood Press, 1984.

Stokesbury, James. *A Short History of Air Power*. New York: William Morrow, 1986.

Stolz, Gerd, and Eberhard Grieser. *Geschichte des Kavallerie-Regiments 5 "Feldmarshall v. Mackensen."* Munich: Schild Verlag, 1975.

Stone, Norman. *The Eastern Front, 1914–1917*. New York: Charles Scribner's Sons, 1975.

Strachnan, Hew. *European Armies and the Conduct of War*. London: Allen and Unwin, 1983.

Stülpnagel, Joachim von. *75 Jahre meines Lebens*. Düsseldorf: Selbstverlag, 1960.

Suchenwirth, Richard. *Command and Leadership in the German Air Force*. USAF Historical Study 174. New York: Arno Press, 1969.

———. *The Development of the German Air Force, 1919–1939*. USAF Historical Study 160. New York: Arno Press, 1968.

Taylor, Michael. *Warplanes of the World: 1918–1939*. New York: Charles Scribner's Sons, 1981.

Taylor, Telford. *Sword and Swastika*. New York: Simon and Schuster, 1952.

Teske, Hermann. "Analyse eines Reichswehr-Regiments." *Wehrwissenschaftliche Rundschau* 12, 5 (1962): 252–269.

Tessin, Georg. *Deutsche Verbände und Truppen, 1918–1939*. Osnabrück: Biblio Verlag, 1974.

Thomas, Georg. *Geschichte der deutschen Wehr- und Rüstungswirtschaft (1918–1943/45)*. Vol. 14 in *Schriften des Bundesarchivs*, ed. Wolfgang Birkenfeld. Boppard am Rhein: Harald Boldt Verlag, 1966.

Trythall, Anthony J. *"Boney" Fuller: The Intellectual General*. London: Cassell, 1977.

Vigman, Fred. "The Theoretical Evaluation of Artillery after World War I." *Military Affairs* 16 (1952): 115–118.

Völker, Karl-Heinz. *Die deutsche Luftwaffe, 1933–1939*. Stuttgart: Deutsche Verlags-Anstalt, 1967.

———. *Die Entwicklung der militärischen Luftfahrt in Deutschland, 1920–1933*. Stuttgart: Deutsche Verlags-Anstalt, 1962.

———. "Die geheime Luftrüstung der Reichswehr und ihre Auswirkung auf den Flugzeugbestand der Luftwaffe bis zum Beginn des Zweiten Weltkrieges." *Wehrwissenschaftliche Rundschau* 12, 9 (1962): 540–549.

Volker, Wieland. *Zur Problematik der französischen Militärpolitik und Militärdoktrin in der Zeit zwischen den Weltkriegen*. Wehrwissenschaftliche Forschungen, Abt. Militärgeschichtliche Studien 15. Boppard am Rhein: Harald Boldt Verlag, 1973.

Volmert, Johannes. *Ernst Jünger: In Stahlgewittern*. Munich: Wilhelm Fink Verlag, 1985.

Walde, Karl. *Guderian*. Frankfurt am Main: Verlag Ullstein, 1976.

Wallach, Jehuda L. *The Dogma of the Battle of Annihilation*. Westport, Conn.: Greenwood Press, 1986.

———. *Kriegstheorien. Ihre Entwicklung im 19. und 20. Jahrhundert*. Frankfurt: Bernard und Graefe Verlag, 1972.

Walzdorf, Bernhard. "Die getarnte Ausbildung von Generalstabsoffizieren der Reichswehr von 1932 bis 1935." *Zeitschrift für Militärgeschichte* 2 (1963): 78–87.

Weeks, John. *Men against Tanks*. New York: Mason/Charter, 1975.

Westphal, Siegfried. *Erinnerungen*. Mainz: Hasse und Koehler Verlag, 1975.
Whaley, Barton. *Covert German Rearmament, 1919–1939: Deception and Misperception*. Frederick, Md.: University Publications of America, 1984.
Wheeler-Bennett, John. *The Nemesis of Power*. 2d ed. London: Macmillan, 1964.
White, B. T. *British Tanks and Fighting Vehicles, 1914–1945*. Shepperton, Surrey: Ian Allan, 1970.
Wilson, Dale. *Treat 'em Rough! The Birth of American Armor, 1917–1920*. Novato, Calif.: Presidio Press, 1990.
Winton, Harold. *To Change an Army: General Sir John Burnett-Stuart and British Armored Doctrine, 1927–1938*. Lawrence: University Press of Kansas, 1988.
Wohlfeil, Rainer. "Heer und Republik." Vol. 6 in *Handbuch zur deutschen Militärgeschichte, 1648–1939*. Frankfurt am Main: Bernard und Graefe Verlag, 1970.
Wohlfeil, Rainer, and Hans Dollinger. *Die Deutsche Reichswehr*. Frankfurt a.M.: Bernard und Graefe Verlag, 1972.
Wynne, G. C. *If Germany Attacks: The Battle of Depth in the West*. Westport, Conn.: Greenwood Press, 1976; reprint of 1940 edition.
Zeidler, Manfred. "Luftkriegsdenken und Offiziersausbildung an der Moskauer Zukovskij Akademie im Jahre 1926." *Militärgeschichtliche Mitteilungen* 27 (1980): 127–174.
Ziemke, Earl. "The Soviet Armed Forces in the Interwar Period." In *Military Effectiveness*, vol. 2, ed. Allan Millett and Williamson Murray, 1–38. Boston: Allen and Unwin, 1988.

## DOCTORAL DISSERTATIONS

Barthel, R. "Theorie und Praxis der Heeresmotorisierung in faschistischen Deutschland bis 1939." Leipzig Universität, 1967.
Boyle, Thomas. "France, Great Britain, and German Disarmament, 1919–1927." State University of New York, Stony Brook, 1972.
Burke, Richard T. "The German Panzerwaffe, 1920–1939: A Study in Institutional Change." University of Michigan, Ann Arbor, 1972.
Doughty, Robert. "The Evolution of French Army Doctrine, 1919–1939." University of Kansas, Lawrence, 1979.
Post, Gaines, Jr. "German Foreign Policy and Military Planning: The Polish Question, 1914–1929." Stanford University, Stanford, Calif. 1969.
Rolak, Bruno J. "European Military Thought in the 1930s." Bloomington: Indiana University Press, 1968.
Sperling, Heinz. "Die Tätigkeit und Wirksamkeit des Heereswaffenamtes der Reichswehr für die Materiell-Technische Ausstattung eines 21-Divisionen-Heeres als Ubergangsstufe zu einem kriegsstarken Aggressionsinstrument des deutschen Imperialismus (1924–1934)." Militärgeschichtliches Institut der DDR, Potsdam, 1980.
Spires, David W. "The Career of a Reichswehr Officer." University of Washington, Seattle, 1979.
Velten, Wilhelm. "Das Deutsche Reichsheer und die Grundlagen seiner Truppenführung: Entwicklung, Hauptprobleme und Aspekte." Westfälische Wilhelms-Universität, Münster, 1982.

# INDEX